Renaissances

T0372677

One of the most distinguished social scientists in the world addresses one of the central historical questions of the past millennium: does the European Renaissance deserve its unique status at the very heart of our notions of modernity? Jack Goody scrutinizes the European model in relation to parallel renaissances that have taken place in other cultural areas, primarily Islam and China, and emphasizes what Europe owed to non-European influences. *Renaissances* continues that strand of historical analysis critical of Eurocentrism that Goody has developed in recent works such as *The East and the West* (1996) or *The Theft of History* (2006). This book is wide-ranging, powerful and deftly argued, and draws upon the author's long experience of working in Africa and elsewhere. Not since Toynbee in *The Study of History* has anybody attempted quite what Jack Goody is undertaking in *Renaissances*, and the result is as accessible as it is ambitious. This book will be of interest to students of the Renaissance and of the history of western civilization more generally, to anthropologists, sociologists and all those with an interest in the construction of modernity.

JACK GOODY is Emeritus Professor of Social Anthropology in the University of Cambridge and a Fellow of St John's College. Recently knighted by Her Majesty The Queen for services to anthropology, Professor Goody has researched and taught all over the world, is a Fellow of the British Academy, and in 1980 was made a Foreign Honorary member of the American Academy of Arts and Sciences. In 2004 he was elected to the National Academy of Sciences and he was elected Commandeur des Arts et Lettres in 2006.

Renaissances

The One or the Many?

Jack Goody

CAMBRIDGE
UNIVERSITY PRESS

CAMBRIDGE
UNIVERSITY PRESS

University Printing House, Cambridge CB2 8BS, United Kingdom

Published in the United States of America by Cambridge University Press, New York

Cambridge University Press is part of the University of Cambridge.

It furthers the University's mission by disseminating knowledge in the pursuit of education, learning and research at the highest international levels of excellence.

www.cambridge.org
Information on this title: www.cambridge.org/9780521745161

© Jack Goody 2010

First published 2010

A catalogue record for this publication is available from the British Library

Library of Congress Cataloguing in Publication data
Goody, Jack.
Renaissances : the one or the many? / Jack Goody.
    p.   cm.
Includes bibliographical references and index.
ISBN 978-0-521-76801-6 (hbk.)
1. Renaissance.   2. Europe – Civilization – Foreign influences.
3. Europe – Relations – Asia.   4. Asia – Relations – Europe.
5. Civilization, Modern.   I. Title.
CB361.G67 2009
940.2'1 – dc22   2009031005

ISBN 978-0-521-76801-6 Hardback
ISBN 978-0-521-74516-1 Paperback

To Eric Hobsbawm, historian extraordinary,
for his ninetieth birthday

'In my end is my beginning' (T. S. Eliot)

Contents

Plates

Credits: (1) British Library, London, UK / © British Library Board. All rights reserved / Bridgeman Art Library; (2) and (3) Edinburgh University Library, Scotland / with kind permission of the University of Edinburgh / The Bridgeman Art Library; (4) Ken Welsh / The Bridgeman Art Library; (5) Photo by Eliot Elisofon / Time & Life Pictures / Getty Images; (6) The Bridgeman Art Library; (7) Victoria & Albert Museum, London / The Stapleton Collection / The Bridgeman Art Library; (8) Famen Temple, Fufeng, Shaanxi province; (9) and (10) National Palace Museum, Taiwan

Acknowledgements

I am most grateful to Prof. Khaled El-Rouayheb of Harvard University, to Prof. Amrit Srinivasan of the Department of Humanities and Social Sciences, Indian Institute of Technology, Delhi, and to Dr Joseph McDermott of St John's College, Cambridge, for reading and commenting on the joint chapters, 4, 6 and 7, respectively. Dr McDermott was especially helpful with the illustrations. I am grateful to Dr Sudeshna Guha for reading chapter 6; and to the most useful readers for the publisher. I have to thank Peter Burke and Ulinka Rublack, experts on the European Renaissance and Reformation; John Kerrigan and Sukanta Chaudhuri; Juliet Mitchell, whose comments have been most helpful throughout; my colleagues at St John's College, where I have done the bulk of the work; the rest of my family for encouragement; my collaborator Stephen Fennell; and those who have helped with the preparation of the manuscript, Mark Offord, Melanie Hale, Sue Mansfield, Manuela Wedgwood and others. I am particularly grateful to the Leverhulme Foundation for awarding a grant to finish this rather wild enterprise and to the College for administering it.

Introduction

I see this book as a culmination of a series of endeavours that I have made over the past years. This attempt was to query the assumption of earlier advantage of the west in attaining capitalism, modernity, industrialization and even printing, leading to the kind of division between those societies with which the anthropologist traditionally dealt and those the sociologist and the historian elected to study.[1] Let me explain how I got there. The cut between traditional and modern societies was embodied in Dumont's works on India which he contrasted with the Christian west,[2] and this again was implied in Durkheim's and Lévi-Strauss's conception of China as a primitive society compared with Europe, the first in relation to religion, and especially in his essay with Mauss on *Primitive Classification*,[3] and the latter in his treatment of kinship in the *Elementary Forms*.[4] How, I asked myself, was this 'primitiveness' to be reconciled with Joseph Needham's assessment of Chinese science as being so much in advance of the west until the period of the Renaissance; or with the assertions of various sinologists that until the beginning of the nineteenth century, China's was the major world economy, the exporter of manufactured products (ceramics, silks, as well as lacquer and tea, which were transformed if not manufactured)? There had to be something wrong somewhere and to that misapprehension Watt and I certainly contributed[5] when we pointed to the positive role of the phonetic alphabet in the achievements of ancient Greece (rather than employing an account in terms of the Greek genius) and contrasted that with the supposedly difficult part played by logographic scripts in China, in ancient Egypt and in Mesopotamia. It became important therefore to show, in the *Domestication of the Savage Mind*,[6] that a 'great transformation' occurred in all literate societies as the result of the invention of writing, not simply

---

[1] On the relationship between capitalism, modernity and industrialization, see my *Capitalism and Modernity* (Goody 2004).
[2] Dumont 1963.   [3] Durkheim and Mauss 1967 [1903].
[4] Lévi-Strauss 1949.   [5] Goody and Watt 1963.   [6] Goody 1977.

with the alphabet but with all scripts, in what Gordon Childe called the Urban Revolution of the Bronze Age.[7] And that this was highly significant as far as culture and social organization were concerned.

It has been objected that instead of the binary division, for example, between savage (*sauvage*) and domesticated societies, I was introducing a similar divide between oral and literate ones. But my difference was not a binary one since it took account of other changes in the means and mode of communication, the human invention of language in the first place, the role of different forms of writing (script types), of changes in the writing materials (tablets, papyrus, parchment, paper) and in the marking instruments (reeds, brush, pens); with paper there was the question of roll or book, the advent of woodblock printing, of moveable type, of the printing press, the rotary press, of the electronic media and finally of the internet. All of these altered the potentialities of 'a knowledge society'. In addition there was the use made of these. So a consideration of these factors was important in plotting the general course of world history to take into account the mode of communication as well as that of production and of destruction (coercion). Instead of looking only at the negative aspect of logographic writing, it was essential to appreciate the positive side as well. This form of non-phonetic writing meant that China could export its culture over different linguistic areas which constituted an enormous internal market not only for material goods but also for the circulation of written information. Indeed I would now argue that instead of this form of writing being an impediment to development, it may represent the way of the future of world civilization.[8]

I followed this work on the social effects of literacy with two other studies of particular aspects of cultural activity, that is, the preparation of food[9] and the cultivation of flowers,[10] in which I tried to show the other similarities between the major cultures of the east and west of the Eurasian continent, in addition to writing, and at the same time to contrast those of sub-Saharan Africa which had remained largely oral. In both of these fields, the east had at least an equally elaborate culture as the west: the high cuisine of China (with India and Islam) compared with France and Italy, and the use of flowers in India, Persia, China and Japan (whence came many varieties of our domesticated plants, especially fruit) compared with our own use of floral motifs in art and in life. Like writing, both of these complex features had something to do with the advances in agriculture and the economy generally that had been made with the use of metals (together with the plough and the wheel) in the various changes that occurred in the Bronze Age. These changes produced a complex,

---

[7] Childe 1942.   [8] Goody forthcoming.   [9] Goody 1982.   [10] Goody 1993.

advanced agriculture and urban life, leading to the differentiation of economic classes and hence to that of forms of preparing the food they ate, to the types of cooking, as well as to the domestication and use of 'aesthetic' plants both for personal celebration and for ritual purposes. Neither high cuisine nor domesticated flowers were found in sub-Saharan Africa (except marginally), nor indeed was writing, since the Bronze Age never reached that continent (though later on iron-working did), despite the complex forms of culture it displayed in other ways. I have examined the differences due to the influence of writing on various aspects of social organization, on religion, on economics, on politics and on law,[11] and in another publication even on kinship, although this difference was the result of the associated economy more than communication itself.[12]

These studies led on to a more general one in which I reconsidered the differences sociologists had found between the east and west, in terms of rationality and accounting systems (especially Max Weber), in terms of modes of production (in the work of Marx and many others), finding these suggestions questionable, at least until we arrived at the Renaissance or the Industrial Revolution. So I needed to examine the widespread thesis that since the Bronze Age there had been a parting of the ways between east and west, the latter leading to Antiquity, to feudalism and to capitalism, the former to Asiatic exceptionalism, which was marked by despotism, by irrigation (rather than by rain-fed) agri-culture, that led away from the flowering of the arts and sciences that the west experienced, not only in the Renaissance but also before the period that saw the rise of the bourgeoisie and of financial capitalism, all of which were deemed to be interrelated. In my study *The Theft of History*, I examined the work of various authors, trying to show that the achievements of the ancient world, remarkable in many ways, were not as unique as the theory about the origins of capitalism and modernization in the west demanded and that feudalism represented a collapse of the urban civilization of the Bronze Age, not an inevitable stage on the way to capitalism. In other words, the hypothetical divergence between east and west was much less obvious than that demanded by ethnocentric, teleo-logical European historiography, which crystallized in the mid nineteenth century at a time when the west clearly had an important advantage in the economy and in the information society more generally. Not all of this was Marxist by any means; he and Weber were representative of a much wider set of views, common in this respect to most Europeanists. But there had been much more of a parallel development across the Eurasian continent, based upon an exchange economy. In this products and

---

[11] Goody 1986.   [12] Goody 1976.

knowledge were transferred over the long term. No part of this vast area had a monopoly and the balance of advantage between the parts changed over time. Both had early forms of mercantile capitalism, as Braudel and others have pointed out. And if the west later developed more complex financial forms in connection with the Industrial Revolution, that was an augmentation of earlier activity and did not involve the invention of something altogether new called 'capitalism', *tout court*, but an elaboration of existing techniques and procedures.[13] Equally Elias's concept of the civilizing process and Needham's of modern science seemed to privilege a western movement towards modernization rather than considering a wider process of social development.

The historian Perry Anderson had seen the concatenation of Antiquity and feudalism at the Renaissance as being the critical factor which differentiated the west in the course of the rise of capitalism (which, as I have suggested, could be seen as having 'arisen' much more widely in Eurasia), and writers like Marx, Weber, Wallenstein and many others thought the period of the Renaissance was critical in the process. So it obviously was for Europe, a catching up by looking back to Antiquity which the Middle Ages had made necessary. But periods of such a looking back seemed to me a characteristic of literate societies more generally, wherever they were found. So too were bursts forward (golden ages) in such circumstances. Where Europe differed, and here I depended to some extent on my account of the history of representations,[14] was that to make such a burst forward, in the subjects of artistic works for example, the culture had to partially free itself from the restrictions imposed by a hegemonic, monotheistic religion, namely Christianity, and to open up to the wider world of classical, 'pagan' or polytheistic Greece and Rome. And the same recourse to a more secular way of thinking helped the new (or 'modern') science, as did the development of non-theological scholarship in institutions of higher learning, in the universities of the west. It was the desire, not to abolish nor disregard, but to modify the idea of European uniqueness either in Antiquity or in the Renaissance, that led to the present study – not to deny Europe the undoubted advantage it had in the nineteenth and twentieth centuries, but to see that advantage in its historical and cultural context, as a temporary phenomenon, as we see clearly from current events in China, India and elsewhere.

If I have emphasized the cultural achievements of the eastern civilizations, that is because the usual European accounts place too much stress

[13] Goody 2004.
[14] Goody 1997b. It was not simply the worship of images but their creation too. But as I have argued earlier, there was always an impulse to iconism which appeared in the Catholic Church, but was later rejected by Calvinism.

on their 'backwardness', which seems a very nineteenth-century view from the industrialized west. Today that 'backwardness' seems distinctly temporary, like that of Europe in the early Middle Ages. The negative role, at certain times, of the Abrahamistic religions seems to me crucial in accounting for the impact of the Renaissance and the Jewish Emancipation, as well as the frequently conservative approach to knowledge of Islam. But in making this point, I may have slightly highlighted the achievements of the one and downplayed those of the other. If so, it is a corrective that was to be made, given the continuing trend of much social science, not only western.

This book, then, follows on from earlier work. In addition to working in Africa, I have long been interested in trying to look at European history and sociology in a comparative way (as befits an anthropologist) and this study attempts the same kind of enterprise with regard to that very European institution of the Italian Renaissance, to which we all look back. As I have said, it argues that all literate societies have periods of looking back, when the old is re-established sometimes with a renewed burst of energy, leading to a flowering of the culture. They have also periods when the religious element is played down, leading to humanistic episodes that provide humans with greater freedom, both in science and the arts. In these areas this suspension of belief was not unimportant and looking back to the pagan classics certainly eased the path.

In chapter 1, I discuss the general problem of the Renaissance in a comparative perspective. In the second chapter, I shall examine one aspect in the Renaissance of knowledge in Europe, namely the foundation of what is often said to be the first medical school in Europe, at the University of Montpellier, in order to bring out the contributions of other cultures, Arabic and Jewish, to the rebirth of knowledge in that continent, knowledge which came from the other literate cultures. Chapter 3 returns to the theme of comparative renaissances and looks at the importance of the growth of secular knowledge and the conceptualization of the religious. That movement seems intrinsic both to the Italian and to the Song Renaissance in China as well as to various cultural efflorescences in Islam. Chapter 4 deals with the cultural history of Islam in some detail and this continues for Judaism, India and China in chapters 5, 6 and 7. Chapter 8 attempts to sum up the discussion.

In the text I have tried to avoid diacriticals and have therefore adopted Pinyin (without diacritics) for Chinese and have followed Romila Thapar in *A History of India* for the spelling of Indian words as well as F. Robinson in his *Cambridge History of Islam* for Arabic. The translations from French are my own.

I want to say a word about the illustrations. It would be unthinkable to produce a book about the western Renaissance without giving some idea of its achievements in the visual arts. Yet this represents only one part of its activity. How would one represent visually its attainments in what has been called 'modern sciences'? By a sketch of a 'black hole', or a drawing of a pipette? In a parallel fashion we can find no adequate visual representation for the Abbasid achievement in science (and in translation) when the visual field was dominated by the Abrahamistic prohibition on figurative representation. What I have shown here for Islam comes mainly from Iran and Afghanistan, or from the Mughals, all of which were much influenced by Chinese painting. Western Islam was more aniconic. It produced its own Renaissance in intellectual activity, especially around the great library at Cordoba and later the palace of the Alhambra, but painting was virtually absent. India had a strong visual tradition but this was rarely individualized. There are, however, significant examples from the productive periods. China was of course the simplest. Not only did it have a flourishing tradition of painting but works were individually acknowledged, and in some cases recognized as masterworks.

1   The idea of a renaissance

Beginning with the 'first lights' (*primi lumi*) of the fourteenth century, the Italian Renaissance has often been seen as the critical moment in the development of 'modernity', in terms not only both of the arts and of the sciences, but from the point of view of economic development also of the advent of capitalism. That this was certainly an important moment in history, even world history, there can be no doubt. But how unique was it in a general way? There is a specific historical problem as well as a general sociological one. All societies in stasis require some kind of rebirth to get them moving again, and that may involve a looking back to a previous era (Antiquity in the European case) or it may involve another type of efflorescence.

My own polemical background is this. I do not view the Italian Renaissance as the key to modernity and to capitalism. This seems to me a claim that has been made by teleologically inclined Europeans. In my opinion its origins were to be found more widely, not only in Arabic knowledge but in influential borrowings from India and China. What we speak of as capitalism had its roots in a wider Eurasian literate culture that had developed rapidly since the Bronze Age, exchanging goods, exchanging information. The fact of literacy was important because it permitted the growth of knowledge as well as of the economies that would exchange their products. As distinct from purely oral communication, literacy made language visible; it made language into a material object, which could pass between cultures and which existed over time in the same form. Consequently, all written cultures could at times look back and revive past knowledge, as was the case with the humanists in Europe, and possibly lead onto cultural efflorescence, that is, to a definite burst forward. Especially in religious matters, this looking back may be conservative in character rather than liberating, in the areas of the arts or the sciences. Or it is of course possible that a cultural liberation of this kind may not involve a looking back. But in a significant number of cases the two are linked together and it is into these parallel events in other literate cultures that I want to enquire, not to deny some uniqueness of western achievements but to contextualize and explain them.

What were the main features of the Italian Renaissance from a comparative point of view?[1] Firstly, there was the revival of classical knowledge, as in the work of the humanists, which had long been set aside by a hegemonic religion. The notion of a renaissance has a somewhat similar feel to that of a *revenant* about it, as Toynbee claimed, something that comes back from the dead. That is what happened in the Italian Renaissance which was a rebirth, not only a coming back from the dead (of the Dark Ages) but also a revival of a 'dead' literature, the classics, which were 'brought back to life'.

In his multivolumed *A Study of History*, Toynbee looked upon a renaissance as 'one particular instance of a recurrent phenomenon'.[2] The essential feature of this genus was '[t]he evocation of a dead culture by the living representative of a civilization that is still a going concern'.[3] Here we are not only concerned with the looking back but also with a burst forward, a flowering. Toynbee does indeed argue that there were such renaissances in other parts of the world, especially in China. However, the idea of a burst forward remains implicit and he does not link the event to literacy nor yet to the secularization of knowledge.[4] In this extraordinary work, however, he does offer a more comparative approach to the Renaissance but one which is also more fragmented in that he treats separately 'renaissances of political ideas, ideals and institutions', 'renaissances of systems of law', 'renaissances of philosophies', 'renaissances of language and literature' and 'renaissances of the visual arts'. My own study accepts the breadth of Toynbee's approach but tries to deal with the problem more holistically.

Toynbee sees the Renaissance both in Christianity and in the Song period as being respectively Christian and Buddhist under a Hellenistic or Confucian 'mask'.[5] It is true that certain aspects of these traditions were incorporated but others, especially the hegemonic claims to truth, were necessarily rejected. This is not to say they reinstated earlier doctrines; they invented an approach which represented neither the one nor the other but a new flowering. Toynbee, with his persistent metaphor of the

---

[1] While the name for the period, Renaissance, was not an early one, right from the time of Petrarch it was realized a break had been made with what was known as the Middle Ages.

[2] Toynbee 1954: 4.   [3] Toynbee 1954: 4.

[4] My use of the metaphor of the *revenant*, which runs tirelessly throughout Toynbee's work, was quite independent. The extremity of his ghostly metaphor is to be found on pp. 128–9 of vol. 9, where it gets quite out of hand.

[5] Toynbee 1954: 166.

revenant, does not fully appreciate the theoretical importance of a new birth, an efflorescence, which is intrinsic to the idea of a renaissance. Toynbee's problem, like Spengler's or Collingwood's,[6] is concerned with the 'spirit', with ideas, not with the other aspects of the period, for example its commercial activity. He also conceives his spirit in terms of the 'native genius', whatever that may mean. Rather he advocates Bury's attitude which talks of discarding 'medieval naïveté and superstition, in assuming a freer attitude towards theological authority' and of calling up 'the spirit of the Ancient World to exorcise the ghosts of the Dark Ages':[7] gradually the ancient world was excluded in favour of 'modernism' over the course of the Enlightenment.[8]

Secondly, there was also a partial secularization, a restriction of the intellectual scope of religion, which was entailed by this looking back to a pre-Christian past. Not so much, it should be said, an abandonment of the religious life but a reconsideration of the long-term appropriateness of Abrahamistic religion to control science and the arts.[9] There was the revolution in both areas, which the Florentine enterprise and the Scientific Revolution involved.[10] This revolution meant putting on one side those earlier religious restrictions in the arts and on 'scientific' knowledge about the world, implying a measure of demystification of knowledge and of life generally. Thirdly, there was the economic and social transformation of Europe beginning in Italy which was central to the achievements of the Renaissance,[11] and which, according both to Marx and Weber, led to 'modern' society.

In Europe the actors did think this change significant, even if they did not speak of it as the Renaissance. The humanists saw themselves as establishing a golden age by going back to Antiquity. Clearly not all had changed. The Gothic continued, despite the later advent of the new style, based on Roman architecture. In politics the struggle between the princes, the church and the populace went on. The economy grew. The arts and sciences were renewed. In Fontenelle's words, '[a] reading of the Ancients cleared the ignorance and the barbarity of preceding centuries ... It suddenly gave us ideas of Truth and Beauty which we would have taken a long time to reach'.[12]

---

[6] Toynbee 1954: 56.   [7] Bury 1924: 48; Toynbee 1954: 67.

[8] See Toynbee's discussion (1954: 68–9) of the ancients and the modern in Fontenelle 1716 [1688], Wotton 1694, Swift 1704 and Bayle 1697, a predecessor of Diderot's *Encyclopédie* (Diderot 1772).

[9] For the continuity and even expansion of other areas of religious activity see Crouzet-Pavan 2007 for Italy and see Rublack 2005 for the Reformation.

[10] The first was the subject of art historians like Berenson (1952), the second of historians of science like Needham (1954–).

[11] Jardine 1996.   [12] Fontenelle 1716 [1688]: 147.

We are unlikely to find all these features occurring together anywhere else, but each feature may have its parallels in other parts of the world. Historians have spoken of other renascences in Europe, the Carolingian in the late eighth and ninth centuries, and another in the twelfth century making way for the scholastics. Some have even found a 'Renaissance' in the work of Bede of Jarrow (673–735 CE) and Alcuin of York (735–804 CE) but this was part of the Carolingian Renaissance; the Englishman Alcuin was a friend of Charlemagne. Even before that, Bolgar writes of the revival of classical studies in the early Irish monasteries (from 458 CE). But this was essentially a revival of the teaching of Latin to speakers of Celtic and Germanic languages which led them to the classics, the content of which was dangerous. As St Gregory said to Bishop Desiderius, 'the same lips cannot sing the praises of Jove and the praises of Christ'. You should not 'spend your time on the follies of secular literature'.[13] The work of pagan authors was condemned by Alcuin, Hraban and St Gallen.[14] Nevertheless, some classical learning inevitably came back into Christian culture. Others have even extended the concept abroad, where periods of efflorescence (not necessarily involving a rebirth but a flowering) have sometimes been characterized as a golden age. We want to examine these other times in other literate cultures in Eurasia where the specific term has been used but also to look at periods of dramatic change that seem to offer some parallels, and then to pursue the question of common features.

The early Italian humanists of the fourteenth and fifteenth centuries, like Petrarch who was trained at Bologna, were constantly looking back to a 'golden age' of letters in ancient times; 'les temps revient', involving the work of searching for ancient manuscripts. These would tell them not only the proper way to write in Latin, or to represent, but also the right way to live, not by rejecting the world but by being part of it, the active life (of the town) rather than the contemplative life (of the monastery). This move did not mean that churchmen were not involved in 'humanism'; they were in some numbers. But the efflorescence went further than simply looking back to Antiquity; it has been claimed that Petrarch developed the concept of the individual and this represented the birth of 'modern man'.[15] Venice was to be *la nuova Constantinopoli*, mainly due to its close connection with the Near East, which one historian describes as 'this ancient part of an eastern empire existing in the west' (by Byzantium).[16] Meanwhile, Florence was the second Rome.

---

[13] Bolgar 1954: 96.   [14] Bolgar 1954: 127.   [15] Crouzet-Pavan 2007: 57.
[16] Crouzet-Pavan 2007: 86.

First of all, let us look briefly at the impact of the Italian Renaissance in Europe. The idea of a renaissance, as we have seen, is central to European history of the modern age. Not only did it serve to characterize a rebirth of artistic and scientific activity but it signalled the take-off into economic prosperity, 'capitalism', world conquest and 'modernization', all of which are closely interrelated. The Renaissance is defined as 'the birthplace of secular modernism'.[17]

For Europeans this was a specific phase of early modern history, unique to that continent, and one without which 'modernization' would not have happened. The Renaissance seems such a dramatic period to us in Europe partly because of the twilight that preceded it. As far as the visual and dramatic arts and the sciences were concerned, it was a necessary beginning but very much linked to the relative darkness of the preceding period when a hegemonic religion had dominated all these fields. The revival of classical culture did not mean any less religious activity for most people but it involved a pagan and secular element in art, portraying the existence of mythical classical gods, as in the paintings of Botticelli. At first, painting did not immediately relinquish religious themes but it widened its content to include portraits, classical myths, courtly scenes, the representation of landscapes and even of ordinary existence as in the Dutch oils, thus becoming increasingly secularized. At the same time, the theatre too emerged from its long sleep since the Greek and Roman periods. Popular drama had continued but there was nothing comparable at the level of 'high culture'. First of all, this revival saw the performance of exclusively religious plays in the shape of mystery or miracle drama; eventually there was the secular, sometimes based upon classical or on historical themes. In sculpture too, there was already some figuration in relief in Gothic art, but three-dimensional representation was largely confined to religious themes. Now other persons, other themes were included.

This gradual awakening followed a Dark Age, an idea that has been challenged but, in my opinion, ineffectively so. For if there had been a rebirth there must also have been a death, in this case the death of the classical civilization which is today held to be so central to European culture. That death occurred with the fall of the Roman empire, partly causing a decline in the European urban economy and the cultural life that took place there. But cultural life also suffered from the spread of the Abrahamistic religions that not only forbade forms of representation such as theatre and the visual arts (except later in Catholic Christianity for religious purposes) but to some extent music and dance as well

17 Eckstein 2005: 6–7.

as other forms of play including cards, encouraging puritanical activity more generally, around sex for example. For Augustine (354–430 CE), man was born in sin and needed a prince to guide him. Moreover, his religion also inhibited scientific enquiry into the natural world by insisting that God was already omniscient, knowing all. In all these spheres Christianity required its own literature, not that of the pagans of Rome and Greece. Reading this was not intended to widen the mind so much as to confirm beliefs. He writes: 'Indeed he is no true man that knoweth not and worshippeth not Christ. What needeth all these digests, codes, glosses, counsels, and cautels?...Thou shalt then be greater than Plato or Pythagoras with all their travails and numbers; than Aristotle with all his quirks and syllogisms.'[18] Initially all three religions excluded much scientific activity and knowledge from mainstream teaching, largely in clerical hands and confined to religion, although some obviously took place. As we shall see, in Islam the natural sciences were later taken up in certain liberal (humanistic) periods, especially in courts, libraries and around medical schools. The latter were something of a special case as healing the sick was always a permanent aspect of human existence which medicine sought to ameliorate. And amelioration involved seeking better ways of treating illness, in most respects an open question whatever the formal ideology. In literate societies another subject that gave rise to separate instruction was law but it was clearly not open-ended in the same way as medicine, though it always required the application of general principles to particular cases.

The role of the monotheistic religions in holding back knowledge is interesting, for they are often assumed to represent the vanguard of civilization, mainly because they come from Europe and the Near East. We need to be reminded, as the classicist Vernant[19] has indeed done, that there is no universal rule whereby religions progress or evolve from the polytheistic to the monotheistic. The very 'rational' Greeks were polytheistic; so too the Chinese; some would even claim that Catholics have become so. For the differences are in some aspects not all that great. Generally, polytheistic religions too have the notion of a creator god, a supreme being, so that the possibility of monotheism is buried in polytheistic beliefs, as the history of Egyptian religion makes clear.[20] Far

---

[18] Augustine 1945: 426; he also wrote: 'There exists in the soul...a cupidity which does not take delight in carnal pleasures but in perceptions acquired through the flesh. It is a vain inquisitiveness dignified with the title of knowledge and science...To satisfy...this diseased craving...people study the operations of nature, which lie beyond our grasp when there is no advantage in knowing and the investigators simply desire knowledge for its own sake' (Augustine, *Confessions* 10:35: 54–5; trans. Chadwick 1991: 210–12).
[19] Vernant 2006 [1979].   [20] Assman 2001 [1984].

from being the most 'rational' form of religion, the monotheistic ones were in practice the most hegemonic, allowing less room not only for alternative versions of the 'truth' but also for independent enquiry and in the Abrahamistic ones, for the most part, for the development of the representational arts. That was not the case in China or in Greece where both scientific and artistic traditions were strong. Monotheism may have meant a certain coherence, aiming at universalism, but it was a religious coherence, a coherence of the 'irrational' which was in many ways damaging to the development of the both sciences and the arts.

As mentioned, in the post-classical period the representative arts, like the sciences, also suffered. Naturalistic representation was restricted, especially figurative. The role of the Abrahamistic God as creator was a monopolistic one. Consequently many of the creative arts suffered. So looking back to the pagan period in European history meant a certain freeing of the mind. We have to draw a sharp line between the artistic accomplishments of the Renaissance and those in the sciences, in the widest sense. In the arts, you could go back to Roman and Greek architecture, sculpture, theatre, and start from there. But there had been a radical discontinuity, with only a small contribution from other cultures. The same with music, fiction and, to a lesser extent, poetry. The 'puritanical complex' meant that these activities were abandoned. Neighbouring religious cultures were equally ambivalent. However, in the knowledge 'industries', some continuity has been maintained partly through the Arab connection, the contents of which fed back into the west at various points in time, though here too objections were raised to what did not have transcendental backing.

This freedom is not always how the progress of art has been portrayed. Berenson, the art critic, wrote, 'the thousand years that elapsed between the triumph of Christianity and the middle of the fourteenth century have been not inaptly compared to the first fifteen and sixteen years in the life of the individual'.[21] That statement presumes Europe grew continuously from the coming of Christianity, the moment of 'triumph'. But that religion meant the introduction of Semitic notions of iconophobia, and only later allowed, in the Roman Church or in the Byzantine icon, the development of art as long as it was confined to religious themes. In earlier classical Greece or Rome matters had been very different; a secular art was encouraged, for example at Pompei where sex was a prominent topic in a way that was scarcely possible in Christendom at most periods, especially with a celibate priesthood and a puritanical ideology. Of course, as time went on, religious art increasingly included a secular background

21 Berenson 1952: 4.

(as well as sex in the literature of Chaucer and Bocaccio); but it was
virtually not until the Renaissance that completely secular painting was
legitimated. That had partly to do with ideological shifts but was also a
matter of patronage, which was increasingly neither of the church nor of
the court but of the bourgeoisie, involving the rebirth of the city and of
urban life. The result is clear in the attention now given to nature. Most
'[p]ainters of the early Renaissance were aware of landscape elements in a
way altogether unknown to painters of the Gothic past, when landscape
was treated symbolically'.[22] Landscape had of course long formed an
essential aspect of Chinese painting. But that came much later in Europe;
it was Dürer who produced not only the self-portrait[23] but dwelt on the
visual aspects of small creatures. And soon after, in the 1510s and 1520s,
the artists of the Danube school, especially Albrecht Altdorfer and Wolf
Hüber, 'started, for the first time in Europe, to treat figureless landscape
studies on panel or paper as an independent speciality'.[24] The Renaissance broke with the past. 'While Christian themes and representations,
with the Madonna and child always popular and ubiquitous, continued
to dominate the interest of Renaissance painters, there was a proliferation of purely lay art and sometimes pagan subject matter.'[25] It was only
possible for historians of art, like Berenson, to draw a continuous line
in its development from earlier times because they saw the 'triumph' of
Christianity as the beginning of things, continuing down to the Renaissance. In fact, continuity never existed and therefore the problem needs
looking at again, in a comparative way.

In this context there was also the question of the status of the
painter. During the Middle Ages, he was an artisan who carried out
the instructions of his patron-employer to the best of his abilities; art did
not require independent invention. An art market gradually emerged in
the Renaissance, where each prince or republic wanted the best artist.
And with the increasing laicization of the subject matter, more scope was
given to imagination and innovation. That market reached its peak in the
Low Countries, where the bourgeoisification of patronage was more pro-
nounced; in Italy the process was always caught up with the aristocracy
of the city, even in republics such as Florence or Venice. If demand was
sufficient, the artisan could establish an atelier, a shop, where he would
train and employ apprentices and would supervise their work. Then the
painter was free to choose his subject, as in genre painting, without
having as an artisan a prearranged position as a member of a *famiglia*.
But much portrait painting still today implies a designated patron.

---

[22] Beck 1999: 10.   [23] Other Italians had already done so.
[24] Bell 2007: 186.   [25] Beck 1999: 7.

Portrait painting was very much part of the view of the Renaissance as the progenitor of modernism, the notion that it represented the beginning of individualism. That quality is seen as characteristic of capitalism (via the entrepreneur) and is especially evident in painting, especially in the large-scale portraits (and sculptures) of particular individuals, particularly lay ones. This view was critical to the still influential work of the mid-nineteenth-century historian Jacob Burckhardt in *The Civilization of the Renaissance in Italy*,[26] where Florence is seen to have 'torn the veil that enveloped medieval minds with a tissue of faith and prejudices' and to have allowed man to be a spiritual individual. This was supposed to be one of the major themes of the Italian Renaissance: 'the development of the individual'.[27] And its particular manifestation is the growth of (realistic) portrait painting and of the autobiography. But leaving aside for the moment the growth of autobiography, this scenario, so beloved by European historians of the Renaissance, is most unhistorical. Portraits existed in Antiquity; they existed in Buddhist and other paintings in China; there is nothing new (modern) in the Renaissance portrait except when it is viewed against the background of the restrictions of medieval Christian art which in some respects held to the iconoclastic tradition of Abrahamistic religions.

In Islam, that tradition continued and, as recounted in chapter 4, some miniature-painters in Turkey were horrified at the idea of one of their company being commissioned to produce a large portrait of the sultan Mehmet, which was realistic, from life, capable of being on a wall where it might even be worshipped. Yet this was precisely what was happening in the Italian Renaissance. Realism was the aim, so too was individuality, and both features appeared even in group portraits and in religious scenes. Gradually, art became more realistic, as in landscapes, and included large figures, with the donors of religious paintings included at the side. There followed religious (and mythological and court) scenes where well-known living individuals were represented in the crowd, then individual portraits of great men, and eventually the Dutch genre paintings and portraits of ordinary people. But the 'realism' and 'individuality' were not only to be associated with 'modernism' for both were present in earlier societies. In art both had been obviously set aside by the Abrahamistic religions. But individuality was not a sudden invention; the anthropologist Evans-Pritchard discovered this quality among the Nuer of the southern Sudan.[28] In painting, it is very much an aspect of the 'rebirth', the renascence, stimulated by a return to classical paganism and

---

[26] Burckhardt 1990 [1860]: 63.   [27] Crouzet-Pavan 2007: 346.
[28] Evans-Pritchard 1940.

rejection of the Abrahamistic antagonism to representation, especially to realistic representation of the secular.

In sculpture there was a very distinct move to resurrect the Greek (and Roman) tradition. In architecture too classical models had an extensive influence down almost to the present day. That was less the case with the representations of literature, except that there was more emphasis on the epic, with Virgil acting as a guide for Dante to the other world, with poems like Ariosto's *Orlando Furioso* and others. Classical themes were constantly taken up by Shakespeare in England, by Racine in France, as well as references to classical mythology in the poetry of Spenser and many others. But in painting, the influence was rather limited to classical themes, which certainly gained great currency after the virtual imprisonment of painting in Christian themes over one thousand years. That move led to a secularization of painting (as with other arts, such as music), which reflected the process of secularization taking place throughout society.

The figuration involved in sculpture and in secular painting was antipathetic to that new religion. A pagan bust might be transformed into a Christian effigy, as happened at Conques in the Auvergne with the head of an unnamed emperor that became that of Ste Foy.[29] But even religious sculpture or painting was originally disallowed, partly no doubt because of its 'pagan' origins. The same was true of that other jewel of the classical world, its theatre, the performance of which was again forbidden. In Christian Europe the great theatrical tradition of the Greeks and Romans was set aside and eliminated. The plays were no longer performed, the theatres fell into disuse, leaving spectacular ruins, though some were defaced or actually destroyed. There are references to the plays of Terence being read in church schools to help with the learning of Latin, but not of any performance. Folk theatre continued but was condemned by the church as a 'mumming' or 'disguising', pagan in origin, misrepresenting humanity. We may see the late medieval mystery plays performed by the town guilds in Chester and elsewhere as being indications of a move towards dramatic representation by the urban population but the content was of course the Bible story, an elaboration of the tropes that the literary historian Chambers had seen as making their appearance in the church services.[30] A kind of more or less secular drama did make its appearance in northern France in the shape of 'clerk's plays' connected with the guild of St Nicholas, whose deeds they celebrated; that was in the tenth century. Otherwise we have to wait for the Italian Renaissance to witness the emergence of the theatre

[29] Goody 1997a: 75.   [30] Chambers 1903.

proper with a repertoire of secular drama, after a gap of a thousand years.

Then the humanists of the Renaissance went back to the writings of the ancients which had been significantly set aside by Christianity. Clearly resurrection of an earlier culture could be done with writing in a way that would not have been feasible in a purely oral one. It is often claimed that oral compositions were preserved in a rigid fashion over the centuries, for example in the Vedic works in India or the Mazdean in Iran. But what proof have we, or can we possibly have? The fixity of the oral composition cannot by definition be known before writing itself; any alternative assumption is pure supposition. Where we have evidence of recent oral compositions, recorded over time, we are impressed by their capacity to change, except of course with very short recitations. That point was made most forcefully to me when I recorded the long Bagre myth ('the First Bagre') of the LoDagaa of northern Ghana which I had supposed was a fairly set performance, as I was so often assured. A central feature of the first recording of the Black Bagre was built around the ascent of one of the original two men to Heaven with the aid of the spider and his web which provided a sort of ladder. There in Heaven God showed him and a woman he met there (the 'slender girl') how to create a child, about whose ownership they then proceed to argue. The visit to Heaven[31] seemed so central a part of this myth that I was amazed some years later to record another version ('the Second Bagre') where only a glancing reference was made to such a journey and where the creative role was played not by God (the High God, *Na-angmin*) but by man himself and by the beings of the wild (*kontome*). No one could now reconstruct the details of the voyage to Heaven from the slight references that existed (nor have they done since, as far as I know) except for myself, simply because I had written down the previous oral recitation. Once I had done so, mine became the 'authorized' version that could be resurrected at any time.[32] That was the difference in the means of communication, between the written and the oral.

So, except at a very general ('mythical') level, a precise resurrection of the past is possible virtually only in a written culture and there it has frequently occurred in Europe and Asia since the Bronze Age. Inherently conservative in written cultures, religion had its own part to play in this looking back to the texts. That made it in many respects more conserving, I have argued, than the religious activity of oral cultures which is more eclectic, more inventive, not constrained by a text. It is not always remembered that early texts were often designed to be read aloud; that is,

---

[31] Goody 1972: 230f. line 477.   [32] For the Bagre see Appendix 3.

they may have served as prompts for speech, perhaps summaries, rather than full-blown literary manuscripts. In Christianity, the search for the 'truth' involved a re-examination of ancient texts to find the real faith. Others had done this before; the Cathars, Wycliffe, Huss, but with Luther and the Reformation and the Renaissance the process gained a renewed vigour. For Christians the attempt to reconstruct the words of God or of Christ was a central aim of 'renaissance' scholarship. This looking back to the text might take the form of a 'reformation' or, in other religions, of 'fundamentalism'. It may look back, for example, to the Old Testament and discover that there God had allowed 'polygyny', hence it should be institutionalized as in the Mormon Church. The same with aniconism, for God forbad the making of images of living creatures. But looking back also means looking forward and arranging things differently in the present. This certainly happened with the Counter-Reformation of the Catholic Church, which sought to combat Protestantism and went back to the text. It represented a renewal of religion.

In religious terms, the looking back takes the form of a 'reformation' or perhaps simply a reference back to what the divine has put down in writing. It is a reform because looking back involves a process of clearing away the accumulated dross. Recuperation was seen as a stimulus of or justification for a new start; indeed all such movements necessarily involve innovation as well as the recuperation of earlier texts or knowledge. This is true for other secular fields, such as philosophy. The works of Plato reappear in the west and give rise to new forms of Neoplatonic thinking. It is a process that is in no sense confined to the west. The same happens in China with Confucius. What was distinctive about Europe was the extent of the collapse of earlier knowledge, partly to do with the coming of a hegemonic, monotheistic religion, as well as to the extraordinary amount and areas of the ancient inheritance that were ready for a rebirth when that faith loosened its hold, that is, when a measure of partial secularization intervened. There was never the continuity with the classical world that much later scholarship presumed. The Austrian scholar Kristeller begins an essay on 'Renaissance Humanism' with the words: 'In the Western tradition that began with classical antiquity and continued through the Middle Ages down to modern times, the period commonly called the Renaissance occupies a place of its own and has its own peculiar characteristics.'[33] But this continuity was fictional, heavily interrupted.

The evidence of earlier civilization never entirely disappeared, either here or in the Near East. For change in Europe also involved the

[33] Kristeller 1990: 20.

containment of religion. In some respects that process looked forward to
the Enlightenment; indeed the Renaissance already encouraged a certain
measure of anti-clericism, even of atheism.[34] Not that for most individuals religion was less active; fraternities flourished, including those practising flagellation; gifts and legacies to or through the church multiplied;
lay orders flourished throughout Christendom; the church reformed. Of
course, in the case of the Jews emancipation meant getting out of the
ghetto, but that was not only a place where Christians had placed the
wandering Jews of the diaspora. It was also a place of refuge where you
could practise your own religion.

A renascence or reformation such as was experienced in Europe (which
I distinguish as the Renaissance or Reformation), then, is in principle
possible in any literate society, in other words, ever since the Urban
Revolution of the Bronze Age, because writing enables one to refer back
to the 'visible speech' originating in earlier times, then to rebuild on that.
Renascences were not restricted to western Europe. There had been some
earlier revivals in Europe. Fifth-century Greece after all had looked back
to the work of Homer; so too Alexandrians went back to the work of the
fifth century producing 'imitations of existing genres', literature became
'an instrument of education'.[35] And that continued to be the case in
Rome. Of course, much else happened outside the bookish sphere, both
in Hellenistic times (with scientific work) and in Rome (with the creation
of towns); but education – a literary education – always involved a looking
back. In the Middle Ages education was even more conservative, since it
was conducted in 'dead' languages. In the time of the church fathers there
was some ambiguity about the 'pagan' heritage of Greece and Rome.
All distrusted things pagan but some such as Jerome viewed the study
of the classics as profitable. Others like Augustine were less convinced
while some like Gregory the Great, two centuries later, considered it all
'outmoded'. Bolgar regards this extremism as representing the view of a
'small and highly articulate minority' who argued from 'premises well-
grounded in Christian belief that the world in general was evil ... that the
satisfaction of bodily needs ... had no real importance in the eyes of a
jealous God' and that man's true end was contemplation in a desert cell.[36]
But a minority though they were, they turned out to be 'the keepers of the
Christian conscience' and dominated education and learning. Individual
authors thought otherwise. Clement of Alexandria, working in the eastern
tradition, saw all Greek literature as going back to Jewish sources and
hence as contributing to the scriptural tradition.[37]

---

[34] Crouzet-Pavan 2007: 511, 532; Gilli 2004.   [35] Bolgar 1954: 20.
[36] Bolgar 1954: 48.   [37] Bolgar 1954: 49.

As the historian Peter Burke points out, there were also 'renaissances' of classical learning in Byzantium, but collapses too.[38] In the east it was at the beginning of the seventh century that Phocas shut down the University of Constantinople, and the new centre of higher learning which opened in the following reign 'was controlled by the Church'.[39] But in the eighth century, the rise of the iconoclastic movement brought 'disaster to Christianity and Hellenism alike' which led to the closing of the college and the burning of its books.[40] Bolgar speaks of an eleventh-century renaissance and of a period of 'ecclesiastical Hellenism' following the iconoclastic period when in 863 there is the founding of a university by Bardas, which is said to have had an educational programme that compares with the one that transformed Europe in the seventeenth century; 'rising capitalism' was not present and new ideas were discouraged. The eleventh century involved a deliberate cult of ancient Greece and what has been called a 'nationalist revival'. This was the Comnenian revival. It was followed by a counter-attack by the church and by the disastrous invasion of the west and then by a further, 'Palaeologue Renaissance' which involved a more serious return to Greek culture and an educational reform. The church went on the retreat against this intellectual revival that encouraged secular knowledge. Plethon was 'the most influential Platonist of his day',[41] a humanist who was exiled by the church, one of a batch of scholars who came to the Council of Florence, of one of whom, Argyropoulus, it has been said that he was 'in every way equal, if not superior, to the Italian Humanists among whom he worked'.[42] Byzantium did not take the same course as the west, partly because it was so embroiled in war (against the Turks) and partly because the church 'was there to circumscribe the action of secular studies which, properly followed, were bound to fill men's heads with pagan ideas'.[43]

One also had renascences within Islam that looked back in a secular sense to the Greek classics, as well as religious reformations that looked book to the Quran. Their own achievements also fed into the Italian Renaissance. In Islam, periods of stasis, involving the dominance of the religious, followed by periods of movement, as in many cases with activity with a more secular trend, were not uncommon. One of the reasons that periods of flourishing in Islam, and maybe elsewhere, too, seem less important, less history-changing to us, is the fact that changes from a more religious to a more secular approach, between periods of relative conservatism and even regression and those of effervescence, were more regular and less absolute in non-European cultural environments, having

---

[38] Burke 1978: 4.   [39] Bolgar 1954: 62.   [40] Bolgar 1954: 62.
[41] Bolgar 1954: 86.   [42] Bolgar 1954: 86.   [43] Bolgar 1954: 89.

the character of oscillations between two opposites rather than that of a final break with restrictive circumstances, which is how the European Renaissance appears to us. There was little of the continuity of secular activity which institutionalized education, particularly at the tertiary level, provided after the Italian Renaissance.

As we have seen, there were many areas where, in societies with writing, the recuperation of earlier texts was important, in science but also in a religious context. Texts were transmitted through schools, which is where reading and writing were taught. Literate societies always had schools which constantly look back to what has been written in the past. Moreover, even though these societies may practise what I have called (in perhaps a questionable way) 'restricted literacy', with reading and writing often constrained by the religion to which literacy is indebted, the opportunities for reading to open out the mind (which is what humanism did to a largely religious education) are in a sense always present. But it was often an intermittent, even a dangerous process, as the case of Aristotle in medieval times reminds us, for his work was forbidden in thirteenth-century Paris. The possibility of reviving any particular work from the past, of the classics for example, obviously depends upon its state of preservation and its location, often hidden in a monastic library. Of course, there was a differential likelihood of particular types of written works being preserved. In medieval England this was most likely to occur in a monastic library. But most libraries were small and largely religious. Some collections of books such as that of the Earl of Warwick have more representation of the lay secular romance, but often in French. In fact much writing did not survive and shorter poems were particularly vulnerable to loss, and recorded, if at all, on less permanent materials, like a wax tablet or jotted down on a fly-leaf of another, weightier tome.

Islam was particularly well placed in relation to conservation since it had some enormous libraries, though access itself was sometimes limited as they often depended on a court. In Baghdad Avicenna (Ibn Sina, 950–1037) consulted the immense collection which contained many books he claimed not to have seen before or since. But not only individuals had access to these collections. In the tenth century they were the focus for gatherings of men of letters and science at the local court, as in Aleppo, Shiraz and in Cairo.

The size of these libraries was sometimes very large, especially for the times. In the tenth century the library of al-Hakim II in Cordoba consisted of 400,000 'books' according to Almaqqari,[44] and 600,000 according to the Lebanese monk Casiri.[45] This was at a time when the

[44] Almaqqari 1855–61: 256.   [45] Hariz 1922: 110.

largest library in Christian Europe is said to be that of the monastery
of St Gall in Switzerland; it had 800 volumes. Chaucer's clerk had a
'large' personal library of thirty books. But of course what constituted
a 'book' was very important; it might have been a few sheets or a long
volume. In any case, the difference in size of holdings between Islam and
Europe is extraordinary. And it is partly due to the fact that the east of the
Mediterranean, and the Near East more generally, never experienced the
great decline in learning that occurred in the west; in England for example
it has been suggested that after the Romans literacy itself apparently
disappeared along with Christianity itself and many useful arts. When
Christianity returned, it excluded 'pagan' learning but retained Latin as
a lingua franca of the church in the west of Europe, and that provided a
sort of opening to the past. In the east (not in western Europe after the
schism) Greek continued to be used in Byzantium; that usage preserved
many works of learning, some of which were translated into Arabic at
the court of Baghdad in the ninth and tenth centuries, and eventually
formed part of the knowledge of the European Renaissance.

Islam was of course not the only source of learning, important as it was.
In the Renaissance, classical knowledge of Aristotle and other writers
came not only from Muslims but also from the Greeks of Byzantium
despite the 'mutual antagonism' of the two churches. This was the case
with the translations made by William of Brabant in Greece circa 1273,
where he had probably been sent to learn Greek.[46]

In Islam one main factor that promoted the numbers of books and the
circulation of information was not only the common use of the sacred
language, Arabic, but the advent of paper, which made use of waste (rags)
and of ubiquitious vegetable materials rather than the skins required for
parchment or indeed rather than the papyrus imported from abroad.
Paper came originally from China, and was then acquired by the Arabs
after the tenth century. Europeans first encountered it in Constantinople
and therefore called it *pergomena graeca*, despite the fact that all the
paper used there came from Muslim sources.[47] Its manufacture first came
through Islamic Spain, then went to Catalonia when Jaume conquered
Valencia (in 1238) and Jativa, subsequently to Italy[48] where it prospered
due to the plentiful supply of water. In northern Italy in the thirteenth
century paper-making spread but was also improved. The power of the
water in fast-flowing Appenine streams could be harnessed to drive the
wooden hammers used to pulp linen and rags. The process was similar
to fulling and to crushing mineral ores and was much more efficient than

---

[46] Toynbee 1954: 134–5.   [47] Spufford 2002: 255.
[48] Crudely in Genoa in 1235; see Burns 1981.

using pestle and mortar, as in the Near East and Spain whose paper the Italian variety soon replaced.[49] The manufacture of paper in the rest of Europe took time; in England it was only made, as distinct from imported, in the late fifteenth century, after the advent of printing and then only of a rough kind. White paper in England had in effect to await the coming of French Huguenot refugees at the time of the Revocation of the Edict of Nantes in 1685.

Whether using paper or parchment, this was a manuscript culture in which writing became valued as a form of art (as in calligraphy) as well as a mode of communication. But the one had an effect upon the other. Illuminating books, whether in Burgundy or Istanbul, was an extraordinarily time-taking task, demanding great skills. 'Publishing' other books was often a matter of copying classics, which limited the circulation of information in concentrating on what had already been written rather than on new works. However, the latter undoubtedly increased with printing.

That too was invented in China. The diffusion of the written word by mechanical means meant the possibilities of a yet wider growth in the circulation of knowledge, and hence in the accumulation of knowledge itself. In China, woodblock printing began as early as the eighth century.[50] In the Song period (960–1279 CE) the popularity of the civil service examination stoked the demand for the relevant books and drove the hand copy of these texts from the shelves by the eleventh or twelfth century. Otherwise, only slowly did the imprint replace the manuscript as the primary means for transmitting written culture. The turbulent period from the mid Tang (618–907 CE) to the early Song had repeatedly seen the loss of old books; over the eleventh century the government felt a compelling need to print a large number of medical texts as well as the Confucian classics, the Buddhist canon, imperial edicts, almanacs, contract forms and ephemeral sheets on the examination results. By the end of the twelfth century, printing was flourishing in northern Fujian, the centre of cheap popular printing.[51] Elsewhere this was not necessarily the case; for example, in the lower Yangzi printing only became dominant in the sixteenth century (save for the Confucian classics for which there was a constant demand). By the mid Ming commercial considerations including the use of moveable type had made printing much more competitive than formerly, so there was a significant expansion. Even so, manuscript production continued to be used in certain spheres of communicative activity and the changeover was gradual. Although printing was invented in China, it did not seem to have had the sudden,

---

[49] Spufford 2002: 357.   [50] McDermott 2006: 43.   [51] McDermott 2006: 48.

revolutionary, effect that it appears to have had in Europe where it was combined with the press.[52] That is to say, when printing came in the west, for most purposes the use of manuscript quickly faded out, anyhow for books; in the Chinese case the two processes persisted together over a long period. There does not seem to have been the rapid efflorescence of the written word that accompanied the coming of the printing press in the west. There this transformation had to do not simply with the use of moveable metal type and paper, which the Chinese also had, but with the use of an alphabetic script and the press, which they did not have. Combined with the radical breakthrough to secular knowledge and to secular arts, the printing press lay at the heart of the Italian Renaissance and the revival of classical knowledge.

Printing in the west, like the alphabet, has been seen by some as a uniquely European development which contributed profoundly to the growth of education, knowledge, freedom and even democracy. Those who have made these claims have drawn their conclusions largely from the study of their own literary heritage. So too with the argument made by the critic Ian Watt and myself[53] regarding literacy in ancient Greece (and hence the subsequent European tradition) that the use of a simple method of alphabetic writing had contributed much to that civilization. Our claim played down the Asiatic origin of the consonantal alphabetic script in Phoenicia, which spread to many eastern cultures, and the great achievements that could be made with other forms of writing (as with logographic writing in China). The literary critic Marshall McLuhan[54] and the historian Elizabeth Eisenstein, in her fine study, confined their research on printing and its revolutionary impact to the one continent and to this particular change in the means of communication. Their work ran the danger of attributing too much to Europe and too much to printing, though the addition of the press itself was unique. The same problem occurs with the literary historian Walter Ong's comprehensive studies on changes in education in the wake of printing.[55] These various innovations were not purely European and have to be seen in a comparative light, as does the Italian Renaissance itself.

That saw the rebirth of aspects of European classical civilization, epitomized by the crowning of Petrarch in a reconstituted ceremony in Rome,[56] and somewhat later it was stimulated by the circulation of its texts in print. At this time there was also an opening up of new possibilities, with the coming of the printing press encouraging not only the much wider circulation of earlier works but also of new ones too, such as

---

[52] Eisenstein 1979.   [53] Goody and Watt 1963.   [54] McLuhan 1962.   [55] Ong 1974.
[56] The poet's crown was awarded to Mussato twenty-six years before.

Elizabethan drama. So while that change in the means of communication was often employed initially simply to reproduce the classics, it also gave a much wider circulation to new ideas, in the arts as in the sciences. The accelerated movement of information meant that those developments had a wider and more immediate audience throughout Europe, leading in time to more rapid responses, to swifter corrections and thus to the accumulation of tested propositions about the natural world. That movement was critical to what the historian of science Joseph Needham and others refer to as the birth of 'modern science' when European achievement in that area began to pull ahead of that of the Chinese. Now, as the eighteenth-century American president Jefferson said, the printers would never leave us standing still and the printing house, the collective home of metalworkers as distinct from the more solitary work of the scriptoria or even of the wood-carving workshop, was a centre for discussion as well as for reproduction.[57]

That 'unrest' applied widely beyond printing and affected the sciences as well as the arts. Although it is Renaissance painting that commands the visual attention, there was much going on in other intellectual fields. The period is intimately connected with the Scientific Revolution, and Renaissance men such as Leonardo covered both fields, as did John Donne in his poetry. However, in comparative terms, the arts and the sciences need a distinct treatment. The arts are essentially local (or localized); they can hardly be considered outside a specific cultural context, European Christendom for example, or Buddhist China. But the sciences are more universal, with systems of counting spreading from India, to Islam, to Europe, as with 'Arabic' numerals, and astronomical data gathered in Beijing being used in Spain. It is worth remarking, recalling our discussion of forms of writing, that alphabetic scripts are heavily local but that hieroglyphic (iconic) ones are not tied to phonemes and are therefore universal linguistically. The difference between the arts and sciences affected not only supply but demand. The Arabs did not translate Greek literature but they wanted Greek science, which held true of 'other cultures' more generally. Nevertheless, despite the relative universality of the sciences, Europeans see their continent as providing the springboard for 'modern science' as in J. D. Bernal's study of *Science in History*,[58] which pays no attention at all to Chinese science (not modern!) but only to Europe – with a nod to Islam.

More generally, that 'unrest' meant that the resurrection of classical texts, both then and later, led to the frequent reference to classical, pagan religion in addition to Christianity. Dante's *Divine Comedy* and,

[57] Cited by Innis 1951: 24.   [58] Bernal 1954.

post-Renaissance, Milton's *Paradise Lost* make much use of classical 'mythology' as well as of Christian themes, the one composed before printing, the second after, but both subject to humanist influences. In looking at the classics, the authors understood they were dealing with 'myths', i.e. with what was not literally true, for they would not have used the term 'myth' of the Old Testament story; that was 'true' at another level. The re-emergence of classical mythology, which the first Christians understood to be an aspect of earlier, pagan religion, was not altogether new. In the first place, it had continued to be an element in the reckoning of time, not only of daily reckoning in the form of Saturn's day, but also of the months, such as December, the tenth month. In the second, Europe continued to be surrounded by the material remains of classical culture. In the third place, classical literature continued to be read because Latin was not only the foundation of the Romance languages but was the language of communication and worship within the western church, just as Greek was in the eastern.

But this reference back increased enormously with the various renascences and their search for texts, which led to a great revival of interest in ancient mythology and in all things classical. Islam also had a language, a spoken language (Arabic), that was largely devoted to the religion and with which it was often identified. God's language was the language of the Book; the Quran could be written in no other. But all that the reader had to look back to in pre-Islamic Arabia was some poetry and little else (apart from the Greek works which were studied in the Levant). It was the same with Judaism, which insisted upon the use of Hebrew for religious purposes and, eventually for the new nation of Israel, displacing the Yiddish, the Ladino and partly too the Arabic from daily use as well. But Christianity had no local, Near Eastern, equivalent as a lingua franca. Although many of its early Scriptures had been in Aramaic, the New Testament was soon translated into Greek and Latin – to some extent both languages of pagan conquests, which brought with them all their classical baggage. Christian fathers of the church, aware of the dangers, attempted to compose and substitute their own literature in those languages for the classical, partly for teaching in the remaining schools that survived or, more likely, were refounded by the church.

Apart from this looking back, the Italian Renaissance itself was followed by an efflorescence of culture at many different levels, in the arts obviously, the rebirth of secular painting, of secular drama (and the theatre generally) just as was the case for knowledge of the world, for example with the Scientific Revolution. The two were not altogether independent since the looking back was to a more secular, 'pagan', age where worldly enquiry and the arts were freer. Moreover, for all these various fields,

the flowering of that Renaissance was obviously connected with the economic revival of European trade and manufacture, begun earlier, not
only within Europe but especially of the trade with the east in which Italy
was a dominant player. The fall of the Roman empire as a result of its
internal and external problems, and later on the Arab conquests, had led
to a drastic collapse in trade in western Europe as well as to a decline of
urban life. One obvious indication of the collapse that took place after
Rome is what happened to the famous roads they had built. Some of
these paved highways turned into country tracks, fit only for pack animals. Stone bridges were not repaired until eventually the ecclesiastical
bridge-building charities took an interest in the twelfth century, with the
revival of trade. Obviously travelling merchants had a harder time before
this reconstruction took place, leading to what in northern Italy has been
called the 'road revolution' of the thirteenth century.

The collapse of the urban economy initially hindered the growth of
the towns and the bourgeoisie. The economy rested not so much on
urban exchange as on rural activity. The development of that economy,
particularly the application of animal traction and the use of the plough,
had of course been part of the achievement of the Bronze Age. With
the downturn in the exchange economy in the west following the end
of empire, the 'surplus' rural production was siphoned off by landlords
who built up large manors, together with large courts, which became
the centres for luxury consumption. Part of these luxuries came from
the east in return for bullion from the silver mines, or for raw materials
such as wood and other metals, which the east needed then as now. In
general, the growth of permanent courts, as distinct from the circulating
variety so common in the early Middle Ages, meant the development of
towns with their specialist workers, artisans, merchants, who catered not
only for the urban and rural populations but also engaged in the luxury
trade for the nobility and their hangers-on. The courts, in their governing
role, took increasing proportions of the surplus in a cash economy, much
of which was spent in war or in building, especially the construction of
large palaces for living and ruling, and huge churches and chapels for
worship, for thanking God for his bounty. At the capital the king's court
often attracted the dwelling of his lesser nobles, who established their
own courts nearby and increased the demand for luxury goods. In the
thirteenth century, bishops also built large houses in the capital from
which to administer their domains, as did the bishop of Winchester in
Southwark or the archbishop of Canterbury at Lambeth. The towns were
however small, especially compared with parts of the eastern world such
as China. 'Since classical antiquity no city in Western Europe, not even
Lombard Milan, had exceeded around 30,000 inhabitants, until the late

twelfth and early thirteenth century. The new opportunities for rulers
and their nobility for living on money incomes away from their rural
estates made the growth of cities possible again in the west for the first
time for three quarters of millennium.'[59]

Trade already began to revive in the eighth century when the commerce of Venice restarted with the Byzantine and Islamic worlds which
had not suffered the same decline as the west. There had been some
communication between Europe and Asia along the northern route to
the east via the Baltic, but commercially it was not of great importance.
With the trade of Venice, the Mediterranean reopened, importing manufactured luxury goods, especially silks, perfumes, porcelain and spices
from the east, and exporting raw products, metals, bullion and eventually some woollen goods in return.[60] Woollen cloth was exported in great
quantity to Mediterranean countries in the second half of the twelfth
century from Champagne, England and Flanders. But the woollen cloth
of Flanders was of better quality and drove the others from the market
in the middle of the thirteenth century; two years later, that of England
recovered. One historian speaks of the 'fabulous fortunes',[61] tied to its
commercial success. Gradually trade revived more generally and so too
did Italy's manufacture, with the adoption of the production of paper and
of silk from the east and the export of finished woollen cloth in exchange.

The importance of trade to the Renaissance is clear from Spufford's
study of late medieval times. Trade and commerce developed in Italy,
its first home, with the opening up of commerce, internally within
Europe, especially to courts, but also to the eastern Mediterranean with
the growth of east–west exchange. Production and commercial activity
spread to other Italian towns, to Genoa, to Florence, to Bologna, to the
Amalfi coast, which in turn colonized parts of the Aegean and Black Sea
coasts. It was the great trading cities of north and central Italy which
led what has been called the 'commercial revolution' of the thirteenth
century, creating the 'striking prosperity of the metropolitan groups'.
'It was this handful of very rich men of the newly enlarged Florentine
state, the Pazzi, the Pitti, the Strozzi, the Ruccellai, and above all the
crypto-princely Medici themselves who were among the first to patronize humanists, painters and sculptors, and, of course, to build, or rebuild,
their *palazzi* in the new "antique" fashion of the early Renaissance.'[62]
In all these activities Venice was one of the main leaders, at the same

---

[59] Spufford 2002: 93.
[60] The importance of luxury is stressed in the work of Sombart (1913 [1911]) and of Veblen (1925 [1899]).
[61] Crouzet-Pavan 2007: 315.   [62] Spufford 2002: 82.

time heavily involved in the Mediterranean trade and colonization in the east. Indeed, from the twelfth century, when trade had greatly increased, agents from Venice, Pisa and Genoa set up colonies in Constantinople, Alexandria and Acre.[63] The calculus of profit and loss was now carried out with Arabic numerals made known to Italians by Finbonacci's *Liber abbaci* (1228) which made many forms of reckoning more manageable.[64] Literacy made possible the diffusion of new techniques. Indeed, the *crédit bancaire* was obviously related to the use of writing and eventually of the printed word. And with the revival of trade came the efflorescence of the arts and of knowledge, as was the case elsewhere. Both required support, by patronage or by sale, from courts, landowners, church or traders, who contributed so much to the learning of the period. All art initially required patrons. If it were not the religious paintings commissioned first by the church or later by some politicians, then it was the court or in the Netherlands the bourgeoisie. Art was inevitably where the money was, the church, the court, then the expanding merchant and manufacturing class. In Europe most activity of this latter kind was in the textile trade, as among the Medicis of Florence where art flourished. The historian Peter Spufford asks '[i]s it more than coincidental that it was in these two optimistic decades at the beginning of the fifteenth century that patronage was available that helped the stylistic transition from late Gothic to early Renaissance to begin?'[65]

The Italians themselves spread out not only to the east but to the largest centres in Europe, to London by 1250, to Bruges a little later, in both places joining up with the smaller Hanseatic trade of the Baltic region where the League distributed Asian and other luxury goods. In London, the Italians included four groups, the Venetians, the Genovese, the Florentines and the Lucchese. They were not only involved in the wool trade and in banking but in eastern goods; the Venetian galleys brought round Asian pepper for the north.

The decline of commerce also had the opposite effect in the relative stasis in the Near East after the fifteenth century. Turkish and Egyptian commerce with East Asia was affected negatively by the navigation of the Atlantic powers round the Cape of Good Hope; although the trade did not stop altogether with the opening up of the direct sea route, the new journey made considerable inroads into the trade in spices and cotton goods. Moreover, some of the exports which had been at the heart of their commerce now moved increasingly westwards through the Mediterranean and to the Americas. In particular, the two Indian cultigens, sugar and cotton, went to the New World, as well as Ethiopian

---

[63] Spufford 2002: 19.   [64] Spufford 2002: 29.   [65] Spufford 2002: 489.

coffee, while the manufacture of cotton and silk textiles and paper became primary factors in Europe's new industries. All this meant a dramatic change in economic circumstance of the Islamic Near East, which also affected the arts and the knowledge industries.

It is clear that commercial activity meant that literacy was in great demand in the west, partly for sending letters between various establishments, partly through keeping the accounts of more complex transactions. The pressure on education was now from lay merchants as well as those working for the state and the church. All of these required literate personnel.[66] For example, price lists were an important part of commercial information which led in turn to various newsletters. So the pressure came from the business community for their sons to read, write and calculate, and they employed tutors to that end. We find a lay teacher of boys in Florence in 1275. The teaching profession blossomed out on the secular level and schooling expanded to take into account the nature of commercial transactions. Especially valuable was the work of Fibonacci, *Liber abbaci*, which we have mentioned, published in the early tenth century after a journey in the Arabic world and introducing Indian numbers to Italians, which allowed for more complex mathematical operations. The end of that century saw an invention of double entry book-keeping in Genoa or Tuscany, which was diffused by Pacioli's *Summa de arithmetica* printed in Venice in 1494. As Spufford remarks, 'Secular, vernacular education was well-established by the early fourteenth century.'[67] The commune of Lucca, for example, the home of the earliest large-scale production of silken clothes in the Christian west, with machines probably derived from China, in the mid fourteenth century funded a teacher of reading and writing as well as one for arithmetic and others too in order to keep up the educational infrastructure (silk was of course produced in Islamic Sicily and in Andalusia). In these commercial cities in northern Italy most artisans were literate. '[T]he cities that did most to promote education, like fourteenth-century Lucca, gained correspondingly commercially.'[68]

This commerce clearly encouraged demand, which in turn encouraged production. 'As well as a demand for better housing, better food and drink, and better clothing, there was also in every capital city a prodigious demand for conspicuous display such as gold and silver plate, or bronze and enamel from the Meuse valley, the Rhineland and Limoges, pearls from the Persian gulf, or diamonds, rubies and other gems from India.'[69] Much of the lavish clothing came from Italy which was a huge

---

[66] Spufford 2002: 28.   [67] Spufford 2002: 29.
[68] Spufford 2002: 410.   [69] Spufford 2002: 119.

workshop as well as being the centre of art. It also imported cloth and
other valuables from the east. All areas were dominated by Italians so
that this exchange was closely connected with the Renaissance. Indeed,
from one standpoint, art was just another commodity required by the
rich, the aristocracy or by churchmen. And most activity centred around
courts, both big and small, which in turn needed a bourgeoisie to supply
them. Exchange of goods in turn encouraged the exchange of information
throughout Europe. In 1471 the mathematician Johannes Müller wrote:
'it is easier for me to keep in touch with the learned of all countries, for
Nuremberg, thanks to the perpetual journeying of her merchants, may
be counted the centre of Europe'.[70] 'The technology of the western style
of printed book was itself disseminated within Europe along the routes
of trade, just as the printed books themselves became items of continent-
wide commerce.'[71] So too with many religious ideas, earlier the heresy
of of the Cathars, then the plague, as well as art itself, which all became
items of transfer as did other aspects of the Renaissance itself.

Spufford gives a useful account of the European merchant in medieval
times who was critical in this exchange, but his work is about Europe and
there is little indication of trading relationships that stretched indirectly
well outside that continent.[72] But the transfer not only of goods but
of information between east and west was enormous, especially with
the establishment of trading colonies at Istanbul and Alexandria in the
tenth century. While to confine a survey of trading activities to Europe is
thoroughly understandable, it does leave the reader with the impression
that the west always led the way, as with printing and the alphabet, which
was not at all the case.

For Europe there was another aspect to the contact with the east; the
revival of European trade and other relations meant mixing with another,
non-Christian, culture, as in their recent book the cultural historians Jardine and Botton have explained for Turkey, and that, like the return to
the works of the ancients, meant a greater interest in what other cultures,
other religions, had to say. Arabs and Jews had long been experiencing just
this, in India and in China. Together with a more general scepticism,[73] a
measure of secularization was generated by contact with other religions
which was beneficial both for the advance of science and for the freeing of the arts. But secularization of itself did not necessitate a rebirth,
though that took place with the discovery of classical culture. The greater
freedom of manoeuvre could also come about through the loosening of
bonds within a hegemonic religion. With outside stimulus, this loosening

[70] Spufford 2002: 390.   [71] Spufford 2002: 411.
[72] Spufford 2002.   [73] Goody 1998, chapter 11.

happened elsewhere too, as for instance in the Jewish emancipation in northern Europe (in the south a measure of freedom had occurred much earlier) where there was no rebirth but rather an efflorescence. As the historian Eric Hobsbawm has pointed out, emancipation did not take place in the north until the early part of the nineteenth century, much later in some cases, and when it did, it was 'like a lid coming off a pressure cooker'.[74] Jews suddenly took a vigorous part in the theatre and the visual arts as well as in science, in fields which had not been open to them earlier. As was the case with the better-known Italian Renaissance, religious control of the arts, resulting in a measure of iconophobia, was swept aside, leading in this latter case to a 'Jewish Renaissance' in the whole range of the visual arts. Iconophobia was exchanged for iconophilia in an extraordinary transformation. Efflorescence was not a rebirth, a return to earlier glories; there was no tradition of figurative representation (apart from certain marginal cases) to go back to. Painting and the visual arts, like natural science, were imported from outside. The west, on the other hand, did look back.

The other point has to do with the founding of institutions which are now so important to modernity and which crystallized the secular approach to the arts and sciences. Much has been written about the beginning of universities in Europe in the twelfth century from the cathedral (rather than the monastic) schools, at Salerno, Montpellier, Bologna, Padua, Paris, in the thirteenth at Oxford and Cambridge. This development is taken to be a significant feather in the European cap, the creation of an institution of all the local scholars, not of universal scope (as universities might imply). That was certainly an important point of growth, but again it was not unique; it was considered to be so in western Europe only because of the earlier collapse of learning, especially higher learning, and ignorance of other societies. Under the Greeks and Romans, higher learning had of course existed, in the Lyceum and in the Academy. To the east of the Mediterranean, even after the fall of Rome, such schools continued to operate and philosophy was taught in Alexandria until Justinian suppressed it as pagan in the fourth century, here as elsewhere. But the great library at Alexandria, partly destroyed by the Romans, continued until Muslim times. As with other literate religions, the first preoccupation of the Arabs when they occupied a town was to build a mosque, construct a hospital and open a free school, a centre for teaching literacy, largely religious, which implied a library. In Cordoba, Abd al-Rahman III (Abderam, r. 912–61), father of al-Hakam II, did all this but also founded public libraries in the main cities and in his

---

[74] Hobsbawm 2005.

capital reunions of scholars and poets took place in 'academies', either in the palace or in the houses of the learned, and these included women of high rank. There were academies of medicine, of mathematics, of history and poetry in Cordoba.[75] Higher learning did not come to a halt with Islam but continued at courts such as that of al-Mamun in Baghdad with its school of translators from the Greek. Later on there were the madrasas such as Al-Azhar in Cairo, founded in the tenth century, which began a tradition of religious instruction similar to that of later European and Buddhist universities. The madrasas, which were started in Iran in the eleventh century, were independent of mosques, privately endowed schools which concentrated on Islamic knowledge. However, the 'foreign sciences' continued elsewhere, informally rather than institutionally, except perhaps in medecine where the *maristan* hospitals also existed independently. For instance, in Cordoba we find in the Alcazar a library which, as we have seen, contained a much larger collection of books than any in northern Europe. The extensive monastic library imagined by Umberto Eco in *The Name of the Rose* does not really reflect the reality of northern Europe at that time. At the founding of the University of Cambridge, the library was minute compared with that of Cordoba. In the fifteenth century there were only a few hundred books, representing a far from universal coverage of human knowledge even for the time. It was mainly religious, adapted to the training of literate priests. Some have seen the growth of universities in Europe as being the key variable in the birth of what Needham calls the 'modern science', of the Renaissance, of modernity itself. But in a world perspective they were not unique and in their teaching were closely tied to the dominant religion. They too had to break out into secular studies. The influence of the church remained strong, though now limited intellectually. Even well on in the nineteenth century, fellows of colleges in Oxford and Cambridge were automatically able to act as priests. It was a feature of the Lucasian chair, the second holder of which was Isaac Newton, that the holder did not have to belong to a college and did not therefore have to be ordained.

Universities were not unique to the west nor to Islam, except in their name. They are reported from Nalanda and elsewhere in Buddhist India possibly in the Gupta period (third to sixth century);[76] there were many others. The sinologist Mark Elvin finds 'analogies to Universities in China', the best known of which was the 'Great School' run by the government during the Song dynasty, which was organized around examinations in mathematics and medicine. We may be sceptical about the

[75] Hariz 1922: 19.   [76] Thapar 2002: 306.

running of higher education by governments, associated with mosques or indeed in having groups of scholars attached to courts and their libraries, as in Cordoba. But there is no reason to think these were less free intellectually than the early universities in Europe, closely tied as those were to the church and to the training of priests and administrators.

After the decline of Rome, higher education was seriously interrupted in the west but it continued relatively smoothly in parts of the east. However, I want to avoid leaving the impression of total discontinuity in the west in contrast to the continuities of the east. Constantinople, in the Levant, had its nomadic invaders which led to some disruption. The great library of Baghdad was destroyed by Mongol conquerors who were said to have used the books to build a causeway across the Tigris. There were also more ideological attacks. The creation of libraries was followed in many cases by their active destruction – in China, under Islam, and elsewhere. There was not only the accidental damage of war or by an 'act of God', but it could be the deliberate policy of an invader, as in the treatment of the Baghdad library, or it could be a result of the rejection of the kind of knowledge they contained, as with Caliph Omar and the library of Alexandria under the Arabs. Caliph Omar considered as worthy of destruction the books that did not conform to the Word of God as presented in the Quran. Nor was this attitude essentially different from that of St Augustine and other apologists for Christianity such as Justinian, who closed down the teaching of pagan philosophy in Athens and elsewhere for similar reasons. The west had apparently no parallel examples of book burning, until the Nazis, but books were often excluded from the canon, libraries were much smaller, in England monastic collections were dispersed at the Reformation (to be collected by Archbishop Parker at Corpus Christi, Cambridge) and there was always the Catholic Index. In fact the disappearance of books was a recurring phenomenon throughout the history of the written word, in China as in Europe, be it through the destruction of libraries, the censorship of individual books, or even their deliberate burning. But in written cultures rebirth, renascence, had also led to the recovery of some past learning, of former achievements; it is an aspect of literacy and of writing that such recuperation is possible.

I say throughout the history of the written word for here we are in the presence of a widespread phenomenon. However, more or less since the Renaissance we seem to have reached a point of what, for the economy, Rostow saw as the initiation of continuous self-sustaining growth.[77] There are some blips in knowledge systems, of which the religious efforts to redirect the teaching of evolution could be considered one, with the

[77] Rostow 1959.

control by political regimes falling into another category. Growth in systems of production and exchange has always taken place, technology has regularly advanced, though the state and religion have occasionally tried to stop it. But knowledge systems have been the subject of definite restrictions, not only those internal to the field but external ones due to outside interference. What we now find in Europe is self-sustaining growth, not only in the economy but in systems of knowledge, at least of 'scientific' ones. There is clearly a vectorial process in other civilizations too but there are also blips, periods of stasis or rejection. Such periods of interruption are probably no longer possible (especially given worldwide communication via the internet), at least on a large scale. Growth in information and growth in the economy are undoubtedly connected; the new universities of Europe may have provided a distinct, independent, institutional environment for knowledge, and technology may have reached the stage when the heightened rhythm of achievement is impossible to reject, either of that or of science. We may have reached a point of no return in knowledge systems too. The idea of 'self-sustaining growth' as a characteristic of the 'modern' is not altogether mistaken. Modern societies do seem to have embarked on a different course. But not altogether different. Change is characteristic of earlier societies and even modern growth has its setbacks, its intermissions. More significantly, growth in one particular cultural unit may stimulate another; intercourse is global, as the modes of communication and of transport have extended more widely and become more rapid.

The development of more or less continuous intellectual growth may have characterized the European university since the time of the Renaissance, partly through the secularization of knowledge, partly through world domination, partly through economic and scientific development. But it would be wrong to see this development as arising only from the looking back to our own cultural past, to the revival of Antiquity. Firstly, all fields are not to be treated in the same way; the arts had a different trajectory from the sciences. Initially the pursuit of science, under all religions but most acutely under the Abrahamistic ones, brought religion into some disagreement with an enquiry about issues on which God or the supernatural was considered to have spoken. For this situation to change, a measure of secularization had to take place; this also occurred in other cultures where there is little doubt that the supernatural inhibited the realm of enquiry into the natural world by providing divine answers to questions which science demanded should be open to investigation. However, periods in which freer thinking and action were encouraged existed elsewhere too and were described as 'humanist' by the Jewish historian Zafrani for Islam; they involved a limited setting aside of religion and hence offered a degree of liberalization of thought, what Max Weber referred to as a 'demystification', what the historian Keith Thomas called the 'decline of magic', a process that happened segmentally in other spheres. In the law, for example, the king's justice was always distinct from ecclesiastical courts but increasingly took over the jurisdiction. That process of freeing activity from religious control was even more obvious in the visual and dramatic arts which had been the subject of heavy taboos, in Europe circumscribed until the Renaissance by allowing only religious themes.

One also needs to reckon with the contribution of Muslim culture to the Italian Renaissance, not so much of Islamic religion, though as an alternative to the Christian account its presence encouraged the querying of specific beliefs and hence may have served to promote the secular. Clearly Muslim influence was less in the figurative arts, where early on during the Iconoclastic controversy Christianity had discarded certain taboos against representation which were retained by Islam and Judaism until recently. Already allowing religious art, in the Renaissance Christianity went back to classical models, while Islam like Judaism pursued the ban on graven images. So the other Abrahamistic religions had little or no influence on the visual arts, though Islam did have on abstract design and on architecture especially in towns like Venice.[78] In literature the influence was less clear cut. For instance, Dante's great work is said to have been influenced by Islamic accounts of Muhammad's nocturnal travels.

The resurrection of another literary genre, fiction, which had virtually disappeared in Europe after the fall of the Roman empire, may also have been influenced by Islamic and Indian traditions of narrative storytelling. Some forms of Italian poetry, such as the sonnet and the *canzoniere*, seem to have originated in southern Italy and to have been affected by the highly Islamized court of Norman Sicily. But most significantly, the troubadours of twelfth-century Languedoc, celebrated as the originators of European love poetry, almost certainly owed much in their style, content and prosody to Islamic achievements in Spain and elsewhere. Love poetry (*ghazal*) comprised a special category in that tradition and it was composed by the Abbasid poets from 750 CE whom the Islamist H. A. R. Gibb calls 'the true humanists of Islam'.[79]

Some fields such as philosophy may appear to have owed little directly to Islam, because, as the philosopher Richard Rorty has argued,[80] philosophy as we know it was a product of the Antiquity–Renaissance line of western thought. In fact not only Europeans but the Arabs looked back

---

[78] Howard 2000.   [79] Gibb 1950.   [80] Zhang 2006.

to that Greek learning, to Plato and to Aristotle. In humanistic periods Islam distinguished philosophy from theology, contributing something of their own to that field. But the later European tradition hardly included the Arabic philosophy of Averroës (although he has been described as the father of secular thought in Europe) or the Jewish one of Maimonides, explicitly at any rate, though these writers had their influence.[81] In the social sciences the work of the historian Ibn Khaldun (d. 1406), author of the *al-Muqaddimah*, which often referred back to Aristotle, was quite neglected until the present century and even in Islam was hardly followed up. All in all, the greatest debt of Europe to Islam and the east was in the hard sciences but not in religion nor in the arts.

Nevertheless, it is important to recognize the debt to Islam in these other fields in order to disabuse ourselves of a measure of that self-congratulatory, ethnocentric element that marks so much of our thinking about the role of the Italian Renaissance in the present and past world situation. Otherwise we are likely to misunderstand the nature of advances in science; for example, a Eurocentric attitude seems to distort the position of Salerno or Montpellier in the discussion of the history of medicine, as we see in chapter 2. The problem is that in Europe we so often draw a direct line from Antiquity through feudalism to the Renaissance and the rebirth of Antiquity, that we not only exclude the contribution of others but overlook the fact that as far as many aspects of knowledge were concerned the direct line between the classical world and that of the Renaissance had been decisively broken with the collapse of secular education and its eventual replacement by church schools which paid little or no attention to alternative ways of thinking and acting. Nor, of course, did the Near East escape the effects of religious ideology on education and on knowledge. But the deleterious effect on science seems to have been less strong under Islam, partly perhaps because of their literary inheritance from the Greeks[82] but mainly because of the persistence of urban culture. That persistence meant the continuation of both trade and schools.

The notion of alternatives (of societies as well as in such societies) is essential as it recognizes the non-intrinsic nature of cultural supremacy, that is, it does not attribute advantage or backwardness to a permanent quality of the culture such as genius or spirit or mentality but to factors that can change over the course of time. History is rarely written from this point of view but is often essentialist in its approach, often ethnocentric.

---

[81] Khalidi 2005.
[82] Aristotle for many was known as the 'first great teacher', Robinson 1996.

My own interest in the comparative study of the Renaissance clearly has a political dimension. Contemporary leaders continually refer to the contributions made to the modern world by Judaeo-Christian civilization. Islam is set aside although it belongs very firmly to the trilogy of major religions based upon some of the same sacred texts, going back to classical knowledge, and having many of the same values. But not only is Islam often excluded from the European account of the Renaissance but so too are India and China, some of whose achievements reached Europe through an Islam that stretched from southern Spain to the Far East. And their achievements were very considerable. In the latter case, Joseph Needham has argued that until the sixteenth century, Chinese science was in many cases in advance of Europe. And in the economic sphere, anthropologist Francesca Bray has described the country as the major exporter of manufactured goods in the world before the nineteenth century and only then, according to the sinologist Kenneth Pomeranz,[83] did the Great Divergence occur. India too was ahead of Europe in some respects, for example, in the use and production of cotton before the Industrial Revolution and intellectually with its 'Arabic' numerals and mathematics. These cultures were not simply sitting back, waiting to be overtaken by a renascent Europe. They made their own contribution to scientific, technological and economic advance, contributing to the European Renaissance in the process. But the result of drawing and emphasizing an exclusive Antiquity–Renaissance line has been to exclude non-European cultures from the growth of civilization. I will not speak further of the political implications except to argue that at times this exclusion, thought or unthought, encourages an almost racist fallacy of superiority towards the rest of the world. Some such feelings are doubtless justified since the nineteenth century, some would argue since the Renaissance. Islam and other societies may argue for a moral superiority but in the nineteenth century the west outstripped all others in economic and military might, as well as in education. What is quite illegitimate, and calls forth the epithet 'racist', is, on a quasi-genetic basis, to project this superiority backwards into earlier periods for which the evidence is lacking.

This problem of ethnocentric history did not start with the Renaissance, nor yet with the classical civilizations. For Antiquity was conceived as a period different from the Bronze or even the Iron Age, quite distinctively European and separate from Asia, a period that started Europe off on the unique path to modernization. No one else had an Antiquity, no one else had democracy (Greece invented it!), just we Europeans. But

---

[83] Pomeranz 2000.

was that actually the case? The Phoenicians in Tyre had a democratic system; they also invented our alphabet. So too had Carthage, a colony of Tyre. But Carthage, a Mediterranean rival to Greece and Rome, has been largely written out of the Antiquity script. I do not want to go all the way with the thesis of the cultural historian Martin Bernal's *Black Athena*, but the manner in which the Semitic-speakers have been excluded from western history does seem to have parallels with the treatment of the Arab contributions to the Renaissance. The Asian input to communication in the form of the Semitic (consonantal) alphabet (even though with this 'literacy' it provided Christian Europe with its scriptures) has been set aside, as has democracy in Tyre, Carthage and elsewhere. The whole weight of classical, humanistic, learning was concentrated upon the Greek and Roman societies which created Antiquity, European Antiquity, as a form of civilization which had to be differentiated from the Bronze Age cultures of the Near East and Asia in view of developments, and which was revived in the Renaissance.

They were of course different from Egypt and the Near East but the attempt to cut this off in a radical way, as Europeanists have often done, has been disputed by scholars like Bernal and in fact by the very Judaeo-Christian tradition, although it is reinforced by the contemporary inclusion of Israel in Europe for many purposes.

It would be more accurate to see a flowering of the Bronze Age in the whole ancient world around the Mediterranean, including the Near East, a flowering which received a drastic setback with the fall of the Roman empire, and in some respects with the advent of all the Abrahamistic religions, although both the negative and the positive aspects have to be balanced out. The eastern Mediterranean always kept its commercial and intellectual links with east and with central Asia. Moreover Europe itself revived again economically after contact with the Levant which had never lost its urban culture, its Asian trade and its tradition of learning in quite the same way, although there too were many setbacks. Part of our study of the Renaissance means reviewing these other traditions of development.

Should we then see the European Renaissance as part of a wider rebirth of culture and knowledge that included the Islamic world from the ninth century when they were translating Greek texts in Baghdad, then producing paper and establishing a large library in the city that is now the locus of so much civil and military strife? As Fernand Braudel emphasized, the inland sea, the Mediterranean, became a node of communication once again, beginning with Venice's early revival in the eighth century. The mortal remains of St Mark were acquired from Alexandria in the ninth, the bronze horses decorating his church came from the Hippodrome of

Constantinople during the devastation caused by the Fourth Crusade of 1204. But trade meant the exchange of knowledge, of 'culture', as well as of goods (and sometimes of stolen goods, as in the case of St Mark). The bringing of his remains to Venice 'represented a great boost to the city's ability to expand its trade in the eastern and southern Mediterannean, to become an important point of departure for pilgrimage to the Holy Land, and to establish herself as . . . the "hinge" between Europe and the East'.[84]

Certainly we have to view the Mediterranean as a lake, in the manner of the historian Braudel. Its banks were intercommunicating even in ancient times. It is not a problem of whether a specific feature or particular object was transmitted between ancient Egypt and Greece, between one part of the coast and another, but given the seafaring peoples on its shores, what was impossible? Grain, olive oil, African red ware, all were traded. The fields of the south supplied the towns of the north. Why should the same societies not have been exchanging information? European Greece was not cut off from what is now Asiatic Turkey. Indeed, it possessed many important cities on the Ionian coast, such as Miletus, Ephesus, Halicarnassus and others, and it exercised much influence in Persia, central Asia and in northern India. They were also communicating with what are now the Syrian and Lebanese cities to the south, inhabited by Semitic-speaking Phoenicians whose settlements stretched from Ugarit to Tyre and further south to Canaan and Israel and on to Egypt and present-day Tunisia and Spain. Too often we think of Greece and Phoenicia as cultural units. So in a sense they were, but not in any self-enclosed way. These were seafaring peoples with their backs to the mountains, whose natural movement was often over the water. Exchange was in their blood. They wanted metals, European metals, which remained important for the east, as for all societies after the coming of the ages of Copper and Bronze. For these they travelled widely and would be well aware of each other's institutions so that the knowledge of particular modes of government and representation constituted a common pool. Hence we should see the distribution of the particular types of democratic government around the Mediterranean as part of an interacting system of goods, institutions and ideas.

But the Mediterranean itself was clearly not self-enclosed. There was no boundary with the Near East, with Iraq and Persia. And the Islamic religion stretched right across central Asia to China, just as China traded to the Near East and established settlements along the way. So too of course Christian (Nestorian) and Jewish communities existed all along

[84] Carboni 2007: 15.

the Silk Road, which was later used by Italian traders. So Chinese culture touched upon the Mediterranean in a variety of ways. Muslims themselves recognized the importance of this link for knowledge as well as for trade. The Hadith has a saying, 'Pursue learning (*ilm*) from the cradle to the grave even as far away as China.' The Chinese had their own trading quarter in Baghdad, the founder of which city, al-Mansur, also exchanged embassies to the west with Charlemagne. Then there were other links of the Near East with India, both overland through Iran and by sea from Egypt, Ethiopia and Arabia. One thinks of the Indian sailor shipwrecked in Egypt whose story Ghosh traced from the Geniza documents in his book *In an Antique Land*, and of the Roman establishments at Arikamedu and Musaris in southern India, connected with the spice trade. Then there was the arrival of Semitic-speakers from the Mediterranean area, all of trading stock, with the monophysitic Christians supposedly led by St Thomas,[85] with the Muslims who settled on the west coast, with the Jewish inhabitants in Cochin and further north whose activities are so vividly portrayed in the documents found in Cairo.[86]

So, yet wider networks affect the cultural shifts, the wide-ranging Muslim sphere stretching from Spain to Canton and the northern borders of China that transmitted paper, porcelain, gunpowder, silk and other commodities, as well as information (in astronomy for example), and the Indian Ocean one that shipped pepper, spices, cotton goods and knowledge such as Indian ('Arabic') numerals, which Needham considers may even have originated in China (at least the concept of zero). The notion of a purely European Renaissance has recently been criticized by Brotton, in *The Renaissance Bazaar*, where he writes 'once we begin to understand the impact of eastern cultures upon mainland Europe (c.1400–1600), then this traditional understanding of the European Renaissance collapses'.[87] His own enquiries have been towards specifying the contribution of the Near East to events in Europe, a point that is certainly well taken. But it is not only a question of *their* contribution to *our* Renaissance but whether similar rebirths occurred elsewhere.

Alongside communication and the flow of goods and ideas between networks of exchanging cultures, there were of course parallel developments (the *commenda*, for example, a method whereby merchants shared risks and profits) some of which arose out of the internal elaboration of distinct merchant societies, as they distanced themselves from court and religious hierarchies. Particularly intriguing are the parallels in bourgeois

[85] These Christians of south India were Nestorians who were condemned as heretics by their fellows in the fifth century and may have fled to India as early as the sixth.
[86] Goitein 1963.   [87] Brotton 2002: 3.

society that appear in Clunas's discussion of written materials on connoisseurship in China which appeared at about the same time as this activity was developing in Europe, undoubtedly an independent development. It was similar with the secular theatre which made its reappearance in early Tudor Britain a little before *kabuki* theatre emerged among Japanese merchants in the seventeenth century (both the No plays of Japan and of classical theatre Kalidasa in India were of course earlier). An elaborate haute cuisine and culture of flowers were found in China earlier than similar developments in Europe and the Near East; they were not borrowed but were manifestations, first of a differentiated elite culture, then one mainly consisting of the bourgeoisie, largely merchant, in both areas. Sociologically the practices had their roots in similar conditions.

The Renaissance and the Reformation are clearly European events, and ones that have been given iconic status in the development of modern society. My present interest is directed not to eliminating their significance in Europe, nor to proposing that their origins lay partly overseas (though some elements certainly did), but to querying their uniqueness and hence the position given to them in world, as distinct from European, history. The uniqueness of the Reformation is a minor theme for present purposes. It is the Renaissance that lies at the centre of my concerns, and here I want to confine my attention to similar activities outside Europe, their comparative neglect and what that implies for European historiography. I turn now to consider an aspect of the non-European contribution to the Renaissance in Europe.

2   Montpellier and medicine in Europe

I begin with Europe in the early Renaissance and with a particular focus on the south, largely in order to show the links with other cultures, especially to Muslim, Jewish and through them to India and to China. This transmission is relatively well known but rarely sufficiently emphasized in Europeanist accounts of the Renaissance nor of the growth of learning in the west, which was not so different from its history elsewhere as many would propose. The 'revolution' was the result of our post-Roman 'backwardness'. I show this in the field of medicine, at what was said to be the earliest such school in Europe, and one of the first institutes of higher learning, the Faculty at Montpellier, though its priority is disputed by Salerno. It is important that this achievement was happening in scientific or technical knowledge, since so much emphasis has been placed upon the artistic contribution of the Italian Renaissance. However, we need to consider the sciences as well as the arts; but we are so accustomed to the glorious paintings, to its music, to its theatre and to its fiction, all of which activities were recently reborn in secular form after a considerable hiatus. It was the same in science.

The argument about pan-European continuity from the Bronze Age onwards up to the Renaissance, as well as about the importance of non-European contributions to the latter, and therefore to modern society, is clearer in the sciences than the arts, for here there has been a measurable progression over the centuries. Technologies have grown in efficiency, from healing and time-keeping to missiles of mass destruction. On the other hand, on the theoretical side our knowledge has been held up by religions which have claimed the sole authority. But if we look at the situation from the standpoint of the history of European science, that has gone forward by leaps and bounds, with many literate cultures making a significant contribution. Joseph Needham has shown the great steps that China took before the emergence of what he calls 'modern science' in the post-Renaissance west. India too made important discoveries, especially regarding numbers and medicine. As with other branches of knowledge, Christianity showed some resistance towards medicine in that illness was thought by certain of its apologists to be a divine scourge meted out for wrongdoing; for some that remains true even today. But other Abrahamistic religions were more positive in their attitudes to private and public health. Islam did develop the institution of the hospital (*maristan*) where medical treatment and investigations were both carried out. These hospitals served as a model for European ones.[1] They made use of the classical research of Galen and others employed by the Nestorian Christian doctors at Gondeshapur, an Iranian town that the Arabs took over and where Hellenistic traditions were continued. Arab doctors came to practise there, so too did the Jews who lived in their midst. It was certainly the case that in the medieval period Arab scholarship in this field was much more advanced than in Europe, having learnt not only from Greek but from Indian and Chinese sources as well. Moreover, Muslim doctors contributed much of their own, including the text books that formed the basis for medical teaching in Europe over several centuries. Indeed, in the early medical schools Arabic was a compulsory second language, just as Latin was in the other universities in Europe.

The neglect of the Arab contribution to knowledge has nowhere been clearer than in this history of medicine. Outside the work of specialists, cultural historians have attempted to draw a line directly back from present practice to Antiquity and have tended to exclude other contributions to that domain. The question either of tracing the European genealogy directly back to the classical world or of allowing for the fact that a distinct contribution has been made from outside is well illustrated in the history of medicine at Montpellier. I start with an account of the origin of the Montpellier medical school written by a Lebanese doctor named Hariz who had studied there. His book (of 1922) disputed versions of the beginnings of that school, which was formally founded in 1230 and which constituted a critical institution for the development of European medicine. The rise of the great medical school was seen either as a purely local development (an outcome of European 'genius') or one that built more widely upon classical learning and practice (also of course European). The author of the book presents an alternative view. He was a Lebanese Christian but of course Arabic-speaking and insisted that both Montpellier, situated near to Muslim Spain, and Salerno, the other early European school of medicine located close to what had been a Muslim regime in Sicily, were heavily influenced by Arabic medical writings and practice.

In Roman times the Mediterranean constituted a network of communication routes between north and south. North Africa was part of the

---

[1] Elgood 1951: 153.

empire, indeed provided much of its cereals and its oil, not to speak of its artisanal products and the gold from across the Sahara. The famous *annona* that supplied cereals to the major urban centres in Greece and Rome came from the coastal plain of what was later the Maghreb, of Tunis (Afriqua) and of Tripolitonia. And where there was trade there was also the exchange of information and arts and crafts, with wonderful mosaics coming south. Previous to Rome this area of course had its own civilization including writing coming from the east of the Mediterranean in the town of Carthage. This northern interest continued in post-Roman times with Ostrogoths coming across from Italy and taking possession of the African plain (which the Visigoths too tried unsuccessfully to take), mainly because of its productivity. The Straits of Gibraltar did not represent a real barrier. Semites, both Jews and Carthaginians, were found in the port cities on both sides of the Mediterranean and traded with one another. Later on, across the Straits at the invitation of the Jewish population, much harassed by the Catholic Visigothic rulers, and of various discontented Visigoths themselves, came the Arab–Berber Muslim army of Uqba ibn Nafi of 711. As before, Semitic-speaking peoples continued to communicate across the Mediterranean and in some cases across a religious divide. So medical practices were not confined to the south but spread northwards when the idea that sickness was due to 'original sin' became weaker.

In the early years of the Christian era, Jewish communities had been scattered all around the Mediterranean, both sides of which were included in the Roman empire as well as further north. Bordeaux, for example, had long been known for its imports, signs of which were found in the homes of 'orientals', of Jews, Syrians and Greeks.[2] In the sixth century, pottery, oil and wines of Gaza were being imported through Marseilles, before the great agricultural decline of that century. There was of course important trade across the Mediterranean until the Vandals appeared in the fifth century. In all these areas Semitic groups were installed including Spain itself, under Visigoth control. However, it was when that kingdom (previously Arian) was converted to Catholicism in 589 with the conversion of Recarred in Toledo that severe anti-Semitic measures were taken, leading to a migration of Jews to France and to welcoming the Muslim conqueror across the Straits of Gibraltar.[3]

In their discussion of medicine in Montpellier, in the course of a book on *Les Juifs du Midi*, the local historians D. and C. Iancu trace the

[2] The connections were especially strong in the trade in tin and the town was linked to Narbonne and Marseilles in the Mediterranean as well with Britain (Etienne 1990).
[3] Labouysse 2005.

formal beginning of the medical school at Montpellier to 1181 – even earlier than Hariz – to the decree of Guilhem VIII providing for the freedom of teaching there. Montpellier became the centre of medical knowledge brought in by masters from every part of the Mediterranean world. Ancient science and that of the Arabs were propagated in practice and were in a large part translated by Jewish doctors, especially those in Toledo and those from Andalusia who fled to the Langedocian town of Lunel in the twelfth century.[4] In the second half of the thirteenth century, for example, Moses ibn Tibbon translated into Hebrew almost a dozen medical works by Maimonides, al-Razi, Avicenna and others. The growth of medicine in southern France was of course only part of the process that included the preservation in Iraq and reception in Europe of Aristotelian philosophy. But the establishment of a school in Montpellier was important because it did involve a change in Europe. Eventually European scholars made direct access to the Galenic corpus but it was the Islamic world which had preserved the bulk of the material. Equally the new universities, which had earlier rejected the Aristotelian corpus, now accepted it, in itself a measure of secularization.

Lunel is an old town, some twenty miles east of Montpellier, which may have been founded by Jewish refugees coming from Palestine after the sacking of Jericho by Vespasian in 68 BCE, and landing at Villa Portus, the Gallo-Roman port on the coast of Lake Magio. There were further reasons for the Jews subsequently to quit Palestine in the coming two centuries. Or they may have come earlier as part and parcel of the Phoenician trading venture, which had occurred in the south of France since the eighth century BCE, for in the ninth there had been a treaty between the king of Tyre and the rulers of Israel and Judah (were they envisaging joint ventures with their communities abroad eventually joining together, as Bernal suggests?[5]). Or they may have come with Roman settlements like the one at Cologne founded in the first century BCE, or that in Italy at Pompei. In any case, whether through exile or trade, the Jews were widely dispersed throughout the Mediterranean, north and south. And there was continuing communication between the settlements. As Brotons writes of Samuel ibn Tibbon much later, Lunel was the place of his birth but 'he lived equally at Marseille, at Toledo, at Barcelona and even at Alexandria'.[6] This to-ing and fro-ing was good not only for trade but for the transfer of information and for the maintenance of a distinct religion. And when it did not take place in person, there was communication by letter.

[4] Iancu 1995: 57.   [5] M. Bernal, private communication and forthcoming.
[6] Brotons 1997: 199.

There were Jews in all the trading ports of the Mediterranean, according to Josephus. He writes of a whole scattering of communities in the
east during the Roman period and of their close relationships with the
Phoenicians. The Jews were part of those Levantine peoples who were
great voyagers, not primarily to spread monotheism (though this happened) but for mercantile reasons. In the Mediterranean they searched
for metals, but they also established merchant colonies in India and
China. So too of course did the Persians, Armenians and later on the
Muslims. The inland sea itself, as Braudel pointed out, was a large lake
which had frequent communication between both sides, with grain and
oil coming to port-cities on the northern side and with manufactures and
materials going south. The *sigillata* ware exported from Arezzo, Graufe-
senque (Millau) and Lyons (Lugdunum) via Narbonne was only one of
these items, later to reverse direction with the pots being made in North
Africa. At all these ports there were Semitic sailors, Carthaginians, Syrians and Jews intermingled, and it was to these centres that refugees fled
from the east when they were attacked. So it is highly likely that, in one of
these ways, Jews were at Lunel long before the foundation of the medical
school at Montpellier, which was the neighbouring town.

There they dated from the tenth or eleventh century, those from Lunel
from the beginning of the Christian era. 'Montpellier should not forget
that it was to Lunel, for the most part, that it owed the beginning of
its Faculty of Medicine.'[7] There were important Jewish schools at Narbonne as well as Lunel which, according to Brotons, taught the liberal
arts as at the School of Alexandria. This seems doubtful, given the che-
quered history of that school. But, on the other hand, instruction was not
confined to religion and the Kabbala, as we see from the comments of
Benjamin of Tudela who visited in 1160. These early Jews were engaged
in economic activities such as the fulling of cloth, but activities expanded
with the arrival first of exiles as a result of the anti-Semitic policies of the
newly Catholic Visigothic king at Toledo in 672; others were the later
refugees from Spain in 1034 when they came from Muslim lands. It was
undoubtedly this latter contingent, affected by the Moorish renaissance
in Andalusia, which brought a whiff of this rebirth of knowledge to Lunel,
leading to subsequent events in Montpellier. Both Narbonne and Lunel
appear to have taught medicine yet earlier but were certainly stimulated
by the refugees from Andalusia. In the second town, they formed the
Havora de Lunel (a fraternity) which has been called a university or an
academy.[8] There, as a result of the influx from Muslim Spain, scholars
translated from Arabic to Hebrew, whereas in Toledo it was from Arabic

[7] Brotons 2005: 183.   [8] Brotons 1997: 189.

to Latin. These translations included many Jewish works as well as others relating to medicine and philosophy. For example, in 1212 Samuel, from the same famous family of Ibn Tibbon exiled from Spain, who provided both translators and rabbis, produced the Little Canon of Galen with Arabic commentary, as well as Aristotle's *Meteorology*, Ptolemy's *History of Alexander of Macedonia*, not to speak of the Jewish philosopher Maimonides, who wrote in Arabic. The translations of his son, Moses, included the medical work of Averroës, the *Principles* of al-Farabi, the *Elements* of Euclid, Ptolemy's *Almageste*, the *Aphorisms* of Hippocrates, a work by al-Razi, and an introduction to medicine by Hunayn ibn Ishaq. These translations may sometimes have been ordered,[9] paid for by rich members of the community who were often doctors, but the father, Samuel, also composed many original works of a religious character. In fact religion was never far from the thoughts of this family. For example, there were the letters of Abba Mari to Ben-Addereth, the rabbi of Barcelona, complaining of the decline of Jewish studies, of the preference for philosophy and for the allegorical interpretation of the Bible. Addereth wanted to excommunicate all those who occupied themselves with such philosophy. Here again religion encouraged medicine but discouraged other forms of knowledge. Nevertheless the Jews were instrumental in bringing in knowledge, especially medicine, accumulated by Andalusian Islam to Montpellier and stimulating the Renaissance north of the Pyrennees.

There had been many important medical men in Islam who relied not only on classical texts but added from other sources as well as incorporating their own work. In Persia al-Razi (865–925) produced fifty-six medical treatises, some of them original, among which some were translated into Hebrew by the Ibn Tibbon family in Lunel in the thirteenth century. Al-Razi made a diagnostic distinction between measles and smallpox, leading to their distinct treatments. Innoculation against smallpox was a significant feature of Arabic medicine and was of course brought to England from Turkey in the eighteenth century; it also crossed the Sahara and established itself in West Africa before the coming of European medicine.[10] In western Islam, there was also Abu al-Qasim (Abulcasis, 936 – c.1013) of Spain, who is described as Islam's greatest surgeon, introducing 'rational surgery' to Europe, for the practice of dissection had gone into abeyance from the time of Alexander; he combined eastern and classical learning in a way that shaped European medical practice before the Renaissance. A court physician (for the court was a main centre for the patronage of medicine), he wrote *al-Tasrif* (The

[9] 'sur leur demande', Brotons 1997: 205.   [10] Achebe 2001.

Method), based upon the work of the seventh-century Byzantine scholar Paul of Aegina, as well as upon his own observations. In the twelfth century, the book was translated by Gerard of Cremona in the reconquered Toledo and remained the leading treatise on surgery in Europe for the next 500 years, being preferred to the work of Galen.

The medical practitioners in Arab lands included both Christians and Jews. Despite the notion of the responsibility of God for all illness, the former followed a training, for there was nonetheless a call to relieve pain and disease. As a result they could practise the healing craft more easily than other sciences. Medicine also brought a living to rabbis, monks, philosophers and others. Health was a preoccupation in and for all regimes (especially public health) and so medicine continued to advance even under those religious systems that discouraged other forms of natural knowledge as being unnecessary in the light of God's omniscience. In Judaism, for example, medicine was 'the intellectual field in which pre-emancipation Jews were already established in the wider world'.[11] In Damascus and Baghdad, such doctors were called to court to treat the rulers, depending on their expertise and not on their beliefs. But many from these groups also worked in the *maristans* (hospitals), healing the poor as well as the rich, and these Islamic institutions were widely taken as models elsewhere.

Before the foundation of the Faculty of Montpellier, medicine in Europe was often limited in scope and practised within religious establishments like monastic hospitals.[12] While there was sometimes a conflict with theological doctrines, medical specialists were always needed. Thus there were important Jewish schools at the synagogues of Béziers, Lunel and Narbonne in each of which medicine was taught and practised.[13] These schools were associated with places of worship and education and had close relationships with Arab scholarship in Spain. So from the twelfth century the town of Montpellier attracted 'hispano-arabic' doctors because of its considerable commercial connections with Spain and with the Mediterranean world more generally.

Montpellier was situated Septimania, the coastal region of the French Mediterranean which had been under an earlier Visigothic regime, then Arian, running between Perpignan and Marseilles. For more than forty years (725–67) it became subject to Muslim rule when Arab forces who had conquered Visigothic Spain, now Catholic, made a raid towards

[11] Hobsbawm 2005: 16.
[12] In the Visigothic kingdom of Toulouse, the officers selected the doctors and professors (Labouysse 2005: 32).
[13] Hariz 1922: 91.

Poitiers and were repelled by Charles Martel and his cavalry in 732. Under Arab rule in the eighth century (although it was reconquered between 760 and 768), there was an area occupied and apparently ruled by Jews who were in contact with their co-religionists in Baghdad.[14] Islam was more hospitable (tolerant) to other religions of the Book than Christianity if we can judge by the continuing presence of Christians and Jewish communities under Arab rule, even today. Whereas there are now no traditional distinct Islamic communities contained within Christian Europe outside the Balkans where remnants of Turkish rule remain, though there are of course very substantial new immigrant populations from Muslim lands which do enjoy a certain tolerance and a very limited autonomy.

The Jews of Septimania were part of a long-established community. The towns in which they concentrated were open to others, since the idea of segregation only came from northern Europe in 1084.[15] When Benjamin of Tudela visited these communities he commented on the prosperity of the towns where the inhabitants had established schools largely for religious purposes. He speaks of Montpellier as having the greatest Jewish scholars of the time as well as many others studying the Talmud. However, a later traveller, Kalonymos ben Kalonymos of Arles, reported the intellectual element as consisting of pseudo-scholars and so-called 'doctors or astronomers',[16] perhaps because it was not sufficiently orthodox. The south encouraged a more integrated and cultivated Judaism than the north, one where the strict regulations issued by the Vatican at the Lateran Council (1215) were often disregarded partly because medicine was so important among the Jews of the Middle Ages but also because of a more open approach. Béziers, for example, with a large Jewish community and its own synagogue had also been hospitable to the Cathars – and earlier to the troubadours; indeed there was a spirit of laicism, even of anti-clericalism, in much of the Midi at this time. It was this reputation that was in part responsible for the invasion of the town by the Albigensian crusade under Simon of Montfort (1209) and the subsequent massacre of the population and the installation of the French royalty.[17] Under northern Catholic rule there was some hostility; and later the Council of Béziers of 1246 excommunicated Christians for calling upon a Jewish doctor ('for it was better to die than owe your life to a Jew').[18] This was a religious rather than an ethnic problem, but even so monasteries and bishops were known to use Jewish doctors. Like Spain the Midi was always more hospitable to Jews, especially to doctors who

[14] Zuckerman 1972.   [15] Iancu 1995: 30.   [16] Iancu 1995: 24.
[17] Bourain 1986: 96.   [18] Iancu 1995: 57.

were often leaders and representatives of their communities, intellectual as well as commercial; for the practice of medicine was also a way in which a rabbi or other religious personage could gain a living. Regarding Montpellier, both Jewish and Arab doctors worked in the vicinity of the school, as well as later as in the school itself, before and after it was established. While Jewish doctors had their own traditions, they learnt much from the Arabs, in the Near East, in North Africa and in Spain. Later, the books they translated, especially in Toledo into Latin and the vernacular after the reconquest by the Christian world, were used in medical schools in France and Italy (particularly in Padua).

Medicine was not the only sphere in which Arabic influences played a decisive role, spurring on the revival in Europe of both scientific enquiry and practice. Nor would later European developments towards what we consider modernity have been possible without the groundwork of Arabic scholars, who searched for frameworks that unified knowledge derived from ancient models with later religious doctrine (appendix 2).

In their various ways, these teachers listed in the appendix were concerned with the problem of the relationship between faith and reason, between a hegemonic religion and a freer enquiry into the world, as well as with the reconciliation of theology and rationality, even science, for no one could reject the former except on pain of death. But an opposition between the two had been there from the very beginning, though religion continued to be important, even for some accountants and other professionals. What was at stake was not the rejection of religion but a widening of the sphere of 'rationality' and extending the role of enquiry; that represented a partial secularization of knowledge which led to its growth, including of science, as well as to an expansion of the arts.

Returning to medicine, the equally famous medical school at Salerno in southern Italy had a history similar in some ways to that of Montpellier. Originally a Roman town, it was already known as a medical centre which continued to operate under the Byzantines. It was also near Arab Sicily and was twice attacked by Islamic forces although it held out each time. Nevertheless, the influence of Arab medicine there was very considerable. The school itself was known in the tenth century, perhaps already in the previous one.[19] At that time, a Jewish scholar usually known as Donnolo, who had been a prisoner of the Saracens, wrote medical treatises for the school in Italian.[20] The institution became particularly famous in the time of Constantine the African, born in Carthage of Jewish or Arab parents (and thus possibly descended from one of the

[19] Hariz 1922: 28.   [20] According to Clot (1999: 270), he wrote a text in Hebrew.

Carthaginians whom Bernal suggests were absorbed into Judaism). He had travelled extensively in the east, acquiring medical knowledge wherever he went. When he returned to the Mediterranean, he was welcomed in Sicily now under the Norman duke, Robert Guiscard, and in 1068 he arrived at Salerno where Arabic medicine was already well known, partly through the advent to the papacy of the mathematician Sylvester II (who as Gerbert of Aurillac had studied those sources near Barcelona) and partly owing to its proximity to Sicily which, as we have noted, had been occupied by the Arabs before being reconquered by the Normans (between 1061 and 1091). As the result of his travels, Constantine, who was now a Christian, was well acquainted with Arabic medicine and when he eventually joined the monastery of Monte Cassino, he translated many works that were to inspire a 'medieval renaissance' in Europe.[21] Some of these works (often offered without acknowledgement and therefore wrongly suggesting a Christian or European origin) were used in the medical schools of Montpellier and Paris over several centuries and as a result Constantine has been called 'the restorer of medical literature in the West'.[22] In the second half of the thirteenth century there was a dispersal of knowledge from southern Italy, following the internal conflicts between Guelfs and Ghibellines, the party of the emperor and that of the pope, and several professors emigrated to establish themselves in other parts of Europe, including France, most notably one Roger of Palma from Salerno. They brought with them the tenth-century works of Abu al-Qasim (Abulcasis) with its 'rational surgery', that is, based upon the dissections of humans, a subject that it had been difficult to advance in a region dominated by the Abrahamistic religions because of the reverence given to the human body preserved in its entirety; it is still difficult to bury an incomplete corpse in Israel. Thus both the great schools, of Salerno and Montpellier, were the repositories of Mediterranean knowledge. And it was not only medicine that spread from southern Italy. The Italian national dish of pasta also seems to have Sicilian roots[23] and so too did the silk-weaving industry. This came from Palermo where it was encouraged by Frederick II, and went to Lucca (and then to Bologna, north Italy and Lyons).[24] Indeed, that Islamic, later Norman territory was even more important for what was to come. 'It was in Sicily indeed that those rational practices of government which during the Renaissance were to form the necessary corollary of capitalist development emerged for the first time in their full power.' It has been called 'the first modern state. It had no supernatural aims.'[25] Unfortunately, this is

---

[21] Hariz 1922: 30.   [22] Hariz 1922: 38.
[23] Toaff 2000.   [24] Blazy 2001.   [25] Bolgar 1954: 243.

seen as 'an expression of the inner character of the society they served', with feudal relations and the medieval church having only an 'episodic significance'.[26] The description is right; the reasoning is unacceptably essentialist, and in effect excludes the influence of Islam; medieval Sicily was no less European in spirit than the Renaissance because alternation was built in here as elsewhere.

In his history of the medical faculty of Montpellier,[27] Bonnet recognized the early role of Arab and Jewish doctors (the latter belonging to what he calls the University of Lunel) in providing treatment. In the south of France they had introduced competent medicine to the Goths before. In this merchant territory, doctors were known as *médicine-epiciers* (doctor-grocers) combining both roles. That was prior to the establishment of a faculty by the decree of Cardinal Guillaume Conrad, a papal legate, in 1220. Indeed, that decree may have its origins in the desire of the Christian church, in strongly Catholic times, to bring the practice and teaching of medicine, often by foreigners, under the control of the bishop of Maguelone who appointed the chancellor. Conrad had earlier fought against the Cathar movement in southern France. Yet even earlier had been the decree of Guilhem VIII, lord of Montpellier, who wanted to protect the interests of Christian doctors; some references to medical activity are already found in the twelfth century. But although Bonnet recognizes the importance of their early teaching, he nevertheless sees Arab civilization as unable to innovate and unable to 'support substantial acquisitions in medicine' mainly because of their lack of anatomy.[28] So in its own account Montpellier went back to Greece, back to the mythical founder of the town, Hercules, who is reputed to have foretold a city of traders. And it was therefore founded on Greek principles – as the saying went, 'Olim Cos, nunc Monspeliensis Hippocrates', 'Hippocrates, you were formerly of Cos, but now of Montpellier.'

This thesis about the development of medicine in Europe presents us with an example of ethnocentric, teleological history. At the time when these historical accounts were written in the nineteenth and twentieth centuries, medicine in Europe was undoubtedly in the ascendancy, but that position of superiority was now seen as a matter of long-standing, a direct development of the inheritance from Greece and Rome. It was a notion that displayed some of the features of what it is not entirely wrong to describe as racist thinking.

That view was characteristic of the European approach to many of their undoubted achievements in the Renaissance and after, when the accepted version of events was that the movement was based on a return to and

---

[26] Bolgar 1954: 243.   [27] Bonnet 1992.   [28] Bonnet 1992: 27.

adoption of the classical tradition, disregarding those very important elements that had been contributed by Arab and other traditions of learning, especially Indian and Chinese. To turn the Renaissance into a purely European event, seeing it as a single, once-and-for-all phenomenon, is again a manifestation of arrogance (and historicism) that displays a disregard for the contributions of these other cultures (all extensive literate ones). That disregard leads to a misunderstanding not only of the past but of the future path of cultural history; an important part of the picture is that *all* written cultures experience phases of rebirth (renascence) or reform (reformation), nor has this process yet finished.

After the Arab expansion Islamic medicine developed, especially in the south-west Persian town of Gondeshapur noted for its hospitals and its doctors, some of whom came from India and others from all around the Near East. Indeed, Persia had connections with China (via the Silk Road) as well as with India. There had been a strong influx of medical practitioners to this corner of Persia which was patronized by the Sasanian king, Chosrues I, when the decrees of Justinian, who had closed Athens in favour of orthodoxy, led to the flight of Nestorian Christians to Persia and Iraq. The followers of Nestor had been condemned by the Councils of Ephesus (431 CE) and of Chalcedon (451 CE) for stressing that the divine and human natures of Christ were distinct, not unified (while accepting that he was one person). Their influence spread along the road to China (until the time of Timur the Turk) where they founded churches, and they received considerable recognition from the Arabs to whose culture they made substantial contributions, although speaking Syriac, with their classical texts. Indeed, the Nestorians often welcomed the conquerors in preference to the Greeks of Byzantium who had rejected the learning of ancient Greece. When the Arabs invaded Gondeshapur in 638, the exact sciences were taught there, including medicine, with Nestorian doctors following the teaching of Galen and Hippocrates. They mingled Greek with Ayurvedic medicine, having a constant intercourse with India. Chosrues had indeed sent his physicians to the south to bring back Indian works on medicine, as well as the Book of Fables (*Panchatantra*) and the game of chess. Beginning in the fifth century, the Nestorians had started to translate various Greek texts which they received through the schools of Antioch and Edessa. In the eighth century they began to translate their scriptures and other writing into Arabic, as that language rapidly took over from local dialects, mainly because in Islam it was the sacred language of the Book. The Arabs acquired much knowledge from the inhabitants who were called upon to treat rulers like the Abbasid ruler al-Mamun in Baghdad; in fact Nestorians were physicians to the caliphs over six

generations.[29] That particular ruler tried to encourage Muslims to enter
the profession and to learn, especially from the Greeks, and he nominated
Hunayn ibn Ishaq (known in Latin as Johannitius), who was born in 809
in a Nestorian Christian tribe, to go with others to collect manuscripts
for translation. The latter spent his life making versions of Plato and Aristotle as well as of Galen, Hippocrates and Dioscorides. So too did others,
mainly Christians. Indeed, as doctors Nestorians continued at Baghdad,
where there were also Jewish 'academies', and they even worked in Syria
until the end of the ninth century. Then they composed directly in Arabic,
as, for example, did Hunayn himself as well as the Melkite Christian Ibn
Luqa. In Baghdad they established 'a real school of medicine'[30] which
existed until the twelfth century when, with the decline of the Abbasid
caliphate, other schools were founded in Syria at Tripoli, Damascus and
Karak, mainly with Greek Christian doctors. The end of the Baghdad
school of medicine itself came with the advent of the Mongols in 1258.[31]
Through this school, Islam came to have its own renascence of classical learning, especially in medicine, when the Greek texts were translated
into Syriac or Arabic, in which languages Hunayn produced an annotated
list of as many as 129 works by Galen. In the eleventh century some of
these were then translated into Latin, a process that initiated a further
renewal (renascence) of the Galenic tradition. Others were translated
into Hebrew at Lunel about the same time.

Of course, medicine proceeded along a large number of lines, developing its local and international pharmacopeia, public health and many
other aspects. But the rise of surgery in medieval Europe (and elsewhere)
was particularly interesting as it involved the rejection or modification of
religious taboos about the body, and hence a certain measure of 'secularization'. Up until the Renaissance, medical texts relied heavily on
the anatomical knowledge set down by Galen in the second century CE.
Galen had to work on apes because for religious reasons humans could
not be dissected. As we have seen, his work was translated from Greek
into Arabic in Baghdad and came to western Europe through the Islamic
world. Thus the teaching of anatomy at Salerno, where the earliest dissection of humans apparently began, again took place with the revival of
Galen on apes (via Baghdad) and developed with the studies of Abulcasis
on humans. But the roots of this school went back further, as we have
seen, although there was certainly a strong input from Arabic medicine in
all spheres. In subsequent centuries the university in Italy most associated
with dissection and contributing so much to anatomy and to surgery was

---

[29] Troupeau 1995: 228.   [30] Troupeau 1995: 230.
[31] Troupeau 1995 for an account of this school.

Padua, founded from the secular University of Bologna, which taught Roman law, and much influenced by Arab medicine. It was there that we encounter the name of Mondino de Liuzzi (1275–1326) as Professor of Medicine. Though there are other contenders for priority, he is said to have reintroduced the Alexandrian practice of dissection (associated with the name of Herophilus, c.375–280 BCE) into Europe, holding a series of public demonstrations; even so, he himself read from a text (of Galen or a commentator) while a barber-surgeon carried out the actual dissection. In 1315 he published *De anatome* which was used in medical schools for the next 300 years. Padua established an anatomy theatre in 1490 and many doctors flocked there to study, including William Harvey, the English discoverer of the circulation of the blood.

The case of medicine, then, demonstrates how indebted Europe has been to its Islamic neighbours for the resuscitation of scientific enquiry. Once the change was triggered, though, the impetus generated led to sustained and independent progression, partly because the institutionalization of learning through universities, hospitals and academies led to the kind of 'self-sustaining growth' that came to characterize the economy. For in addition to contacts and exchanges with the external world, there was also the further dimension of internal development, of 'social evolution', in technological matters. That is to say, a culture reaches a particular state in the production, say, of medical knowledge, or going further afield, of the making of iron, and it tends to build on this and to move towards the next level of complexity, but this is only really institutionalized in Europe with the Renaissance. However, this process produces, even in earlier societies, a parallel development that happened most obviously in Mesoamerica where urban civilization and writing appeared without any straightforward exchange with the rest of the world.[32] During this period in Europe the theory and practice of medicine obviously advanced in hospitals, in consultations and in libraries where this process was stimulated externally by Arab, Jewish and other eastern knowledge, but internally the crystallization of scientific learning came not only with the work of monastic infirmaries, with the omnipresent desire for better cures but much later with the advent of printing to the west, which ensured the rapid diffusion both of text and of diagrams. The latter contributed significantly to the work of Vesalius (1514–64), who was of Flemish origin and studied Humanae Litterae at Louvain in 1529. From there, he went to medical school at the University of Paris (1533–6) and learnt dissection. Because of war he returned to Louvain where the influence of Arab medicine was still dominant.

[32] Adams 1966.

Following a prevailing custom, in 1537 he published for a dissertation a paraphrase of the work of the ninth-century Persian physician al-Razi. He then attended the University of Padua, which, as we have seen, had a strong tradition of anatomical dissection, probably influenced by Salerno in the south. In January 1540, breaking with the reliance on Galen, as had Abulcasis and Liuzzi before him, Vesalius openly demonstrated his own method, which was now diffused through printing – doing dissections himself, learning anatomy from cadavers and critically evaluating ancient texts; Galen, he declared, was of limited use as he had worked with animals since cutting up the human body was forbidden to him. Vesalius then published his work *Fabrica,* or the Seven Books, on the structure of the human body. For this he himself supervised the drawings in Venice in 1542, a town already open to the new learning, and in 1543 he took the wood blocks plus the manuscript to Basel for printing. His work has been described as 'the culmination of the humanistic revival of ancient learning' but it was not only ancient learning in the classical sense: his training was based upon the Arab tradition as well as on his own detailed observations, the results of which he circulated widely through his printed works. What becomes apparent in Vesalius's case is the role played by the change in the mode of communication in medical advances. In this case it is the printing press which allowed for the wide circulation of insights and observations, but already writing itself had been of great importance in, for instance, the circulation of case histories. In China, for example, medical material was collected in provincial gazettes, and printed warnings sent out about the spread of disease to the provinces.

The medical schools of Montpellier and Salerno were not simply resurrecting the works of Galen and Hippocrates (and continuing from there). In the first place, these texts were being reinstated partly by virtue of the Arabs. In the second, the Arabs had themselves made many additions to medical knowledge as well as accepting those from further east. In the third place, the profound gap between the classical authors and the rebirth of knowledge was partly due to the advent of a hegemonic religion which clamped down upon the cutting up of human bodies (made in 'the image of God'), as did the other Abrahamistic religions, and promoted the moral attribution of illness to divine agency. Academic medicine only flourished again when God was allocated a narrower sphere of interest.

European scholars frequently discuss the Renaissance as if it were the direct rebirth of classical learning, as if the seed of knowledge were lying there ready to sprout on its own, given favourable external conditions, whereas that rebirth was strongly mediated by Islam and was stimulated by works written in Arabic like those of the Persian al-Razi in medicine, and the commentaries of Averroës (Ibn Rushd) on Aristotle and Plato, not to speak of their own important contributions and those of countries further east. But in the dominant paradigm the Renaissance is thought of as a European rebirth of Europe; that was the idea of the humanists in relation to their revival of the classics, and it was an idea that held sway not only among the public at large but for many scholars in history and the social sciences. What is peculiar about Europe is this necessity for a revival that results from a significant discontinuity with Antiquity in medicine and in other sciences, a discontinuity created by collapse, by conversion and then by feudalism. Nevertheless, Europeans have constructed a historical continuity of development from Antiquity and then to the Renaissance by looking back and reviving that Antiquity. But that trajectory in fact suffered a radical interruption. The road between the past and the present was distinctly uneven, as is clear from the history of medicine.

It is easy to see why Europeans traced the revival of medicine, and culture more generally, back to the ancients, to a culture which they considered to be the starting point in a line leading directly to the modern world of industrial capitalism. In the first place, the Arabs themselves owed a lot to the Greeks – so it was relatively easy to 'degrade' them to the status of mere transmitters of information from one point to another. Secondly, medieval Europe was surrounded by the physical remains of the classical period while Greek and Latin survived as ecclesiastical languages as well as being encapsulated in our reckoning of time. It seemed logical to want to revive past glories that had virtually disappeared under the pressure of northern invaders, from internal contradictions but above all with the conversion to a new religion that tightly controlled worldviews, and which was soon to accumulate a vast and imposing estate.[33] However, drawing a line directly back to classical Antiquity necessarily meant creating a purely European genealogy of learning and culture generally, that is to say excluding the contribution of Islam and, through Islam, that of India (from whence we get 'Arabic' numerals, acquired by Gerbert of Aurillac), or of China. Or if these were included, it was as an appendage to the classical tradition.

The case of Gerbert (945–1003) makes the error very clear since it was he that introduced a numerical system, completely essential for calculation and science in the modern world, which came through the Arabs but was developed in Asia further east. Gerbert had been sent from Aurillac in the Auvergne to the monastery of Vic, near Barcelona, by Count Borrell in 967 as a promising young scholar and he spent three years there, reading in its fine library. He worked on the subject of the abacus,

[33] Goody 1983.

on Indo-Arabic numerals, on the astrolabe, and in geometry he tried to fill in the fragmentary Euclid that was all that was available in the west. At this early stage he acted as a channel for the transmission of Arabic learning which had been brought to Catalonia by Mozarabic migrants from Muslim Spain and was collected by the Latin church. Later he became a teacher in Germany and then at the schools of Chartres and Rheims, 'preparing for the religious, literary and scientific renaissance of the eleventh century'.[34] The role of Arabic learning in the range of subjects on which he worked was clear. His studies led to the adoption of the 'Arabic' numeric system as an alternative to the clumsy and inefficient Roman one, so that the calculation and mathematics basic to 'modern science' became much easier. Later, as Pope Sylvester II, he was in a position to spread their use.

The place where he worked was significant. Barcelona had been under Islamic rule and remained in touch with Islamic learning, especially through the migration of Mozarabs. One important factor in the patent superiority of Islamic medicine and science at this time was the circulation of knowledge under Islam, which was both wider and more rapid, due largely to the use of paper. Libraries were plentiful, and in general accessible to scholars. In Baghdad, al-Mamun established the House of Wisdom (*bayt al hikmah*) in 832; in Basra there was the Home of Books; in Mosul students were supplied with paper; in Cairo the court library had 18,000 books of 'foreign sciences'. The Dar al-hikma founded by Caliph al-Hakim in Cordoba in 1005 had reading rooms, paid librarians and provided pensions for students. In northern Spain, Gerbert benefited from the depth of this written culture.

This network of libraries secured the transmission of part of classical knowledge, in medicine and other spheres, as well as the Arabs' own contribution, which had to go through a process of translation. Hunayn had already done this for the works of Galen in the ninth century. For Europe they had to be translated anew. Those of Constantine the African, mainly consisting of Arabic works, were however done into Latin. The same was true of another great period of translation at Toledo in the twelfth century when the town had been reconquered from the Muslims and various scholars used it as a base for producing Latin versions of Arabic works. Gerard of Cremona for example had gone to Toledo in order to learn Arabic so that he could read Ptolemy's *Almagest* (written in Alexandria in the second century CE), a text dealing with mathematics and astronomy which was not then available in Latin. All his subsequent life Gerard stayed in Toledo, which had been a centre of Muslim learning.

[34] Hariz 1922: 24.

There he translated (or had translated) some eighty works including some by Aristotle, Euclid and Galen.

Translation was important not only for handing down the earlier classics like Galen but also for transmitting knowledge that had accumulated and been developed, in other cultures, other traditions (for example, the work of al-Razi). Translation has an interesting cultural effect. It sets knowledge above any particular religious or cultural tradition; it secularizes and generalizes learning. The exchange of information in this way resembles the exchange of goods among traders. One is not concerned with the belief systems of the trading partner but rather with his capacity to exchange, even his creditworthiness. These traders crossed cultures and they transferred both goods and knowledge. Muslim merchants were found around the canals of Venice, Christians in the streets of Alexandria. Indeed, in each town the foreign merchants had their own lodgings, *fonduq* in Arabic. Inevitably they exchanged information about products, about techniques, about culture, and about ideas generally. So there was a transfer not only of goods but of information. Christian exchanged with Muslim, Muslim with Hindu, Hindu with Buddhist or Confucian. The further results of the transaction depended on the quality of the information, in this case of medical knowledge.

It was this level of exchange that helped produce many parallel patterns of learning and performance across the Eurasian continent, often by the more rapid 'circulation' of information through the use of paper and of printing. Such exchanges tend to be excluded from most accounts not only of the Renaissance, but also of the whole journey towards modernization. That happened especially with changes in the means of communication, deemed essential to the modern world. Printing was held to have emerged from Gutenberg, and well before that Europe was said to have developed a unique alphabetic system. Earlier European discussions of Antiquity saw the alphabet emerging in Greece but in large part it was developed by Phoenicians. The classicist Havelock plus myself and Watt attributed the Greek achievement to the use of the alphabet rather than to their 'genius',[35] certainly a refinement, but we did not take fully into account the remarkable possibilities of the Semitic consonantal alphabet that produced the Jewish (and Christian and Islamic) Bible. Finley poses something of the same problem with democracy which he attributed to Athens but which was also found in Phoenician cities on the Asian mainland, and elsewhere too. Printing of course was invented by the Chinese, long before Europe, even using moveable metal type (but not the press). Indeed, this early mechanization of writing was one of their

---

[35] Havelock 1963; Goody and Watt 1963.

advantages in developing natural science. As for numbers, the classical Roman system was abandoned in favour of the Arabic (Indian) system which proved more efficient and laid the basis for 'modernity', making calculation much easier.

The history of the medical faculty in Montpellier is an epitome of this aspect of European studies, not only of the science of nature in the eleventh, twelfth and thirteenth centuries but of what I may clumsily call Euro-humanism more generally. By looking back to the work of Galen and Hippocrates, one can construct a European tradition which leads chronologically to the remarkable intellectual and technical achievements of the nineteenth and twentieth centuries, as running in a direct line from the classical to the modern, involving the rebirth of the fourteenth to the sixteenth centuries (the Italian Renaissance). But that is to ignore three points. Firstly, the drastic loss of much knowledge in western Europe in the Dark Ages and beyond, partly the result of religious restrictions. Secondly, the role of the Muslim tradition in the Renaissance, not only in making available translations of lost Greek texts but in contributing much knowledge of its own. And thirdly, the achievements of other traditions, the Indian and Chinese, not only in the sphere of medicine but in many other aspects of the sciences as well as the arts, in what from many points of view must be considered as a joint enterprise of the literate societies of Eurasia.[36]

In the end the thinking behind this supposed European uniqueness is partly based upon a clash model of the contrast between cultures, civilizations and religions, Christianity (the west) against Islam (the east). That model does not account for very much. Of course there were conflicts between Muslims and Christians, as between Muslims and Hindus, Catholics and Protestants, Sunnis and Shiites. And there were small-scale troubles as well as larger pogroms, even after the establishment of a European and international political system. It is the same on the individual level as on the cultural. These worldviews are thought to be irreconcilable. But there has also been consistent interchange between human cultures and between human beings, especially under conditions, market or not, where one individual or group is involved in exchanging with another. This has led to cooperation rather than to conflict, to the international or intercultural transfer of knowledge. What we need for this aspect of culture is not only a clash metaphor but also a flow chart, and the study of the 'reprise' of European medicine seems to be paradigmatic.

---

[36] This chapter owes much to Dr Paul and Dr Hélène Bras of Bouziques, to Dr Gilbert Lewis of Barnes and, for a visit to Salerno, to Prof. Vanessa Maher of Verona.

3   Religion and the secular

One important aspect of the return to classical knowledge was that it
circumvented the earlier dominance of a hegemonic religion and led to a
measure of secularization, partly by returning to pre-Christian times and
to a pagan mythology. Not that at this time the worship of Christianity
diminished but the world became more pluralistic, more segmented;
and within the classical world there was of course a non-transcendental
tradition.

There was always a built-in contradiction for Christianity since it
constituted a rejection of much of the Roman world and its gods. But this
it could not altogether avoid. As with its language which continued, especially in the Church, knowledge of the classical gods did not disappear
from society for it was enshrined not only in the reckoning of time and
in the geography of the Heavens, where Venus held her own in the night
sky, but in literature itself. Although drama was not performed because
of an objection to representation, Latin plays, like those of Terence, continued to be read in order to improve one's mastery of the language which
was kept on for ecclesiastical purposes even in the German lands with no
Romance heritage. So Terence was studied in 'grammar' schools, even in
the north where Latin was part of the tradition of the southern invaders.
In poetry too in that language (the lingua franca of religious discourse),
which was read and composed, the gods lived on. It is true that there was
a movement among some Christians, such as St Augustine of Hippo and
again St Jerome, to discount pagan literature and to substitute a purely
Christian poetry and prose.[1] However, despite these tendencies, literacy
in the church and mainly outside meant literacy in Latin so the earlier
pagan texts continued to be available to the *clerici*. Indeed, an important

---

[1] Augustine quotes Corinthians approvingly, 'knowledge puffs up, but charity edifies'
(1945: 269), and he comments '[u]nto the angels, the knowledge of all temporal
things . . . is vile' (1945: 270); knowledge comes through God and is of his, not of man's,
creation. Not a potential model for a knowledge society.

element in the continuing history of the book in Europe consists of the story of the preservation and rediscovery of classical literature, which had hitherto been largely set aside, up until the time of the Italian Renaissance itself – a process that has been well recorded[2] and began even in classical times with collectors gathering earlier manuscripts. This collection did not of course involve a setting aside of religion, as happened to some extent in later Europe, but it was the result of an elitist bibliographic concern with past achievements made possible by the fact of literacy. However, in the Christian period the problem of retrieval became aggravated because classical literature was less appreciated and hence less conserved. Some libraries nevertheless continued to keep classical manuscripts, not so much those of wealthy individuals but those of monastic establishments. Here there were certain outstanding collectors, beginning with Cassiodorus who established his monastery at Vivarium in Calabria in the sixth century CE. Then with the spread of schooling and learning more generally in the Carolingian period, there is a wider resurgence of interest. Thus, as a result of literacy, knowledge of classical gods and of classical literature had a kind of half-life throughout the Middle Ages, renewed, revived and extended at every renascence until we arrive at the Italian Renaissance itself.

So, partly because of the continued use of Latin as a language of communication, partly because of the enduring presence of Roman ruins in their midst, the classical world was never far from peoples' eyes and ears. That world was pagan and secular and its products should therefore have been set aside by the faithful. But the existence of written texts meant that that world could not be entirely neglected, so classical learning was a sub-theme throughout the Dark and Middle Ages of Europe, coming out in bursts of activity from time to time, as at the Carolingian renascence or that of the twelfth century, stimulated by Andalusia. These bursts did not 'last' and their impetus fell away. The Italian Renaissance was different, partly as Burke suggests,[3] because of the coming of print to Europe when a more widespread literacy became possible, but also because of the institutionalization of learning in the universities.

In intention, then, the Italian Renaissance was a revival of classical culture, the rebirth of Rome, beginning perhaps with Petrarch in the 1330s or 1340s, perhaps before, since a generation earlier saw Giotto and Dante, whose interests were not entirely 'medieval'. Not everybody embraced this return to classical models with equal alacrity. In his treatise *Lucula noctis* (c.1405) Dominici, for instance, an important cardinal, diplomat and anti-humanist, saw the return to classical culture as a return

---

[2] Reynolds and Wilson 1968.   [3] Burke 1998: 60.

to paganism, a view that had been also expressed by early Christians.[4] Still, the majority of intellectuals and artists were searching for antique models.

All this had happened before. In early Christianity the classical tradition had been rejected so that in Byzantium, for example, there was a 'dark age' which had a devastating effect on the survival of classical culture. From the middle of the seventh century interest in the production of secular literature had completely disappeared[5] and no secular manuscripts were copied during the period of the iconoclastic controversy. After the turn of the ninth century there was a gradual emergence of scholarly activity in this field in what had been called 'the first Byzantine humanism'. The second was the so-called 'Palaeologue Renaissance'. My usage of secular here applies to spheres of human action, not necessarily to an outlook that dismisses all transcendental reference. Most individuals move between the two, even in the simpler societies. A segmental approach is often neglected in current debates which tend to universalize one or the other.[6]

The Italian Renaissance again encouraged some secularism and speculation. According to Bousma,[7] that happened (in Padua) the generation before Petrarch, based at the papal court in Avignon, and Petrarch's 'major contribution was to Christianize what had formerly been a secular movement'.[8] This contribution enabled humanism to prosper but diminished its appeal to the Italian city states. 'In their attempt to recover and to master classical language and literature, the humanists inevitably began to build the foundations of an autonomous secular culture.'[9] They distanced themselves from institutions of higher learning, most of which were associated with the church, and 'privileged experience over theology'.[10] They even took Roman republican politics as their model, a model that some see as having filtered through to the English Civil War.[11] Indeed, the University of Bologna was founded to teach Roman not canon law, largely for urban administration and for trade rather than for the clergy. And in its turn Padua was founded by Bologna, an important trading city that adhered to the imperial regime (the Ghibellines) rather than to the ecclesiastical (the Guelfs).[12]

Before the coming of the monotheistic, Abrahamistic creed, the religious activity ('paganism') that preceded it was not as monopolistic

---

[4] Burke 1998: 31.   [5] Gutas 1998: 177.   [6] See Bakhle 2008.
[7] Bousma 2002.   [8] Jurdjevich 2007: 249.   [9] Jurdjevich 2007: 251.
[10] Jurdjevich 2007: 251.   [11] Skinner 1978.
[12] Of course, law was taught and practised before Bologna, even by professionals. But it was handed down through private instruction and apprenticeship (as in offices of earlier solicitors) rather than in law schools (Bolgar 1954: 143).

as Christianity but rather polytheistic, the worship of many gods. The way that polytheism, as well as paganism, are generally conceptualized can be misleading with regard to one important aspect: the names suggest to us a consistency and fixity in the pantheon of the respective culture, which is far from accurately reflecting the state of affairs as it would have been experienced from within. There certainly were fixed points of reference, but the pagan supernatural was a field for invention, where new cults jostled with old, and in which worldviews allowed for alternative perspectives. This stands in stark contrast to written monotheistic religions and their rigid adherence to an established regime.

The difference between the two is partly due to the tendencies of literate religions. If one can look back to 'writings' of this kind, one is caught up in the return to texts. That brings with it a problem relating to my earlier argument that writing tends to force one to make a binary choice. To take an everyday example, the drawing up of a list of vegetables and fruits; in a written list you have to categorize the tomato as one or the other, whereas in oral speech it can more easily be a vegetable in one context and a fruit in another. The same happens with much more abstract concepts where written ideologies tend to come down on one side of the fence or another for the sake of 'consistency', for example, in the case of broader ideas on the side of either evolution or of creation. Oral cultures do not promote a binary division in the same way. Contemporary society has two very distinct, mutually exclusive ways of accounting for the appearance of man on earth – evolution or creation, whereas in oral recitations, like of those of the Bagre of northern Ghana, one version may stress the creation of the world by God, the next may emphasize the contribution that Man Makes Himself.[13] Consistency over time is not such an issue, since you cannot check by looking back. Oral memory traduces.

Having said this, even the greater certainty of the text may in practice be qualified by a measure of doubt on the part of the reader, one that may eventually lead to a reformulation of ideas. In religion this can be justified as a return to the real meaning of the scripture. Doubts of this kind are at the basis of the agnosticism with regard to the supernatural that one finds in different forms in both written and oral cultures, though writing is likely to produce a more definitive ideology. So that, even in hegemonic religions, the written text will not totally define belief; equivocal material as in the Apocrypha reflects the fact that such religious ideologies do not succeed in suppressing all alternative questioning about the universe. Of course, Roman and Greek religions were literate and so too were religions

---

[13] Goody 1998.

in the east, but these were polytheistic and not monopolistic in the same way.

However, any system of beliefs contains potential contradictions and actual lacunae that may lead to questioning by members of the congregation, all of whom have their own experiences of 'the sacred' and can add their own gloss to what they have been taught. But despite the fact that there is room for alternatives like Catharism to make an appearance, hegemonic interests tend to dominate thinking over a large range of intellectual and political activities, especially where this domination is reinforced by an omnipresent hierarchy of powerful priests, as in early Christianity.

Thus written civilizations continue to display an aspect both of certainty and of doubt, of dynamism and of conservatism, the balance between which varies at different times. From one standpoint, the recording of knowledge in writing makes it easier to subject it to inspection, to reflection and to modification, as in the case of some early types of comprehensive lists, such as the *onamasticon* of ancient Egypt, and as with the encyclopaedias of Song China. People may go on to modify these accounts on the basis of their experience. On the other hand, writing may also give rise to fixed ideas that resist change, especially in texts of a religious kind seen as composed by the deity or by those in close contact with him. Consequently Christians today find themselves referring to a fixed text composed some 2,000 years ago, Jews somewhat longer, and Muslims somewhat less long ago. In a purely oral culture the ideology would have changed gradually over the years sometimes more or less in line with other movements, but in written cultures religious statements are often frozen in time and have to be more deliberately abandoned or reinterpreted.

When a text refers back in this way to ancient times, there is bound to be a discrepancy between what is related about the past and what occurs in the present. Watt and I argued that this happened in ancient Greece when myths were written down; as time passed the gap between past and present grew and scepticism arose when the ancient texts were seen to be inappropriate.[14] Or they were viewed not only as unrepresentative of the present, but also as giving no satisfactory account of the past, unless interpreted 'allegorically' rather than 'literally', as pertaining to 'myth' rather than to 'history'. That discrepancy is a variable quantity; obviously some tales and sentiments are more time-specific than others, in their outlook, their morality and in their worldview; some may be wider and more general and therefore more universal in their application.

---

[14] Goody and Watt 1963.

We may not see this scepticism as a move towards secularization but it is. For the move was already made by the ancients. Of Thucydides, Finley writes that 'history was in the most fundamental sense a strongly human affair, capable of analysis and understanding entirely in terms of known patterns of human behaviour, without the intervention of the supernatural'.[15] How different this approach was from that involved in the idea of 'the Lord of Hosts' or an account of the events leading to the conversion of Constantine, the events related to a hegemonic religion that claimed unilateral supremacy over life and death. But, as we have remarked, elements of scepticism were not altogether absent from even the most rigid of religious beliefs.

The question of scepticism and secularism is especially important in studies of the natural world, where the conflict between religious ortho-doxy (the words of the Holy Scripture, written down many centuries before) and the contemporary opinion of scientists and others is not sim-ply about the past. The problem persists among the Christian Right in the USA, among many Muslims and Orthodox Jews. It is a general problem for all societies with dominant world religions. In the words of Mir-Hosseini and Tapper, the 'situation [in Iran] was the latest eruption of two universal tensions; between religiosity and secularism, and between despotism and democracy'.[16] Democracy is partly involved with secu-larity (not inevitably but as a tendency), because the rule of the people usually implies the actuality of a secular rather than a transcendental power. Not that parlements are irreligious; some, as in Puritan England, think of themselves as guided by God, but in making their decisions, these popular assemblies may deviate from orthodoxy which needs to be maintained by a certain degree of authoritarianism, either political or religious. However, a measure of secularism is also necessary to be able to pursue free enquiry in science or in other spheres of knowledge, just as it is required to pursue the kind of government that a modern democracy demands; that is difficult in areas where religious beliefs are not com-partmentalized, that is, where the world is not partly secularized, as it tends not to be with contemporary Catholics and Protestants in Northern Ireland, or with Sunnis and Shiites in Iraq. But there are of course less violent manifestations of religious conflict even in predominantly secular societies, ones that often turn around education in religiously oriented schools.

Theology is thus to be contrasted with philosophy. According to Renan (2003), philosophy had always been promoted at the heart of Islam but from 1200 the theological took control. In Europe Greece is regarded as

---

[15] Finley 1972: 20.   [16] Mir-Hosseini and Tapper 2006: 9.

founding philosophy, starting with Thales (624–546/5 BCE) among the Ionians (hence in Asia), according to Diogenes Laertius,[17] with Athens being 'the mother-city of philosophy'. Philosophy differed from theology representing an alternative set of secular, 'rational' beliefs, and in the medieval period the two conflicted. Philosophy even produced its non-belief, non-religion, in the shape of Cynicism, beginning with Diogenes (and perhaps with Antisthenes, the propagator of atheism, a rejector of religions). Cynicism itself was concerned with a vagrant, ascetic life (the path to happiness), an assault on all established values and a body of literary genres particularly well adapted to satire. Indeed, the emperor Julian saw Cynicism not as a type of philosophy but as something man had practised down the ages, as secularism, as a permanent feature of humanity, a way of life.[18] Others disagree, saying that while Cynicism was never a school of philosophy in the strict sense, it did have a series of specific beliefs that shared a beginning and an end. However, the argument seems to go part of the way with Julian in seeing Catharism and anarchism, outside the classical period, as being later manifestations of Cynicism. In other words it has about it elements of the anti-authoritarianism and the rejection of luxury that characterizes many oppositional movements of a political or religious kind (counter-cultural) in elite societies, as well as a note of the agnosticism which, alongside religion, is widespread in all human life.[19] In this respect the attitude is both pagan and disbelieving, hence providing a secular approach which ran quite contrary to many 'spiritualistic' interpretations involved in the Abrahamistic and other religions, though unlike them Cynicism and agnosticism were rarely dominant.

The relationship of secularism to materialism, which Thales is also seen as initiating, is clear, since if carried through both would exclude a supernatural explanation. It is no use looking for these doctrines in oral cultures, since supernatural explanations are part of the fabric. That is not to say there is no room for such thoughts on the part of individuals who may well be agnostic, and in any case certain areas, such as agricultural production, may be partly exempt, for as Malinowski[20] showed in the case of the Trobriands, religion or magic only applied to aspects of their activity.[21] However, it is only with writing that we effectively talk about such doctrines as philosophical, perhaps because we can then read them as external objects, out-there, that endure over time as well as space. And partly too because it is writing that encourages (perhaps produces) the kind of reflexivity that is intrinsic to philosophy

[17] Diogenes Laertius 1925 1: 14.   [18] Dudley 1937.   [19] Goody 1998.
[20] Malinowski 1935.   [21] See also Worsley 1997 on different kinds of knowledge.

as a discipline. However that may be, it is in fact Thales who one is often looking back to in this regard. In his recent book on Materialism in a series on the history of philosophy, Charbonnat[22] goes back to this writer but then reports the virtual elimination of the subject between the first and seventeenth centuries, only showing some faint beginnings with the Renaissance. So far so good, since the argument reinforces my claim about western society in that period. But Charbonnat's problem, which is the problem for most western philosophers, is that he excludes consideration of any other civilization, despite the fact that books have been written on *lokayata*, Indian materialism, and that Needham has seen the presence of this doctrine as being critical for the growth of science in China. Societies other than European, post-Greek, are not considered to have had materialistic (or secularized) beliefs, nor indeed to have had 'philosophy'. This seems a thoroughly ethnocentric view, teleological in view of later industrial developments, and exactly why we need to look carefully at whether the west was unique in having a renaissance.

Thales is sometimes said not only to have founded philosophy but to have 'invented rationality' in the sense that human intelligence suffices to know the world.[23] The first part of the claim is certainly wrong, the second not necessarily so, since to put a belief or even an attitude in writing as he did is a way of universalizing and crystallizing it. For the first time, it is said, knowledge was independent of myth or religion.[24] Charbonnat links this emergence to the predominance of a slave society, giving the elite enough leisure for speculation. I see this efflorescence rather as the further development of a mercantile culture in small states, combined with a ready form of literacy which greatly facilitated the circulation of knowledge. Thales, who made his money in the olive market, is said to have made many voyages where he mixed commerce with science. Rather than the presence of slavery being the main booster of the economy in Greece, it was surely the mercantile economy, based on trading artisanal goods and the search for metals, that boosted the Aegean economy, as it did that of much of the eastern Mediterranean and indeed the whole of the inland sea. An emphasis on the one led perhaps to a neglect of the other.[25] It was this mercantile regime, centred on a seafaring culture, that resulted in the many contacts with Phoenicia (and hence the alphabet and much else), the Phocean settlement at Marseilles, and the fifth-century voyage of Phocius from that city into the North Sea beyond, as well as the incessant movement to Ionia (Asia Minor), to the Persian empire and to Egypt, which brought them in touch with the sciences and

---

[22] Charbonnat 2007.   [23] Charbonnat 2007: 55.
[24] Charbonnat 2007: 54.   [25] Finley 1973; Goody 2006.

with other writings of the great empires of the ancient Near East. It was a similar impetus that led to the Phoenician colonization of Carthage, of Spain, of Sicily and Sardinia, of trade with Cornwall. Related to the Phoenicians were those other neighbouring Semites from the Asian seaboard, the Jews, who also dispersed throughout the Mediterranean, long before the forced emigration of the diaspora, mixing in many of the same commercial settlements as the Phoenicians. That merchant activity did not stop. Greek shipowners like Onassis, Italian traders like Marco Polo, Portuguese explorers like da Gama, Spanish sailors like Christopher Columbus, Muslim voyagers in the Indian Ocean, all speak to the maritime and commercial past of the Mediterranean. It was this area of small city states that gave rise to the relatively independent writings of the philosophers, including 'materialists' like Thales who developed aspects of sceptical and agnostic thought that were already present in oral cultures but required the act of writing to emerge as a 'philosophy'.

However, the Greeks themselves were not altogether as free of spiritual restrictions upon free enquiry as some modern apologists have supposed. Babylonian calculations of the length of the year were more accurate than all others and from there Anaximenes of Miletus (fl. c.545 BCE) was given permission to set up a sundial in the Spartan capital. At the same time his pupil Anaxagoras left Persian Clazomenae in Anatolia to visit Athens, then coming to fame under Pericles.[26] He taught there but when he came to deal with heavenly bodies, the 'superstitious Athenians' summoned him to trial for impiety in his teaching about the sun – and for being pro-Persian. He was forced to flee for his life, though Pericles saved him. The study of astronomy became 'illegal' in Athens but 'the Orient continued to refine its scientific results', which is why Olmstead writes of Persia as having 'science without theology'. Athens still had restrictions on knowledge though not as severe as in the regions of the Abrahamistic religions.

While both Thales and Heraclitus were committed to the exploration of nature without the intermediary of the supernatural, they looked upon the problem of explaining the world from a monist standpoint, one thinking of water as the general principle, the other of fire. Thus they approached nature in a way that resembled myth. Scientific enquiry demanded an openness of investigation but setting the supernatural on one side went part of the way. Of course, the Greeks, despite their 'rationality', worshipped shrines and gods, but no one of these tried to adopt a hegemonic position in regard to nature. Medieval Christianity did, which was why the Italian Renaissance was so important in limiting the scope of

[26] Olmstead 1948: 328.

religion, both in the sciences and in the arts. In this process, the looking back to classical theory and practice was of the utmost significance.

Thales was followed by Democritus of Abdera (460–370 BCE), the proponent of atomic theory, who thereby effectively excluded the supernatural from the study of nature for the world was made up of particles (*atomon* or indivisible), and therefore an explanation came from within and not from without. Democritus had travelled widely in Egypt and Persia at the height of Athenian achievement. It was a time when medicine and mathematics flourished, both largely emancipated from the supernatural, at least as far as concerns their pursuit as intellectual disciplines (for this was the time of the specialization of knowledge). Not that transcendent doctrines were inexistent, either as theory or in practice. In theory Socrates took that route and in practice individuals went to whatever source of healing served them best, including the gods. But nevertheless science was established as partly independent of the supernatural.

Democritus, who declared that 'man is that which we all know', is presumed to have visited Babylonia and other countries in the interest of astronomy. 'Only the atoms and the void exist in reality', he concluded. He was welcomed in the orient as a fellow-student and absorbed the learning of Nabu-rimanni, subsequently introducing Babylonian discoveries to his own countrymen though Athens remained 'infertile soil for the scientist', for 'the prejudice against science was yet strong'; as Democritus announced, 'I came to Athens and no one knew me.'[27] His astronomical work was continued by Eudoxus of Cnidus, the father of scientific astronomy and the immediate precursor of Euclid; he was a pupil of Plato who also spent time in Egypt where he came under the influence of oriental mathematicians. But Plato himself had been a pupil of the ageing Socrates, who saw little use in studying astronomy or anything that God had not intended man to know. Even in 'pagan' societies such as Greece where there was no Abrahamistic religion, the influence of the supernatural inhibited enquiry into the natural world. This anti-scientific attitude was very much against the thinking in oriental science which influenced the Orient in many ways. It was certainly not in Europe that everything began; science was a more international product.

The atomistic and sceptical philosophy of Democritus was followed by the Athenian materialist Epicurus (342–270 or 271 BCE), whose family emigrated to Samos in Asia Minor where his father, like him, was head of a school. His teaching expanded during the Roman period until the end of the empire and the coming of Christianity, especially through Lucretius and Philodemus. His atomism led him to be profoundly critical

[27] Olmstead 1948: 340.

of religion and myths. For atoms were permanent features of the universe through the conservation of matter and did not require creating by some transcendent being. Getting rid of these beings gets rid of fear.

All this was anathema to Christianity, which in a hegemonic manner imposed its own version of creationism; independence was no longer possible, philosophy was in the service of God.[28] That was mostly the case under the Abrahamistic religions. There were a few thinkers that have been called 'heterodox' even in the Muslim world, for example, Omar Khayam (1040–1123) and to some extent Averroës (1126–98). The latter was a faithful interpreter of Aristotelian doctrine who was condemned by Muslim orthodoxy but pardoned by the sultan. In western Christianity there was also a limited attempt to gain some freedom from religious orthodoxy, especially at the school of Chartres in the twelfth century, which tried to divorce philosophy from religion. Guillaume de Conches produced comments on *Timaeus* and sought to show the consistency of Plato with Christian belief, better to understand nature. In the same way Roger Bacon (1212–90) tried to reconcile faith with natural causation by obtaining a 'conditional liberty' to study the latter. Both referred back to Plato. In the thirteenth century Siger de Brabant was an Aristotelian (accused of 'averoism') who drew attention to philosophical contradictions in Christian creationism. Others followed, appealing to Greek sources in an attempt to reform the thinking of the church (and sometimes the church itself). One among them, Nicolas d'Autrecourt, who taught in the faculty of arts at Paris in the fourteenth century, was called to Avignon to defend his thesis, which included the statement, close to the thought of Epicurus, that 'nothing could be born of nothing'. He was held in prison there for six years and eventually retracted and his books were burnt. Thus heterodoxy was snuffed out by the power of the orthodox church.

Science is caught up in the doctrines, or at least the method, of materialism. It has been said that science is materialist and that materialism is the only philosophy compatible with the scientific programme. It is a necessary aspect of the emancipation of the experimental sciences relative to theology – in the modern west with the naturalistic method of the seventeenth century. That led to an egalitarianism in law, when inequality was no longer protected by a transcendent view of the world. Nevertheless it did not altogether set aside deism nor indeed pantheism, even though it could be consistent with atheism. Nor was it inimical to morality, as has often been supposed; indeed, this is where contemporary 'humanism' claims to fill the gap. Despite 'Intelligent Design', despite the implicit

[28] Charbonnat 2007: 142.

injunctions of many writers, religion is not a necessary aspect of every human action. Indeed, the history of materialism has been marked by the torture of thinkers, executions, exile, blocked careers, the denial of liveli-hood, the suppression of opposition by a hegemonic religion, a struggle that has often centred on the control of schools and universities, institu-tions that are central to the production of (written) thought and of the next generation.

The position of Islam provides an interesting slant on a religious regime of the typically hegemonic kind and its conflict with the secular in the shape of the political. There was always a degree of opposition between the dominant Islamic religion and the political powers, e.g. in the Sunni caliphate, for the latter had to take pragmatic decisions which could not always measure up to the principles of the former. An opposition of this kind was bound to arise under any religious dispensation, which explains the frequency of secular political regimes even in countries with a hege-monic religion; in fact regimes that do not differentiate between the two aspects are few and far between. That is not to say the regimes them-selves have become completely secularized; they still observe some major tenets of the religion but they draw a distinction between ecclesiastical law and civil law, as happened increasingly throughout Christian Europe, whereas the demands of the religious life suggest there should be no such distinction. Since the religion was hegemonic, it wanted to govern all. Whereas the notion of representation, e.g. in democracy, means that the law, and hence in theory people's conduct, could be changed by the deci-sions of the popular assembly, in response to particular situations rather than to divine principles. But the distinction is similar in authoritarian regimes, where supernatural demands and present policy diverge. Of course, the opposition occurs with other, non-hegemonic, types of reli-gion, in India for example, where the conflict is often overt between *artha* (political economy) and *dharma* (religious purity), or in castes between the Kshatria (warriors, the territorial rulers) and the Brahmans (priests, the representatives of the divine). There is a split between the secular rulers and the representative of the divine, but here never with quite the same intensity as with prescriptive monotheism.

Following the Renaissance, the west partly solved this problem by 'humanizing' religion and by making its scope more restricted, e.g. to the Sunday church service. This was not a solution which then appealed to Muslims. Much Islamic learning was directly challenged by the secular philosophy of the west which followed the Enlightenment and threatened the extent of its belief in God, which has defined the Muslim civilization. The west, however, had not by then abandoned its belief in God (though in 2007, 30 per cent of French people now have), but that belief was rationalized in a way that largely confined him to a minor appearance. That process of diminution has not touched Islam in the same way although 'modernism' and earlier a form of humanism have made inroads for the scientific sphere. But the fact that the west has secularized part of life has only made it more difficult for Islam. India and China have rarely sought to define their culture by religious criteria alone but with its Abrahamistic background Islam has done precisely this.

Hegemonic religions, initially, allowed little room for the secular. Christ had said, Render unto Caesar, but soon the aim was to make the ruler a Christian in order to convert the whole state as part of a Holy Roman empire, the Kingdom of God. The same was true of Islam. The head of the country was the caliph ('successor') or imam, the leader of the faithful. But there was in fact often a tension between the political (the sultan and the independent, hereditary governors) and the religious leader, even though the former was meant to rule in God's name, as the Defender of the Faith. That was the problem for the Shiite movement which refused to accept the legitimacy of the rule of the Sunni ('orthodox') caliphate. For them, in the absence of the imams (they await the twelfth, the Mahdi, the 'Imam of Time'), no worldly power is legitimate.[29] Muhammad was of course successful both as a religious and as a political leader, initiating his reign as a conqueror as well as a prophet, not only of Arabia but tentatively outside. However, conquest was primarily the result of the leader having God's support; religion was essential to earthly history, as it was in the case of ancient Israel and for Constantine at the battle of Milvian; indeed, as it has been throughout history, God was the God of Hosts, the secular ruler needed the support of the divine.

I do not wish to try to establish a relationship between expansionism and conquest on the kind of scale practised by Christianity and Islam (and by Judaism itself in its earlier times of military glory) and militant, hegemonic monotheism; however, these beliefs undeniably had a profound impact on the life of the communities that embraced them. One can probably see something of what happened in Africa today when Christianity or Islam takes over from polytheistic (and oral) practice in a particular area. Many villages now have their huge church, their communal mosque or elsewhere their synagogue, where (schisms apart) the entire congregation gathers to worship, as distinct from the small groups of people attending different shrines at different times and for different reasons. The church towers above the rest of the community, just as the vicar stands out at one level, the bishop at the next, the pope at the

---

[29] For an outline account of the position in recent Iran, see Mir-Hosseini and Tapper 2006.

next. The other Abrahamistic religions did not have a similar hierarchy to Christianity but they were nonetheless hegemonic in the way they took over the lives of their congregation, managing the ceremonies of birth, marriage and death in an exclusive way; Jews had to marry Jews, and Muslims and Christians too were endogamous. Co-religionists welcomed one other in childbirth and said goodbye to each other at funerals; religion dominated these aspects of their personal lives. It is sometimes forgotten that so hegemonic were the religions that even the personal names of the next generation had to be chosen from a limited range taken from the Holy Book, and that was true of all the Abrahamistic religions.

The church dominated family life not only in imposing individual rites of passage, of birth, marriage and of death, but also in changing the nature of kinship and marriage. Many of the restrictions it imposed had specifically to do with the church,[30] with marrying a fellow member, and, I have argued, with its desire to accumulate property. Much later the Protestants did away with some prohibitions on the grounds that they were not laid down in the Book (a return to the Bible), as indeed was the case with some other later accretions to the religion, such as the Sacraments, Purgatory, dispensations and the multitude of saints.

In Europe regimes gradually became more secular. Initially the bishop wielded much political power over a region. Even in fourteenth-century France he might be in charge of half a town, such as Rodez in the Rouergue.[31] The other half was the king's town, administered quite differently. And even he of course ruled by the Grace of God. Gradually the population of the towns or communes asserted themselves, in relation both to the church and to the prince, each of whom might display more or less authoritarian or even tyrannical features, with the powers of the prince giving way to a qualified 'democracy' and those of the clergy to a selective secularization. At some moments, and specifically during the French Revolution, the powers of both were annulled, giving rise not only to the guillotining of the aristocracy but to the worship of Reason in preference to that of the supernatural, and to the consequent destruction of some castles and some churches. It was part of a process leading to 'democracy' and to secularization, at least in the form of compartmentalization.

However, hegemonic religions are not simply hegemonic politically (as is the case today in Israel as in many Islamic countries) and personally, but hegemonic over the arts and sciences, and even knowledge in general. That was very much the case in the early days of Christianity where

[30] Goody 1983.   [31] Wroe 1995.

figurative representations were at first forbidden and then only allowed in a religious context. All high art was religious, not simply because the church was a very significant patron but because the ideology embedded in the Old Testament decreed it should be so. Or rather the phase of Semitic aniconism disappeared in Catholicism, which eventually allowed even the High God himself to be portrayed, but high art permitted only religious figuration – of course, in Judaism and Islam no figuration at all was allowed, except in special circumstances and at some courts. As discussed earlier, at the time of the Renaissance in Europe there was an enormous burst forward when it became possible to represent classical (pagan) scenes. Lorenzetti's famous *Allegory of Justice and the Common Good* was painted around the walls of the meeting place of the Nine, the elected rulers of the Siennese state. Spufford writes that it is 'one of the earliest examples of a purely secular painting to survive'.[32] He means of course in the high culture of Europe since secular painting was of course common in Rome. Its later appearance was a *rebirth*, a renaissance, such as increasingly characterized Europe. When secular painting returned, classical deities partly took the place of Christian ones, mythical figures in an Italian landscape (which had already appeared in the later medieval religious works). And then the classical figures disappeared, leaving an Italianate landscape. Meanwhile the much more bourgeois art of the north gave rise to portrayals of everyday scenes, interiors of houses, outdoor fairs, seascapes and genre paintings. In later Judaism, emancipation led to a similar breakthrough. But in that religion (as in Islam) there was not really a change in the framework of religious space; the synagogue remained impervious to non-abstract art, the cemetery out of bounds to floral tributes. Even emancipation in Judaism did not challenge the aniconism in these spheres.

In the medieval period the great achievement of Christian art lay in architecture, in the building of magnificent cathedrals, which were later decorated with sculpture and stained glass, towering monuments that reached to the skies. But these were religious buildings and their construction illustrates the preoccupations of medieval society and the enormous concentration of talent and of wealth at the disposal of the church. That was not however the only form of building. Medieval warfare needed the castle, which produced its own (less elaborate) architecture, and the lay rulers needed palaces and mansions. But the church clearly won out over the nobility and the palace, at least until a much later period.

Following the iconophobia of the Old Testament, early Christianity had rejected forms of representation, such as sculpture, painting and

---

[32] Spufford 2002: 88.

the theatre. Gradually representations of a religious kind were allowed and aspects of landscape and still-life appeared in the background of these paintings. But the classical tradition of secular painting as found in Pompei existed no more. Although there was some continuity in the forms of art in the Christianized Roman world, and no doubt the majority of its members accepted icons that promoted the new faith, there was an important current of iconoclasm to which a number of important figures subscribed. For Augustine art was 'unable to be true', for Epiphanius, bishop of Salamis, who died in 403, art was 'lying'.[33] In any case, it was only religious art that was permitted; the 'naturalism' of Rome was abandoned and while cultic painting was allowed, there was some intellectual ambivalence which was resolved into iconoclasm under the Protestants. The three-dimensional sculpture of the Greek world was also condemned, although in a religious context there were some figures and relief sculpture on buildings, in stone or in wood, that came back with the Gothic. In both these cases, secular painting and free-standing sculpture only returned in force with the early Italian Renaissance, with the *primi lumi* of the fourteenth century. Michelangelo's statue of David was the first nude since Antiquity. It was the same with theatre. While all such dramatic representation was at first forbidden in Christianity, with classical theatres being deliberately destroyed (as at Verulamium, St Albans), although it continued at the 'folk' level despite condemnation by the church, this returned first in the form of liturgical tropes, then in mystery plays and clerks' performances before giving birth to the secular theatre of the Renaissance. It was the same story with written fiction, a mode that was not encouraged during the Dark Ages. Narratives restarted with tales of saints' lives; they gave way to the romances which became popular in late medieval times, often largely based upon earlier epics which became widely diffused and popular among various classes and which often spoke of pagan gods.

The revival of the secular renascence relates to the extension of literacy. As one editor notes, in the thirteenth century Oxford began to contribute to 'the over-production of clerks' which, 'by breaking the bounds set between ecclesiastics and laymen, played an important part in the secularization of letters'.[34] It was then that 'romance' was established in English, that such storytelling became popular, even if some of the clergy denounced all minstrels as 'ministers of Satan'. But '[t]hough there are moments in the fourteenth century when the preponderance of the clerical over the secular elements in literature seem as great as ever, by the end of the Middle Ages the trend of the conflict is plain. It is the church

---

[33] Elsner 1998: 248.   [34] Sisam 1953 [1921]: ix–x.

that draws back',[35] as imaginative literature eventually wins full secular liberty, under French influence, from ecclesiastical Latin. This liberty corresponds to a new freedom of form: the long alliterative line in poetry gives way to rhyme, which develops at the hands of the *trouvères* and the minstrels, though in the course of time these practitioners gave way to 'the men of letters'. Such changes were felt first in the larger centres rather than the country districts, although the third quarter of the century saw the revival of the alliterative tradition of non-rhymed verse. That was again followed by a reversion to the big-city tradition in Gower and Chaucer when for the first time 'a layman, working in English for secular purposes . . . ranked among men of letters'[36] and followed continental models. The miracle and mystery play developed all over Europe even earlier, heralding the return of drama in that continent, albeit ambiguous for the church, that gradually moved outside the sacred space to be taken over by the city and its guilds, again a sign of secularity even if the subject remained religious. But the plays are reluctantly transformed into English rather than Latin (or French) drama. For the church, however, '[l]iterary composition as a pure art was not encouraged. Entertainment for its own sake was discountenanced.'[37]

Literature seems to have been less dominated by religion than the visual arts, especially with poetry, which was more inclined to celebrate the old gods. In England it remained influenced by Anglo-Saxon religion, especially in *Beowulf* and in the early English *Sir Gawain and the Green Knight* as well as in the saga literature, although in Chaucer's various works there is a Christian theme (often satirical), as in the anonymous *Pearl*. There are strongly secular elements in Arabic love poetry (*ghazal*) too and in the Jewish equivalents in the Hispano-Maghrebian tradition. In prose we have the secular Anglo-Saxon Chronicles. But it was not until the Renaissance that, with the coming of humanism in Europe, literature was virtually emancipated from religion. It became 'fundamentally secular', and in many spheres looked back to the pagans; according to Reynolds and Wilson, 'the thin but unbroken tradition of lay education [i.e. classical] in Italy had doubtless contributed to this'.[38] In their review of the transmission of classical learning, these authors write of an Italy which had already enjoyed a much earlier renascence in the first half of the sixth century and then of the blossoming of Visigothic culture in Spain in the late sixth and early seventh centuries with the achievements of the writer Isidore of Seville (c.560–636). His *Etymologiae* spread rapidly throughout Europe and contributed greatly to medieval

[35] Sisam 1953 [1921]: xiii.   [36] Sisam 1953 [1921]: xx.
[37] Sisam 1953 [1921]: xxxi.   [38] Reynolds and Wilson 1968: 110.

education. Essentially it was in the other spheres that a break had to be made with the predominantly religious, but there were previous efforts to look back which had some humanistic repercussions.

Not only the arts but knowledge more generally suffered from the demands of religious hegemony. Much of what had been accumulated in the efflorescence of the classical period was now doomed to at least partial oblivion. In Christianity, as in Islam and Judaism, schools became church schools primarily engaged in transmitting religion and religious knowledge.

There was a difference in medieval education and learning between the cathedral and the monastic schools. The former were more humanistic: 'in the monasteries all pagan poetry . . . came to be regarded as . . . sin'.[39] The former, however, guided by a master appointed by the bishop, taught the Quadrivium and formed the basis of later universities as with Bologna, Chartres, Paris and Rheims, which served professional rather than purely religious aims. There was between 1000 and 1150 a strong move in the knowledge of classical material but this was accompanied by the fear that Christian civilization 'should be undermined by the popularity of pagan ideas'.[40] A reaction took place in the second half of the twelfth century which was followed by the Age of Scholasticism.

The negative effects of Christianity on scientific thought are empha-sized by the Islamic historian al-Masudi in the tenth century. He writes '[d]uring the times of the ancient Greeks, and for a little while during the Byzantine [i.e. Roman] empire, the philosophical sciences kept on growing . . . They developed their theories of natural science . . . until the religion of Christianity appeared . . . ; they then effaced the signs of philosophy, eliminated its traces, destroyed its paths, and they changed and corrupted what the ancient Greeks had set forth in clear expositions.'[41] For instance, in map-making Christian maps of the Middle Ages regressed from the detailed map of the Greeks and Romans, anyhow until the Islamic maps such as Idrisi's in his Book of Roger (1154) and later in northern Europe the sixteenth-century maps of Mercator. The early Christian seventh-century map ('T-O') has been called a 'rather spare diagram'. Ptolemy had to be rediscovered just as most sciences had to be reborn. This is another example of the loss of information under Christianity. In the words of Ibn Gumay (d. 1198), the personal physi-cian of Saladin, 'the Christians considered it a fault to study intellectual matters and their kings cast away the care for medicine and found read-ing Hippocrates and Galen too tedious; thus, it fell into disorder and its condition worsened'.[42] In opposition to Christian Byzantium, the

[39] Bolgar 1954: 191.   [40] Bolgar 1954: 201.   [41] Gutas 1998: 89.   [42] Gutas 1998: 91.

Muslim Abbasids looked back to Greece and encouraged translation into Arabic. The Alexandrian physicist Oribasius and Paul of Aegina had seen that a limited instruction was continued at Alexandria and this was taken over by the Muslims and developed by the caliph al-Mamun. If it were not for this man, '[a]ll the sciences of the ancients . . . would have been forgotten, just as they are forgotten today in the lands in which they were most specifically cultivated, I mean Rome, Athens, the Byzantine provinces'.[43] The work of the Alexandrian doctors much influenced that of al-Razi and later of Abulcasis. The importance of his conservation (or indeed rebirth) of Greek knowledge is brought out in the famous dream of al-Mamun where he meets with Aristotle, implying that the caliph was the preserver of the didactic, rational, mode of thought.

It was Augustine's attitude the Renaissance reversed by its appeal to the ancients. It was these ancient writers who cultivated philosophy rather than religion, which was multiple rather than hegemonic. Philosophy was 'pagan', secular, even at times not spiritual at all. The humanists saw it as an addition to Christianity but in fact its study often moved in another direction altogether.

It was not until the 'economic revolution' of the fourteenth and fifteenth centuries, with its rapid growth in commercial and financial exchanges, especially with the east, allowing for the relative independence of towns and rulers, that a greater freedom emerged. The pre-eminence of Rome and the Catholic Church over things intellectual and political no longer went unchallenged. Venice in particular gained an independence from the papacy. Universities and courts offered alternative careers to the church. Universities in northern Italy were now sometimes directed by laymen rather than clerics. The towns had greater resources which made them less dependent. At the same time there was an intellectual revival. Observation rather than deduction was promoted both in astronomy and in botany. The Italian universities trained many doctors and gave courses in the natural sciences; Copernicus (1473–1543) was one of the beneficiaries. Their research was given a wider distribution by the coming of the printing press, for the diffusion of the book helped to break the clerical monopoly on knowledge. Burning books no longer had the same effect since they were produced in numbers. But books also led to the rediscovery of classical, pagan, authors.[44] This intellectual emancipation gave greater weight to a naturalism which saw science and religion as distinct. Baconian experiment joined observation to create a new form of science, involving the naturalization of knowledge. But the Catholic Church still stood out against some of these developments and in 1516

---

[43] Ibn Ridwan, cited Gutas 1998: 93.   [44] Charbonnat 2007: 170.

a decree prohibited diffusion of the doctrine of heliocentricism. On the
religious side, the books of the Protestant Ramus were forbidden by the
Parisian theologians and he was forced into exile, eventually to be killed
in the St Bartholomew's massacre of 1572.

Nor was orthodoxy of belief confined to Catholicism. While some areas
may have been freer, Jewish orthodoxy gave Spinoza a hard time and the
Protestants continued to propagate creationism. With the opening up of
trade round the Cape of Good Hope and the development of America
and the Atlantic, the Mediterranean lost much of the importance it had
had during the Italian Renaissance and it was the north-west of Europe,
England, Holland and France, which took over the lead, not only in commerce and finance but in matters intellectual as well as in the colonization
of the rest of the world. Only then was there substantial change in these
matters. But medicine and the curing of disease had its own momentum.
So too did technology in other spheres. Apart from medicine, the other
field which science dominated was in the naval yards.

In the growth of a more secular attitude, Padua had been important
for a number of reasons. Witt looks upon it as the place where humanism
began.[45] As a city it was under the rule of Venice whose commercial
activities especially with the east made it virtually independent of Rome
and therefore of ecclesiastical control. It was also rich enough to support
independent scholars and publishers. Most of the northern Italian cities
came to participate in this commercial wealth and to establish universities
and city states.

One major figure of Renaissance science in Padua was Pietro Pomponazzi (1462–1525) who carried out his medical studies there and eventually became professor of natural philosophy, after which he taught at
Ferrara and Bologna. He got into trouble with the clergy as he denied the
immortality of the soul as well as the supernatural character of miracles,
which he tried to explain by Aristotelian methods; in 1516 the clergy of
Venice publicly burnt one of his books. However, he was by no means a
materialist, believing like Aristotle in a separate supernatural world which
did not influence the sublunar and which had its own rules which were
auto-determined and capable of examination by mankind. So the early
naturalists of the period went further than what we may describe as the
heterodox thinkers of the Middle Ages, and looked back to Greek times.
They did not renounce the creationism of Christianity but they saw the
supernatural as operating outside the human sphere.

Pomponazzi influenced many other scholars. So too did the University
of Padua, which pursued its enquiries by going back directly to the Greek

[45] Witt 2000.

texts. In 1497 the Venetian senate established a chair in Aristotelian studies to be examined in the original language. Many of the great figures of European science passed through this university, not only Copernicus but Gallileo, Bruno and Vesalius.

In the fourteenth century medicine developed, especially with the demands of the inhabitants of the growing towns, whose wealth made the universities more independent and freer of the control of both clergy and state, as with Bologna, Padua's founding institution, for Roman law. They even began the dissection of bodies. Thus a natural science started to develop and to gain its autonomy, though it still had its ups and downs. In neighbouring fields, the scholar and printer Étienne Dolet was burnt at the stake in 1546 as a relapsed heretic, but he had also published Rabelais and Erasmus. Writers still required a patron or protector, which were more abundant in the independent towns and at the independent courts. Nevertheless, in 1574 the young Geoffroy Vallée was hanged in Paris for putting his name to a deist tract. Bruno moved from one place to another in Europe partly to avoid the Catholic Inquisition. Escape was more possible than before, especially by residing among Protestants who had broken with the domination of the prevalent orthodoxy.

So what had been heterodox thinking in the Middle Ages now became part of a much broader movement, confining the church to operate mainly in 'spiritual' spheres. Religion was partly separated from philosophy. Science gained a certain autonomy and lived along with religion, especially as that became increasingly rationalized.[46] For most people religion and science were not completely separated; those early naturalists nevertheless left the supernatural sphere to the clergy, while they were concerned to remove religion from nature.

But this did not always work. Guilio Cesare Vanini (1585–1619) studied law in a religious college in Naples before going on to Padua where he worked on scientific questions. He opposed the Roman interference in political matters and was recalled to Naples. Instead of going back he fled to England where he converted to Anglicanism, but he was later arrested by the archbishop of Canterbury. He escaped to Paris but, though it had royal approval, his search of nature was condemned by the Sorbonne and he went off to Toulouse to work as a medical doctor. Nevertheless he was condemned by the church and burnt. Philosophically he was close to Bruno and suffered the same fate, indicating once again how necessary the Renaissance and subsequently the Enlightenment were for the freedom of knowledge.

[46] Charbonnat 2007: 174.

The suppression of alternative views continued through the eighteenth century. In France Diderot (1713–84), organizer of *L'Encyclopédie*, was imprisoned in Vincennes and he suffered repeatedly from the censor. In the end he had the patronage of Catherine of Russia but otherwise had little security. The Baron d'Holbach (1723–89), a model for Franklin, Priestley and many other intellectuals of the period, had to publish anonymously even on the eve of the French Revolution and his London publication of the *Social System* (1773) was put on the Index and forbidden by the police. Other books were burnt publicly. When the Revolution came, it took an anti-clerical turn in favour of the worship of Reason. Science and knowledge were freed from religion. In the following nineteenth century, prison and censorship were no longer options for non-believers, although the Index continued to exist in Catholic regimes and more generally the laws of blasphemy (rarely invoked) applied to attacks on religions; while in the Near East challenges against Islam or Judaism were more usually countered by legal means. The Abrahamistic religions gave up their monopolies of the truth reluctantly and slowly, clinging to infallibility despite the increasing speed of intellectual developments in the nineteenth century; Charbonnat notes that the decline of the influence of the church was related to the dominance of institutions of knowledge at the heart of intellectual life.[47] Thus in the work of Marx and Engels, the philosophy of the natural sciences not only set aside divine intervention but led back to pre-Christian times, to the classical philosophies of immanentist persuasion, like Epicurus and Democritus on which the young Marx wrote a thesis.

Pre-emancipation Jewry had no possibility of such a recourse to a quasi-secular tradition outside medicine; for while they were involved in the translation of the Greek classics, they themselves had no equivalent past of their own to which to look back, though later on individual members made a break-out to the thought of the Islamic or Italian Renaissance and later to the Enlightenment. Such a move required them to reject some restrictions of their religion; indeed, sometimes it involved conversion to another creed or possibly even to atheism. The Polish philosopher Maimon, a seeker after knowledge of all kinds, writes of the iron grip of the rabbis in Galicia on all written learning at the beginning of the nineteenth century. In northern Europe contact with the post-Renaissance life of Christian Europe, or rather with Catholic Europe since the Italian Renaissance at first made little impression in Orthodox Russia, gave Jews the opportunity to pursue the arts or the sciences.[48] As in aniconic Islam, not only were the representational arts largely taboo, but at certain

---

[47] Charbonnat 2007: 406.   [48] Hobsbawm 2005.

periods when religion predominated, the 'ancient sciences' of the classical period (and elsewhere) were forbidden. As Caliph Omar reportedly declared, what went against the Holy Book should be burnt. Yet there were other periods in Islam which were 'humanistic'. They involved an alternation with the dominance of the religious account when knowledge of the ancient or 'foreign sciences' were revived and extended, for this learning was essentially secular and often denounced by orthodox opinion.

That denunciation of the secular was an aspect of hegemonic religion, not so different from the ambivalent attitude of St Augustine to classical texts. On the other hand there were other Muslim rulers, in Baghdad and Cordoba for example, who built up considerable collections of writings at a time when libraries in western Europe were very small. Given the greater possibility of looking back and adding to past achievements through books, which can take the form of resurrecting neglected glories, Zafrani is right to find periods of 'humanism' in Maghrebian–Spanish civilization; around Cordoba in the tenth century when Averroës and Maimonides were writing, there was a revival of interest in Aristotle as well as in more general issues and in other traditions. Looking back involved an approach that was wider and more secular. And this wider learning in Islam in turn stimulated the twelfth-century renascence in western Europe.

Justinian closed the philosophical schools in Athens in 529 CE. But in Mesopotamia and Syria one had to know Greek to read the Bible and the writings of the church fathers, so at the same time scholars read science and philosophy in Greek, especially after 363 when St Ephraem set up his school at Edessa, teaching Aristotle, Hippocrates and Galen. When this school closed, the professors went to Syria, including Gondeshapur. So that when the Abbasids appeared in 750, all the works of science were translated, sometimes from Syriac, sometimes directly from Greek.

In Europe, the 'inevitable conflict' between Arab philosophy and Christian theology came at the beginning of the thirteenth century with the founding of the University of Paris. The masters and students of the cathedral school of the town came together in one body in 1200 and were recognized by the king and by the pope as a *universitas*, already important in the previous century in attracting European students, and whose teaching was divided between religious and scientific studies. From the first years, translations of Aristotle and his Arab commentators, especially Averroës, made their appearance.[49] Soon translations were made straight from Greek texts coming from Constantinople (as with William of

---

[49] Gilson 1944: 386.

Moerbeke, 1215–86), although at first the teaching of Aristotle was forbidden because of pantheism (at Paris but not at Toulouse). But avoidance was not easy, given his work already in circulation and the evident success of his account of the physical world. So Aristotle became increasingly acceptable, especially with St Thomas Aquinas and the Dominicans. But for theology, as at Paris, it was the method, the dialectic, that was important; science was subject to the superior interests of theology, but Oxford on the other hand was freer 'to put at the service of religion the mathematics and physics that the work of Arab scholars had shown them'.[50] It was closer to the empiricism of Occam in the fourteenth century. Moreover, there was not only a divide of this kind, with Oxford being more interested in Arab science than Paris, but the latter tended to see all study of letters (in classical languages) as being pagan and therefore to be avoided.[51] But there were tendencies against such religious hegemony in Orléans as in Oxford, the study of law at Bologna and medicine at Montpellier, that were revived and renewed by the humanists at the Italian Renaissance.

These periods of renascence often involved a measure of humanism, in this context a measure of secular learning, though the humanists generally did not see themselves as secularists but rather as forming a bridge between Christianity and the classics, as rationalizing religion. How did this come about? Again it is due to one of the characteristics of the written word. The very existence of written world religions implied the existence of the school to learn the text – Muslim schools, Jewish schools, Hindu schools, Christian schools. But while the schools focussed on religion, they taught reading which entailed the possibility of reading pre-Muslim Arabic poetry and Greek learning as well as the Quran; in the Christian case that looking back could not exclude going back to pagan (classical) times. In other religions too literacy would lead beyond the Book. This was not the intention. Muslim schools, like the others, were involved in the teaching of religion. Indeed, with the founding of the madrasas in the eleventh century, 'foreign sciences' ('natural science') were formally excluded; only religious learning was taught. The natural sciences were passed down in separate institutions such as medical schools or as practical technology or else informally. The same was true of Judaism, initially of Christianity, and largely with Hinduism or Buddhism. Schools were required to teach people to read the scriptures on which the religion was based; the scriptures laid down the divine view of the world and in theory required no supplement from outside. Religious practitioners were therefore the first schoolteachers, with the possible exception of China.

---

[50] Gilson 1944: 397.   [51] Gilson 1944: 406.

But teach someone to read and you teach him or her to read not only the scriptures, although efforts were often made to limit reading to these and to appropriate texts. You would also teach him or her to read (and possibly to write) other materials which have been composed with different aims in view. For even early religious traditions had their doubters; agnosticism and scepticism are widespread if not universal features of human society.[52] In this sense humanism involves the emergence into the light of an approach that would otherwise remain in the shadows; while European humanism was Christian, embracing the pagan classics, there was also another non-theistic or polytheistic element.[53] For the arrival of a dominating and dominant world religion does not succeed in suppressing all alternative pictures of the universe. We are reminded of this in the history of the Italian miller, arrested for his unorthodox beliefs, who saw the world as a ball of cheese inhabited by human worms eating their way out.[54] These alternatives will be attacked, as the miller and the Cathars were attacked by the Inquisition and declared heretical, but agnosticism and alternative beliefs continued. Science was also attacked, as happened to Darwinism in the nineteenth century, and today in parts of America and Turkey; it too may become hegemonic but it is in principle evidence-based. The result of these tensions is a struggle for power that in earlier times might bring about the temporary emergence of the one or the other, as an alternative system of beliefs as it were. But in the longer term the struggle has only one outcome; in most contexts the wider view of science prevails and it is the religious one that retreats. Today in western Europe, religion is highly compartmentalized, highly confined, having given way to science on many issues. For if one takes Genesis literally, then the evolutionary doctrine is blasphemous. Only by taking the Book in a metaphorical manner can it continue to be recognized as an 'authority'.

The alternation I refer to only ceased with the institutionalization of the secular, the creation of what Oppenheim called 'a great organization' out of the knowledge industries, in the shape of the universities, research institutes and knowledge-based associations such as the Lyceum and the Royal Society.[55] These provided a permanent base for the secular, scientific approach, the equivalent to that of the supernatural view offered much earlier by the church and its schools from which it had gradually dissociated itself. The emergence of the universities, it is important to stress, was not a sudden and unique accomplishment of Europe in the late Middle Ages; schools were essential to the teaching of reading and

[52] Goody 1998: chapter 11.   [53] Crouzet-Pavan 2007: 489.
[54] Ginzburg 1992.   [55] Oppenheim 1964.

writing that marked the Urban Revolution of the Bronze Age, and they required some further education for those becoming teachers, leading to training colleges and to higher education, though at first this training was largely limited to religious knowledge. For schools were usually organized by priests who were required to read and teach the scriptures to others. Hence they often had some training in order to do so. But in Renaissance Europe the religious and the secular gradually diverged, the religious not being displaced altogether (except under a few recent regimes) but rather confined, perhaps to specialist theological colleges and to special periods in state schools, making space elsewhere for an approach that led to the dominance of 'humanism' in major areas of human endeavour.

But in later Europe humanistic studies were more explicitly defined by those Italian teachers of the early Italian Renaissance who were called *humanisti* and who taught *studia humanores*. These humanistic studies involved a return to the written works of Antiquity, and their efforts were to some extent paralleled by the return of religious writers to earlier textual material in order to correct the translation of the scriptures – and so reform the church. But although the *humanisti* combined the two activities, the classical and the Christian, the first were obviously 'pagan' in inspiration and hence permitted a wider exploration of the material world than ecclesiastical hegemony allowed; they were no longer bound by the established religion which had for so long inhibited enquiry, but gave more attention to the secular dimension of knowledge. As already noted, two tendencies were involved here, the looking back to earlier literature (which saw a rebirth, a renascence), and an opening towards a freer, secular, even pagan, interpretation of the world.

In this way, the question of 'humanism' was closely associated with the Renaissance. But the word has expanded its meaning in several directions not all of which are pursued here.[56] Not that religion was set aside, but it was given a more 'rationalist' justification, more in tune with ancient philosophers, placing somewhat less emphasis on ritual and the transcendental, a demystification more in tune with the work of Protestant reformers who were also looking back to discover the true religion and its associated values. But while most humanists attempted to use ancient texts to reconcile Christianity and the classics, in a manner we have inherited, nevertheless the 'return of the gods' in the Renaissance inevitably queried Christian beliefs leading to some discussion of atheism.[57] Today humane, human, humanitarian or humanist values are ones that do not require a specific religious belief but are essentially secular. These are

---

[56] See Southern 1970: 29ff. for a fuller discussion of the meanings of humanism.
[57] Crouzet-Pavan 2007: 489.

often thought of as universal but what we find is that they in fact represent the spread of certain recent values (westernization, 'modernization', even globalization) across the world, values such as western democracy, western education (schools), western health services, western and Christian tolerance, western (modern) science, western or Christian love and the family. I do not deprecate these supposedly European values, which we generally see as 'humane', certainly as secularized, but I do want to argue that they have not long been characteristic of the west, except possibly in a very particular form, certainly not in the way that would justify Europe claiming for itself a monopoly of such values, if only because that implies a lack of humanity in others.

This position is not a question of taking up a simplistic anthropological view of the relativity of human values. But we nevertheless need to look more closely at the situation in hand. That is often problematical since in the course of conquering the world, the west has become deeply involved in justifying its invasion of the lands of others by proclaiming its 'civilizing' mission, its spread of the Christian religion with its supposedly unique virtues of charity (caritas), of tolerance,[58] of individualism[59] and of 'human values' generally. With secularization these came to be seen as 'human rights' to which all are entitled (but if rights are reciprocal with duties, by whom?). And do they include the right not to be invaded, not to be imposed upon?

The idea of that 'civilizing' mission has to do with the spread of Christianity and what contemporary politicians refer to as Judaeo-Christian civilization, neglecting the fact that there were three, not two, Abrahamistic religions in the Near East having the same sacred books and many of the same values, values which were and are shared by others. In this respect Christianity is seen by some of its practitioners as being a particularly tolerant religion, though this characteristic was remarked on as only subsequent to its influence by humanism. In fact, as I have remarked, there is a measure of intolerance, of exclusivity, in all written religions, especially monotheistic ones, as compared with oral beliefs, which are more accommodating and have no founding text to restrict them.[60] In the past, these creeds have clamped down upon the secular. But written religions certainly differ amongst themselves. Broadly speaking, the monotheistic creeds were less tolerant, were more hegemonic, than the others because polytheistic religions are by definition more pluralistic. However, there are also different degrees among the monotheistic ones. Because of the diaspora, Judaism was until recently rarely in a position to exercise tolerance towards others, only to receive intolerance;

<hr />

[58] Lewis 2002.   [59] Dumont 1963.   [60] Goody 1986.

now an Israeli state has been established as a religious one, excluding others from full membership. But between Christianity and Islam, who both found themselves in a dominant position in different parts of the world, the latter had a consistently more tolerant attitude towards other 'peoples of the Book', though this situation has now changed with the increased secularization of the post-Renaissance west. After the Christian reconquests in Spain and Italy, Muslims were violently expelled or else forcibly converted; that situation has changed but there are still those who want to define Europe in religious terms. In Islam, on the other hand, Christian sects were usually allowed to practise their faith openly, in Turkey, Egypt, Syria and elsewhere. They paid extra taxes but were permitted to stay, work and live; to this limited extent, the state took account of other denominations. Not always, but in general.

It is automatically assumed by many that since the Renaissance we have seen the progress of the 'civilizing process' of humanitarianism, if not of humanism, of a 'rationalized', secular version of Christianity, bringing in less cruelty, more consideration for others, more tolerance, more humanity. I do not want to deny or relativize this idea altogether. It is absolutely basic to the work of Norbert Elias[61] that has been particularly influential amongst western historians. Civilization, in his account, began in the European Renaissance. Certainly there has been greater attention paid to the use of handkerchiefs, which he singles out as a mark of civilization, but at the same time as this apparent 'progress' there were the terrible forms of genocide, in colonial conquest, in Nazi Germany, in former Yugoslavia, elsewhere too, with which (initially at least) Elias does not try to deal. The last century has certainly been the one of war, of mechanized war, which suggests the Panglossian process has not been clear cut. However, there are other related problems in Elias's account relating to modernization and the Renaissance. Firstly, he neglects non-European 'civilization', which is inadequate in view of what we know of China, Japan, India and Islam, which we shall review. Secondly, even for Europe he sees the 'civilizing' process as beginning with the Renaissance, that is, with what happened in Florence in the sixteenth century, at the time that many historians have seen as the birth of capitalism and of the bourgeoisie, whereas in some respects this movement saw itself as looking back to classical culture.

Many such as Burkhardt, Berenson and others have seen developments in the Italian Renaissance and in the Reformation (in the writings of Max Weber and many others) as intrinsic to the progress of the western world, to modernization, to 'capitalism', both as essentially European. But is that

---

[61] Elias 1994 [1978].

in fact altogether the case? Earlier renascences were certainly to be found in Europe, that is, periods for which historians have used the concept, e.g. the Carolingian renascence, the renascence of the twelfth century, the early Italian Renaissance. As we have seen, the renascence of the twelfth century, and in a different way the later one, was stimulated partly by contact with Arab learning. Islamic culture also had its 'humanistic' phases in which earlier learning was revived and brought to light. There were clearly periods in the history of Islamic societies when knowledge systems were dominated by a concern with the scriptures. There were others, as in tenth- to twelfth-century Andalusia and the Maghreb, when this was less true, periods that involved looking back (anyhow among the 'learned') to earlier, more secular achievements, to earlier texts, as well as looking forward to new creativity. Although with the establishment of the madrasas, Sunni schools were only for religious teaching, there were periods which saw some scholars not only return to their own classics of a more secular bent (the poetry of pre-Islamic writers, for instance) but also look back to the works of Greek and other authors, translations of whose enquiries had been incorporated in their own tradition (where they were known as 'foreign science'). In other words, there was a long-term alternation between periods or positions that stressed the authority of the Book and those that permitted, invited, even encouraged, wider enquiry.

The stimulus for any of these more secular periods is not always purely internal. There may well have been some influence from outside, as was later the case with the Jewish emancipation and with the Italian Renaissance itself. As we saw with medicine in Montpellier, in Christian Europe there was not simply an internal move towards the classics, away from the hegemony of the church and towards new forms of expression. There was also a wider movement that involved an influence from outside which is generally disregarded in discussions of the Renaissance, thus preserving European uniqueness and self-determination. There are some historians, especially historians of science and technology though economists too, who have considered the impact of other traditions on the Italian Renaissance, but they have been in a minority. Undoubtedly most Europeans see themselves as the post-Renaissance heirs of a particular continental tradition, and in certain cultural fields, such as the figurative arts, they need not look elsewhere. But in others it is different, as Brotton has recently argued in *The Renaissance Bazaar*,[62] as Howard has shown for Venetian architecture[63] and Caskey for the Amalfi coast.[64] Of the utmost significance in this rebirth has been the east's influence in the recovery of economic and urban life, given that it had never declined in

[62] Brotton 2002.   [63] Howard 2000.   [64] Caskey 2004.

the manner of the west. It continued to develop its Bronze and Iron Age cultures, in which east and west initially ran parallel courses, developed their mercantile societies in interaction with each other. After the fall of Rome, Asia avoided the 'Decline of the West', a decline which we can characterize as 'European exceptionalism', until that was changed in so many spheres by developments from the sixteenth century. Those developments raise another question that I will take up later on, namely of internal movements that are not limited to one culture but may affect all vaguely equivalent societies, continent-wide in this case, that is, the expansion of trade and manufacture, of knowledge and artistic life, in distinct communities that may influence each other but which may also be part of parallel changes that are taking place in quite different parts.

But before we can consider this problem, we need to look at the other major societies in Eurasia. If I am right in thinking that all literate societies are potential candidates for renascence and reformation, I need to examine the past of Islamic, Indian and Chinese regimes. I suggest that in this, as in some other respects, Europe was not as unique as has been claimed. For in the Italian Renaissance, as I have said, looking back to the classical period also meant giving less room to Christianity and to the religious generally and therefore more space to the secular, as was stimulated by a trend to ancient philosophy and the dominant classical view of the world, pagan and polytheistic. Of course, it was also true that looking back might also be to the religious text which is in principle unalterable; indeed, written religions necessarily involve such a return to the Book. That return could lead to reformation as it could to fundamentalism; it has the effect of breaking the pattern into which established religion has fallen, and may point forwards either to new solutions or backwards to old ones.

The Italian Renaissance had many facets. For humanists, it led to the rebirth of classical civilization, and the wedding of philosophy with religion. For science, it meant not only the return to a more open tradition of investigation, partly with the help of the Arabs, but it involved in effect a revival of enquiry into nature. In the arts too, a new era began, which in part resulted from a rebirth of an earlier, more secular, civilization, but also the creation of a new forward-looking culture. That was at a time that experienced not only the revival of Mediterranean trade but also 'the expansion of Europe' and the conquest of both the east and the west, leading to settlement in the west at the expense of the local population, to colonization and eventual withdrawal from the east. However, it was not simply a one-way traffic from Europe that was involved in this efflorescence of culture. Merchant and exchange activity was expanding throughout Eurasia, in both directions. The earlier developments in

Chinese trade and science are well known, and to some extent what was happening internally in the west was also happening in the east. For example, the east had long known refinements of the kind Elias sees as part of the 'civilizing process' emerging in Europe after the Renaissance, refinements which in the Asian cultures are evidenced by the elaboration of food and of flowers. In the arts we have the development of painting, poetry and the novel in China; in Japan in the seventeenth century we have the establishment of *kabuki* theatre, using some religious themes but in a largely secular context and directed to the growing merchant communities, just as often the Elizabethan theatre in England.

I started this book with the statement that renascences and reformations take place in all written cultures because of the very nature of (written) texts. In Christian Europe the return to earlier texts was also to the pagan classics. It opened the door to a different thinking, including the secular. The same happened intermittently in Islam which also resurrected classical learning. I see these alternating periods as occurring in other civilizations, though they were especially important in the hegemonic Abrahamistic religions. Lewis[65] regards the separation of the religious and the secular as one of the advantages of Christianity. That certainly took place politically, as with Guelphs and the Ghibellines. But I would argue that, despite the words of Christ, that separation did not happen in many spheres until the Renaissance with the substantive institutionalization of secular knowledge. But secular government had long since established itself, as had the lay economy. Indeed, similar developments already took place in ancient Egypt and in the classical world. But in western Europe with its hegemonic religion, the process of intellectual and artistic separation had largely to await the re-establishment of a more complex culture, through trade on the one hand, a degree of secularism on the other, with its various burgeoning renascences looking back to the pagan knowledge of the sciences and the arts. A more long-standing secularization began with the European Renaissance when various educational forums institutionalized independent enquiry outside a religious frame. But that was a slow process, the establishment of such knowledge in the form of schools, universities, academies, foundations. For example, at St John's College in Cambridge the first lay master was not appointed until 1908 with R. F. Scott;[66] previously all had been in holy orders. Only with the university dispensation of 1882 did fellows cease to have to be ordained and remain celibate. The religious life lived on for a long time and its imprint is very much in evidence even today.

---

[65] Lewis 2002.   [66] See Miller 1961: 96.

What I have been concerned with in this chapter has been the problem of breaking through the restrictions of a dominant religion, the confinement of that religion to a more restricted field, or alternatively other ways of circumventing these limitations. The placing of boundaries on the overwhelming intellectual and artistic influence of an Abrahamistic religion seems a very important factor in these developments.

4   Rebirth in Islam

with S. Fennell

In the Islamic world the process of looking back has taken place not only in the secular sphere, a rebirth of knowledge in both the arts and sciences, but in the religious sphere too, people returning to the Book not only every day in worship but also as a recurrent inspiration for specific purposes of reform. This chapter is exceptionally long because we are trying to assess cultural revival in the various countries of the Islamic world. This enterprise involves considering periods of decline as well as efflorescence and reviewing its cultural history as well as the economic and political and religious features that affected this – a tall order but one that we cannot escape. We are looking here not mainly at Islam's contribution to the Italian Renaissance but to rebirth within Islam, especially the Abbasid translation movement, the *Buyid* renaissance, similar activity in Mamluk Egypt, in Ottoman Turkey, in Andalusia and in the nineteenth-century *Nahda*.[1]

Following Muhammad's death in 632, from the years of the early caliphate and through the century or so of the Umayyad rulers, the Arabs quickly conquered the adjacent area of the Near East which the Greeks and Romans had earlier ruled, including Egypt, Syria and Mesopotamia, and subsequently the central and western coastal states of North Africa, and central Asia as well as virtually all of Persia, thus ending the Sasanian empire founded at Fars by Ardashir I in 226 CE. The Arab invasion of the Near East unified an area which had been divided by the struggle between Persia and Byzantium, a struggle that produced the 'disastrous wars' of 570–630 which were 'generated by the economic barriers raised by the division into East and West', and specifically the absence of free access to the main trade routes.[2] For the first time since Alexander, the reunification occurred, even in agriculture where an exchange of plants, vegetables, fruits as well as techniques fed the Abbasid 'revolution' and

---

[1] On this chapter, see especially the work by M. G. S. Hodgson, *The Venture of Islam*, 3 vols., 1974.

[2] Gutas 1998: 12.

94

provided much of the wealth of the early empire. At the same time, on the level of learning, paper was introduced from China. Commerce was of fundamental importance. The foundation of the Arab capital in Baghdad by the Abbasids in 762 meant that ships could sail from Siraf, the port of Basra in the Persian Gulf, to India and south China, a trade in luxury goods that brought silk, spices and porcelain back again. The very expansion of Islam produced a common language of high culture throughout the Nile–Oxus region, together with 'a great cultural florescence';[3] the sudden and staggering linguistic penetration of Arabic and Arabisms even in the Iranic sphere is evidence of the great influence it had. There was now a centralized empire with one official language and with trade replacing booty as the fiscal basis of society. When the Abbasids, a Hashemite family, took over from the Umayyads in 750 CE, the latter having initiated caliphal rule (and distally related to the Prophet), the former descended from one of Muhammad's paternal uncles, an early looking back took place, both to classical Greek knowledge and to earlier Islam.

Trade was widespread throughout Islam, by sea and by land, along the inland Silk Roads and by water to India, south-east Asia and China. Coins circulated, cheques existed as did letters of credit, the *commenda* (cooperative trading arrangements) and banking institutions. Trade was basic to any renascence. Compared with Europe, where the exchange economy had greatly diminished, in Islam trade grew.[4] In the tenth century the centre for all this exchange shifted from Iraq and Persia to Egypt and the Indian Ocean. Very important in this were the Karimis, 'a unique group of capitalistic entrepreneurs',[5] supported by Saladin (r. 1174–93), who came to dominate the routes between east and west; by established *funduqs* all along the way, which operated as 'virtual stock exchanges',[6] their risk-laden activity stretching as far as Ghana in West Africa. Some of the merchants who operated family businesses amassed amounts which were as great as the richest merchants in India or in China, and they established banks which loaned to sultans. Information was exchanged as well as commodities. And these items were produced not only in households but also in early factories. Textiles were regularly fabricated in 'royal factories called Dar al-tiraz'[7] which existed all over the Islamic world, including Spain, Sicily and especially Baghdad in the tenth century, mainly for royal but also for private purposes. The economy flourished, and so did intellectual activities.

---

[3] Waldman 1997: 109.   [4] Labib 1969: 81.   [5] Labib 1969: 82.
[6] Labib 1969: 85.   [7] Labib 1969: 87.

Unlike the other cultures we will be discussing, the Muslim world found itself repeatedly undergoing a kind of renaissance even in the Italian sense, since there was the actuality of returning to 'foreign sciences', that is, to the learning (but rarely the creative literature) especially of Greece and Rome and to building on that. They also looked back to earlier regimes. For example, the Abbasids (750–1258 CE) buttressed their legitimacy by going back and emphasizing their position as heirs to earlier, pre-Islamic traditions of leadership (as did the later Buyids, with more credibility), building a new capital near the old Sasanian one of Ctesiphon (Kasifiya). Their court became highly elaborate, especially during the reign of Harun al-Rashid, the contemporary of Charlemagne. Harun drew on Jewish and Christian as well as recent converts as administrators; the Barmakids, formerly a Bactrian family of eminent Buddhist priests, were amongst the earliest supporters of the regime, and subsequently wielded great power as viziers under al-Mansur, al-Mahdi and Harun al-Rashid. From shortly after their accession, the Abbasids and their viziers were generous patrons of the arts and sciences, and because the power which made their takeover possible emanated from Merv (Magiana) in Khorosan, a formerly Seleucid (Persian) and Graeco-Bactrian centre of learning which remained most influential throughout the early Abbasid dynasty, the inflow of both Persian and Greek culture was a concomitant of the expanding trade economy. The 'literary florescence'[8] which followed was facilitated by the advent of Chinese paper, produced in mills set up in Samarkand with the aid of Chinese captives following the battle of Talas in 751 and, at the instigation of the Barmakids, by the mid 790s in Baghdad itself. Paper superseded the older media of vellum, which was expensive, and of papyrus, which was fragile, often uneven, susceptible to mould, not durable in moist conditions and had to be imported. With the resulting proliferation of written culture came growth in the translation of foreign works, which had already begun on a smaller scale in the Umayyad capital of Harran. Foremost among the sources were works in Persian, Syriac and particularly the Greek classics, thus providing a channel through which older writers could be revived and taken up by the Islamic tradition.

The previous dynasty, the Umayyads (661–750), had succeeded the early caliphate and established themselves at Damascus. They were followed at Baghdad by the creative Abbasid dynasty. The more cosmopolitan-minded head of the Abbasid clan introduced Christians, Jews, Shia and Persians into the Arab army, the local government and the central administration of the empire, though the Shia enfranchisement

[8] Waldman 1997: 114.

did not extend to the caliphate itself. The cultural and political broaden-
ing of recruitment to the imperial administration was a vital ingredient in
the success of a wider Islamic civilization in the centuries that followed.

When al-Mansur formalized the transfer of the capital from Harran
to Baghdad in 762, he was in fact moving to an already existing Persian
settlement of that name, and the architects he chose to design the city
delivered not so much an adaptation as a continuation of Sasanian Persian
architecture of the Umayyad and pre-Islamic eras. The indebtedness of
early Islamic architecture to Zoroastrian building was considerable, and
the name of the new capital Baghdad (from Middle Persian *bhag-dad*,
'god-given') bore the acknowledgement of a non-Abrahamistic god. This
represented a certain looking back.

Nevertheless it is clear that, as with the classics in Europe, the translation and study of many of what were referred to as the 'foreign sciences', although a rebirth, repeatedly faced resistance by the religious,
as did the political regime generally. Indeed, the Zoroastrian convert Ibn
al-Muqaffa (d. 760), secretary to the uncle of al-Mansur (r. 754–75),
suggested the regime should follow pre-Islamic models, since under the
auspices of the *ulama* (the learned men) the law might undermine caliphal
authority. A caliph's legitimacy derived from his being the spiritual ruler
of Islam and al-Mansur's son and successor, al-Mahdi, declared that the
caliph was the Protector of the Faith against heresy and had the right to
declare what was orthodox. Yet the caliphate and its state apparatus were
not directly involved in developing holy law, Sharia, and indeed there
developed a conflict between them. As a result, the Sharia was never
the sole source of law.

Al-Mansur's reign marked an increasing openness to Persian artistic cosmopolitanism and al-Muqaffa was known as a brilliant Persian
scholar. He also translated Sanskrit works on logic and reason as well as
the *Kalila* (a book of animal stories). Astronomical works too were rendered into Arabic in the early period, as were mathematics. Both literary
and scientific culture were strongly encouraged.

While they continued to maintain administrative as distinct from religious courts, until the reign of al-Mamun, al-Mansur and his successors
persecuted the Manicheans as heretics. Islamic orthodoxy was indeed
strengthened. Under the early Abbasid caliphs the puritanical zeal and
legislative ambitions of theological scholars gradually gathered momentum, and it was during Harun al-Rashid's time that al-Shafi (767–820)
founded the discipline of Islamic jurisprudence[9] and the four main

---

[9] He seems to have been the first to reflect on the various sources of Islamic law and to
reason about how to derive positive injunctions from them.

schools of Sunni law started to emerge around recognized masters. The resistance to caliphal 'interference' in holy law became more organized. He was viewed as the protector of the all-encompassing law which was now declared divine rather than human. An examination of theological allegiance (the *mihna* or 'ordeal') was imposed on officials, judges and other scholars, which the *ulama* however resisted as al-Mamun favoured Mutazili theology. For the Mutazilites, influenced by Hellenistic ideas, the Quran was a divine creation.

During the later ninth century Islam split into different regimes, yet all of these were held together by the acceptance throughout of one Sharia-based law and one religious language, as well as by the ongoing exchange of goods and ideas over the area it dominated, through all of which communication was greatly improved. Whereas centralizing politics slowly foundered, religion, economy and culture provided the durable factors. At the same time, despite its spread, one should not exaggerate the penetration of Islamic culture itself amongst the peoples of the empire; the Jewish, Christian and other populations, which had provided many early converts, remained numerous, both within and outside the Arab heartlands, and even after the increase in conversion in the years from al-Mansur to al-Mamun, the Muslim proportion of the empire as a whole still accounted for rather less than a fifth of the inhabitants, and less than 10 per cent in many areas.

As far as religious knowledge was concerned, Islam of course looked back not only to its own canon but, partly on the authority of the Quran itself, to the earlier Abrahamistic religions, to Christianity and particularly to Judaism, both of which had been present in the Arabian peninsular before the time of Muhammad. With the coming of Islam both these of course became respected as religions of the Book; in the Old Testament above all, both looked back to Abraham and hence to a monotheistic creed, and in their ritual each religion relived events that took place at the time of its founders. As religions of the Book, all three went back to these writings in their daily worship. Under these circumstances the potential for movements of reformation was always there, and these indeed materialized at times and places when a consensus returned to the Book in a somewhat different spirit, arguing that people had got the wrong reading or had fallen away from its injunctions. Indeed, both Christianity and Islam may be seen as radical reformist reactions of this kind to Judaism.[10] Within Islam itself, to retain favour with God it was necessary to go back to the original teaching. Therefore reformation was always on the cards, as it was for the Berber Almoravids in the extreme northwest

[10] See Quran, especially sura iii.

of Africa and southern Spain, for the Almohad princes who displaced them, and for the later Wahhabis, the puritanical reformers of the desert whose faith informed the Senussi of the Libyan sands (as well as Colonel Gaddafi, the Royal House of Saudi Arabia and, to some extent, the Taliban of Afghanistan). The latter brought upon themselves the wrath of much of the world by blowing up the Buddhist statues of Bamiyan and thus reasserting the early iconoclastic faith of their fathers, a belief which was also embodied in earlier Judaism as well as being held by the first Christians and later by many Protestants (especially Calvinists). All this represented a turning back to the pages of the scriptures and the rejection of what were considered later accretions. In that sense what took place was a reformation, a renewal, so that later interpretations were declared inadequate and even heretical. Within each branch of these religions a struggle took place (as it still does – most notably today in Iraq, but also in Jerusalem and in Northern Ireland). But a reformation of this kind is the opposite of a renascence, since it looks back to a fixed text of divine origin (hence unchangeable) and does not lead to a leap forward in knowledge or in culture generally.

For the Muslim, most learning is also an act of worship; the acquisition of knowledge was a duty of each individual. But there was a strong divide between religious knowledge, which centred upon the Quran, and the type of 'foreign science' such as the Greek, which was obviously secular. It was these 'foreign sciences' that were the primary subject of the early Abbasid translations. These constituted a revival of this knowledge and kept certain of the topics, and the Greek texts themselves, alive to be revived again for the Italian Renaissance. Until the twelfth century none of these works from the Greek or Arabic reached Christian Europe. But in Sicily, Greek and Latin works in Arabic were used during the Arab occupation of the ninth, tenth and eleventh centuries; a very lively hybrid culture continued from 1091 under the Norman kings, but the atmosphere of religious and cultural tolerance that had grown up from the time of Arab rule finally broke down in 1224 with the Crusades when the last Muslims were banished from the island. This cosmopolitanism had not been without its consequences, however, for Italian intellectuals had come into contact once again with the works of Antiquity, as can be seen particularly with the medicine which was taken up by the school at Salerno.

A similar influence was felt in the Islamic west, as we have seen in the previous chapter. As well as the religious sciences, then, in Islam there were other fields that had their own developments and prestige, especially medicine and other 'foreign sciences' blessed by the Prophet. For all types of learning, towns were important educational and commercial

centres where the student would come and study (although religious
learning was also important in the desert monasteries like the Christian
St Catherine's). In later Islam, however, the Sunni madrasas only rarely
taught anything but religious knowledge and the ephemeral observatories did not offer much continuity to scientific advance, though hospitals
offered greater security for medicine. In the Arab heartlands, the first
madrasa (or higher school), which has been discussed as a prototype
for the European university, was founded by the Seljuq (Turkish) vizier
Nizam al-Malik in 1067. They were colleges 'teaching the study and
propagation of the Sunni version of Islamic law', which first appeared in
Ghaznaid Khurasan but spread throughout Iran and further west. They
succeeded in enlarging the body of *ulama* and most were founded by sultans and other rulers. But in scope they were in general highly restrictive.
'Under the tolerant Shia Buyids, individualistic scholars had studied the
philosophy and literature of Greek and Roman Antiquity and pursued
lines of speculation condemned as un-Islamic by more narrow-minded
co-religionists. The Seljuq triumph effectively curtailed this humanistic
renaissance.'[11] Subsequently, the madrasas with their 'religiously based
and formerly quite narrow syllabuses' became the 'intellectual centres'
but only for religion.[12]

The madrasas, then, were largely confined to the religious texts, with
the *ulama* offering commentaries on commentaries. There was little or
no instruction in science which was confined to other centres: to libraries;
for medicine, to hospitals; for astronomy, to observatories; and for technology, to places such as arsenals (an Arabic word). Except in the latter
cases, science was not institutionalized and was therefore more vulnerable to attacks of various kinds. Otherwise learning was conservative and
often elitist.[13] But the *ulama* were at least international and their members were involved in much travelling throughout Muslim lands. This
meant the frequent transfer of information. For example, notable in the
seventeenth and eighteenth centuries was the export of knowledge from
Iran to India, and then the subsequent movement of outstanding Indian
scholarship to Egypt and west Asia, where it helped to revive the whole
field of learning.[14] The spread of Islam meant that all teaching was in
Arabic although later the Quran was also available in Persian.

Despite the diffusion of many manuscript books, the basic transmission of knowledge in Islam was personal, from master to disciples, like

[11] Irwin 1996: 40.
[12] It is rarely possible to generalize across all times and places in Islamic civilization.
In Ottoman Turkey, Safavid Persia and Mughul India some rational sciences were an
established part of the curriculum.
[13] Robinson 1996: 220.   [14] Robinson 1996: 230.

many arts and crafts in Europe. For one of the main features of learning was its face-to-face character. A book, which was of course handwritten, should be learned from a scholar who would give the pupil a certificate and he in turn would keep a genealogy of learning, a list of his masters, that is to say an *isnad*. This relationship was based on a manuscript culture and was threatened by the relative anonymity of print coming much later from Europe, as some leading scholars in Egypt recognized. Others welcomed these new ways of spreading Islam and of democratizing knowledge, but nevertheless print was at first abjured. There followed eventually a general adaptation of most of the new means of communication. In print, religious texts became more widespread, making it possible to study them outside the authority of the madrasa and of the *ulama*, who were increasingly marginalized by changes in the transmission of knowledge.

The *ulama* and from the tenth century the Sufis (Ar. *sufiyya*) were missionaries, the latter also having great mystical poets, such as Hafiz (d. c.1390), Jami (d. 1492) and Rumi (d. 1273) whose followers formed the Mevlevi order in his memory. There was a tension between the two. Sufi worship was marked by the use of music and dance. The Sufi were tainted with heresy, and the Spanish Sufi al-Arabi, who preached the doctrine of the unity of being, including God, was accused of pantheism. The Sufi espoused a version of 'popular Islam' in preference to the Sharia.[15] Both, however, revitalized Islam and this led to increased criticism of the 'rational sciences'. Saints' cults in their turn were also criticized and puritanism dominated some areas, notably in the work of al-Wahhab (d. 1787), the reformer whose teaching of the *jihad* became popular in North Africa.[16] Reformation and 'spiritual renewal' were constant features of Islam.[17] There were ups and downs in time, especially as far as secular knowledge was concerned. In Andalusia, there was the reign of caliph al-Hakam, who was the patron of the learned and brought a huge library to his capital, in quantity similar to that of the Abbasid princes in Baghdad. He was followed by his minor son who was then succeeded by the prime minister.

Islam also had a scientific tradition of which it has been said that it was 'crucial to the development of universal science in pre-modern times'.[18] For example, Saliba and others have stressed the contributions of Islamic

---

[15] Mainstream Sufism adapted to the law but saw an inner meaning. This was the synthesis achieved by al-Ghazali and reigned until modern anti-Sufi Salafism.

[16] Muhammad only uses the word in the general sense of striving (in the interests of the faith, in this case), e.g. at sura ix, 19–20.

[17] Irwin 1996: 37.   [18] Saliba 2007: 1.

science to the European Renaissance. This development took place, for example, with regard to perspective. In a recent book (2008), Belting

shows how the measurement of fictive space in perspective did not originate, as we have come to believe, in early 15th century Florence with Brunelleschi, Alberti, and Ghiberti, but had been developed four centuries earlier by the Arab astronomer and mathematician Abu Ali al-Hasan Ibn al-Haitham (965–1039), known as Alhazen. Alhazen's tract on the theory of visual rays, *Kitab al-Manazir* (The Book of Optics), was first published in 1028 in Cairo and circulated from the 13th century onwards at western universities in a Latin translation entitled *Perspective*. In due course the manuscript was re-named *Thesaurus Opticae* in a 1572 edition published in Basel.

Alhazen laid the mathematical foundations for calculating the refraction of light, thereby refuting the ancient idea which assumed that the eye emits rays. Not only was he the first to experiment with the camera obscura, he also taught that what we see originates in the brain. The acceptance of such concepts presupposed a rationalist, experimental way of thinking that was practised at some Arabic courts, but which, before the Florentine Renaissance, manifested itself in the west only in exceptional instances, for example in the case of Roger Bacon.

Belting maintains that, to some extent, this medieval Jewish and Arabic knowledge was simply taken over without acknowledgment by Renaissance artists and authors or attributed to ancient western sources. From the mid-19th century, colonial hubris in trumpeting the western development of perspective precluded recognition of its Arabic roots. Educated Europe elevated the Renaissance and its capital Florence into a fiction of an aesthetic against outsiders.[19]

Neither development would have existed unless Islam had had its own incorporation of Greek learning in the shape of the 'translation movement' in Baghdad at the time of the Abbasids. Of Greek science Leclerc[20] has written of the Arabs that they brought to the assimilation of their science an enthusiasm and soon surpassed them. 'For five or six centuries they held the scepter of enlightenment and civilization.' Much of this knowledge they transmitted to the west but when the Renaissance came, 'education gave birth to ingratitude'. This was not linguistically a rebirth since the Greek language was still spoken and used administratively in Syria. So knowledge of Greek learning was partly continuous in many Christian and Zoroastrian centres in the east and one could speak of 'living scientific traditions'.[21] On the other hand, Greek learning was largely rejected by the Christians of Constantinople and so the Muslims welcomed it partly as a result. There was a distinct hiatus in the European tradition which was partly filled by Islam. 'By the seventh century this Byzantium high culture was inimically indifferent to pagan Greek learning, having left behind the stage of confrontation characterizing the previous age of the church fathers. Hellenism was the defeated enemy.'[22]

[19] Pokorny 2009: 51.   [20] Leclerc 1876.   [21] Gutas 1998: 16.   [22] Gutas 1998: 18.

It was only the aggressive promotion through the translation movement of the Abbasids in Baghdad where a new 'multicultural' society developed which renewed Hellenism in a way that Damascus had not.

Greek–Arab translation started with the second Abbasid caliph, al-Mansur, the builder of Baghdad. 'In the beginning of Islam', wrote the Andalusian historian Said (d. 1070), 'the Arabs cultivated no science other than their language and a knowledge of the regulations of their religious law, with the exception of medicine ... on account of the need which people as a whole have for it.' God Almighty gave the rule to the Abbasids, when 'peoples' ambitions revived from indifference and their minds awoke from their sleep'.[23] The caliph caused to be translated the much-illustrated *Kalila wa Dimna*, animal tales from Sanskrit, as well as Aristotle on logic and Ptolemy's *Almagest*, Euclid's *Elements* and other works.[24] He was especially interested in astrological history, an interest he derived from the Sasanians, and which legitimized his rule, making him a leader in knowledge. This connection revived earlier Persian civilization and looked back to pagan times. For the Persians believed all knowledge to come from the Avesta but had been scattered by Alexander to Greece, India and to China. The Sasanians brought 'some of this knowledge together as the Arabs were now doing through their translation movement'. First there was a Sasanian 'renewal' and then an Arab one.[25] There was a rebirth of knowledge conceptually and in reality which was believed to be predicted in the stars and this idea of recovery through translation was essential both to the Sasanians and to their successors, the Abbasids, where the renascence 'received institutional and financial support' based upon commercial and imperial success.[26]

A great deal of the translation was carried out by the Christian community in Iraq, for the Nestorians did not have to justify the pursuit of philosophy within the framework of a religious system that was fundamentally inimical to Greek thought.[27] The Jews of Baghdad, who numbered some 40,000 in the twelfth century at the time of the visit of Benjamin of Tudela and included the Radhanite long-distance merchants, as well as many bankers, excelled in medicine and astronomy, but had little to do with translation until much later in Spain.

The birth of science in early Islam was thus also a renascence, since what was happening involved to some extent a rebirth of ancient Greek and other science through translation. For some time before the advent

---

[23] Gutas 1998: 31.
[24] Gutas 1998: 143–4. There had been translation from the Sanskrit into Pahlavi in pre-Abbasid times, especially of astronomical tables. But it was during the reign of al-Mansur that an Indian embassy arrived, a member of which brought along tables that were translated and published as *Zig al-Sinlhind*. They were used by al-Fazari.
[25] Gutas 1998: 45–6.   [26] Gutas 1998: 54.   [27] Kraemer 1986: 76.

of Islam to the Levant there had been a translation of Greek classics into another Semitic language, namely Syriac, especially in philosophy and in theology but also in astronomy and mathematics. In the early years of the sixth century at least twenty-six medical works of Galen were rendered into Syriac by the Nestorian Christian priest Sergius of Resh Ain, who had studied medicine in Alexandria and worked in Mesopotamia;[28] and several other Nestorians did similar work.[29] Owing to the use of many of these Syriac versions in the Academy of Gondeshapur in western Persia (to which many Nestorians had fled the Byzantine persecutions in favour of papal orthodoxy, sometime before the invasion of the Arabs), some of the material found its way into the Quran via Muhammad's companion and medical consultant Harith ibn Kalada, who had studied at its medical school around the turn of the seventh century.[30] This was at a time when Indian medicine and astronomy, in Pahlavi and Syriac translations from the Sanskrit, were already widespread in Persia and Iraq; and the transmission of scientific knowledge continued into the seventh century, when we find scholars in the town of Edessa again translating part of the medical work of Galen. The Muslim conquest of Egypt in 639–42 brought Alexandrian knowledge into the orbit of Islam, although the great library of the museum had mostly disappeared. But well-stocked private collections also existed and these gave Islamic science its first push, especially in Galenic medicine and philosophy.

So before the coming of the Abbasid dynasty, we find the teaching of medicine, astronomy, accounting and measurement in Syriac, stimulated by the presence of Nestorian scholars. Subsequently the gradual arabization of the administration under Islam was accompanied by the translation of many scientific works into Arabic. Most translations were from the Greek, but in mathematics, the calculus owed little to them and much to Babylonian, Persian, Indian and possibly Chinese sciences as well as to local activity; about twenty Indian books were translated which were especially important in astronomy.[31] Much of this work, particularly in the scientific sphere, was later translated into Syriac or Arabic in Baghdad in the ninth century under the guidance of the Abbasid caliph al-Mamun; even before the Arab conquest, the Hellenistic

---

[28] Sarton 1927: 423–4.   [29] Khairallah 1946: 24.

[30] Siddiqi 1959: 6–7; Porter (1997) denies there is any evidence for such a school, but this seems to be a quibble on the meaning of 'school'; medicine was certainly studied there and we find a great hospital (*bimaristan*) established by the Sasanian emperor Shapur I in the third century. The literature documents a major medical centre in the sixth and seventh centuries. The *bimaristans* were (free) hospitals with specialists in particular diseases and presumably there were many smaller infirmaries of various kinds.

[31] Djebbar 2005: 72.

traditions of Athens were continued in medicine by Nestorian Christians working under the Sasanians at Gondeshapur, a number of whom later moved to Baghdad and became royal physicians, engaging also in medical research.[32] With the coming of the Arabs, who wanted to see their own 'sacred' language established, the Nestorians and other learned communities rapidly adapted to Arabic in the translation of their own religious texts (though their own language was Persian, with Syriac for science). The main translations, as we saw earlier, were the work of Hunayn (809–73), who came from a Nestorian Christian tribe and was sent by the caliph to gather manuscripts, including at Byzantine Constantinople. Aramaic (i.e. Chaldean-speaking) Christians and a few Jews were essential in this process of translation, which was done largely at the House of Wisdom (*Bayt al Hikmah*), the great library established at Baghdad in 825.[33] These groups were spread widely through the area, including Baghdad, and translated, especially in medicine, but neither had a state and court of their own to set up public libraries or telescopes and were largely dependent on the patronage of others. The efflorescence of Greek learning was most evident within the sciences, largely astrological and medical though also optical, arithmetical and geometrical; there was little interest in literature. Djebbar and others have written of the 'golden age' of Arab science (not simply translation but their own) which later influenced Europe in so many important ways.[34]

It was not simply a question of propagating Indian and Hellenistic achievements but of developing disciplines hereto unknown, especially algebra. These calculations were at once theoretical and referred to the problems in contemporary society, for example to the works of jurists regarding inheritance. So it was not unusual to see algebra taught in legal-theological schools such as the Nizamiyya of Baghdad. Other scientists were specialists in the observatories. Experimentation was also present. It has been argued that we have to get rid of the idea that a scientific renaissance in the sixteenth century had no precedent except in Greece. Islam made its contribution.

The extent of commercial and religious contacts meant that information flowed in from all Asia. It was in the mid ninth century that an anonymous author published a book entitled *Information on China and India*, which contained descriptions of the coasts of the Indian Ocean and the China Sea, showing the extent of Islamic operations. The contribution

---

[32] Gutas 1998: 118.
[33] Gutas 1998: 56ff. However, the term 'house of wisdom' appears to be one for palace libraries in general which clearly existed in pre-Islamic times.
[34] Djebbar 2005.

of Indian mathematics to Arab and hence to European sciences was clear cut.[35] At the beginning, in the Arab lands as in India, calculations were made in the dust or sand. They were given greater permanence with the use of wax tablets and a stylus, but greater still was the advance in the development of knowledge with the coming of paper and ink from China; this acquisition precipitated a genuine revolution in literate culture since it permitted its cheaper and more efficient accumulation, distribution and storage.

Meanwhile in the east even political fragmentation led to a further period of florescence (870–1041) after the Baghdad of al-Rashid and al-Mamun. Regional courts competed as patrons of culture with the Abbasids in the east and with each other elsewhere. Cultural creativity was so noticeable that this period is often called the Renaissance of Islam.[36] The decline in power of the Abbasid caliph al-Radi meant that political power rested with the chief emir, with the former becoming the titular sovereign of the Islamic world. The dismemberment of the empire was followed by the ascent of the Buyids, who entered Baghdad in 946 (where they ruled until 1055). The Shiite Buyids, who were mercenary soldiers from south of the Caspian sea, gradually founded a kingship (emirate) of their own, one of many smaller dynasties to do so following the decline. When they entered Baghdad, they deposed the Sunni caliph but later proclaimed his son, and an 'efflorescence of learning' took place under further Greek influence during their reign.[37]

All in all, the brilliant heritage of Hellenistic learning had been no less keenly admired and eagerly embraced in the Islamic world than later in the west. The works of Aristotle and Plato, and those of their successors and later competitors, Stoics, Pythagoreans, Neoplatonists, were duly incorporated in Muslim scholarship and in turn deeply influenced Islamic theological, mystical, scientific and political thought. The Hebrew world of course had also been impregnated by the Greeks, especially with the conquests of Alexander. Indeed, one of the recensions of the Bible was in Greek and the Jewish philosopher Philo of Alexandria (20 BCE 50 CE) was strongly influenced by Platonism. Throughout the Near East, Greek became 'the language of culture'[38] and even a few of the Qumran statements are in that language. But what the Greeks had accomplished in the fields of mathematics, astronomy and optics was redigested, systematized, elaborated and in many cases corrected or improved upon by Muslims and by others working under their hegemony; extensions of the work of Euclid and Archimedes, large-scale correction and adjustment

---

[35] Jacquart 2005: 56.   [36] Waldman 1997: 115.
[37] Kraemer 1986: 152; see also Frye 1965.   [38] Herrenschmidt 2007: 179.

of that of Ptolemy, and the further development of the medical system of Galen were amongst the achievements of this era.[39] Astronomy too was developed. Writing at the end of the tenth century, al-Biruni recognized his time as exceptional, prodigiously fertile in this respect.[40]

The impetus of translation was not only provided by the Abbasid court but, from the time of the caliph al-Mahdi (775–85), by merchants and high functionaries. What helped this process was partly the emergence of an important Arabic scientific community, but also the advent of paper in the ninth century which meant that information was more readily communicated, especially with the build-up of large libraries. For the manufacture of paper caused a very real 'revolution' in the democratization of knowledge.[41] It meant that reproduction was much easier, leading to a trade in books. The patrons for these works included not only the court but also merchants and other wealthy individuals. That interest led in time to an increased demand for translation and hence to the further rebirth of ancient knowledge, especially Greek, which involved a local search for old manuscripts.

But if the Abbasids experienced a rebirth of Greek scientific literature, how is it that they did not have a full renaissance of culture in the European sense? Firstly, the rebirth was of a limited kind, embodied in the 'translation movement', primarily for astrology, astronomy and mathematics. This did not involve the same all-round admiration of classical culture and an attempt to return to it in the Italian sense; there were no efforts to resurrect ceremonies, as with the laureate, with architecture as in Palladio, sculpture as in Donatello, nor in literature generally. It was confined to science and to some extent philosophy, and it was in these limited fields that it led to an efflorescence.[42] But otherwise the Islamic religion held fast; there was little long-term secularization as we have seen occurred in Europe. In Islam the looking back was more segmental; religion was less affected (although the Aristotelian dialectic had its influence in some quarters) and secular knowledge was less institutionalized, especially after the coming of the madrasas with their stress on religious learning. It has been argued by Gutas[43] that there was no incompatibility between science and religion (in practice or in the Quran), but not everyone saw it this way and at certain times contrary opinions dominated the Islamic scene. Moreover, throughout there existed a strong current against certain secular developments, as in iconography (illustration) and as with the means of communication (printing), both of which closely affected the development of science. In general we can speak, as Zafrani

[39] Robinson 1996: xx–xxi.   [40] Jacquart 2005: 102.   [41] Djebbar 2005: 32.
[42] Gutas 1998: 151.   [43] Gutas 1998: 166.

does for Andalusia, of an alternation between periods of greater 'human-ism' and periods of greater religiosity (that have been called 'orthodox', but in Islam objections have been raised to that term).[44] A similar alter-nation took place in Christianity. The 'renascence' in Constantinople meant the end of the rejection of the Greek (pagan) tradition. And the 'first Byzantine humanism', together with the revival of the ancient sci-ences after 'the horrors of the "dark age"',[45] was related to the influence of the Graeco-Arabic translation movement. But these were temporary movements towards a more secular understanding, not the more perma-nent shift that we found in the Italian Renaissance. Religious authority always reasserted itself. And that seems to be due the fact that at the beginning of the thirteenth century, some European universities offered a more favourable framework for the diffusion of secular (as well as religious) knowledge. Taking over from the schools of monasteries and cathedrals, they provided assembly points for students coming from all over the continent; they institutionalized the change.[46]

From the ninth century, this subsequent effort resulted in continued local research, experiment and publication in the sciences, as in the work of al-Khwarizmi (d. c.848). In the field of mathematics he had combined Hellenistic concepts (such as procedures for cancelling derived from Dio-phantus's work) and Indian methods (such as Brahmagupta's research on quadratic equations), and his name gave rise to the word *algorithm* from the term for 'restoration' (elimination of negative quantities in an equation) in the title, when translated into Latin, of his major work *al-Kitāb al-Mukhtaṣar fi hisāb al-Jabr wa'l Muqābala* ('Compendious Book on Calculation by Restoration and Balancing'). His book (now extant only in Latin translation) on the Indian decimal system was undoubt-edly among the main factors in the westward transmission of the now universal method.

With regard to the great achievements of Arabic sciences, what even-tually was their importance in Europe or in the world? The translations of course were significant in preserving Greek knowledge, but also the research stimulated by these. Many of the important discoveries of the Italian Renaissance were affected by work done under Islam. The pul-monary circulation was already described by Ibn al-Nafis and he may have influenced the theologian-doctor Michael Servetus whom Calvin had burnt at the stake. Was Copernicus also influenced in his planetary

---

[44] See Gutas 1998: 168.   [45] Gutas 1998: 186.
[46] Jacquart 2005: 89. Ones attested at the beginning of the thirteenth century were: Bologna, Paris, Oxford and Modena. After Cambridge (1209) several more appeared (Valladolid, Salamanca, Montpellier, Padua, Naples, Toulouse) by the end of the 1220s.

models by the work of Ibn al-Shatir of Damascus?[47] But despite the existence of the golden age, Djebbar sees a decline in science from the twelfth
century, partly because of socio-economic factors, but also because of
ideological restrictions as in the madrasas, such as the ban on dissection,
though in this case, the taboo was not confined to this particular period
or to Islam but was more general.[48] However considering the Buyids and
the astronomical work in Afghanistan, even after the Mongols, there was
certainly no complete disappearance of scientific activity.

This period of political instability for the Baghdad caliphate in the late
ninth and early tenth centuries was largely due to their Turkic soldiery,
but that instability proved no barrier to cultural activity; Iraq underwent
what has been described as a 'cultural flowering',[49] producing some
of the most striking figures of early Islam, the Mazandarani historian
and theologian al-Tabari (c.839–923), the theologian al-Ashari (c.873–
c.935) and the Sufi mystic al-Hallaj (c.858–922). With considerable
success, the dynasty of Buyids from the Caspian tried to maintain the
brilliance of the court of Baghdad, especially in the field of speculative
thought. In the Buyid-patronized circle (*majlis*) of al-Sijistani, there was a
powerful outpouring of philosophical thinking on a wide array of topics,
inspired by an interpretation of Neoplatonic doctrine and applied to a
metaphysically sophisticated vein of Shiite Islam.[50] Partly due, perhaps,
to the style of the Persianate viziers and princes, with their mode of religious tolerance and the liberal patronage of art, science and literature,
and partly to a conception of God that developed within al-Sijistani's
and the other major schools and associations of the day, philosophy and
'humanist individualism' developed to a degree that was unprecedented
in the Islamic world.[51] Looking back over the pattern of acquisition
and use of ancient thought over the whole of the Abbasid Age, and
indeed throughout the history of Islam as a whole, it is this period, under
Adud al-Dawla and his successors in the late tenth century, that invites
comparison with the Renaissance activities of the likes of Ficino and
the Florentine Academy under the patronage of Lorenzo de Medici. But,
apart from their dynastic tombs in Rayy and minor buildings in Baghdad,
the century or so of Buyid power saw little by way of an architectural or

---

[47] Although Copernicus's theory was heliocentric and al-Shatir's geocentric, Roberts and
Kennedy say the mathematical details were identical (*Isis* 1959: 227–35).
[48] But see Saliba 2007. There is an account in Ibn Masanayh as to how he was forbidden
by al-Mamun from dissecting human beings but although this does not appear to be
expressly forbidden in Islamic law, it seems not to have been practised in medieval times.
Similar inhibitions existed in Judaism and in early Christianity.
[49] Waldman 1997: 117.   [50] Kraemer 1986: 211ff.   [51] Kraemer 1992: 13–20.

graphic legacy, by marked contrast to the calibre of the intellectual activity they produced.

Kraemer, who gives the most forceful account of this Buyid Renaissance, refers to 'a classical revival and cultural flowering within the soil of Islamic civilization'.[52] But this movement was also taken up in neighbouring states such as those of the Hamdanids of Syria and the Samanids of Persian Transoxania (whose capital, Bukhara, had its own 'wonderful library'), though the latter looking back to Sasanian rather than to classical times. The principal expression of this renaissance was a 'philosophical humanism that embraced the scientific and philosophical history of antiquity as a cultural and educational ideal'. Alongside this was a literary 'humanism', epitomized in the word *adab* and cultivated by poets and others. It was marked by individualism, by personal expression, by literary creativity, at the hands of cosmopolitan scholars 'united by the pursuit of wisdom, the love of wisdom'. The ambience was also 'permeated by a spirit of skepticism and secularism', plus 'rebellion against convention'. But though intellectually alive, it was also a period of social and economic decline. The Buyids sought in the glory of culture the legitimacy for the power they had acquired by military means.

The middle of the 'Shiite century' led paradoxically to the revival of Sunni Islam, together with the emergence of a second language of high culture, namely New Persian. Two Iranian dynasties arose, the Samanid (819–999) in Bukhara and Samarkand, and the Ghaznavid, who replaced them and extended to India, especially to the Punjab. The Samanid court attracted leading scholars, such as al-Razi and Avicenna, as well as the poet Firdawsi, whose work brought ancient Persia into Islamic history. The subsequent Ghaznavid court (977–1086), the most celebrated ruler of which gave 'a very generous impulse to the Iranian renaissance', was also the home of great scholars, including al-Biruni (973–1048), who studied astronomy and physics and left an account of Indian life.[53] This was the great period of Muslim art in Iran, much influenced by China and mainly confined to the predominantly courtly work of book illustrations (and some portraits of rulers).

Lopez[54] has argued that the European Renaissance, for all its cultural grandeur, was a period of economic disaster. That was more or less true of the Shiite Buyid period, when we find a socio-economic downturn but great cultural affluence. This period witnessed the emergence of a wealthy and influential noble class, when an urban society, with its proliferation of courts, provided the framework for creative enterprise. Merchants and scholars moved from place to place, trade expanded, towns became

[52] Kraemer 1986: vii.   [53] Wiet 1961: 134.   [54] Lopez 1962.

more cosmopolitan. Princes and their viziers were patrons of the arts and sciences. The age was bracketed by the outstanding figures of Alfarabi (d. 950) and Avicenna but it had a host of lesser scholars who met in courts and in academies, many of whom were humanists whose object was to revive the ancient philosophic legacy, with Aristotelian thought predominant. But the 'Shia century' of the Buyids came to an end with the Sunni restoration under the Seljuq Turks with its stress on orthodox Islam.

The activities of scientists did not end altogether with the slowing down of translation. In fact Gutas speaks of a burst forward at the end of the tenth century with the foundation of the Adudi hospital in Baghdad in 982. This was during the Buyid period when he also refers to a 'cultural efflorescence'[55] as described in Kraemer's book on *Humanism in the Renaissance of Islam*.[56] These humanists were successors to the *dictatores* of an age dominated by secretaries.[57] If translation now diminished, it was because so much had already been translated and there was now more demand for the results of original, up-to-date research.

In this respect Islam is indeed said to have experienced a long golden age, between the eighth (or ninth) and the sixteenth centuries.[58] Science developed outside madrasas and therefore precariously, for example, in the observatory that was built at Maraghah in western Iran, and used by Nasir al-Din Tusi (1201–74), who criticized some Ptolemaic views. His work was translated by the Byzantines into Greek and ultimately reached Copernicus and others who employed aspects of it (along with the work of al-Shatir) to develop their own heliocentric theory.[59] In medicine, which was more securely based in hospitals, there were the works of al-Razi and Ibn Sina. Considerable achievement was made in mathematics, especially by the three Persians, two of whom we have mentioned, al-Biruni of central Asia, al-Khwarizmi, as well as by Omar Khayyam (1048–1131), the poet.

In chemistry, which was not distinguished verbally from alchemy (as with astrology and astronomy), the Arabs pursued experimentation with metals and other products. They were also the first to perfect the manufacture of soap as we know it today (from sodium lye and olive oil), and further refined the arts of distillation (including of perfume) and of glass-making (especially in Syria), which were eventually picked up by France and by Venice respectively. The extent of Islamic civilization

---

[55] Gutas 1998: 152.   [56] Kraemer 1992.   [57] Kraemer 1986: 209.
[58] Djebbar 2005, though this claim is controversial, for in the seventeenth century there was significant intellectual development in various parts of the Islamic world.
[59] Robinson 1996: 228.

meant that for natural history, of plants, for example, the available spec-
imens came from far and wide. In the compendium of Ibn al-Baitar (d.
1248) of Malaga, probably the greatest botanist of the medieval period,
the author gives the names of plants in Arabic, Persian, Berber, Greek
and in the Romance languages.

Medicine was another field in which Islam made significant contributions, not only in reviving Greek knowledge but in experimental work
of its own and in the organization of hospitals (the first major one of
the Islamic period being in Damascus), which had a significant influence on the European Renaissance. Hospitals were places of enquiry. In
the twelfth century Ibn Jubayr describes the one built in Cairo by the
sultan Saladin who chose an administrator among the learned men and
entrusted him with the pharmacy which allowed for the preparation of
medicines and their prescription according to their virtues.[60] We have
already commented upon Montpellier, but Salerno in Campania was
also claimed as the oldest known medical school in Europe: a medical
school in nearby Velia was thriving in Ciceronian times and had moved to
Salerno following the fall of Rome. Having later been in Byzantine territory, it retained a strong link with Greek medicine throughout its heyday
in the tenth to thirteenth centuries. It was also Greek medicine that
the Carthaginian Constantine the African claimed to restore at Monte
Cassino during the eleventh century, but Greek medicine that he had
acquired through Arab works and that gave western Europe its first full
view of the scope of Galen and Hippocrates.

Hospitals were important not only for healing the sick but, especially
given the prevalence of literacy, because they allowed for the collection
and comparison of cases which in turn led to advances in medical knowledge. That knowledge consisted not only of the curing or alleviation of
disease, whether by surgery, by pharmacopoeia or by their healing rou-
tines, but also of preventative medicine, of hygiene, public health, diet
and exercise. In all these spheres an important contribution was made
by Islam (as well as by Judaism and Christianity), especially as many
mosque complexes (like other religious houses elsewhere) had hospitals
attached to them. Although surgery was at first restricted by the difficulties with dissection, animals continued to be cut up in Judaism to
determine whether they were undamaged and kosher. Surgery was also
important in dealing with wounds acquired in warfare as well as with
those caused by mutilation, widely practised as a punishment; both of
these encouraged the development of techniques of grafting.

Though politically and economically problematic, the tenth and
eleventh centuries were periods of unexampled cultural ebullience in

[60] Jacquart 2005: 104.

Baghdad as in the wider Islamic world.[61] It was these centuries that could boast the most dazzling array of Muslim philosophers and scientists:[62] this was the age of Avicenna, of the mathematician and physicist Ibn al-Haytham (d. 1039), and of the religious thinker al-Ghazzali (d. 1111). The cosmopolitan outlook of the age was evident in the openness of gaze in works such as al-Biruni's description of Indian life.

Nevertheless this achievement did not lead to a permanent dominance in the scientific field. There was an alternation, as 'traditionalism' conflicted with 'reason'.[63] The golden age was followed by a certain stasis in Islamic sciences, attributed by Djebbar to Christian aggression, to economic reverses in the Mediterranean and to the brutality of the Mongol conquest.[64] Internally there was a diminution in economic activity as well as what he calls an increasing conservatism of scholars, which seems to refer to the dominance of religious considerations (an alternation, in other words). Many writers on Islam diagnose such a kind of long-term shift in patterns of traditionalism and cosmopolitanism, and sacralism and secularism.[65] The so-called intellectual stasis in Islam happened to be contemporary with the rise of Europe and the acquisition by Europeans of much of Arab achievements. According to Jacquart,[66] the apogee of the European 'Renaissance' of the twelfth century was heralded by the reconquest of the city of Toledo in Spain,[67] where, with the patronage of its bishops, much Arab writing was translated, especially by Gerard of Cremona (1114–87). By the twelfth century in Spain and Andalusia the two 'civilizations' were closely interrelated, with the east contributing significantly to the west. Much of the spirit of confessional and cultural tolerance (*la convivencia*) that had preceded the Christian reconquests in this area would continue for some centuries, and the considerable cross-pollination of artistic and intellectual interest was a vital ingredient of European culture.

The efflorescence was not limited to science and to scientific translation but like Europe it included literature in Arabic and Persian, although not much figurative representation. It was also found in Khurasan (known there as 'the Irano-Islamic Renaissance') under the Samanid kings

---

[61] See Lopez 1962 and Kraemer 1992 on the paradox of poor economy and cultural splendour.
[62] Crone 1996: 31.   [63] Kraemer 1986: esp. p. 115.
[64] Some of the reasons given for the so-called decline are purely 'whiggish', as in the explanation of why 'Islam' did not have a 'scientific revolution'. The claim is more controversial than Djebbar suggests, for greater devastation than by either the Crusades or the Mongols was caused by the Black Death of the mid fourteenth century, which may have wiped out a third or half of the urban population.
[65] Kraemer 1986 and 1992.   [66] Jacquart 2005: 88.
[67] Alphonso VI of Castille retook Toledo, from which he had in fact already been exacting tribute, in 1085.

(819–999), in Egypt under the Fatimids (also Shiite) as well as in Spain under al-Rahman III (d. 961) and his son, the bibliophile. In Syria, too, there were the Hamdanids (905–1004). But it was not only the courts, largely Shiite and often Persianized, but also a series of enlightened viziers together with other scholars who established informal schools and intellectual circles, above all patronized by secretaries and by government officials. Much of this cultural activity, in which Christians and Jews often took part, was connected with book dealers, at whose establishments they might meet as later in printing workshops.[68]

This was especially true of Andalusia and of the Umayyad court at Cordoba, founded by a branch of the Near Eastern dynasty and initially established as a refuge in 756 but which eventually declared itself a caliphate. However, it was with the collapse of this centralized Umayyad rule in 1031 and the establishment of numerous *taifa* or 'party kings' in southern and central Spain that once again fragmentation and efflorescence really took place. At the time the permeable Christian–Muslim frontier of Spain meant that the writings on love of the prolific Cordovan minister Ibn Hazm (994–1064) may well have influenced the poetry of the troubadours in the south of France.[69]

However, words were different; the graphic and plastic arts experienced a repression rather than a renaissance, due to a strict interpretation of the scriptural injunction against figurative representation. Apart from religious painting in the mainstream of Christianity, the Abrahamistic religions had remained largely iconophobic. Some others (such as Hinduism) have resisted a representation of their High God, but in the monotheistic ones there was no other; all figurative representations of the spiritual were thus 'idols', false gods. And even to represent God's creation was a threat to the uniqueness of the sole creator, a blasphemy against his name. He alone accounted for the creation of the world and further enquiry was unnecessary. As a result all three Abrahamistic religions originally followed the commandment, 'Thou shalt not make unto

---

[68] Kraemer 1986: 286.

[69] Goody 1998. There are a large number of these poets in all stations of life whose work is partly preserved and will certainly have influenced Occitan and Catalan verse of the eleventh and twelfth centuries; the description of horses, plants, women, birds and other aspects of nature, and the types of poetic conceits, figures, attitudes and refinements one finds in the troubadour works are absent from medieval Latin poetry proper, but are there in the Hispano-Arabic corpus, stemming ultimately from the early Abbasid poets like Abu Nuwas. Some of the phrases and conceits (such as that of the language of the birds) we still find a century later in Chrétien de Troyes. The earliest surviving remnants (the fairly basic songs of William of Aquitaine) are for the most part monorhymed (the same rhyme throughout the poem). Even the earlier *chansons de geste* are written in a mono-assonance pattern that is not common in medieval Latin poetry, whereas monorhyme is a regular feature in Arabic verse.

thee any graven image.' In Christianity the iconoclastic controversy came down in favour of those who could represent figuratively saintly persons and the human as distinct from the divine side of Christ, but painting was only for religious purposes as in the Byzantine icons. However, Judaism until recently and Islam, even today in many places, continue to hold to the original prohibition which applied to figurative art, to theatrical representation, to secular fiction.

This prohibition did not, however, mean there were no periods of artistic efflorescence in the Islamic world. In poetry there obviously were, often returning, apparently with little compunction, to earlier, pre-Islamic models. Both Iranian prose and poetry, as in Firdawsi's *Shah-nama*, experienced what Miquel speaks of as a 'renaissance'.[70] At least this work displayed a spirit of purist restoration, for in both the prose version and the subsequent epic versification (with rhymed couplets), Firdawsi largely avoided the Arabic locutions that had accumulated in the centuries since the Muslim conquest, preferring and extensively documenting the Pahlavi diction which preceded it.

It was also the translation of Indo-Persian texts into Arabic in the course of the eighth century that promoted *adab*, a sophisticated prose literature incorporating a set of refined urban manners. Indeed, a local movement known as *shu-ubiyya* arose in reaction to the privileged status of ethnic Arabs in Persia and other parts of the empire that preferred non-Arabic texts.

The period is also spoken of as the golden age of Arabic music, the practice of which being 'obligatory for every learned man'.[71] By means of the lute (which had developed its classic form during the previous century in the Arab–Iranian–Byzantine region), this music would be later introduced from Baghdad to western Islam under the Umayyad and Berber dynasties of the following centuries, and eventually to western Europe where it was so important in the Renaissance. This development occurred most notably under the virtuoso Ziryeb who emigrated and established a school in Spain in the ninth century, which became a defining moment for Hispanic Muslim music. However, he had a much wider influence on the high culture of manners in the west.

This era was undoubtedly the golden age of Arabic literature, profiting in this case too from the many influences from other high cultures.[72] The transmission of literature was accomplished by the 'humanists of Islam',

---

[70] Miquel 1995: 177.   [71] Schimmel 1997: 67.

[72] This notion of a golden age is a nineteenth-century construction; the themes (often homoerotic) and style (highly ornamental and mannered) did not find favour with western Orientalists and westernized Arab literary critics.

as the Arabist Gibb has described those poets who represented the 'new style' such as the blind Persianate poet Bashar ibn Burd (741–84) of Basra and the Hijaz-born Iraqi Abu al-Atahiyah (748–828). The classic Beduin style of poetry was still common and enjoyed prestige well into the Abbasid age when it was developed by grammarians. But a good deal of poetry was now written by those outside the strictly Arabic tradition and a new dimension, a 'new style', was added, both in the composition of verse and in the range of topics, a process that gained pace in the ninth century. Lines like these (from Bashar ibn Burd) signalize that quite openly secular spirit is abroad:

> But for Allah, O'Abda, I had no lord
> Until, that is, your face became my Lord.[73]

This secularism inherent in the work of these avant-garde poets was partly a revisitation of elements of the pre-Islamic *qasida*, but took on new dimensions in the Abbasid period and was not without its risks. Its topics included new attitudes to love, and took many forms. Amongst the vanguard (and probably the greatest) of the Arabic poets was the gay Persianate Abu Nuwas (750–810), who was much patronized in Baghdad and equally adept at laudatory, contemplative, erotic, witty and cynical verse. He had a prodigious command of the language and a disarmingly frank and versatile turn of amatory expression, making him one of the most influential of all Arabic poets, a model for libertines and holy mystics alike, though naturally disapproved of by many of the traditionalists. For a time a royal tutor at Harun al-Rashid's court, he spent a good deal of his life in exile and in prison, due to politically inopportune pieces, which included blasphemy and homoerotic debauchery, at times (somewhat reminiscently of the Roman poet Catullus) bordering on rape. In addition he gave a poetic portrait of the sexual mores of the day. But the heretical side of Abu Nuwas's worldly love was not wasted on the wider Islamic world; we see it notoriously in late twelfth-century Khurasan, in the work of Farid al-Din Attar and in that of the mystics who read him. This was a highly secular verse that ran up against orthodox religion.

In the purely secular context, some writers even developed a tradition of celebrating wine and love. Then, as we have seen, there was also the composition by the Persians of poetry, especially in the *shu-ubiyya* movement (demotic and anti-Arabocentric) which injected new blood into an ancient tradition. A century after his death, the influence of Daud and his amatory mode (d. 910) spread to western Islam and was manifest in the work of Ibn Hazm (probably of Christian convert background) whose

---

[73] Bashar ibn Burd 1972: 13, 15.

'Ring of the Dove' (*Tauq al-hamamah*) may well have been among the models for troubadour poetry; despite his being an eminent theologian and jurist, the secularist spirit of the day was such that he would, like his blind Andalusian confrère al-Ama al-Tutili, contradict the Quranic permission of polygyny or compare his girlfriend with the holy Kaaba in Mecca.

During the Abbasid period, a sophisticated literary prose developed alongside poetry, but this development was not entirely without cultural risk, however; the Arabs had hitherto cherished prose primarily to transmit religious knowledge, and any new monuments of admired prose were in some sense competing with the Quran and with the narrative elements of the Hadith. Secular influences triumphed, but dangerously. Ibn al-Muqaffa was even executed for some of the Zoroastrian elements evident in his prose works.

Following the decay of Abbasid military control in the late ninth century, the formation of new states led to a reaction against the domination of the Arabs and in Persia what Miquel has called 'la renaissance des lettres iraniennes'.[74] Already during al-Mansur's reign in the mid eighth century, as a part of the *shu-ubiyya*, there had been a softening in the repression of Persian cultural achievements. The following century saw the composition of a number of versions of the Panchatantra, none of which survive in their entirety. This practice of translation of course limited the personal creative input in these works, but in those decades there were other sources of innovation and inspiration open to Arabic literary prose. Many legends existed, which were used by public storytellers, but they relied increasingly on a written version rather than 'an uninterrupted oral transfer'.[75] This popular material often included scurrilous elements, and the growing use of this in the written form previously reserved for religious and other serious material gradually overcame the forces of conservatism. But the tension between the religious and the secular traditions was always present. The taste for entertainment 'seems to have set off a religious reaction' that considered jokes as not altogether compatible with Islam. Ambivalence and contradiction were evidently present, at least at the societal level.

Islamic pre-eminence in abstract representation (as distinct from the religiously forbidden figurative) in architecture and in the minor arts has been important since early times; Arabic and Arabesque art certainly remain a significant force in the international aesthetic traffic of the present day. However, the 'Golden age' of Arab art, the period which saw its greatest dominance on the world stage and the strongest internal

---

[74] Miquel 1995: 177.   [75] Pellat 1976.

dynamism, was undoubtedly in the medieval period.[76] One symptom of its ascendancy in the Baghdad caliphate of Abbasid times during the eighth to ninth centuries was its becoming the subject of aesthetic scrutiny. However, there are other periods of Islam which were undeniably 'golden' in their own way: the Buyid one, the Umayyad in Cordoba, the Maghreb and Egypt under the Shia Fatimids (tenth to eleventh centuries) as well as under the Mamluks, Spain and North Africa under their Tunisian rulers, the Almohads (twelfth to thirteenth centuries), and the steppe-empires of the Mongols (thirteenth to sixteenth centuries).

From 1250 the Mamluk period coincided with powerful artistic activity in the Syrio-Egyptian area. In Granada, as well, the Umayyad and other caliphs built great palaces outside the towns, as at Samarra, where the courts provided 'a freedom of action with respect to religious prohibitions'.[77] There one found figurative representation not only of animals but also of humans, including dancers with bare breasts. So that in this context figurative art was at times possible, even if vulnerable. There was some figuration in Persia and Afghanistan under Chinese influence[78] and hence some in India at the Mughal court (particularly in miniatures), some at other courts, but until the colonial period little in the west of Islam. The Berber renewal was led by an opposition to figuration and luxury. Even today Muslim puritans, such as the Taliban, continue with their objections to figurative art.[79] However, with the advent of Mongol-Chinese culture a tradition of painting was established in Herat in Afghanistan. That was part of a process of segmental secularization. When the Mongols came to Baghdad, where they were said to have thrown the books from the library to make a bridge across the river Tigris,[80] according to Pamuk, a famous calligrapher, Ibn Shakir, fled in the direction from whence the Mongols had come and became an illustrator. 'At that time, no one made illustrations because the Koran forbade them, and painters weren't taken seriously.'[81] He painted the world as 'from a minaret', 'all things from clouds to insects the way the Chinese envisaged them'. From the late twelfth century there was a temporary growth of figurative imagery in eastern Muslim lands. The final flowering of refined art at Herat, one of the major centres partly

---

[76] Achour 1995: 310.   [77] Achour 1995: 332.

[78] Or under Indian Buddhist, or even Hindu influence: both religions had monasteries throughout the region.

[79] The Quran generally endorses the Jewish Torah (incl. Exod. 20.4, Lev. 26.1, etc., esp. Deut. 5.8 on man-made likenesses), and indeed reproduces the thrust of most of the Commandments, but not this one.

[80] Saliba 2007: 235. In any case, there was a considerable destruction of libraries, the Tigris said to have become the colour of printer's ink.

[81] Pamuk 2001 [1998]: 401. This incident may be an imaginative creation of the author.

because of its proximity (via Badakhshan and the Wakhan Corridor) to China, occurred at the end of the fifteenth century when the great Persian miniaturist Kamal al-Din Bihzad (1450–1535) was active. The new art centred on the illustration of books, very different from the type of European painting which was full-sized and realistic and hung on walls. It consisted of a form of miniature painting that was produced by book-art workshops attached to courts, a type of art which could more easily set aside the prohibitions of Islam (plate 1). All khans, shahs and sultans, writes Pamuk,[82] love painting, at least while they are young, then religion takes over. But ambivalence remained. Shah Tahmusp I (1514–76) was himself a master miniaturist but later closed down not only his very important atelier but, in so far as he was able, destroyed all the books he had produced. So too Sheikh Muhammed of Isfahan widened the scope of painting to include erotic scenes, but later came under the influence of a pious sheikh and went from place to place getting rid of the manuscripts he had illuminated. He burned down Prince Ismail Mirza's large library containing hundreds of books[83] because the prophet had warned that on Judgement Day Allah would punish painters most severely, for he alone is the 'Creator' and others cannot give life to the lifeless.[84] They can only pretend.

It was this fear of Allah that inspired the followers of Nusret Hoja of Erzurum[85] and which led to the death of the painter Elegant Effendi, a master of borders and edges, around which Pamuk's novel turns. For it was not only extremists who felt an ambivalence towards painting. That sentiment emerges even in the history of the miniature painters themselves who tried to destroy their own work, and that lies at the centre of the whole story. This historical novel is called *My Name Is Red*. The hero, Red, was critical of his uncle, Enishte Effendi, who had spent time in Venice, the city of contact between east and west, and was asked by the Turkish court to imitate their manner of portrait painting. Each Venetian portrait was of a recognizable human face and, hanging on a wall, might become the object of worship as a real likeness, a figurative representation, whereas in the Herat style the painter did no more than 'complement a story'.[86] The western kind of illustration might become a 'false idol'; you believe in the picture itself. That form of composition

---

[82] Pamuk 2001 [1998]: 198.
[83] Pamuk 2001 [1998]: 190. Both Mohammed of Isfahan and Prince Ismail Mirza may be inventions of the author.
[84] According to al-Bukhari's hadith, written fully 200 years later, perhaps around 830; there are also other, less severe hadiths on this topic transmitted by him.
[85] Nusret Hoja is probably based on the puritanical Mehmed of Birgi (1522–73).
[86] Pamuk 2001 [1998]: 132.

meant moving away from 'Allah's perspective'[87] and placing something else at the centre of attention. For this reason, the sultan wanted his portrait 'hidden in a book', not open to the world. Pamuk writes of one character 'that the illuminations Enishte Effendi hired him to gild were slowly evolving from simple ornamented pages into full-blown illustrations, pictures moreover that bore the marks of Frankish blasphemy, atheism and even heresy'.[88] If these illustrations had been part of a story, or seen from Allah's viewpoint and not street-level 'perspective', it would have been different. The miniaturist's style was something else. He draws a picture not from real life like the Venetians but from memory and from a story.[89] Nevertheless there is a connection between miniatures and other forms of painting. 'Manuscript illumination leads to painting, and painting, in turn, leads to – God forbid – challenging Allah.'[90] The problem is always present for the Muslim, even though it may not always have been altogether explicit in the Quran.

In all this development of arts and sciences under Islam, towns were clearly important as centres of trade, patronage, schools and learning. In the traditional European view, their own towns were the ones associated with freedom of thought and of government. A certain political enfranchisement emanated from their very economies for the commerce could finance other activities; money and power were never far removed. But European towns were not alone in this, despite Weber;[91] in Islam too they were the places where things happened. There was a considerable amount of self-government in an Islamic town; while the earlier caliphs tried to affirm their authority over religious doctrine, al-Mamun attempted to establish a civil government and to oust the *ulama*. It was al-Mamun who invented the role of the *muhtasib*, a market official who also looked after what was right and wrong in the town (asserting both commercial and moral probity) according to his understanding of the Quran.[92] As far as social control was concerned it was also the case that from 776 to the mid 830s the state maintained itself by employing Turkish mercenaries, but individual Muslims also had the duty of upholding Islamic order; *hishba*, a concept used from about 1050, was the primary call of every individual to preserve the right and to prevent the wrong. But nevertheless authority was always divided between the political and the religious spheres.

With regard to the dominance of religion in many civil affairs it is significant that along with the school even the town market and the

[87] Pamuk 2001 [1998]: 135.   [88] Pamuk 2001 [1998]: 295.
[89] Pamuk 2001 [1998]: 325.   [90] Pamuk 2001 [1998]: 312.
[91] Weber 1966 [1921].   [92] Musallam 1996: 176.

hospital were clustered around the mosque; and the market gave financial support to these and other complexes. A similar grouping took place in Christianity where the abbey might provide hospital facilities not only for monastic inmates but for the public at large, as well as offering education for the local children. Religion dominated these various activities in a hegemonic fashion. Nevertheless in the west Roman Antiquity seems to have left some remnants of a more secular system of civil government, whereas in Islam the market inspector had a specifically religious as well as a civil function of seeing that prescriptions were observed. But in both east and west the town had a similar job to do.

Towns of course meant trade as well as learning. The traditions of Islam were said to have 'reflected the mercantile environment in which they were formed in their special concern for fairness, honesty, covenant keeping, moderation, law and order, accountability and the rights of ordinary human beings'.[93] These features are attributed by the author to the religions of the earlier Axial Age, but in fact they are important to exchangist societies everywhere, especially law and order; the institution of 'market peace' was prominent even in early non-centralized societies in West Africa.[94] They were especially important in Islam since the extent of its territories and of its trade was vast. The Islamic lands stretching from Spain to India and the east constituted 'an enormous, contiguous, relatively stable, low-duty commercial zone'[95] in which there was much exchange not only of goods but of ideas and of people travelling freely. As the Frenchman Chardin remarked in the late seventeenth century: 'In the *East* Traders are Sacred Persons. 'Tis on that account especially that the Roads are so safe over *Asia*.'[96] As in much of Africa and elsewhere, traders were protected persons.

Already before Islam, the Yemenis had been in touch with the east and had developed sea routes down the East African coast and across the Indian Ocean to India. Indeed, the entire Afro-Asian seaboard as well as all the large rivers appear to have been well travelled since Harrapan times. After the Jews from the first century CE, Christians also entered the Indian peninsular, especially in the early fourth century, followed by the Sasanians in the late sixth. With the development of these trade routes the Arabs were brought into a greatly expanded network of communication in the fifth and sixth centuries, a prosperous period in which they shared in the trade running from the Near East through Mecca

---

[93] Waldman 1997: 104.   [94] Goody 1967: 104.   [95] Dale 1996: 64.
[96] Chardin 1988. Similarly in the so-called Pax Mongolica under Genghis Khan, and again under Timur (thirteenth and fourteenth centuries), it was said that a man could walk from one end of the empire to the other (i.e. from Anatolia to the China Sea) with a bowl of gold on his head without being robbed.

where the important shrine, the Kaaba, became a focus for all the tribes of the peninsular.[97] Islam later developed that trade and expanded as a religion in doing so. Its importance is well illustrated not only by the early settlement in southern India but by voyages even further east; as early as the ninth century over 100,000 Arab merchants were alleged to be at work in the southern Chinese port of Canton.

In the Near East, a renascence developed despite the political fragmentation of Islam and the splitting of the caliphate. One of the early areas to leave the orbit was the region of central Asia. After his father had climbed from being a slave-soldier under the Samanid governors of Khurasan and Transoxiana to being the head of a small independent principality, Sultan Mahmud of Ghazna quickly expanded the realm to include most of Persia and Transoxiana, as well as Afghanistan and parts of India (Punjab, Multan, Sindh, Delhi and coastal Gujarat in the late tenth and early eleventh centuries by means of slave-militias). Although his legitimacy was bolstered by advocating the cause of the Abbasid caliph of the day (al-Qadir), he was the first to call himself sultan, and in doing so was already signalling his relative independence of the caliphate of Baghdad. Despite India being the greatest source of his wealth, he kept a heavily persianized court, gathering round him a group of poets including Firdawsi. This 'golden age' of literature was partly a revival of the earlier work of Abu Nuwas and others. The dynasty survived till 1186, but under the pressure of the Seljuqs, from the west, it was reduced by the mid eleventh century to the areas surrounding what is present-day Pakistan.

Having already been presided over for four centuries by groups and individuals other than the caliphs (including various sultans), the so-called Abbasid era came to a definitive end in 1258 with the Mongol conquest of Baghdad under Hulagu Khan. Over these centuries, the Persian influence on the caliphal metropolis had maintained a certain ascendancy, despite Sunni and Turkic rule in the Persian heartlands. From Genghis Khan's incursions in the 1220s to his grandson Hulagu's establishment of the Ilkhanate in 1255, the Mongol invasions had brought with them both urban and rural disruption, but it was the Black Death of the mid fourteenth century that may itself have killed a third or a half of the entire urban population of the Near East.[98] Despite the bad press they have received from modern nationalist historians of Arab extraction, as well as from Europeans, the Mongols actually patronized scholars

---

[97] The pre-Islamic status of Mecca is open to question. Muhammad's tribe, the Banu Quraysh, were in charge of the Kaaba temple (see Crone 1996).

[98] See Dols 1977.

such as Nasir al-Din al-Tusi, the astronomer and philosopher, and they provided a link between China and the west, being themselves strongly influenced by that civilization. Under Ghazan Khan around the turn of the fourteenth century, the economy of Persia was revitalized, but politically the empire was again soon fragmented into an assortment of lesser regimes. The Turko-Mongolic conqueror Timur brought almost all of Persia under his sway in the late 1300s, and he was himself well versed in, and much in sympathy with, that culture;[99] the tale of his collector's sparing of the poet Hafiz from tax is at least plausible.[100] And so, through the quarter of a millennium that followed the establishment of the Ilkhanate, a very significant trickle of major Persian literary and scholarly talent left its mark on the Arab world. Indeed, apart from the handful of eminent scholars like the Tunisian Ibn Khaldun (1302–1406), the Spaniard Averroës (Ibn Rushd) and the occasional Arab such as al-Kindi, Persia and its environs produced a commanding proportion of the Islamic world's major talents in this period. Its language had taken over as a literary vehicle after the decline of Arabic, and the Persian cultural ascendancy continued from the time of Firdawsi, through to that of Khayyam, Sadi (1184–1283), Rumi (1207–73), Hafiz and their fellow mystics up till the deaths of Jami (1492) and Alisher Navai (1501) of Herat. But it is the case that right from the early Abbasid years we see a paucity of significant figures, scientists, artists or thinkers, coming from the Prophet's own homelands, or even from the wider Arab heartlands that included Syria and Mesopotamia. As Ibn Khaldun would reflect some centuries later, illustrating his view with numerous Persian achievements, 'It is a curious fact that most Muslim scholars, both in the science of sharia and of the intellectual sciences, have been (Persian) non-Arabs.'[101]

Throughout all the main Islamic lands, there was a broad distinction between court and popular culture. The court was the home of written poetry, of classical music and dance, as well as of some theatre and of some figurative art, even though among the general public such activity suffered from the predominant Islamic aversion to forms of representation. At the court level, these activities flourished and declined at different times. At the popular level the arts had a continuous tradition which was scarcely perturbed by the changing practices of the elites. That is why in their case there was no question of a renascence, a golden age or any other sort of flourishing: these latter are phenomena of high culture, though they may have influenced and been influenced by the populace. At the court level the tradition changed from time to time because high culture

---

[99] Chaliand 2004: 75.   [100]Fennell 2005: 237n.   [101]Muqaddimah iv.42.

changed; the class, or anyhow the consumer, aspect of society shifted with the mode and means of production, with exchange but also with the mode and means of communication, especially with the introduction of paper and in more recent times of the printing press, changes which affected the culture more widely, leading for instance to the democratization and mechanization of writing and of the image. While rather than continuity, a rebirth or even a reformation requires some break with the past, at the popular level there was formerly little break. Many fashions have their roots in peripheral or popular folk cultures such as the Lulis mentioned in Hafiz's *ghazals*. But, as in England, folk culture continued as a separate tradition from the higher culture of Shakespeare, for example, despite the latter's use of folk song and despite today's growing conflation of the two.

With the growth of the state Islamic art became something of a court activity. Change in the system was especially noticeable when the Abbasid court disappeared, to be followed by several smaller ones. The culture of the courts was imitated by the bourgeoisie and they encouraged music and art even of a non-Islamic character, for instance at Ghazna southwest of Kabul in central Asia where the capital of the Ghaznavids (r. 977–1086), influenced by the east, became a centre of intellectual and literary life. The difference between court and popular activity is seen most clearly in the dance. Throughout the Muslim domains there was folk dancing at the popular level, a more or less continuous tradition, but at the caliphal, sultanate and subregional courts there were also the harem or palace performers of dancing girls, especially the erotic belly dancers, which were much more subject to fashion and to prohibitions. Apart from these various forms, there was the religious dancing of certain dervish orders, such as the Mevlevi founded by al-Rumi in the thirteenth century, which was disapproved of by some but encouraged by many. The dervish Zikr ceremony was intended as an act of worship, designed to lead to trance and hence to union with Allah.[102] As far as theatre was concerned, there was little activity, even today no native theatrical establishment exists in Saudi Arabia. Puppet theatre was active (a kind of miniature, not truly representational) but the figures were regularly punched with holes to show they were lifeless.[103] Nevertheless some religious theatre did develop at the popular level in Shiite areas such as the Lebanon and Iran in the form of miracle plays which were performed during the fourth month of the year, based upon the murder of the descendents of Ali. In the tenth century parades started, and when the Safavids took over and Shiism became institutionalized in Iran, they became more elaborate, leading

---

[102] Arabic *dhikr*, 'remembrance of Allah'.   [103] Landau 1997: 69.

in the sixteenth century to written compositions and then to drama in the eighteenth. The Passion play of Husayn was particularly popular in Iran, a non-Arabic-speaking country with a long tradition of theatre dating to pre-Islamic times, especially in comic plays, and linked to Asian traditions of representation. This tradition is particularly marked in the marionette theatre which was common in central Asia. Shadow puppets, such as the Turkish *karagoz* ('Black-Eye') and his companion Hacivat, originally from India, were widely performed, with plays of a satirical nature presented by artists who had established their own guild. Many plays, however, even at this level, revolved around religion, although the Ottoman shadow-plays were as bawdy and scatological as anything Rabelais produced.[104] Otherwise there was little except the pageants arranged by the Ottoman court and imitated by the aristocracy throughout the empire. During the nineteenth and later centuries, the Turks subsidized the *ortaoyunu* (middle show) theatre, played without any stage but using musicians in open spaces or in coffee houses. At the popular level, mime shows also existed with historical or erotic themes, especially in Anatolia, where they were a part of the tradition of public storytelling.

It was the Fatimid dynasty of Ismaili Shiites who, beginning their career in Tunisia and conquering Sicily, revived cultural activity in the Near East, founding the city of Cairo to rival Baghdad with the ruler adopting the title of caliph and constructing the great mosque-school complex of al-Azhar, described as the Sorbonne of Islam.[105] The dynasty built up a navy for trade and warfare in the Mediterranean as well as for reinforcing the route to India. Besides patronizing the arts, they also occupied the holy cities of Arabia and spread northward into Syria where in 1004 they conquered the Shiite Hamdanid dynasty of Aleppo. This latter dynasty had seen the presence of two of Islam's most illustrious writers, namely, the poet al-Mutanabbi (915–68) and the philosopher al-Farabi (870 – c.951), who contributed to the islamization of Hellenistic thought and who also tried to reconcile reason and revelation. But for such men there was a practical as well as an intellectual problem, that of their livelihood. Philosophers (*falasifa*) often had to earn their living as physicians, astrologers or musicians and had to compete with more religiously inclined Muslims. This confrontation sometimes led them to question the relationship of revelation to truth, threatening the domination of the former in favour of a more secular interpretation.

The efflorescence of Muslim Spain ran parallel to that of the Near East but slightly later. Cordoba was the centre of cultural life, the seat of the

---

[104] Zeevi 2006 devotes a chapter to the sexual element in shadow-plays.
[105] Achour 1995: 337.

Umayyad ruler who had fled there. Spanish Islam, writes Clot, was the one culture that contributed most to the development of knowledge in Europe; but in astronomy and also mathematics the Abbasids built on the work of Euclid, among others, which only reached the west in the twelfth century. The efflorescence of western Islam attained its heyday under Abd al-Rahman III (912–61). It was about the time of the opening up of Mediterranean trade which Miquel speaks of as involving a renaissance.[106] This renaissance included not only writers such as Ibn Hazm,[107] but music and philology also flourished. Philosophy, medicine and theology were of considerable importance in this and influenced western Europe, often through the translations of Jewish intermediaries. In philosophy there was al-Kindi (d. c.870) and especially Avicenna, who worked in medicine, science and philosophy as well as writing religious treatises. But the most important figure lived in the Almohad kingdom, Averroës (Ibn Rushd), who became court physician in Marrakesh as well as being the great Arab commentator on Aristotle. In the west Sufi poetry achieved its highest point in the work of Ibn Arabi (d. 1240), who shaped the thought of much of Islam in the following centuries.

The achievements were considerable. Proclaiming himself caliph, al-Rahman III built the great mosque at Cordoba, known as 'the kaaba of the west', one of the four wonders of the Muslim world, and he constructed an enormous palace outside Cordoba which was called the Medinat al-Zahra after one of his concubines. He collected the wood and precious stone required to build the palace from many places, including importing Roman columns from Carthage, mosaics from Constantinople and sculptured panels from Jordan, Mesopotamian ceramics and motifs of animals and dancers typical of Samara, the palace inhabited by the son of Harun al-Rashid outside Baghdad. Andalusia was at the height of its powers and exchanged ambassadors with Byzantium whose ruler sent an illustrated copy of Diascorides *Materia medica*. Otto I of Germany also despatched an envoy to Andalusia to protest against Mediterranean piracy, since trade was vital to the regime. Such was his renown that at times the caliph even acted as moderator between Christian rulers.

Like the reign of al-Rahman III, that of his son, Hakam II (r. 961–76), was a time of peace and prosperity. And it was in the reign of the son that Andalusia saw the zenith of Muslim culture in Spain. He it was who attracted intellectuals of all kinds, poets, merchants, travellers, refugees, to his court following the style of the Abbasid rulers of Baghdad. He was

---

[106] Miquel 1995: 165.
[107] Ibn Hazm was remembered in the Islamic world primarily as a religious scholar of the Zahiri school and a 'heresiologist', who also dabbled in prose belles-lettres.

himself well versed in the arts and sciences and built a huge library in the Alcazar of Cordoba containing possibly some 400,000 manuscripts. In the town Hakam started twenty-seven schools, while his example was followed by others who founded many smaller libraries; some of his contemporary rulers were also authors and his example was taken up even in Christian Spain.[108]

Hakam was succeeded by his only son, Hishom. This adolescent youth soon came under the influence of a military man, Mansur, who then seized power and confined Hishom to his palace. In an attempt to show the people his status as a true Muslim, not affected by *falasifa*, Mansur decided to disperse the library and burn all books relating to 'ancient sciences', spurred on by the caliph's own teachers. This act of 'impardonable vandalism' served to slow down the effort which the west of Islam was making to revive the achievements of the east. Their study could give rise to heresy and the *ulama* had to concentrate upon legitimate studies. But the dispersal of books throughout Andalusia led to the renewal of interest in the ancient sciences in all the small kingdoms.[109] This Mansur nevertheless achieved his end which was to make himself seem a good Muslim and which he confirmed by copying the Quran which he always carried with him.

Mansur pursued a very aggressive policy, dependent on war, on Berber soldiers and on taxation. His followers were less successful as rulers and the caliphate gradually drew to a close, with the country split up, partly under Berber pressure, giving rise to the rule of the *taifas* or 'party kings'. This disintegration meant a large number of small courts but nevertheless led to one of the most brilliant periods of Muslim Spain, with one court emulating another.[110] The reign of Mohammed II (r. 1069–90) at Seville, who was one of these 'party kings', was a period in which the arts and letters flourished especially brightly. The town played its part in commerce and was surrounded by a fertile plain which produced oil and cereals that became central to international exchange, especially to Alexandria. It had been his father who was called upon by Alphonso of Castille to give up his territory to the Christians, and with the loss of Toledo to them (1085), the conquests of the Cid and pressure from their neighbours, he eventually called in the puritanical Almoravids from Morocco to help, which delayed the expansion of the north into Andalusia.

At the period when Spain was going through the Reconquest, few Christians suspected that this pagan country 'held in its huge libraries

---

[108] Clot 1999: 137.
[109] Jacquart 2005: 101–2, quoting Said al-Andalusi, *Kitab Tabaqat al-umam*.
[110] Clot 1999: 189.

some of the greatest treasures that mankind has ever possessed'.[111] One
reason for Christianity's lack of interest was that all was already supposed to have been said by Our Lord and required no contribution from
outside. In the twelfth century, that changed, even before the taking
of Toledo. Islam and Christianity met each other, producing a flow of
knowledge northwards. Intellectual Europe could for the first time get
to know all the great works of Antiquity, Aristotle especially. Scholars
rushed to Spain to fill in their knowledge of these works – and those
of Arab authors. European culture was radically changed. 'In a few
years, . . . there was a transformation of minds, that ended if not with
rejecting, but at least no longer as accepting revelation as the point of
departure for everything. One was less inspired by Scriptures, more by
profane philosophers . . . Aristotle was at the basis of the method and
theory of knowledge of Abelard . . . All this was made possible by the
meeting with Islam.'[112] This advance in secular thinking developed with
the taking of Toledo. Pedro Alfonso, a converted Jew, went to England
and cultivated a circle of intellectuals, persuading Adelard of Bath to
study Arabic works abroad where he translated Kwarizmi's tables and
Euclid's *Elements*. It was under Adelard's influence that a more scientific spirit of enquiry developed, leading in the thirteenth century to the
work of Roger Bacon and of Robert Grossetête; the English tradition was
less religious, less Thomist, than Paris. From 1120 the move to translation in Spain intensified, spreading to Navarre in addition to Toledo.
Many intellectuals were involved in this process and networks grew up all
around western Europe. The most important figure in this movement was
Gerard of Cremona, who translated some hundred volumes from Arabic
to Latin, including Ptolemy's *Almagest* and works by Avicenna, Galen,
Hippocrates, Razi, Aristotle and Farabi. His Aristotle was particularly
important for the subsequent development of European thought.[113]

It was the difficult times of the *taifas*, followed by two centuries of
the Almoravids and Almohads, the puritanical Berber dynasties, that
produced the great philosophers and scientists who had the major influence on the civilization of both the Near East and the west. That was
in the twelfth century, the century of Averroës whose works included
many commentaries on Aristotle, a paraphrase of Plato's *Republic*, as
well as studies on meterology and medicine. A number of his volumes
were translated into Latin but the Arabic originals have been destroyed
with the great libraries either by Christians or by Muslims. This activity
of translation was of special significance in the history of the west as it

[111] Clot 1999: 271.   [112] Clot 1999: 273.
[113] On the twelfth-century Renaissance, see Southern 1953 and 1970, and Bolgar 1954.

preserved for Christian Europe some of the work of Greek authors but also the texts of Arabic learning. One of Averroës's own philosophical books was entitled 'The Incoherence of the Incoherence', which was a reply to the Persian Sufi Ghazali (1058–1111), who had composed an attack on philosophy called 'The Incoherence of the Philosophers'. In medicine there was the work Abulcasis (b. 926), who produced an encyclopedia in thirty volumes, the *Tasrif*. He was the first to use surgery, for example, in cauterization, and undertook many clinical observations. He also recommended the study of anatomy and dissection. Subsequently, in geography al-Idrisi (b. 1100), who worked for Roger of Sicily, produced an account of the world (the Book of Roger). And these were a few outstanding men among the many scholars of this period. Nor did things end there. In the two centuries before the Christians took Granada there was 'a brilliant late flowering of Islamic culture, rivalling that of the Umayyad golden age some three hundred years before. The most remarkable remnant of this flowering is the Alhambra.'[114] Miquel observes that with many of the advances of Islam in the later period, of Ibn al-Nafis in medicine, of the philosophy of Averroës, of the history of Ibn Khaldun, there was little follow up; it was taken up above all by the Christians of the west. That was perhaps due to the absence of the institutionalization of secular knowledge such as was found in later western societies.[115]

The history of Islam had started with the movement of the partly nomadic Arab tribes into the Near East. That movement was in some sense repeated by the coming of Altaic peoples from central and inner Asia in the period from 1041 to 1405: the Seljuqs (1055–92), the Mongols (1256–1411) and neo-Mongols (1369–1405) who were divided with the death of Timur. The Turkic Seljuqs ousted the Shiite Buyid sultans from Baghdad at the commission of the Abbasid caliphs in 1055, and Sunni Seljuq rule soon saw the founding of new orthodox Islamic madrasas there and elsewhere whose students were to serve not only in the religious establishment but also in the bureaucracy. As under previous sultans, that bureaucracy contained a very significant number of Persian intellectuals, some of whom were patrons in their own right. The vizier Nizam al-Mulk chose as the head of the Baghdad madrasa the famous fellow-Khurasani jurist, theologian and later mystic, al-Ghazali, who elaborated a strong criticism of hellenizing *falasifa* (in the Arabic tract we have mentioned) as well as of Ismaili thought, a branch of the Shiite faith. He was a great supporter of religion, regarded as a 'renewer' (*mujaddid*) of the faith, of which one was expected at the turn of every Muslim century. But despite al-Ghazali's *Book of Counsel* and a number of other

---

[114] Irwin 1996: 57.   [115] Miquel 1995.

works of advice to the ruler which were produced in the heyday of the early Seljuq sultans when their domains spread over Mesopotamia, Persia, central Asia, Afghanistan and Anatolia, their successors were unable to prevent territorial losses or resist the depredations of the Crusades. Their sovereignty lingered on for three centuries in Anatolia, but elsewhere barely saw out the eleventh century.

Renewal of a different kind came from outside sources. The invasion of the Near East, and indeed much of the intermediary territory, by the Crusaders occurred at a time (1096–9) of much political fragmentation in the Levant, but within a century the combination of local disorder and the uncongenial presence of European invaders presented an opportunity for the general Saladin, who was of Kurd origin. Having already evicted the last Fatimid caliph from Egypt for the ruler of Damascus, he subsequently usurped Syria itself, setting up the Ayyubid dynasty, when the Christian Copts of Cairo experienced 'a real intellectual renaissance'.[116] So too did the other inhabitants. Ayyubid architecture is best preserved in the northern Syrian fortress city of Aleppo, where we see extensive and carefully modernized military fortification combined with the continuation of pious patronage; the foundation of mosques (some of them remodelled Christian churches), Sufi institutions and madrasas went on apace, the latter mostly centring on the teaching of the legal schools that were now firmly entrenched as the pillars of Islamic tradition. The first introduction of madrasas to Egypt was made by Saladin and his Ayyubid successors, built in a Syrian style besides its sultanate and patrician palaces from earlier eras. Even from the time of the Fatimids, Cairo had been a city marked architecturally by the erection of mausolea, for this was where the spoils of conquest were increasing spent. The combination with a madrasa as a pious institution offered the patron a legally irremoveable hold on the premises supporting his mausoleum. It is for this reason so many mausolea, from the Ayyubid and even more during the following Mamluk period, line the Qasaba and central streets of the Egyptian capital. In the matter of style, there was an eclecticism nourished by local innovations and ideas from the older centuries of Levantine and Mesopotamian buildings: the square-plan and octagonal dome-drum combination, the honeycomb (*muqarnas*) recess design, the geometry of the minarets, the use of *iwans* (vaulted halls that were open at one end) and water features and so on – even the occasional borrowing from Christian cathedral architecture. The same applies to smaller *objets d'art*; the years of Saladin himself were known to be relatively unextravagant, but the great demand for intricate trinkets, vessels and other

---

[116] Miquel 1995: 85.

objects of use, including the astonishing array of gadgets produced by the engineer al-Jazari and described in his *Treatise on Automata*,[117] grew up towards the latter end of the Ayyubid period.

Design and taste went to and fro with the course of trade, the fortunes of battle and the provenance of victors, taking old and new ideas with them wherever war, politics and commerce dictated. In this constant movement across Islam, there was not exactly a renascence but rather an efflorescence, in the sense that there was no reanimation of a previously neglected or forgotten culture, but rather the ebb and flow of a civilization in constant contact with others.

The Ayyubid dynasty ruled until the 1250s, when its Egyptian and then Levantine territories were taken over by the leaders of its own 'slave'-recruited (*mamluk*) militia; its northerly retreats would before long fall to the Mongol invasion of Syria. Yet the new Mamluk state proved militarily more than a match for the new intruders. The Mongols traditionally followed a shamanistic religion but in the thirteenth century they ruled over vast tracts of Muslim territory. In tune with the literate culture of the local Muslim elites, their khans patronized learning of all kinds, encouraging scholars from as far afield as China and building a major observatory in Azerbaijan. However, in the mid thirteenth century Berke Khan (d. 1266, grandson of Genghis Khan), and under him the Blue (western) Horde, converted to Islam, which embroiled him in supporting the Egyptian Mamluks in Palestine against the campaigns of his own cousin, Hulagu, and later defeating him in the Caucasus. For a time, Hulagu's successors embraced Tibetan Buddhism, but by the turn of the fourteenth century they too had converted to Islam and sponsored a series of brilliant Muslim writers, such as the Jewish convert Rashid al-Din from Persia, a physician and author of a lengthy and for the time a well-sourced universal history in that language.[118] Rashid al-Din was vizier and court-historian for the Ilkhanate ruler, Uljeytu (r. 1304–16). He wrote the *World History*, probably in Tabriz in 1307, and it was lavishly illustrated some years later (plates 2 and 3). These volumes, which began with the history of the Mongols, were produced in al-Din's scriptorium in the Rashidiyya, which had become a focus for intellectual, artistic, theological and cultural life under the Ilkhans of Persia. He had established an endowment to support scholars and students to enable that institution to produce two copies a year, one in Arabic, one in Persian, for distribution to the major centres of learning in the state. This activity attracted intellectuals from central Asia and the Far East as well

[117] *Kitāb fī Maʿrifāt al-Ḥiyal al-Handasiyyah*, Atil 1981: 255ff.
[118] *Jāmiʿ al-Tawarikh*, the 'Compendium of Chronicles'.

as from Mesopotamia and Iran. Nevertheless, following the failure of the Ilkhanate to expand through Palestine and Egypt, Mongol power in the west also began to disintegrate, with other Turkish rulers taking control, many of them emanating from the military caste that quickly grew from the Mamluk soldiery developed under the ninth-century caliphate. At the eastern side of the Muslim world, the early Delhi sultanate, ruling over much of north-west India (as the eighty-five-year 'Slave dynasty' and the thirty-year Khilji dynasty which followed), was also of *mamluk* origin, and repeatedly succeeded in repelling Mongol incursions. The centre of the sultanate was 'a culturally lively place that attracted a variety of successful persons',[119] that comprised the Qutb complex (including the most massive minaret in the Islamic world, and the uncompleted stump of one eight times the size) built from the remains of the even more extensive Hindu and Jaina buildings, twenty-seven temples of which were said to have been destroyed. These are a reminder of the architectural talent that distinguished the Turkic-Muslim from the Mongol element of the Altaic diaspora which dominated virtually all of east, west, central, inner and south Asia during these centuries.

To the west, the Cairo-based Mamluk state, which had successfully resisted the Persian Ilkhan's invasion of the Levant, prospered despite the apparent political instability of the system; for the first century the average reign of this 'dynasty' was only a few years. The cultural florescence which followed its inception contributed to the cultural dominance of Egypt which had begun under the Ayyubid.[120] Echoing the earlier words of the Chinese in their deference to Beijing, Ibn Khaldun remarked of Egypt, no doubt thinking primarily of the capital Cairo, 'He who has not seen it does not know the power of Islam.'[121] There was a developed intellectual life that included Ibn al-Nafis (1213–88), a physician who as we have seen discovered pulmonary circulation 300 years before European medics learnt of its workings. But religious activity flourished at the same time; a Muslim reformer, Ibn Taymiyyah, living in Mamluk Damascus in the late thirteenth and early fourteenth centuries, wrote against pursuits outside the scope of the Sharia, arguing for the fundamentals of Islam in a manner that would be taken up in the late eighteenth century by the Wahhabi movement; that got him in trouble with the Mamluk authorities of his own day, for his anti-hellenizing credentials are clear to see in *Ar-Radd ala al-Mantiqiyyin*.[122] Again, there was conflict between the demands of religion and those of science.

---

[119] Waldman 1997: 122.   [120] Waldman 1997: 122.
[121] From his autobiography, *Al-Ta'rīf bi Ibn Khaldūn wa Riḥlatuhu Gharbān wa Sharqān*, Ibn Khaldun 1951.
[122] 'Refutation of the Logicians'.

In Egypt itself, the demand for high culture came from the ruling class of Mamluks rather than from the merchants; indeed Ettinghausen argues that conditions there made 'the formation of an extensive, well-to-do bourgeoisie impossible'.[123] But while the Mamluks may have controlled and even inhibited the full emergence of other classes, much of Egypt's wealth came from mercantile activity which was encouraged by the government and ranged far and wide; for nearly three centuries, their territories alone had direct access to the shipping routes of both the Mediterranean and the Arabian Sea. Consequently, the flowering of art in Iran was not as unique as has been claimed. Egypt too experienced a 'renascence' that was built on burgeoning trade, but the clientele differed, although both were dependent upon an urban culture.

This flowering of activity sometimes took place in one sector alone. Musallam writes of 'a remarkable efflorescence' of women in religion in the time of Sakhawi (d. 1497), and of a 'renaissance of women's religious learning'.[124] Al-Sakhawi was a Shafii scholar in the Cairo Medina in the last decades of the Mamluk period; his biographical encyclopedias *Al-Daw al-Lami*, of which *Kitab al-Nisa'* (The Book of Women) constitutes the final volume, lists and gives detail of 1,075 women (otherwise virtually unknown) who were apparently skilled transmitters of hadiths (*muhaddithat*), about the personal doings and sayings of the Prophet. Ibn Hajar al-Asqalani of fifty years earlier had also listed many of these.

The Mamluk dynasty of Egypt began with the brief sultanate of Qutuz (d. 1259–60) and his general (and later assassin) Baibars (r. 1260–77) usurping the remnant of Ayyubid power in Cairo shortly before repulsing the Ilkhan's invasion of their region as well as the threat of Christian crusaders, though the nobility among the latter actually offered aid to Qutuz and it was only the Templars who advocated supporting the Mongols. Baibars was followed by Qalawun who again defeated the Mongols and took over a number of Crusader fortresses despite his prior treaties with them. During his time trade flourished, with merchants from China, India and Yemen bringing valuable goods through Mamluk ports and providing rich revenues for the state.[125] The court gave patronage to the arts and established its own (Mamluk) style. Porcelain was much influenced by the 'blue-and-white' (*qing-hua ci*) and other styles from China, while the geometric and inscriptional intricacy of Mamluk metalwork was imitated in Venice's 'Veneto-Islamic' production.[126] There was a lively commerce and influence running in both directions, for the

---

[123] Ettinghausen 1970: 131.   [124] Musallam 1996: 191.
[125] Atil 1981: 14; see also Howard 2007.
[126] Atil 1981: 55. Cobalted blue-and-white pottery was known in Europe from the end of the sixteenth century, through the late Ming and Qing dynasties; it was mass produced in Jiangxi province from the late Yuan (early fourteenth), and the uptake of its influence

aniconistic aspects of other Muslim dynasties were not to the taste of the Egyptian Mamluks; the influx of craftwares from East Asia and the intervening lands introduced new decorative features, with floral and leaf motifs and fantastic animals including harpies, griffins, qilins (a Chinese chimerical beast), phoenixes and sphinxes, of Chinese, Mongol, Turkic and Greek provenance.[127] If this mutual receptiveness was the case with artistic styles, it was also true of techniques and of uses; Egyptian Mamluk glassware has been recovered in China, from where the Near East also imported Ming porcelain with designs imitating its own metalwork.[128]

A wave of architectural commissioning began even in the days of Baibars and Qalawun, with complexes of imposing domed and minaret-flanked mosques, elaborate mausolea and madrasas which quickly became the hallmark of the Cairo skyline. However, the high-water mark of early Mamluk art occurred during the reign of Qalawun's son, al-Nasir Muhammad. 'With his treasury overflowing with revenues from trade and improved methods of agriculture, he could well afford to be the greatest Mamluk patron of the arts, commissioning magnificent palaces and some thirty mosques, and ordering spectacular objects for both secular and religious use.'[129] Among the works he commissioned were Cairo's first public fountain and the grand aqueduct running from the Nile to the Citadel. But patronage was not limited to the rulers. 'The amirs competed with the sultan ... The wealth of the Mamluk empire and luxury of the sultan's court stimulated artists and architects.'[130] Ibn Khaldun, who lived to see the grandeur of Bahri Cairo, called it, 'the centre of the universe and the garden of the world'.[131] Competition among the elite led to 'an unprecedented explosion in artistic production', as well as to the work of 'men of the pen' such as the Syrian historian and Quranic exegete Abu al-Fida (1301–73). In the course of the fourteenth century, the diplomatic activity of the later Bahri sultans took on a breadth little known to earlier Muslim dynasties, and cordial relations were established with the late Ilkhans, the Golden Horde, various Indian, Balkan and Abyssinian rulers, with the Roman pontiff and the kings of France and Aragon.

However, the Bahri rulers gave way to the Burji (1382–1517), and the state became less prosperous. The rulers made attempts to emulate the magnificent endowments of the earlier sultans and build their own

in Egypt as early as the mid fourteenth century shows how close the Mamluks were to the pulse of world trade.

[127] Atil 1981: 15, 50ff.   [128] Atil 1975, 1981: 55.
[129] Atil 1981: 15.   [130] Atil 1981: 15.   [131] Ibn Khaldun 1951: 246.

mosque complexes, but there was some falling-off particularly in the aux-
iliary arts of metalwork and glass, partly owing to the devastation of the
Black Death. Then in the middle of the fifteenth century, the sultan Qaitbay's long reign (1468–98) witnessed what Atil calls 'the renaissance of
Mamluk art'.[132] He increased commercial activities, and at the same time
built mosques and 'revitalized' all forms of artistic production, including
books; with the spread in madrasas, there was an upsurge in the demand
for ornate Qurans, and the art of book illustration prospered handsomely,
though its more secular glories were mostly lavished on popular books
from earlier periods, like the satirical prose *Maqamat* collections of al-
Hamdhani and al-Hariri, written around 1000 and 1100 respectively,
and the *Kalila wa Dimna* of al-Muqaffa. Due to the heavily military and
administrative focus of Saladin's era (in which the major literary works
were mainly epistolary or biographical), to the relative brevity of the
Ayyubid dynasty, to the non-Arab mother tongue of the founder and to
the early Mamluks, with their slave origins and warrior ethos, there was
perhaps some eclipse of Arab literary and scientific works in the centuries
following the Mongol invasions, though this was punctuated by exceptional travel literature by the likes of Ibn Jubayr (1145–1217) and Ibn
Battutah (1304–77), and the works of Ibn Khaldun, all stemming from
well outside the Mamluk territories. It was a situation that depended
very much upon the region. If we focus on Egypt, its cultural life in the
thirteenth and fourteenth centuries was not less rich than it had been
in previous ones. There were plenty of scholars active in various fields,
such as the logician and jurist al-Sharif al-Tilimsani (d. 1370), one of the
teachers of Ibn Khaldun, the astronomer Ibn al-Shatir (d. 1365) and the
bellelettrist al-Safadi (d. 1363). However, in the visual arts in the wake of
the Mongol incursions it was only the more visible, decorative, practical
and plastic ones that prospered, even in Qaitbay's golden years. Yet in
these arts his reign left a legacy which 'recaptured the splendour of the
past'. The splendour included the interpenetration of styles and motifs
of the Near East, Europe and China, which is evident from the fact that

the most difficult task in the study of Mamluk silks is to identify pieces made in
Egypt and Syria and to differentiate these from the Chinese textiles produced for
the sultans and from the Italian and Spanish imitations of Mamluk fabrics. Chinese silks woven for the Mamluk court employed Arabic inscriptions and heraldic
motifs similar to those manufactured by local artists. Exported to the West, Mamluk silks were in great demand in Mediterranean states . . . and inspired the textile
industries of Granada, Lucca, and Venice.[133]

[132] Atil 1981: 17.   [133] Atil 1981: 223.

The Chinese took great pains to satisfy foreign customers. Some of their textiles with Arabic script made their way to western Europe where they were especially popular in ecclesiastical circles and are now found in various cathedral cities of central Europe and in museums like the Victoria and Albert in London and those in St Petersburg and Berlin. But in Cairo's holdings from the excavations at Fustat, many block-printed, resist-dye cotton fabrics from India are also to be found.[134]

While there was some creative import of Chinese craft-features, as in metalwork, the culture of the Mamluk period was mostly a continuation of that of the Ayyubid, and more distantly of the Abbasid, especially in Mesopotamian wares, for example. Architecture again was not without innovation (possibly the damask inscription carpets, the use of blazons, one or two decorative features, the mausoleum linked with other institutions), but it was largely continuous with Baghdadi and earlier Syrian genres and features. There was a great spread of trade and diplomacy, and some evidence of individual activity among the literary and crafts celebrities, but science was not much advanced while the religious tradition continued to be drawn from existing elements, some recent and some older. Despite the so-called renascence there was not a revived culture as a whole nor yet a great burst forwards as in the Italian Renaissance. The major interaction with China was a striking phenomenon of mercantile activity, with the transferred content being often decorative and for commercial consumption.[135] The 'renaissance' claims are designations of a cultural and economic upsurge, a heyday in some of the artistic crafts and in the more commercial forms of creative productivity, not more comprehensive. The plague, which had once decimated the populace under the Bahris in 1348, returned to the Levant and Egypt at the beginning of the sixteenth century and contributed to the ebbing of political and cultural power. The Mamluks fought unsuccessfully against the Ottomans, finally losing in 1517.

Was there a renascence among the later Ottoman Turks who took over? The Ottomans trained their *ulama* in specialist madrasas to be bureaucrats and this aspect of government was well developed. Their influence was considerable but it 'discouraged scientific, philosophical and even theological speculation', a trend already marked in the late sixteenth century. In 1580, for example, the supreme Ottoman religious official, the shaykh al-Islam, objected to the construction of a new observatory

---

[134] Atil 1981: 224, 225.

[135] From their use on ecclesiastical garments, it seems unlikely that the Mamluk inscriptions on the silks were ever read as such by either the northern European buyers or the Chinese producers.

in Istanbul[136] and the janissaries were allowed to pull it down. That act demonstrated the fragility of knowledge that seemed to query religious orthodoxy. Yet in the same period the Rajput Mughal scholar Maharaja Jai Singh II of Jaipur built observatories at Jaipur, Ujjain, Benares, Mathura and Delhi. Such difference of emphasis, such alternation, was very much a regional matter within Islam.

From the time of the Mongol invasion, however, the Arab heartlands as a whole experienced something of a dark age, a stasis in culture and science, that was further exacerbated by Ottoman domination and by the concentration on military affairs. Within Turkey, the Ottomans had seen the blossoming of Sufi poetry and had encouraged Persian as a literary language as well as Turkish, while Arabic was consigned to strictly liturgical and theological functions. Political and military reversals in the course of the seventeenth century encouraged the adoption of features of European culture at the beginning of the eighteenth, in the 'Tulip Time' as it was called. But even then, cultural features, including the tulip itself and vaccination, were moving westwards.

So the Ottoman hegemony of the Arabic world was not always favourable to artistic activity. In this polyglot empire Turkish multiculturalism existed from early days, but this did not work out to the advantage of any of the subject languages or literatures since patronage was dominated by Turkish dignitaries. For them, most of these regional cultures, including those of the Arab lands, lacked importance. So that even a poet like Fuzuli, born and working in Iraq, could barely afford to write in Arabic; hence the bulk of his poetry was in Persian and Turkish. Even Persian poetry became, for the most part, one of conventional lyric themes.

However, Turkish culture had its own originality and varied cultural achievements, though it is difficult to speak of a renascence in the European sense. On the literary side, Turkish scholars translated much material including from the Greek.[137] Numerous Greek manuscripts were copied in the court of Mehmet II, the Conqueror (1453–81), who was famous for his 'cultured catholicity'. In architecture, Istanbul is known for its attractive skyline. The earlier achievements of Byzantium and of Hagia Sophia were undoubtedly important in this. So too was the Roman architecture for early Christian basilicas. But the magnificence of the Blue and other mosques are not diminished in any way by such links. The range of design in the internal decoration in these buildings is as varied and startling as anywhere in the Islamic world, and the craftsmanship and detail, interspersed with plainer surfaces and contours, indicates a generous patronage. There are the mosaics, the Bukhara-like

[136] Irwin 1996: 69.   [137] See Gutas 1998: 173ff.

dome-clusters, the heavy mix of script-types, the preference for medal-
lions and roseate script-panels, perhaps the extra embellishment of a
column, arch or pendentive, whether in the palace of Topkapi Saray and
its kiosks, or in the mosque complexes of the viziers and pashas. Then
there were the tiles developed at Iznik, the famous silks from Bursa and
the many carpets which were so attractive to Europeans in the Renaissance (and later), appearing often in the paintings of the period. The food
of Turkey is today renowned throughout the world as one of the great
cuisines. It is true that it was heavily indebted to Persia for its cooking,
to China for its tiles and to Europe (or to China and the Near East)
for its military technology, but that mixture of origins is a feature of all
Eurasian cultures and does not detract from its own contribution to the
result. Trade with the later Turkish Near East was a prominent part of the
economic revival of Europe, making possible the Italian Renaissance.[138]
All this may not amount to a 'renascence' in our sense, but Turkish
culture certainly had its moment of flowering.

The Near East saw a struggle between the Ottomans, more particularly
under Suleyman (r. 1520–66), and the Safavids in Persia under Abbas I
(r. 1589–1629). The latter experienced a split between the Shiite leadership of the *ulama* and the secular authority of the shah, a title which was
revived and harked back to pre-Islamic Persia, whereas the Ottomans on
the other hand became more religious in a traditional Sunni way. In the
sixteenth and seventeenth centuries Iran under Safavid rule contributed
to 'a major cultural flowering' through the Persian language and the
visual arts.[139] The development of *falasifa*, including the Ishraqi or illu-
minist school, was encouraged. This was a philosophical group founded
by Suhrawardi (d. 1191), who wished to return to the wisdom of Plato
and the Presocratic and Zoroastrian sages. The movement, discussed by
Pamuk,[140] was influenced by China and affected in turn the surrounding
cultures such as India.

In the west of Islam, in the course of the eleventh century, reformist
movements developed among the Sunni Berbers of North Africa who
were called in to assist in the resistance to the Christian reconquest of
Spain. The Sanhajah confederation of the western Sahara consisted of
several leaders involved in the caravan trade across the Sahara, which had
long been in contact with Islam and gave rise to the so-called University of Timbuktu. One of these leaders went on a pilgrimage to Mecca
(like many others) and brought back a teacher, Abdallah ibn Yasin, to
instruct his followers in the true religious life. In this way the Almoravids
were founded, a group that later conquered Morocco, western Sahara,

---

[138] Goody 2006.   [139] Waldman 1997: 127.   [140] Pamuk 2001 [1998].

Mauretania, Gibraltar and parts of Senegal, Mali and Algeria. They were summoned to help the Andalusians in their struggle with Christianity but in the 1090s in fact the second wave of their invasion had the purpose of removing and replacing the 'party kings' of the Islamic south who had called them. In this struggle with Christianity, Valencia was the only significant addition to Muslim rule, which in their case was strict and reformist, attempting to bring the 'correct' Islam of the Sharia to people fallen into error, be they the Berber and west Saharan converts or the petty *maliks* and *amirs* of Spain. Although the political, economic and religious impact of these reformers was very considerable, during the first quarter of the twelfth century they crumbled in the face of another major movement of the Berbers, the Almohads.[141]

Led by Ibn Tumart from the Atlas Mountains, a one-time *hajji* and student of the Persian mystic al-Ghazali, the Almohads were yet more severe than their predecessors, their founder for example throwing the ruler's sister off her horse for not wearing a veil. He preached a renewal of Islam, arguing for a return to the words of the Quran.[142] Through the middle decades of the twelfth century, the Almohad movement gradually replaced the Almoravids in the Maghreb and in Andalusia, slowing the pace of the Christian reconquest. Despite the puritanical beliefs, its courts acted as the patrons of arts and letters, encouraging the important group of scholars that included Ibn al-Arabi, who would have described himself as a Sufi, and Averroës (Ibn Rushd), the great Aristotelian philosopher. Important achievements took place outside the Islamic community among the Jewish inhabitants of Andalusia, especially in the writings of Moses Maimonides, who was mainly active in Cairo. Although Almohad power eventually began to decline, the successor states were also responsible for many high achievements among Andalusian Muslims, including the magnificent Alhambra palace in Granada, the rival of any European cathedral (plate 4). In the Maghreb too writers flourished, especially those great scholars the traveller Ibn Battutah (1304–68/77) and the historian Ibn Khaldun (1332–1406) who was also a *qadi*; as a historian and the contributor to a number of the modern human sciences, the latter was a considerable polymath.

In the east of Islam, the Timurid Babur had established his reign in India. At this time, many scholars from Persia came there, including poets who went to be under rich patrons. Under that kingdom, a liberal approach flourished. Babur's grandson, Akbar (r. 1556–1605), banned intolerance, abolished the special tax on non-Muslims and encouraged

---

[141] Lopez 1962.
[142] The Almohad were staunch Asharis, but the Wahhabis considered them to be heretics.

an ecumenical attitude. In the arts there was a mingling of Hindu and Muslim traditions, leading to many local developments including the building of the Taj Mahal.

The impact of the Timurid regime took place at the time of the struggle with Europe, which had started its period of expansion and colonization. The opening up of the direct sea route from Europe to the east as well as the conquest and settlement of America in the west was principally a matter of military and naval force, of 'guns and sails'. The arrival of a conquering Europe led to two kinds of reaction from Islamic powers. Firstly, there was the acquisition of the ways of the west later typified in twentieth-century Turkey in the shape of Kemal Ataturk and the Young Turks, which involved a secularization borrowed from the west as well as a kind of local renascence. Secondly, there was an equally strong resistance to things western together with a determination to continue to 'modernize' in the Islamic way, as advocated by the Muslim Brotherhood in Egypt. The former movement was dominantly secular, following the path of the nation state, the second adopted the doctrine of pan-Islam, placing a strong emphasis on religion and on the words and deeds of the Prophet. But this latter movement was not purely conservative for it often sought to renew in religious terms what had subsequently been abandoned, as with the Wahhabi movement which went back to the Book but in order to revitalize current practice, in a way similar to the Reformation in the west.[143] Because of the absence of an authoritarian church, it was frequently the case in Islam that individuals and groups called the faithful back to the written word. In doing so, they also veered away from the secular, which some thought of as not only intrinsic to modern life but as essential in some degree to all forms of central government. The recent period saw an exacerbation of the division between the secular and the religious as well as the associated conflict between the national state and the international religion, in Persia between the shah and the *ulama*. In some parts the proponents of the latter were known as Salafiyah, derived from the word for 'pious ancestors', and were always involved in a looking back. But so too was all written religion as well as the secular learning involved in returning to Hellenistic times, in bringing Aristotle to the attention of one's contemporaries. Looking back was an aspect of all written traditions, not confined to Islam, but in religion one looked back to the word of God, not of man, which tended to make the process much more conservative, even perhaps where a major reformation was involved.

---

[143] The term 'Wahhabi' is a term of abuse used by opponents of the movement. They describe themselves as Salafis.

Looked at over the long-term, Islam was part of the monotheistic religions in the Near East, all of which had Semitic roots. All tried intermittently to revive the achievements of the classical societies in Greece and Rome (the Jews largely through the Muslims) but all were ambivalent about these pagan cultures, differing from them as they did intellectually because of that monotheism and because of their commitment to the tradition of Abraham – at least initially. One important aspect of cultural rebirth in all three meant looking to the classical heritage of Greece and Rome which from their religious standpoint was 'pagan'; this reference involved a switch to more secular modes of thought, stressing reason rather than faith (though the latter could be more or less 'rational'). At times Islam looked back to those 'foreign sciences', including philosophy, but in alternation with an approach that allowed others to look back to the Abrahamistic tradition. It never really institutionalized the secular vision on a long-term basis, as happened in the Italian Renaissance, although a scientific tradition remained part of Islamic culture. In some ways significant rebirths of the thought and practice of others were rather temporary phenomena, except perhaps in medicine, where the healing role was apparent and usually welcomed, and in technology, where progress was often (but not always) encouraged and manifest. But while developments in Islam did take place in other sciences, and in a lesser way with some of the arts,[144] and these certainly influenced the Italian Renaissance, there was less continuity and more resistance than in Europe after 1600. Nevertheless, they had their own periods of florescence and from time to time displayed a rebirth, a burst forward.

The important influence on northern Europe leading to the Italian Renaissance came especially with the military victories of Muslims in the south of that continent. The impact of Arab science burst in on the European world at the end of the tenth century in Catalonia, made a slight progress in the south of Italy at the end of the eleventh and exploded in Toledo and Salerno at the beginning of the twelfth,[145] literally 'illuminating' the knowledge of medieval Europe. Djebbar writes of this 'human culture that prefigured the modern future'.[146] Why did a civilization that had made such advances and contributed so much to Europe's scientific revolution of the Renaissance then fall behind? This is a question that has preoccupied many scholars who have often enough attributed the difference to moral or intellectual causes. But essentialism cannot account for alternation. Nor can the attribution of religious reasons, since all

---

[144] For example, in architecture, Islam may have been responsible for the Gothic arch (Achour 1995: 337).
[145] Djebbar 2005: 161.   [146] Djebbar 2005: 164–5.

Abrahamistic ones had much in common. On the other hand Djebbar points to economic causes, the loss of control of the Mediterranean and at the same time the build-up of Italian trade with the east, a root factor in the spectacular advance of the peninsular. But at the same time a conservativism crept into Muslim culture, secular as well as religious; until recently there was little permanent institutionalization of the secular in universities or academies.

The position of the Arabic lands, mainly under Ottoman domination, changed with the nineteenth century and the coming of the revival or renascence called the *Nahda* which continues in various forms to the present day. This is commonly referred to in English as the 'Arabic Renaissance', and it has been partly the engagement with European forms that has fuelled an ongoing resurgence in graphic and plastic art, as in literature and other activities. Beginning in Egypt and Syria, its early decades showed a very lively linking with the wealth of the older Arabic tradition (a rebirth), and soon produced a striking neoclassical movement in literature.

There was a relatively brief revival of the *qasida* and other couplet-type forms, but these were soon found too restrictive in a world where poets would no longer function as courtiers or suppliants, and where politics bore little resemblance to the old tribal practices of the desert. The effect of this revival on prose was neglible. The neoclassical impulse was of predictably short lease, and what continued to fuel the revolution in thought and literature was less the revived elements of the past than the contact with other modernities; in a sense that began with the new means of communication themselves (in print, photography, film and in representation generally) which increasingly impinged on the life of every Arab. The beginnings of change came with Napoleon's interruption of the Ottoman domination in Egypt, and the introduction of the printing press; fonts were soon cut locally and newspapers and printed works of many kinds proliferated within the space of a few years. The newspaper, which obviously required print and later the rotary press, changed the scale of political participation and altered the outlook of the many. It is this change in the means of communication that Eisenstein has seen as so important in the Italian Renaissance.[147]

Otherwise, while there was undoubtedly a burst forward, modernization did not involve much of a rebirth of a former culture. The main

---

[147] Her emphasis on the changes following from the printing press have been queried by Adrian Johns (2002), but in fact neither writer has introduced comparative material; Eisenstein confines her observations to Europe and Johns to England: neither looks at communication in societies before writing, or indeed before the press.

contribution has been not so much a rebirth of anything past but rather the cult of the new; its culture was stimulated by influences from abroad. There was a little creative use of the past, but although we find these traditional elements used in ever more innovative combinations with new ideas, in the architecture of mosques for example, innovation is restricted because the aim necessarily remains the same, to recall the Islamic faithful to a state of devotion practised by their forebears. It was important for Islam to assert a traditional architectural identity, especially in a world dominated by largely western ideas and corporations.

As elsewhere, in China, India or in Japan, 'modernization' was partly the result of the unequal contact with the west, resulting from the discrepancies in military and economic power as well as in the accumulation of knowledge. But the aspect of rebirth played less part, except on the religious front; in terms of the secular, looking back to classical culture was of little importance, except perhaps for philosophy. It was the contemporary west, and not some past tradition that offered the relevant model, although earlier the west had in turn borrowed heavily for its own Renaissance and had been revived in an economic way by contact with the Muslim Near East and beyond. As elsewhere many aspects of contemporary western life have forced themselves on the Islamic world, leaving little untouched, a process that is part of the globalization of the world's cultures. The *Nahda*, which has been welcomed by many and was a vital source of a modern self-image for recent generations of Muslims, is an aspect of this process, not so much a looking back as a looking around.

In examining Islam more generally, in the early days we see a considerable 'revival' of Greek and even oriental cultures, producing a wealth of translations of scientific and philosophical works that helped to give science a strong burst forward in many fields and later became important for the European Renaissance. Greek learning was often being revived and built on during the course of Islamic history, which alternated between periods when first the religious, then the secular dominated, although both were always present. The secular, and indeed the scientific, was mainly a feature of the life of courts which attempted to collect together great scholars, great achievements and great libraries. Higher education developed in the hands of teachers at religious madrasas, but the secular and the scientific did not take the kind of learned, institutional form that it eventually did in Europe, where the religious gradually became of more restricted relevance in intellectual life. But in Islam this crystallization of a non-transcendental approach never achieved a permanent ongoing context as it did in the west, partly because of the absence of a secularized (or partly secularized) higher education and the prohibition on printing and the press to diffuse knowledge, as well as the decline of the Near East as a centre of trade and of economic activity, at least until the worldwide use of petrol. Things changed somewhat in the early nineteenth century with the founding of the *Nahda*.[148] Otherwise religion usually remained hegemonic, as with Judaism until the Emancipation. However, something approaching a (temporary) renascence, at least in the sense of a flowering of culture, did take place not only among the Abbasids, the Buyids, the Mamluks and even in Mughal India and among the Turks but between the eighth and tenth centuries in Andalusia, promoted by the wealth of that area, with the improvements in water-controlled agriculture, with the introduction of sugar and silk, and of many fruits and vegetables, from the east, and with the speedier circulation of useful information through the use of Chinese paper and the build-up (albeit temporary) of large libraries. During this period the outlines of the modern information society began to emerge more clearly.

---

[148] But *Nahda* is not always considered an Islamic phenomenon, since many of its central figures were Christian Arabs.

5   Emancipation and efflorescence in Judaism

It is unusual to treat Jewish cultural history in terms of a renaissance. I do so here because, despite the constraints of an Abrahamistic religion, firstly, Jews were heavily involved in the intellectual efflorescence of Andalusia and in other parts of Islam; secondly, they contributed to the revival of academic medicine in Montpellier and Salerno (as we have discussed in chapter 2 and in chapter 4 on Islam). Here I want first to discuss their role in western Islam in the Sephardic tradition, and then to look at the extraordinary contribution the Ashkenazi made to the existing cultures of post-Renaissance Europe in the course of what has been called the Emancipation, a transformation that involved freedom not only from limits placed upon them by the dominant Christian culture of the north but more importantly from the restrictions placed upon themselves by their own religion. Both of these required not so much a looking back as a looking around, and the introduction of a measure of secular thought into the body of Judaism, which of course continued to look back to biblical times.

Both involved an important division in Jewish culture between the Sephardic or Andalusian-Spanish Jews and the Ashkenazi or Franco-German branch. The former traced their cultural filiation to Babylonia, the latter to Italy and Palestine. Those in Muslim areas employed Arabic for prose and Hebrew for poetry, the Ashkenazi wrote almost exclusively in Hebrew for internal use. While the southern branch composed secular poetry and scientific works inspired by the Arabs and their translations of Greek scholarship, the literature of Jews in the northern areas was overwhelmingly religious. The Sephardi were also much more integrated into local society and many distinguished themselves not only in secular sciences but in administration. Their communities, however, were almost wiped out by the invasion from North Africa of the more fundamentalist Almohad reformers in 1147–8, driving people to northern Spain and Provence and, in the case of Maimonides's family, to North Africa and Egypt.[1]

---

[1] Cohen 1997: 393–9.

Politically, Jewish society in the Near East was strongly affected first by the influence of the Greeks and then by the Romans, both of whom conquered the area. But although some Jews were Hellenistic the bulk kept to their own ways and their own religion, and rose up against their conquerors. Berenson speaks of 'the anti-Hellenic Jew'.[2] Nevertheless the Greek influence was later felt particularly through the Arabs in Baghdad when the looking back meant that an 'efflorescence intellectuelle' was injected not only into the Arab world but into the Judaic which it contained, especially through Platonic thought. Later on for North Africa,[3] Zafrani speaks of a golden age in wider Jewish–Muslim relations despite the confessional differences – the Jews 'endured tolerance and tolerated compromises'. The very extent of the caliphate regime throughout the Near East meant that 90 per cent of Jews were then included under Muslim rule. They were of course already represented in the Arabian peninsular when the Muslims came to power. They had been dispersed by the Romans but previously had been exiled to Babylonia and it was in Baghdad that there were established two of their celebrated academies (*yeshivot*), the leaders of which (*gaons*) provided an important reference for Jewry in the rest of the world. Muhammad eliminated three Jewish tribes at Medina, suspecting them of complicity with the enemy, Mecca. But others were allowed to stay as *dhimma*, people of the Book.

The Jews in these territories were close to the Muslims in several ways. Firstly, both religions went back to Abrahamistic sources as well as to common values and beliefs. Secondly, they were close physically, sharing the same territorial space. They also had similar mystical sources, since the Kabbala and Sufism had elements in common;[4] so too did the forms of magic.[5] As one Sufi said, 'I am neither Christian, nor Jew, nor Muslim.'[6] Jews and Arabs were very much intertwined and the revival of Greek also brought them together intellectually, for example, in translation which led to the first Jewish philosopher, Saadya Gaon (882–942), who, 'following Graeco-Arab philosophers', developed 'a rationalist religious system in which both faith and reason were involved'.[7] This bringing together of the two realms was a general problem with such religions which each met in different ways. But any meeting was not to the liking of some, including many traditional Islamic students or the majority of Ashkenazi scholars in Europe. For them philosophy was the realm of reason, religion that of faith, while philosophy was always viewed as

---

[2] See Berenson 1950; Julius 2000: 4.   [3] Zafrani 1996: 33; also 1995: 212.
[4] Zafrani 1996: 152.   [5] Doutté 1908.   [6] Zafrani 1996: 159.
[7] Zafrani 1996: 44. The line is from Ibn Arabi; there are similar lines in Attar, Amir Khusrau (*Kafir-e-ishqam, musalmani mara darkār nīst*) and various other writers.

being descended from the Greeks and therefore a little 'pagan'. Any such bringing together, of which the Enlightenment in Europe was an extreme example, was far from easy either among the Ashkenazi or in tight-knit rural groups, for example in a shtetl in Galicia or a mellah in Morocco, where the community was close and any deviation from the law was likely to be reprimanded by vigilant neighbours as well as by the rabbinate; in the most extreme cases it was met by expulsion or by excommunication. Towns were freer, more anonymous.

By the eleventh century the cultural centre of gravity of Judaism had moved westwards from the Near East to Spain. In the golden age of Andalusia, the Judaeo-Arab synthesis, both economic and sociocultural, 'contributed to the great participation of Jewish society in literary and artistic activities, to fashionable occupations, both serious and frivolous, of the flourishing of medieval civilization'.[8] The Jews took part in all these various activities, including entertainment with poetry and singing. Andalusian song was not like northern European music, one part of which was confined to the upper class; here all elements of the population took part. Nevertheless, from time to time the talmudic prohibition bearing on performances with drinking wine took hold, with even innocent diversions being forbidden, such as the singing of slave-girls, a practice condemned by Maimonides. However, in this part of the world religious restrictions were generally more relaxed.

There had already been a tradition of poetry in Judaism, incorporating the Piyyut of Palestine. Starting in the tenth century, when the main centres of Judaism had moved, the production of poetry was greatly influenced by what was happening in Andalusia. Verse became secularized, developing 'progressively the tendency to leave the sacred domain', first of all as an instrument of polemic, then as 'a profane literature of entertainment'.[9] That separation occurred especially among the elite who benefited most from the economic prosperity of a country that was involved in commerce with the vast world of Islam, especially through the Mediterranean – though the enjoyment of poetry was also shared by the less well-off.

Judaism was not immune from adopting some of the patterns of representation of its host cultures, as we see in the decoration of marriage contracts and even of the scriptures in post-Renaissance Europe, in the miracle play of Esther, and indeed in its entire role in the golden age culture of Andalusia. But it was not until the 'emancipation' of late eighteenth- and nineteenth-century Europe that Ashkenazi Jews took a prominent place in such activities in the north, especially with their move

[8] Zafrani 1996: 136.   [9] Zafrani 1996: 126.

to America and elsewhere which involved a heavy commitment to new forms of visual communication running against earlier iconoclasm. And even so, only rarely was there, nor is there today, any form of representation in the holy space of the synagogue or the cemetery. Under the earlier dispensation, neither Islam nor Judaism could undergo an artistic renascence in painting or in the representative arts, such as took place in Florence and elsewhere in Italy, since there was no parallel break-out from a restrictive religion as took place in Europe. Nor was there the same representative past for them to look back to, as with Greek and Roman sculpture, theatre and artistic activity more widely. Judaism had almost nothing but an aniconic history in this respect. Islam, however, did take over a measure of the Greek and Roman tradition in ruling over the lands these societies had earlier possessed. So it was that al-Mamun, following Sasanian and earlier Abbasid tradition, encouraged Hunayn and others to collect Greek manuscripts which were later translated at his court and became important elements of the Muslim world. These documents fell largely in the scientific and philosophical fields. The arts were little affected by this looking back. Apart from some courts, for the most part the appearance of the visual arts had to await the coming of the colonial period. At this time the influence from the west brought its own 'renaissance' to Arabic performance in the nineteenth century, which was not simply a matter of taking over western ways though it was stimulated by Napoleon's intervention in Egypt.[10]

Around the Mediterranean, Jewish as well as Muslim thought was influenced more by the Greek than in the Latin west and north. Originally the Jews rejected classical thought as belonging to the polytheistic, pagan world while they on the other hand had to defend monotheism. It was only with the wider victory of the latter with Christianity, and especially with the coming of Islam, that a more conciliatory view of Greek 'wisdom' became acceptable.[11] Jewish thought in the Islamic lands became hellenized. That process even led to the emergence of a certain secular element in medieval Judaism of the south which encouraged philosophy (and mysticism) 'with rational and religious resonances' but with 'its universalistic tone and dominant humanism'.[12] We see the result in the reconquered Toledo in the encounter between the Ashkenazi traditionalist Asher Ben Yehiel and his colleague on the rabbinic tribunal, Israel Ben Yosef Israeli, representative of the Hispano-Maghrebian culture who defended the laws of reason as against those of religion; the Greek influence was very apparent in the latter's position but did not affect the former's.

[10] Miquel 1995: 104.   [11] Zafrani 1996: 259.   [12] Zafrani 1996: 81.

There was a further 'reformation' in Jewish thought as the result of the expulsion of Muslims and Jews from Andalusia in 1492 (and even earlier). This move profoundly affected both communities and produced 'a spiritual effervescence' among the Jews, especially at Safed in Palestine, leading to the development of an interest in the Kabbala (which was influenced by Sufism) as well as in other fields, all of which were marked by this same mysticism. This was essentially a religious renewal, arising from the catastrophe of what some called 'the third exile', rather than the development of both religious and secular thought that had marked the earlier 'golden age'. The former was the result of separation whereas that earlier experience was very much the result of the Jews having been caught up in Muslim society and, like the Muslims, having undergone a degree of 'hellenization', even of partial secularization. Then there was a symbiotic relationship between the two communities at the level of knowledge, and the Jews became the rivals of the Muslims in philosophy, grammar, mathematics, medicine and astronomy, as well as in poetry and music, all of which were much freer than among Jews elsewhere (except perhaps in medicine).[13] In the west of Islam Jewish and Muslim communities were thus linked together, linguistically and in other respects, in what was an efflorescence for both, displaying an interest in 'foreign sciences' and making considerable additions to human knowledge as well as in certain of the arts.

So the Jews of the Iberian peninsular had a different experience from that of the Ashkenazi of northern Europe. As the latter did with Yiddish, they adopted the language of the dominant community, Arabic (in Andalusia) and, from the ninth century, no longer used their Aramaic vernacular, though they still often used Hebrew script. Saadya Gaon had translated the Bible and many other texts into Arabic, and as we have noted these were accepted by the community as authoritative. All this happened in a society described as 'symbiotic' by Zafrani with 'a great effervescence of Jewish thought and literature',[14] religious but also philosophical and concerned with the sciences of nature. In this cultural milieu, Greek thought was important for both Muslims and Jews. In essence it was from Plato that they elaborated the opposition between matter and spirit. Influenced by the Greeks, Saadya already presented a rationalist view of religion in the ninth century involving both faith and reason, the separation of which was insisted upon by the Pharisean movement. That was what was at the core of the fourteenth-century conflict in Toledo that saw the disagreement between the Ashkenazi and Hispano-Maghrebian Jew to which we have referred.[15]

---

[13] Zafrani 1995: 275.   [14] Zafrani 1995: 246.   [15] Zafrani 1995: 247.

According to Zafrani, Spanish Islam itself was already different from Islam elsewhere, in granting first place to the 'secondary sciences' called speculative although not setting aside religious education, and in giving rise to a certain 'humanism'.[16] That comparative freedom was also true for the Jews living there. He writes of them rivalling Muslims and Christians 'in the domains of philosophy, medicine, mathematics, astronomy etc.'.[17] But at various periods Muslim Spain was governed by different individuals and by different dynasties with different aims, and the balance between religious and secular sciences was very much a matter of change over time, of alternation.

This alternation, which affected all communities, manifested itself in many ways. In Islam there were periods of rigidity, of puritanism, as when the second invasion of the Berber Almohads took over Andalusia and the town of Cordoba in 1140. The intransigence of this dynasty meant the forced conversion of many Jews, including the philosopher and scientist Maimonides. For the religion was now under 'the unrelenting domination of the followers of Ibn Tumart' who adopted 'the rigour of an extreme unitary doctrine'.[18] The imposition of this doctrine meant the exclusion not only of minority religious communities but also of the secular, 'heretical', sciences associated with the Greeks, and of the places where such scientists taught or practised. So at this point in time Maimonides moved to Egypt, which, as Fatimid and Shiite, was more tolerant. What made for this periodic Muslim intolerance was a strict adhesion to the faith and to its omniscience, which in theory prohibited all enquiry into nature. The idea of absolute monotheism was more destructive of the knowledge society than polytheism or spirituality in general since it worshipped a being who knew all and was capable of doing everything, allowing little latitude to humankind itself. At one level 'the problem of evil' threw some doubts upon the goodness of God and put the blame on the incapacity of the 'human individual properly to communicate with the divine'. However, as we have seen, just as periods in Judaism were subject to alternation, so too were they among the Muslims; there were times of humanism and others 'when a prince determined to apply to the letter the rigours of Islamic law'.[19]

In some circles (e.g. that of Karl Jaspers) it has become common to associate the early development of Judaism in the heart of the Near East, and indeed of modernism more widely, with the appearance of the Axial Age which saw the coming of monotheism and of 'confessional religions'. The thesis maintains that the biblical commandments

---

[16] Zafrani 1996: 87.   [17] Zafrani 1996: 89.
[18] Zafrani 1996: 113.   [19] Zafrani 1996: 139.

'reflected the mercantile environment in which they were found in their special concern for fairness, honesty, covenant-keeping, moderation, law and order, accountability, and rights of ordinary human beings'.[20] It is highly doubtful if any of these qualities were exclusively or predominantly associated with monotheistic religions, as distinct from societies further east; the concept of the Axial Age seems part of the attempt to validate the supposed superiority not only of monotheism but of Judaeo-Christian culture as something distinctive, leading inevitably to modernization and to capitalism.

After the diaspora, the Jews in Europe lived in gentile society, where in the north local Judaism had been supplemented by Ladino-speaking refugees from Spain and Portugal, especially after their expulsion in 1492. Jews living in the Mediterranean area had been influenced more by the surrounding (Muslim) culture than those in the Christian north, more integrated into the local society, as witness the growth of Jewish poetry in the eleventh century. This process of integration often involved a partial emancipation and sometimes conversion. In general this change happened earlier in the south, even in Christian societies. Rabbi Leon Modena of Venice (1571–1648) noted the difference between northern European and Italian Jews, some of whom were from Spain. Many of them, he said, keep 'drafts and pictures in their house, especially if they are not in relievo, nor a whole body but only the face'.[21] Icons of a restricted kind were allowed. When the Renaissance came, it had of course a strong influence on Jewish life in Italy, especially among 'court' and 'merchant' Jews, just as had previously been the case among those in Muslim Spain. In the later Maghreb, many looked back to the golden age of their civilization before their expulsion from Spain at the end of the fifteenth century. There they contributed to science, especially medical, to philosophy and to poetry, areas which were relatively neutral in religious terms. Not only did Jews in the south contribute to science, but they even broke the iconoclastic prohibition, choosing to make the word of God beautiful contrary to their religion's rejection of representation. The 'beautification of the commandment' was an obligation which took a variety of forms involving images, especially book illumination and marriage contracts. In the north the change came later and the end of the eighteenth century saw the birth of the Haskala movement. This was the progenitor of Zionism and was obviously influenced by the European Enlightenment, itself the heir to the Renaissance. The Haskala was associated in Germany with the name of Moses Mendelssohn (1729–86), and aimed to get Jews to learn European languages, abandon Yiddish and to

[20] Waldman 1997: 104.   [21] Modena 1637.

'modernize' in other ways. Jews in Germany were much more 'modern' even than those in nearby Galicia, as we see in the autobiography of the philosopher Maimon, who made a pilgrimage to Berlin to become a doctor and met Mendelssohn there. In his search for knowledge he lost his very restrictive faith and at one time he almost became a Christian.

By and large in much of the north of Europe Jewish society remained closed, except for a few men like Spinoza or Marx who abandoned Judaism altogether and some like Einstein and Freud who radically modified their faith. The reasons were clear. At the end of the eighteenth century Maimon writes of 'the rabbinical despotism [of Galicia] which by the power of superstition has established its throne for many centuries'.[22] When he went to Germany to learn the 'truth', he was considered an 'atheist' and did indeed try to become an unbelieving Christian. Secularity was essential to him and he eventually abandoned the faith altogether in order 'to enlighten the Jewish nation'. But he had received 'too much education to return to Poland, to spend my life in misery without rational occupation or society, and to sink back into the darkness of superstition and ignorance, from which I had delivered myself with so much labour'.[23] Maimon was actually refused meals by a Jewish resident of Berlin who saw him as paying so much attention to the 'sciences' (mainly philosophy) that he was considered to have neglected the study of the Talmud. Indeed, he was almost driven from the town because he carried with him some writings of his namesake, the Spanish philosopher Maimonides.[24] The orthodox looked upon all study of the sciences and philosophy as being 'something dangerous to religion and good works', as encouraging the scepticism which was characteristic of some Polish rabbis and especially of Maimon himself.[25]

When the immigrant Jews abandoned their iconophobia and similar restrictions, especially towards the end of the nineteenth century, there was a great burst of activity in many spheres. From being against images, they suddenly shifted to the other extreme. In the cinema they practically ran and owned Hollywood. On the New York stage it was the same. In painting and sculpture, they made enormous contributions. Chagall came from a rural northern background near Yitebsk, migrated to France to be rid of restrictions and to become an influential painter. He was the first major Jewish painter and went to Paris to get away from his shtetl in order to pursue his career. This change in orientation happened within one generation and represented not so much a rebirth as a birth, but none the less one that had many resemblances with the great efflorescence of

---

[22] Maimon 1954: 138.   [23] Maimon 1954: 126.
[24] Maimon 1954: 107–8.   [25] Maimon 1954: 92.

artistic activity that took place in Italy and the whole of Europe in the sixteenth century, involving a partial release from the religious restrictions of the Christian church. Emancipation meant the equivalent release from Judaic ones.

Previous to this period, there had been little representational art in the Jewish tradition. According to Maimonides, just to imagine God in a figurative manner was wrong. Even today there is in effect no figuration in a religious context, nothing except abstraction in the synagogue, neither sculptured monument nor flowers in the cemetery. In the Jewish museum at Prague there is certainly some painting of Jewish ancestors but this is rare. In Europe the essential breakthrough in the visual arts took place only towards the end of the nineteenth century, especially with the massive migration of the Ashkenazi to the New World about 1880.

This period in Jewish life is sometimes known as the Emancipation. But emancipation from what? From the restraints put on the Jews by the Christian community? At least equally important was the release from the restraints that were part of Jewish religion, as the autobiography of Maimon makes clear. Hobsbawm writes that earlier on, while Jews lived in gentile societies, whose languages and cuisine they adopted and adapted, 'only rarely and intermittently were they able, and, what is equally to the point, willing to participate in the cultural and intellectual life of these wider societies'.[26] Jewish education was largely religious and restrictive; it inhibited contact with others and with their learning, except on a very limited front. 'Rabbinical authority banned philosophy, science and other branches of knowledge of non-Jewish origins' except medicine, even, in parts, foreign languages.[27] Only religion was studied, but they did teach all their male flock to read. Learning to make a living was taught not at the school but in the house, so that it was normally his father's trade that a boy followed. There was a distinct opposition here between learning about religion and learning about ordinary life. Education at school should not lead to material advantage,[28] hence a trade was learned in the family and by apprenticeship, producing a certain immobility especially as far as modern knowledge was concerned. Women were rarely included among the 'literati', except some in medieval Spain, and they learnt their religion and their work in a familial context, by imitation. Occasionally they were given an elementary education, but generally in Judaism, as in Islam and early Christianity, women did not play a primary role in the religious life and therefore were not given a religious training.

In northern Europe emancipation took place after the French Revolution of 1789 (when religious creeds were abolished in favour of

---

[26] Hobsbawm 2005: 16.   [27] Hobsbawm 2005: 16.   [28] Zafrani 1996: 315.

worshipping Reason and even cemeteries were secularized) and then
following the revolution of 1830. After 1848 Jews were especially prominent in revolutionary politics, but that applied only to an elite and not
everywhere. However, the attitude of rural conservatism changed radically with the migration to cities when the newcomers took on the urban
values that surrounded them and were no longer imprisoned in the framework of their shtetl or village. It was a migration that took place on
an enormous scale. The number of Jews in Vienna jumped from fewer
than four thousand in 1848 to 175,000 on the eve of the First World
War. Urbanization meant emancipation and when that happened 'it is
as though the lid had been removed from a pressure cooker'.[29] As was
written of a Galician immigrant coming to Petticoat Lane in London,
'[p]erpetually thwarted for centuries by discrimination and insularity
or able to express itself only rabbinically, my grandfather's life finally
exploded, like compressed oil deposits from a suddenly tapped well'.[30]
From being against images, the migrants suddenly shifted to the other
extreme. The change was revolutionary, as in earlier Christendom.
However, this eruption of a large ethnic/religious group of 'outsiders'
into a formally Christian society had other consequences, increasing anti-
Semitism in the towns and the work place. To some the Jews were more
'dangerous' after emancipation than before as there was more intensive
competition for social space.

    In Morocco too, early schools among the Jews were for teaching a dis-
tinct religious rather than a common, secular, curriculum. Remnants of
this division mark many schools to this day. Here they were 'essentially
intended to give the child, especially the boy, the means of participating
in the practice of the cult',[31] to make him part of the community. The
role of the teacher was to augment education received in the family, 'to
teach them to read the Torah'.[32] The aim of education was therefore
not to prepare the child for life but to train him in religion. Elementary
education (at the *heller*) was virtually universal for males, unlike in Christianity or Islam where it was more voluntaristic, and it was completed
with the bar mitzvah at about thirteen years of age when traditionally the
boy had to deliver a sermon in the synagogue. After that, certain pupils
proceed to the yeshiva for a rabbinical education. As a consequence of
the earlier training no male was illiterate; all had a training in religion
which culminated with a ceremony introducing them to adulthood but
also making them members of the cult.

---

[29] Hobsbawm 2005: 16.   [30] Miller 2006: 112.
[31] Zafrani 1996: 309.   [32] Zafrani 1996: 360.

There is no doubt, writes Hobsbawm, that in the minds of the emancipators two changes were essential in the traditional state of affairs: a degree of secularization and education in the national language, both of which went hand in hand.[33] By 'secularization' he means not the loss of Jewish faith but the establishment of a religion that was no longer 'the unremitting, omnipresent and all-encompassing framework of life. Instead, however important, it fitted only a part of life.' The same could be said of the Italian Renaissance; it involved not the abandonment of the Christian religion but its confinement to a more limited area of existence. Education was at least partly, if not wholly, withdrawn from the jurisdiction of the church and linked to citizenship. As a result of the French Revolution, learning in a German public school was initially universal, but in Galicia (and most European Jews lived in Poland) one learnt Hebrew letters in a religious establishment.

Emancipation had happened earlier in a more fragmented, segmented way. As we have seen, there were periods in Spain and the Maghreb when Jews were strongly influenced by the surrounding Islamic culture, when they went back intermittently to Greek and other forms of knowledge. In turn they too influenced the Italian Renaissance. Though Judaism was not known for women participating in the arts, in Spain in the Middle Ages we find a school of Jewish women writing verse including love poetry, which was again greatly influenced by the surrounding Arab culture. Medieval Jews, even males, were not normally poets in a secular sense. In Palestine, the Piyyut was part of the liturgy. But from the tenth century the centre of gravity of Judaism moved from east to west and poetic practice passed to Spain, where it was much influenced by local forms. Imitating Muslim styles, there was 'a tendency to emerge from the domain of the sacred'.[34] Firstly, poetry was used for polemical purposes and then like its local counterparts it became 'a poetry of prestige which expressed taste and love of art, and where one could see a desire to compete with high society and the Christian and Muslim intellectual elites'.[35] So that in many ways tenth-century Spanish Judaism was very different from that of their co-religionists elsewhere.

Emancipation also affected other types of representation both in the form of the theatre and of fiction. The theatre was forbidden to Jews, as it was to Muslims and Christians. Over time there was some relaxation in all three creeds. The Christians were first and eventually allowed religious drama in the form of mystery plays after which the secular was revived in the Renaissance, beginning with Mussato in Italy. In Lebanon, the Shia

---

[33] Hobsbawm 2005.   [34] Zafrani 1996: 126.
[35] From the tenth-century work of Moshe ibn Ezra (1993).

community developed a religious play about the death of Ali. In Europe, Jews produced a drama on the life of Queen Esther which was acted at the festival of Sukhot and was much influenced by the Christian miracle play. Although there was minimal theatrical activity in either Judaism or Islam, a real change took place among the former towards the end of the nineteenth century, creating a tradition of Yiddish drama, together of course with playwrights, actors and *metteurs en scène*. As mentioned earlier, Hollywood got taken up in this burst of Jewish activity, both at the level of performance and of finance, and the new film industry became dominated by their participation, as they became leaders of the American visual media that spread right around the world (though not to such an extent in the written cultures of India or China). This representational activity was also part of a birth rather than a rebirth, connected as it was with emancipation, but it was a break-out from the strict religion of the rabbis rather than from the ghetto of the gentiles. Previously there had been the occasional illustration in the Torah and little else. This change had some similarity with the Italian Renaissance because there too secularization meant the arts were freer to move outward; the artists and dramatists of Christian Europe had found a way around the restrictions imposed by a dominant hegemonic religion that had at first only allowed artistic activity in the sacred sphere. In Christian Europe the major breakthrough to secular representation came with the Renaissance, in Judaism with emancipation towards the end of the nineteenth century among the Reformed, in parts of Islam with colonization and the influence of Europe (and earlier of China).

Some of the 'sciences' were less influenced by the restrictions of religion, some more so. In general, philosophy came under a definite interdict since its speculations ran into problems with religions in that it substituted 'rationality' for faith and could challenge the cleric's vision of the world beyond. But enquiries into this world too might run counter to what was laid down in the Bible and the Quran. Experiment was not welcome where faith had already decided what was the right view. Sometimes experiment was expressly forbidden, as in surgery with the cutting up of the human body. But there were other areas that were relatively free. The practice of medicine, everywhere in demand, made some advance, especially in pharmaceutics since knowledge of plants and their qualities became particularly extensive. Practice and research in medicine was carried out separately in the *maristans* of the Arab world, by Muslims, by Jews and by Christians, in hospitals and universities in Europe. In some technical subjects too like communications (paper-making but not printing) and agriculture (water-control) the Near East saw a number of developments with little interference from religious sources. Moreover, encouraging literacy and knowledge brought fame to dynasties and to courts so here again there was some freedom in various spheres including the arts. While the pursuit of religious learning under Islam took place in the madrasas, work in the sciences was carried out less formally in palaces, in libraries, in hospitals, in observatories and in learned societies. In the sciences, apart from the hospitals and observatories teaching was not institutionalized in the same way as religious knowledge in the madrasas or yeshivas, nor as religious or secular learning in later universities. However, technology was more or less free to advance on its own, whether in medicine, in shipping, in farming or in communication, except for the ban on the mechanization of writing under Islam which excluded printing, either that from China or, with the press, from Europe.

Under all religions, but especially the Abrahamistic ones, an enquiry into the nature of the world came face to face with the transcendental. That is what religion is about. In Islam the secular sciences, known as the 'foreign sciences' or the 'sciences of the ancients', had to be distinguished from the Muslim sciences 'created by qu'uranic exegesis'. 'Relations between the one and the other were open, restricted or qualified, according to the place, the time, and the individuals.'[36] That alternation between the religious and the secular (sciences) marked the intellectual history of Islam and it affected the communities embedded in their midst. There were always individuals and movements that concentrated on the scriptures. There were others who developed the work of the 'secular sciences', especially in mathematics, in astronomy and in medicine. In medicine this work took place in the context of the hospital, much developed under Islam. Astronomy was carried out in the observatory and often promoted in parts of Islam as a means of timing ceremonies. But in general the ancient sciences were not included in a normal Islamic education, certainly as taught in the madrasas. These latter were overwhelmingly for religious instruction. That was not so different in Christianity nor in Judaism. Monastic and cathedral schools concentrated upon religious tuition; until humanism, classical texts did not play a central part in education, though these schools always provided a wider education. In the Jewish yeshiva too, it was religious works that pupils learnt (often by heart). 'Ancient sciences' were pursued by them in hospitals, though since the Jews never had a state after the Roman period, it was in hospitals attached to another creed. Individual rabbis followed a medical career, and taught some medicine to others as well as translating texts from Greek and Arabic, as at Lunel near

[36] Jacquart 2005: 46.

Montpellier. But it was religious instruction that was dominant in their schools.

The fact that Jews had no state of their own but lived where other religions were dominant also meant that they were necessarily influenced by the policies and institutions of the hosts. For example, in the south Jewish medicine was strongly affected by Arab practice, and of course affected that practice in turn. Constantine the African, who brought much medical knowledge to Italy from North Africa and the Near East, was possibly a Jew originally living among Arabs at Carthage. There is much evidence of Jewish practitioners in Arab and in Christian lands. The same applied to other fields of learning, of philosophy for example in the work of Maimonides. Jewish scholars always had a great deal to do with books and with texts as all the males were taught literacy from an early age and, because of their interstitial position, they often became adept at translating from one language to another, especially from Arabic, another Semitic language. In this way they became acquainted with the scholarship and with the writing of others, even of the arts.

But in global comparison these achievements borrowed from their neighbours were initially somewhat partial; with emancipation there was a sudden outburst. Hobsbawm writes of 'the explosive transformation of this impact [of the Jews on the outside world] in the 19th and 20th centuries'; that is to say, since 'the emancipation and self-emancipation of the Jews began in the late 18th century'.[37] Before that, things had been very different. While Jews were often restricted in the occupations and activities they pursued, it was not only external restrictions that confined them but internal ones too. And both were tied to religion. For example, the absence of Jewish artists in the European Middle Ages was partly due to the fact that all art (for example, all drama, most fiction) was specifically Christian (with the church and occasionally the court as patron or recipient) but also because the Bible laid down prohibitions against figurative representation, which the Jews and the Muslims observed although the Christians no longer did, anyhow for religious art. The restrictions were both internal and external.

However, even religious knowledge itself was not completely static. Reformations took place, as in all written religions. Zafrani writes of 'a renaissance of Hebrew studies' in Old Cairo at the end of the tenth century.[38] The Karaites, who trace their origin to the end of the eighth century, rejected orthodox law and appealed directly to the words of the Bible for the authority of their faith. Their opponents were the Rabbinites, who were also compelled to re-examine the actual words of the scriptures

---

[37] Hobsbawm 2005:16.   [38] Zafrani 1996: 70.

to justify their own teaching. All this led to a 're-opening of the Jewish mind and imagination to the actual words of the Bible'.[39] But religion remained dominant. Initially even the secular had to be sacralized in order to be considered respectable. Although the Song of Songs was basically a secular piece of love poetry, we know it only because of its allegorical interpretation which made it suitable for preserving by the rabbis. 'After the close of the canon, we have to wait for more than a thousand years before Hebrew secular poetry appears again on the scene, as an important part of the renaissance of Hebrew poetry in Spain in the tenth century.'[40] But that again was under the outside influence of Islam. In other times non-Jewish models were frowned upon, and there was a reluctance 'to embark on an activity which might be construed to be contrary to the law and customs of the Jews'. However, in Spain they took an enthusiastic part in this rediscovery of the Hebrew Bible and that return to the scriptures affected the subject of their poetry. This looking back occurred in the religious domain but not in the secular, not until later when they became influenced to a yet greater extent by the Arab cultures that surrounded them; then they followed their masters in much of the subject matter of poetry.

In these changes in Judaism, whether occasional or long term, the economy was highly significant. Not only did the growth of all 'leisure activities' require a certain level of prosperity, but trading, in which Jews were often involved, required a measure of both literacy and numeracy, and brought the community into relations with other cultures, as in the case of those who traded so vigorously in the Mediterranean, with the west coast of India, and established settlements in both places.

In conclusion, elements of a cultural renascence, whether as an explicit reference back to what is perceived as a previous, now vanished, period of glory, or as simply a burst forward to a golden age, perhaps an opening up to influences from outside, have appeared throughout the history of written cultures. In the case of the Jewish Emancipation, the efflorescence arose not so much from looking back as from looking around. The stimuli for the departure from purely religious thinking and scholarship were usually provided by influential neighbours – by Islam, by Christian Europe or by the Asiatic world. In the last and the next two chapters I examine written cultures which experienced a renascence in a stricter sense than that which changed the face of Judaism, since these often involved a direct appeal to the past: initially in Islam reference was made to Greek and other texts in translation as well as to the Quran, in India this referral was largely religious, in China it was secular

[39] Goldstein 1965: 16.   [40] Goldstein 1965: 12.

to the works of Confucius and others. But only in the Abrahamistic creeds was there a need to break away from a hegemonic religion, though Islam (and the Sephardic Judaism buried within it) had periods which, if they did not lead to long-term secularization, at least resulted in an emphasis on the 'ancient sciences' and eventually influenced the Italian Renaissance.

6   Cultural continuity in India

with S. Fennell

When we set about evaluating the various periods and facets of Asian cultures from the standpoint of renascences, one of the questions raised by India and by China is that both cultures display a considerable amount of continuity, linguistically, culturally and in other respects. Despite the vicissitudes of the dynasties, the invasions of peoples from the north and the ongoing development of the society, this continuity raises the question of whether any major cultural rebirth was called for since there was not the same discontinuity as in Europe or the Near East. In other words, this continuity excludes the possibility of rebirth but not of florescence. In India, the continual looking back to the Vedic scriptures and to the great epics have provided a more or less constant source of inspiration. At the same time, no hegemonic, monotheistic religion intervened to keep people away from the classics, as happened to the west. Indeed, India always had not only a plurality of gods and religions but also its own tradition of secular thought. So it scarcely required a process of 'disenchantment of the world' to modify any such creed in a secular direction and towards their classics.

The continuity is partly due to the longevity of Sanskrit, the language in which the earliest Hindu texts were written down; it has since been revived many times and still has not only a very substantial and ongoing role in the liturgical, ritual and intellectual life (it is lavishly employed at weddings and other sacramental occasions), but in a few parts is even spoken as a first language.[1] With the exception of the Indian Punjab (where 60 per cent are Sikhs, and Hinduism the largest minority faith), and despite considerable muhallas (neighbourhoods) of Muslims in a number of cities such as Lucknow and Hyderabad, and the sprinklings

---

[1] This is a long established tradition in Mathoor and Hosahalli in Karnataka (where a number of Muslim families also speak it); there are also numerous second-language conversational speakers of Sanskrit in Mohaka near Jabalpur in Madhyapradesh, in Varanasi and in a number of the large temple cities both in the Gangetic belt and in the south.

of those and Buddhists and Christians, both rural and urban, in virtually all parts of the country, the Hindu religion, embodied in these
Sanskrit texts, remains the central one for the majority of people. Buddhism, which was at one time very important, had been largely swal-
lowed up by Hinduism, although it is now making a comeback amongst
the Dalit ('untouchable') community. Jainism is practised among the
merchant sector but is also less significant than it was. Hinduism has
been reformed and reformulated at various times, a process that has
inevitably involved a looking back towards the classical, Vedic scriptures and their commentaries. But as distinct from western Europe, there
was no hiatus with classical culture as there was when Rome declined
and Christianity or Islam arose; despite political conquests, campaigns of
conversion to imported faiths, and repeated diversification and reintegra-
tion of the majority creed, there has been considerable continuity since
early times. Indian science too continued to make some progress between
the sixth and the twelfth centuries, even during the period of Dark Ages in
Europe.

As with the Abrahamistic religions, even in this now iconic culture
there was some tendency in Hinduism towards the non-representation of
sacred objects, at least until the time of Alexander's appearance. According to Partha Mitter, '[a]part from pottery we have little evidence of
art until the third century BCE',[2] while the Vedic scriptures contain no
mention of the worship of images.[3] The first few centuries of Buddhist
art were figuratively aniconic and it was only with the advent of Greek,
or Indo-Greek, art that for the first time the Buddha was figured.[4] It
is also the case, as with Di in China, that the High God in Hindu religion, namely Brahma, is virtually unrepresented in sculpture, and the
most revered representations even of Shiva are non-figurative and phallic
pillars (and indeed sometimes invisible or imaginary ones). We cannot
say that Buddhist art saw a renascence, since there was nothing figurative beforehand to be reborn. But that form of representation came
as an efflorescence marking a new era (plate 5).[5] However, in the later
Hindu tradition itself there was no widespread discontinuity, no sudden
shift from aniconism to figurative representation, from the religious to
the secular or from the partly indigenous, partly Achaemenid-influenced
monumental art of the Mauryan period (still fairly limited), to the distinctly artisanal and partly narrative sculpture of the early stupas around

---

[2] Mitter 2001: 9.   [3] Thapar 2002: 129.
[4] This absence (and the role of Greek art) is now disputed.
[5] In religious terms, aniconism was for the most part a crystallization of tendencies and
elements already existent within Hinduism – perhaps not unlike the Protestant elements
and sentiments pre-existent in Catholicism in fifteenth-century Europe.

the time of the Christian epoch; there was no great explosion in figurative art, and its gradual growth probably resulted from a link between secular political patronage and the Brahmanical institutions that legitimized their rule (plate 6).

There was a looking back to classical times but there was no decisive intellectual break as there had been in Europe, although in certain areas a discontinuity occurred through the Muslim and British conquests. Nevertheless there was no comparable hiatus of a general kind (except, as we have seen, with early Buddhism) and religion did not really involve the rejection of other knowledge in the same way as happened in Europe with the coming of Christianity as a hegemonic creed. Nevertheless, higher education was largely religious and hence restricted. Indian science did not make as spectacular progress as the Chinese, but it was not faced with a theologically aggressive religion whose sacred writings supposedly held all the keys to the universe. Despite the overwhelming religious element, the early Indians recognized 'natural law'.[6] Hinduism did not see itself as at loggerheads with the practical or mathematical sciences, nor as competing for a monopoly of explanatory authority. In any case alternative modes of thought were available, which is important in considering the European Renaissance where the return to the classics meant at least a degree of secularization. As we shall see, Indian science saw periods of obvious vigour and apparent inactivity, of florescence and sterility, but it did not have to reject a divine interpretation in so dramatic a manner as occurred in Europe. While higher education was associated with religious learning – often Buddhist and therefore combatted by Muslims and other invaders – it had always included secular subjects which might be developed separately, as with astronomy and medicine. Moreover, a thread of atheistic thought existed in India, which continued to be present despite the hold of the dominant Hinduism, and was more favourable to scientific enquiry. In other words, there was development in both the arts and sciences over time which meant that the idea of a rebirth was not called for in the same way and change in these areas was slowly evolutionary rather than revolutionary. By referring to this relatively stable continuum we do not imply the sort of unchanging India that was beloved of early European writers like Max Müller and Baden Powell, with an idyllic notion of a static village life. For there was frequent movement in the historical trajectory of the country, in its urban and rural life, in its trade both with the east and west, in its arts and sciences. But in respect of religion and iconography, there was not the discontinuity we find in the west. The social historian Romila Thapar writes of 'the impressive

[6] Subbarayappa, 'Resumé', 1971: 572.

continuity of the major social institutions over many centuries'.[7] In *A History of India*, she elaborates:

[t]hat the study of institutions did not receive much emphasis was in part due to the belief that they did not undergo much change: an idea which also fostered the theory that Indian culture has been a static, unchanging culture for many centuries, largely owing to the lethargy of the Indian and his gloomy, fatalistic attitude to life. This of course is an exaggeration. Even a superficial analysis of the changing social relationships within the caste structure, or the agrarian systems, or the vigorous mercantile activities of Indians throughout the centuries, points to anything but a static socio-economic pattern. It is true that at certain levels there is in India a continuous cultural tradition extending over three thousand years, but this continuity should not be confused with stagnation.[8]

For continuity did not mean immobility but rather a durability of specific features. At times there was considerable differentiation in parts of India, especially with regard to views about the sacred and the secular. There were cultural efflorescences at various times which were often connected with a looking back to Vedic or Hindu religion or to a revival of Sanskrit.

Early on, like the Near East and China, India had an advanced Bronze Age culture, known as the Harappan, which flourished along the Indus Valley and saw the growth of an urban society, together with the many crafts that accompanied it, including a system of writing which has not yet been satisfactorily deciphered. 'The Indus civilization was the most extensive of the ancient riverine civilizations', extending its contacts to the Pamirs (for lapis lazuli) and to Oman (possibly for copper).[9] It was an early literate metal-using society (which entailed exploration), possibly stimulated by the Fertile Crescent, that seems to have developed out of the Neolithic cultures along the Indo-Iranian border. Those began around the eighth or seventh millennium (e.g. at Mehrgarh) with wheat and barley, sheep and goats, together with Indian humped cattle, but no pottery until a millennium later. In the second phase, we find an increasing number of granaries plus the remains of massive walls, almost monumental architecture, and a wealth of new activities, including the use of copper and ivory. In the early third millennium, this culture appears to have led on to the Harappan with its brick-built walled cities but lacking the plough, though with a large granary (possibly),[10] temple mounds and cemeteries in the largest towns, including a great bath at Mohenjodaro, the growing of cotton though not of rice, the making of textiles, and with a

---

[7] Thapar 1997: 43.   [8] Thapar 1968, 1: 19–20.   [9] Thapar 2002: 80.
[10] This granary is now thought to be a 'great hall' (Kenoyer 1998: 64; Guha 2005) and the existence of temple mounds is in some doubt.

proliferation of specialist crafts in the towns which were constructed near to river beds for access to water. In terms of public works, the cities of the Harappan civilization seem to have been well in advance of any other Bronze Age settlement. The mature phase emerged about 2600 BCE, roughly the period of Sargon of Akkad in Mesopotamia. This society continued until about 1750 BCE and judging by the standard of material culture it was remarkably uniform, suggesting a centralized regime that may have contributed to some elements in later Hindu life even today. Thapar notes a reappearance of various objects in Harappan society in later worship – the *pipal*, the bull, female figurines, the Horned Deity. Though this is now disputed, the prehistorian Gordon Childe (like the present excavator, J. M. Kenoyer) was already impressed at the Indian-ness of Harappan culture; he wrote that it was already specifically Indian and formed the basis of modern culture, as in the aspects of the life revealed on seals, such as the one representing what has been controversially called a Shaivaite *lingam*.[11] This specification is an exaggeration; we do not know definitely of such an identification as the script itself has not yet been deciphered. On the other hand, the seals themselves indicate the considerable commerce that took place with Mesopotamia, where writing was closely linked to mercantile activity.[12] Was the notion of writing derived from there? It is unlikely to have developed from local potters' marks, as suggested, since writing was an urban pursuit.[13]

The unity of the Harappan culture is visible in the common weights and measures as well as in the art forms, especially on seals, all connected with worship (or alternatively with children's toys!) including the illustration of positions later used in *yoga*, similar animal representations, supernatural figures and the use of the swastika. The country traded widely, particularly from the dock of Lothal in Gujerat along the (Iranian) Makran coast to Mesopotamia, where Harappan seals have been found, but not vice versa, indicating the dominant direction of trade.[14] The Indus civilization came to a close, probably through hydro-climatic factors[15] rather than by incoming Indo-Iranian-speaking peoples as was once thought

---

[11] See B. B. Lal (1997) who doubts this identification on the grounds that the object is too general. The archaeologist Marshall found no evidence of a temple at Mohenjodaro, and there are alternative explanations for the apparent phallus, the icon for which was fairly widespread in some early cultures (in Rome, for example). As far as Shiva is concerned, the word only occurs adjectivally in the Vedas in relation to Rudra, the god from whom Shiva is supposed to have evolved in the Puranas, where there is no evidence of phallic worship in Vedic times.

[12] Schmandt-Besserat 1996.   [13] Kenoyer 1998: 41.   [14] Kenoyer 1998: 101.

[15] See Appendix to Lal 1997, which discredits the various suggestions of Aryan immigration. For a similar argument, though offering a variety of different reasons, see Kennedy in Erdosy 1995: 46–66.

(the previous language being hypothetically Dravidian, south Indian), and the focus of urban society moved to the Ganges basin. But this early city civilization nonetheless left its mark on subsequent India; the new culture-bearers absorbed something (though possibly not much) of what had already existed. As we have seen, a few motifs, such as the *pipal*, continued down into later history.[16]

The ending of the Harappan period led to what historians have called a dark age, with the decline of towns and the disappearance of both the script and the seals.[17] Afterwards the re-emergence of large-scale town life towards the end of the second millennium occurred in the Gangetic plain and in coastal south India, where the growth of settlements was connected with the expansion of trade in both directions, to Asia and to the Mediterranean. The caste system seems already to have been present and Sanskritic 'literature' (in an oral form) is claimed to have emerged, together with various types of Hinduism and later, in the middle of the first millennium BCE, Buddhism. Iron and the horse also became important at this time.

However, the presence of non-material, oral and religious forms like Vedic hymns is obviously much more difficult to assess. As Whitney long ago declared, '[a]ll the data given in Indian literary history are like skittles set up for being knocked down'.[18] It is claimed that the early texts, the hymns of the Rig-Veda, were composed in the 'Vedic Age' around 1500–1300 BCE, probably in the Punjab.[19] Some would claim the date of 800 BCE for the end of this period, but the text is likely to have been written down only much later in Gupta Brahmi or in the Siddham alphabetic script rather than the presumably logographic one of Harappa. In fact, our earliest extant manuscript is datable only to the eleventh century CE. According to Winternitz, some scholars put the age of the Rig-Veda as far back as between 3000 and 2500 BCE, others at 1000 BCE.[20] The problem relates to the date given for the development of so-called 'Aryan culture' in India. Winternitz rejects the relevance of astronomical material, is dubious about linguistic aspects, regards the cuneiform inscriptions as uncertain, and so goes back to the evidence arising out of the history of Indian literature itself. That turns on the presupposition by Buddhist works of the existence of the Veda, which brings us to 400 BCE for their canon. But from there he goes back further to around 2000 or 2500 as the starting point for the Veda, with the end point between 750 and 500 BCE.[21] He says little about any

[16] Thapar 2002: 85.   [17] Thapar 1997: 36.   [18] Cited in Winternitz 1981 [1907], 1: 22.
[19] Macdonell 1993 [1917]: xi–xii.   [20] Winternitz 1981 [1907], 1: 270.
[21] Winternitz 1981 [1907], 1: 288.

script, except that an alphabetic form in which those texts may have been written was most likely used earlier than the third-century inscriptions (questionable claims have been made for the fifth century) because it was not 'a new invention'.[22]

This remains much too early for Romila Thapar, who writes: '[t]he versions [of the epics] we have today are generally placed in a chronological bracket between the mid-first millennium BC to the mid-first millennium AD'.[23] Of course, the dates are again purely speculative for they depend upon oral transmission. 'The hymns were memorized meticulously and transmitted orally over many centuries before being written.'[24] But how can we possibly know this? It seems to be at odds with what we now understand of the transmission of lengthy recitations. Oral memory, she claims, was developed by repetition 'making the composition almost unalterable . . . Education was in theory open to the twice-born, although the curriculum of formal education was useful largely to brahmans.'[25] This hypothetical 'oral' school sounds very much like an early literate one. Do we know of any reliable precedent for such transmission in the preliterate world? The evidence needs to be carefully evaluated.

Thapar writes of 'myth' that '[o]ral sources were sometimes preserved through being so carefully memorized that the text almost came to be frozen, as in some of the Vedic ritual compositions'.[26] Alternatively, she goes on, it was less frozen and more open, as with the *Mahabharata*. The first is possible for certain types of short verbal material. But we cannot know of continuity for any specific composition, especially a long one, unless there is already a written record. Continuity has recently been shown to be the case with the memorization of the Vedic texts. As with the Quran or the Bible, this is possible where there is a written text in the background. One must remain sceptical of such claims for purely oral cultures, which means opting for the second, flexible alternative for such compositions, and existing knowledge would support this.[27] For transmission of longer recitations over time has been shown to involve not simply minor variations but very substantial changes.[28] This understanding radically affects the question of the continuity of 'non-material' contributions from earlier cultures. However, in India there is a problem even with literary texts since 'the epics, as we have them today, were not necessarily written at a precise point in time'.[29] They have been edited, interpolated and no longer have a single datable authorship.

[22] Winternitz 1981 [1907], 1: 27.   [23] Thapar 2002: 101.   [24] Thapar 2002: 111.
[25] Thapar 2002: 126.   [26] Thapar 2002: xxii.   [27] Goody 1993: chapter 4.
[28] Goody and Gandah 2002: xiii–xxvii.   [29] Thapar 2002: xxiii.

It was this Vedic literature that became the basis for the Hindu religion as well as for the education, including in science, to which it was closely tied. Repeating the words of the Rig-Veda (whenever composed) was an important part of learning for upper-caste males, so important that, as we have seen, many have claimed this work as having been transmitted orally over a long period in the distant past. But in the recent times for which we have evidence of 'oral' recitation there is little doubt that Brahman teachers had written copies of the text to which they could always refer.[30] As in other early literate traditions, especially in religious contexts which are by definition highly conservative (the words of the divine are ineffable, everlasting), the memorization of a written text was a significant part of education. Even when such forms of rote memory were no longer strictly necessary, they were much encouraged for the Quran and for the Bible. One did not really *know* a text until one could recite it from memory, a sentiment often still heard today; ability to recite is commonly regarded as a criterion for knowing one's Wordsworth or one's Shakespeare.

Basham, the cultural historian, argues that 'a long period' must have elapsed between the composition of the lost hymns of the Rig-Veda and the days of Buddhism – perhaps as much as 500 years – so that most of the Rig-Veda would have been composed between 1500 and 1000 BCE. But that is pure speculation buttressed by no convincing historical evidence.[31] That much is clear from the fact that some commentators have even given a date of 6000 BCE for their composition. Basham recognizes that the *Mahabharata* is of little use to the historian, less so than the *Iliad*, the *Nibelungenlied* or the Sagas, which have been edited in the same way in later times. Similar queries about chronology arise concerning the *Ramayana*, where the actual date for the famous battle varies between 3102 BCE and the ninth century, and was '[t]he product of an age very different from the one it purports to describe'.[32] Why cannot the same be true of the Vedic literature as it apparently was of the Homeric in its references to past times?

In India we have an example of a society that is always going back to its roots. But those roots are difficult to discern either in religions or in oral recitations. While Vedic 'literature' was said to have been transmitted orally, it is difficult to know what that means. The corpus is held to have consisted of four major 'texts', the Rig, the Sama, the Yajur and the Atharva-Veda, the first being the hymns of the Indo-European peoples who in the second millennium apparently came from the Iranian plateau, or possibly from the Punjab, speaking a version of Sanskrit. The entry of Indo-Europeans further east into the Mesopotamian world such as the

---

[30] Goody 1987.   [31] Basham 1967: 32.   [32] Basham 1967: 40.

Kassites, the Hittites or the Mitanis has been recorded in the cuneiform texts. Apparently it was they who moved into the Gangetic plain but the newcomers then took up aspects of the local culture; as for Harappan society, as we have seen, it is generally thought today that internal factors, including ecological, were the important ones which brought about its collapse, not an 'Aryan' invasion from outside. Therefore the latter could have come not as conquerors but as immigrants.

The text of the Avesta, the founding document of Zoroastrianism, is said to have been composed in the mid second millennium. The language is close to that of the Rig-Veda and by that time there was of course a consonantal alphabetic script, which was used for Aramaic, available in north Syria (Ugarit). The arrival of the alphabet brought to India by Aramaic merchants led to the development of the Brahmi script which is first recorded in the third century in the Prakrit edicts of the emperor Ashoka. Its use there shows some familiarity, so it may go back 'a few generations'.[33] Radiocarbon and thermoluminescence datings on mainland Tamil Nadu pottery have been said to present examples of Brahmi before Ashoka, for at least as early as the fifth century BCE; but the evidence is unsafe. There was apparently no continuity with the undeciphered, logographic script of the Indus civilization. However, Iranian Aramaic gave birth to a script, *kharosthi*, in north-west India when Achaemenid control over Gandhara took place in 530 BCE as the emperor Cyrus crossed the Hindu Kush. Achaemenid dominance ended c.330 BCE with the conquest of the empire by the Greek Alexander of Macedonia. This Iranian script may have been the one that the remarkable grammarian Panini refers to in the fifth century, although this contention is questionable.

One thing that writing did not make possible but simply explicit was the categorization of plants and animals, a process that is intrinsic to scientific advance and that in itself raises questions of the nature of species. This process is especially notable in the classification of animals, a field that later benefited from the descriptions of particular beasts that were much stimulated by the observations and accounts of the Mughal emperor Jahangir.

It is difficult to divorce Brahmans from writing. In the present day a Brahman has to appear at many a village ceremony bringing a prayer written out (or printed) on paper. Earlier it would have been on palm-leaf or possibly on wood. Their position as ritual specialists and as schoolmasters (transmitters of the Vedic texts) is bound up with their control of the written word, as of course was their role in administration. It is

---

[33] Thapar 2002: 163.

possible that long recitations of the *Mahabharata* type existed before the advent of alphabetic writing, but they would not have taken a fixed form. In court circles there were doubtless praise songs of some length that celebrated the dynasty's history in earlier times, especially in war. But we do not find Brahmans, as a group, as oral historians without the command of writing. Nor do we believe that long oral epics existed unchanged over the decades or even in identifiable form. The Bagre of the LoDagaa of northern Ghana changes a great deal over the relatively short space of time it has been recorded, making the idea of exact continuity difficult to maintain. It is true that the title of the Bagre remains the same, and the recitation is declared to be 'one' by the members, but in fact the name Bagre refers to very different versions; indeed, they are hardly versions of the same 'myth'. Even in the case of the Krishna story, this friend of the Pandavas was not always a god but sometimes appears in the *Mahabharata* as a herdsman. In the Indian case, there is no evidence of the handing down of an oral recitation in the form of the *Mahabharata*, nor can there be. And that it should remain even approximately the same goes against what we know about the limits of oral transmission and memory under these conditions. It therefore goes without saying that to posit the transmission of Vedic recitations or of the Hindu religion in anything like the form we know them today would be impossible (or at least highly unlikely). The religion, like the recitations, would be constantly changing, and not only in minor ways; oral communication involves invention.[34] Winternitz proposes that the Brahmans wanted to 'obtain writing' to 'fortify their power and influence',[35] inserting legends into the epic. It is difficult to see this latter happening without their control of a written means of communication, what I have called the technology of the intellect.[36] In any case, as I have argued, the epic poetry we know[37] is a feature of post-Bronze Age societies where writing in some form was already present.

The question of religion, to which Sanskrit was tied as the 'sacred' language, has affected the growth of culture in the widest and in the narrowest sense. The difference from Abrahamistic ones is notable. Thapar comments that '[r]eligion in early Indian history did not constitute a monolithic force... the idea of a state religion was absent'.[38] Hegemonic monotheism did not exist. The worship of local deities associated with fertility cults was widespread but less popular in the urban areas than the more puritanical sects of Buddhism and Jainism and the *bhakti* tradition of Hinduism. 'A third level included classical Hinduism and

[34] Goody and Gandah 2002.   [35] Winternitz 1981 [1907], 1: 298.   [36] Goody 1977.
[37] In Chadwick 1932, for example.   [38] Thapar 1997: 36.

more abstract levels of Buddhism and Jainism',[39] with a greater emphasis on major deities or on the teaching of the founders. For Hinduism, its measure of flexibility was largely responsible for its survival. Polytheistic religions did not demand exclusive allegiance in the same way as the major religions in the west. There was an 'orthodox' Hinduism, supported by Brahman scholars and their schools, but modifications of that religion flourished, in Puranic Hinduism, for example. Also in the Pallava dynasty of southern India (fourth–ninth century CE), some of the kings took a serious interest in the Alvars and Nayanars, who were religious teachers preaching a new form of Vaisnavism and Shaivism based on the widespread *bhakti* cult of personal devotion. The movement aimed to teach a popular Hinduism, preferring as its medium the local Tamil vernacular to the classical Sanskrit. This new *bhakti* cult represented a measure of change and especially among the lower castes was competitive with Buddhism and Jainism, both of which gradually declined in consequence, the former becoming influenced by Shaivite Tantric cults, though not before it had left its impress upon Hindu thought.[40] Jainism in turn was influenced by local fertility cults, especially in providing each god with a wife. At the same time a more orthodox Brahmanism also flourished – particularly the Shaivite sect from the time of Mahendravarman I (600–30 CE), receiving royal and other endowments of land on which it built temples (such as the complex at Mahabalipuram in the early seventh century) that served as schools of Vedic lore as well as centres of religious art.

Despite the fact that Hinduism had a focus in Brahman orthodoxy in its temple schools, there was the breadth of belief that a polytheistic religion itself entailed, as well as a certain amount of heterodoxy. For the religion continued over the years to incorporate a number of variants, including eventually Buddhism itself. Meanwhile Sanskrit acted as an important medium throughout the first millennium CE, not only for religion (even in Tamil – south Indian – areas, where it forever jostled with the local language in inscriptions, even resulting in a sizeable corpus of dual-language epigraphy) but for the arts as well. While Sanskrit was taken up more at some times than at others, and in some contexts made way for the local vernaculars, it continued as a learned tongue, both written and spoken, throughout the subcontinent, and remained a medium for the composition of plays and poetry. Linguistically there was no great gap in

---

[39] Thapar 1997: 36.
[40] The impact of *bhakti* can be perceived in local politics and religion after the seventh century CE, especially from the Chola period onwards until the sixteenth or seventeenth century CE. In the first millennium CE, Brahmanic worship makes its mark, but to conceive of a Hindu religion then, and for the period of the Vedic hymns, can be misleading.

Indian culture since the use of Sanskrit never died out; its cultural prestige continued but its use had both heydays and doldrums, movements that ebbed and flowed with commercial activity and with the fortunes of political and ecclesiastical patronage. As Toynbee remarks, it could not be reborn as it 'never tasted death'.[41]

Thus, through Sanskrit, there has been a regular looking back in orthodox Hinduism from the very beginning of the written word. This has produced orthodoxy but also not so much reformations as a breaking away to what many regard as new religions, which Hindus later saw as variants of their own, such as Buddhism, Jainism and even Sikhism. The diversity prevalent within even mainstream Hinduism easily explains this view. These new religions were basically anti-caste movements that exploited conflicts in the hierarchy intrinsic to Hinduism, the hierarchy that untouchables struggled against at various periods in Indian history and that eventually led Ambedkar and his followers in Maharashtra back to an independent Buddhism (as 'the neo-Buddhists'), that is, to move outside the mainstream altogether. However, it was not only belief that affected the destiny of this religious tradition but non-belief, 'atheism' too, which Max Müller referred to as 'adevism', without a god. Even though Hinduism was never a theologically prescriptive religion in the same sense as the Abrahamistic ones, it did imply an order of the world which was in some sense God-driven or transcendental. Yet even among the Rig-Veda hymns there are elements of scepticism, for example about the birth of the universe in the Creation hymn:

> Then even nothingness was not, nor existence...
> The gods themselves were later than creation,
> So who knows truly whence it has arisen?[42]

Hinduism was less prescriptive precisely because it retained some of the characteristics of religion formed in an oral culture, whereas the Abrahamistic religions were dependent from the very beginning upon an authority peculiar to the written word.[43] Although India was never under the control of a hegemonic religion, it had a written one that appealed back to the Rig-Veda; and it also developed a number of internal protest movements, including those that totally rejected the Brahmanic regime, indeed rejected all spiritual interpretations as well as the general division between the mind and the body. Such a protest movement was Lokayata, which meant 'demotic, that which is prevalent among the people',[44] and

---

[41] Toynbee 1954: 79.   [42] Basham 1967: 249–50.   [43] Goody 1986.
[44] Perhaps 'material-based', from 'world-relying'; the word seems to have been a Buddhist invention.

was obviously widespread. The question of whether this took a written form is disputed – we know of it mainly from the writings of its opponents who obviously adhered to another (spiritualist) creed. But its main doctrines appear to have been set out in the *Brihaspati Sutra*, said to have been composed around 600 BCE, of which extracts are preserved in the *Sarvadarshansansgraha* of the fifteenth-century Brahman Madhavacharya. But the only extant writing of the school is the *Tattvopaplavasimha* (or 'Upsetting of all principles')[45] by the extreme nihilist Jayarashi Bhatta (sixth century CE).[46]

Lokayata was highly sceptical of the benefits of sacrifice (not only Hindu) and of all beliefs in the supernatural, as well as of the caste system. It was distinctly non-Vedic and seems to have had some affinities with the earlier forms of both Buddhism and Jainism as well as the Ajivikas.[47] It has also been associated by some with Tantric rites and sexual rituals but the essential feature is its opposition to a supernaturalist interpretation of the world:

> While life is yours, live joyously;
> None can escape Death's searching eye:
> When once this frame of ours they burn,
> How shall it e'er again return?[48]

Naturally these worldviews were strongly opposed. But clearly it represents a secular element that was present in Indian thought and appears to have been associated with the work of scientists, especially in anatomy and physiology, just as Needham associated Taoism with Chinese science and just as a secularizing element was critical in the Italian Renaissance.[49] For religious individuals it was more difficult to enquire into fields where their creed considered it had already provided an answer. It was particularly hard to make a contribution in medicine; in theory, believers were often more concerned with the soul than with the body, and moreover in this case the caste system meant the twice-born could not touch dead bodies. Indian medicine was nonetheless very important; this was true not simply of Ayurvedic medicine, but especially of surgery, in which the Indians excelled.[50]

The Lokayata was looked upon not only as the worldview of the common people but also as more concerned with the study of nature and of

---

[45] Literally, 'reality-deluge-lion', i.e. reality-check, reality-scourge.
[46] Abul Fazl still mentions his followers as an appreciable force in the late sixteenth century; they attended a conference held by Akbar (Abu'l Fazl ibn Mubārak 1977–8 [1868–94], 3: 217–18).
[47] D. Chattopadhyaya 1959: xvi.   [48] Madhava Acharya 1914: ch. 1.
[49] Needham 1956: 33ff.; D. Chattopadhyaya 1959: 335.   [50] Subbarayappa 1971: 581.

taking a 'materialist' view, that is, not attributing causation to supernatural forces but rather accepting a more naturalistic standpoint. At the same
time the doctrine accounted for the generation of that world by sexual
activity, as also happened among some non-literate peoples (for example,
in the Bagre myth of the LoDagaa of Ghana).[51] That is, the generation
of the world was associated by analogy with the generation of humans,
with sexual intercourse. Hence the possible interest of the Lokayata in
such activity, as was the case with Tantrism. However this may be, their
approach was inevitably more oriented towards this world rather than the
next, to women, love-making and other popular activities, like Epicurus.
For the Lokayata, there was no God, no soul and no survival after death.

One commentator[52] actually writes of the period when this creed flourished as being a renaissance in Indian history.[53] The materialists talked
of freedom for all individuals. Like the Buddhists they were against Vedic
sacrifices, the memorizing of Vedic mantras, of repetitive rituals, the
caste system, magic and ascetic practices. Indeed, one feature probably
influenced another. 'India had been seething with free thinking and Buddha was the product of this freedom.'[54] The result of this movement,
writes Shastri, 'was the generation and propagation of different arts and
sciences'. Vatsyayara records some sixty-five names of Indian fine arts
which were probably encouraged in this period. It was a renascence in
the sense of an efflorescence, although this did not have the character of
looking back. But it did display a certain disregard of transcendentalism,
which for some was one aspect of the Italian Renaissance. So in both
there was an element of secularity. While art remains mainly religious,
other art did exist, some of it highly sensuous. In Europe medieval art was
'truly religious' with Gothic architecture itself being vertical, pointing to
the skies; the patrons of the work were religiously motivated. In India
the problem was rather different; for all sculpture made use of the female
form and was in the hands of secular craftsmen, who often provided their
work with a sensuous vitality.

The historian D. Chattopadhyaya notes that the Tantrikas too were
able to contribute to the study of the human body because of their materialist outlook; to which they also added the knowledge of alchemy and
of general chemistry.[55] Whereas the orthodox, especially those belonging to idealistic schools, were, as we have seen, actually prevented from
contributing to anatomy because, firstly, they were concerned primarily
with the soul, and, secondly, only lower castes would touch a dead body.
Tantrism on the other hand was affiliated 'to the crafts and professions

[51] Goody 1972.   [52] Shastri 1930.   [53] Shastri 1930.   [54] Shastri 1930: 22.
[55] D. Chattopadhyaya 1959: 335.

traditionally despised', as was Taoism in China; therefore they could investigate these domains without any ideological constraints.[56]

Indian scientific activity depended heavily on alchemy, although it was from the Muslims that the practice was passed to Europe about the twelfth century CE. In the more specific sense, alchemy revolved around two objectives, firstly the transmutation of base into noble metals, secondly, the preparation of the Elixir of Life for attaining immortality. The technique relied upon the processing of mercury and sulphur (which became cinnobar when combined), a practice that demanded a specialist laboratory and initiated assistants, and had purpose-built equipment. The beginnings of this alchemy may have occurred in China in the early centuries BCE, where it was especially associated with Taoism. It did not make its appearance in India until the fifth or sixth century CE, when it was linked with Tantrism and produced a voluminous literature. But it is also connected with ancient Egypt and its ideas were elaborated in Greek theories about the elements. Alchemy, which was practised throughout Eurasia, was undoubtedly the forerunner of and model for chemical experiments in the so-called 'scientific revolution' in Europe, and initially in Arabic these activities were not verbally distinguished. Chemistry proper only emerged in Europe at the end of the eighteenth century, when it offered a mechanical explanation of change.

In what has been called the early historical period (c.500–150 BCE), the consonantal alphabet had definitely arrived and, because of writing, identifiable dynasties for this period are documented in the Puranas. The age in which 'history' appears in India, the age of the Buddha, is 'one of great intellectual and spiritual torment', which produced both philosophers and merchants.[57] At this time Sanskrit became the spoken language of the educated few as well as the written language of the Vedic religion. Some secular writings date from the third century BCE but more important are the inscriptions of the following period. There was already a looking back to an earlier time, to another culture. As a result, in certain spheres Vedic literature was being questioned, giving rise both to doctrines of idealism and materialism, that is, both to Hindu supernaturalism and to Lokayata scepticism; and while orthodoxy continued to hold sway, so too these other alternative traditions were present and the questioning led to the creation of Buddhism and of Jainism, each one emphasizing equality (as indeed did the *bhakti* sects), the democratically organized monastic life, the local vernacular, education and the improved status of women. Moreover, both queried Vedic orthodoxy. Buddhism did not initially make wide use of Sanskrit (preferring the Pali Prakrit)

---

[56] D. Chattopadhyaya 1959: 64.   [57] Basham 1967: 46.

because its main congregation consisted of regional commoners disaffected with the system in which Sanskrit was enshrined. Rather, these religions appealed to merchants who approved the non-Vedic docrine of *ahimsa* ('non-violence', that is, for peaceful co-existence), and as the economy flourished, in return for perceived supernatural aid they contributed to monasteries and to other endowments, as did the women of royal dynasties. This economic activity saw the growth of cities and of the whole economy, the formation of guilds, the role of bankers and the use of coins in the Buddhist and Mauryan period of the fifth century BCE. The new writing, economic prosperity, the non-Vedic religions, increased literary activity, all represented an efflorescence and all are interconnected.[58] However, Buddhist literature is of relatively little importance for the development of science because their philosophy centred around *nirvana* and was preoccupied with eternal considerations, showing relatively little interest in the positive sciences except in the field of medicine.[59] The Jains on the other hand were closer to the Hindus and 'exhibited considerable interest in secular learning and sciences, especially mathematics'.[60]

In the overall exchange of information India was in a favourable geographical position. From early on it had received much knowledge from the Near East, including during the Bronze Age itself. It had contacts with Egypt and western Asia from prehistoric times. In later historical periods, the Achaemenid empire and the Greeks in the north provided a link to the Mediterranean. Rome and Egypt both traded to the subcontinent. With the spread of Buddhism to China, many contacts developed in both directions, also involving scientific exchange. The opening of the Silk Roads and the coming of Islam encouraged yet firmer links.

In astronomy, the Vedic systems were favoured but the development of the stellar zodiac, or *nakshastra* system, may have been influenced by Babylonia. Later on it owed much to the Greeks, though it always added to these foreign borrowings. Equally important were the exports to China, especially of Buddhism, cotton cloth and sugar, beginning about the time of the Christian era. But it was through the Muslims that Hindu learning in this field passed into Latin Europe and hence to the European Renaissance.

In the pre-Mauryan era, Gandhara, with its capital of Taxila (the hellenized form of Taskshalila), which lay astride the Indus, was an obvious

---

[58] Of the Buddhist and Jain texts, Basham writes that they were passed down by word of mouth for centuries (1967: 46) but unlike the Vedas they altered over time. How can we possibly know either? As Basham describes it, this was an age of great intellectual and spiritual ferment!

[59] Sen 1971: 38.   [60] Sen 1971: 42.

place for a cultural efflorescence to take place. It was on the communication route to Iran and was influenced by the Archaemenian empire of Persia; indeed, in c.519 BCE it ended by becoming one of the latter's twenty-two satrapies. That country acted as a channel not only for woollen goods but for Greek art, which together with the Indian formed the basis of much Buddhist sculpture. In these works the mother of Buddha resembled an Athenian matron and a variety of Apollo-like faces appeared in the sculpture. But it was initially a lateral rather than a backward look towards the Greeks who were contemporaries. For a mixture of Greek and Indian culture took place not only through the Persian empire that fought the Hellenes as well as displaying elements of their culture, but when Alexander later conquered the area and established a number of settlements around 327 BCE, thus providing an impetus for trade and communications with western Asia. There is no record of this contact in available Indian sources, except for references to Yavana flutegirls and other slave personnel in the dramas and other related literature, although a number of Greeks reported their own impressions of the east; their uses of literacy were undoubtedly wider. But Alexander is said to have met with Chandragupta Maurya, the first ruler of the Mauryan empire who later fought with the Seleucid dynasty of Iran and moved into Alexander's former territory when it was abandoned by him. This period was followed by an era of friendly relations as well as by the composition in Taxila of a major treatise on political economy, that is, the *Arthashastra* of Kautilya, who is thought to have been Chandragupta's prime minister.[61] However, with his grandson, Ashoka, the dynasty almost came to an end, despite the fact that he built roads and rest houses, planted medicinal herbs and established centres for the sick. His regime displayed an astonishing measure of political and social humanism, with its message of religious tolerance and enlightened ethics. But the empire depended upon land tax and upon a well-paid bureaucracy and army, and such an organization was difficult and expensive to support, despite the improvements in agriculture, some irrigation and the expansion of trade. The arts also flourished. Of sculpture, there are no surviving works from the Harappan period right down to the Mauryan, over one thousand years; but the patronage of the Mauryan emperors, growing material prosperity, western influence, led to a 'revival' of culture, even in the context of political disintegration.[62]

The break up of the Mauryan empire was followed by the rise of a number of small kingdoms in the north (180 BCE–300 CE), but despite the political fragmentation the economy prospered. This was the time

[61] But the authorship and date of the text are both questioned.   [62] Basham 1967: 366.

of the Indo-Greek kings, the last of which was Menander (c.155–130 BCE), called Milinda in India, who was the subject of a written dialogue, *Questions of King Milinda*, with a Buddhist philosopher, Nagasena, as the result of which discussion the king was said to have been converted. Meanwhile the determination of the Han rulers of China to keep out the central Asian tribes led these latter to move into India where they established local dynasties that followed local custom. For instance, royal inscriptions from many parts record donations made to Buddhist monks and monasteries, often by princesses, and also land grants to Brahmans as well as the performance of Vedic sacrifices by the rulers.[63] Plurality was maintained.

In the south, Tamil Brahmi inscriptions of this period record further donations made to Buddhist and Jain monks by royalty as well as by merchants and artisans. These gifts are confirmed by the *cangam* literature, poems in classical Tamil, elements of which were affected by the intrusion of a northern Sanskritic tradition. While rice production flourished in the south, trade with the Romans as well as with the east was also very important. In the north, Babylonian civilization had earlier used Indian woods and both the Romans and the Semites took up the coastal trade route until the discovery of the regular seasonal monsoon which made possible the direct voyage, leading to a yet more vigorous exchange with the Near East. That trade developed especially with the south, on both sides of the Indian peninsular, with Musaris in the west and Arikamedu in the east, partly for spices but also for other luxury objects. Judging from the number of Roman gold coins and the quality of pottery, the trade must have been both extensive and valuable. Culture too expanded; and literature flourished, not only poetry. The popular epics served as a treasury of stories embodied in plays, such as those by Bhasa, foundational for Sanskrit drama; indeed, Bharata produced its own study of dramaturgy. In the sciences, astronomy and medicine were foremost, reflecting an exchange of ideas with western Asia. Two basic medical compendia, by Charaka and Sushruta, were composed around this time.[64] The collections seem to have been written around 100 CE in Taxila and under Gupta rule in fourth-century CE Benares respectively. The material on which they drew probably stems partly from the early centuries of the Buddhist era, reflecting an expansion of medicine in the Mauryan period.

There may indeed have been a little 'golden age' of medicine at that time, perhaps due to the generally higher level of institutional organization in many facets of imperial life, including the military.

---

[63] The first evidence for land grants is from the Satavahana period, not before the first century CE.
[64] Thapar 2002: 258.

Medical knowledge consisted in the consolidation of an already extant body of lore and customs, as well as of Greek medicine from minor Buddhist writings which we no longer possess; the *viharas* (monasteries) were likely places for the gathering of such materials. Together the Charaka and Sushruta compendia, along with the shorter and fragmentary *Bhela Samhita*, constitute a very substantial source for the subsequent Ayurvedic corpus; in their extant form they contain abundant material on diet, the potencies of a very extensive herbarium, sophisticated surgical techniques extending even to ocular and cosmetic surgery, the causes and symptoms of a range of illnesses (including dropsy, piles, various fevers, epilepsy, tuberculosis, asthma and virtually all commonly identified maladies), various types of epidemic, techniques of clinical examination, diagnosis and prognosis, fertility medicine (including aphrodisiacs), gynaecology and foetal care, bloodletting, leechcraft, and the detailing of a considerable pharmacopoeia of animal, vegetable and even mineral origin. Near the end of the Gupta era we also see the detailed treatment of obstetrics in Vagbhata's *Astangahrdaya* of c.600 CE and a systematization of pathologies in Madhavakara's *Rugviniscaya* of around 700 CE which would become the pattern for virtually all the post-Gupta medical tracts.

Ayurvedic medicine clearly grew out of the earlier curing techniques of oral societies. But it was essentially a written medicine. How else would one have the listing of 600 drugs and 300 different surgical operations? The surgery itself was based on dissection and there was a type of Hippocratic oath.[65] The object of Ayurvedic medicine was to maintain a healthy body and mind, dependent on humours but not avoiding surgical interaction (early on, but not later). The production of these texts involved an encyclopaedic knowledge of medical topics, including 'social medicine', history, chemistry, psychology, cosmology and religion. Indian doctors came to Europe with the Greek army which influenced their medicine, but the extent is unknown though it may have included an understanding of the topic of humours.[66] And the influences ran in both directions, as with Arabic and Persian medicine. Indian medical compendia were translated into both languages. Indeed, Persia was influenced by Indian medicine even before the arrival of the Arabs, as we see in the medical centre of Gondeshapur in the fifth century. A century earlier the medical manuscripts found on the trade route from Bactria to China at Kucha in central Asia provide evidence of the spread of such knowledge to the east, including to Tibet and south-east Asia. One interesting aspect of Indian medicine is that it continued to expand and to produce commentaries right up to the arrival of European doctors.

---

[65] Majumdar 1971: 223.   [66] Majumdar 1971: 259.

During the Gupta period (c.320–540 CE) there was a clear-cut cultural efflorescence, for example at Ujjayini, one of the capitals. That period saw a dramatic expansion of knowledge in medicine and astronomy, and among other fields especially in mathematics. Education developed in the monasteries, in the Hindu and Jain *mathas*, and in the Buddhist *viharas*, though it was basically religious, taking up an earlier Vedic tradition. But the teaching environment of a Buddhist *vihara* was less formal than elsewhere and further education of a university type did develop at Nalanda, not far from the old Mauryan metropolis of Pataliputra (today's Patna) in Bihar, consisting of a type of extended quadrivium with grammar, rhetoric, prosody, logic, metaphysics and medicine. It is likely that with an upsurge in institutional organization, the Gupta period coincided with and accelerated a major increase in the use of writing for a variety of purposes. The main written materials used for the study of medicine were the steadily augmented and amended versions of compendia, and in addition the momentum of a thriving university environment must have been a major factor in the augmentation of those writings into the form in which we now have them. In India at this time the decimal system was in full use, as evidenced by the inscription that occurred in Gujarat dated 595 CE; the earliest certain appearance of a zero in a Hindu treatise is in a fragment of 876 CE, well into the post-Gupta era. From there the system spread to Indo-China and Japan and in the west was taken up by al-Khwarizmi in the ninth century and eventually came to Europe in the twelfth. According to a Christian monk of the tenth century, the Indians had a very subtle ingenuity and everybody acknowledged their superiority in arithmetic, in geometry and in other liberal arts.[67] As we have seen, mathematics developed strongly in the Gupta period mainly owing to the fact that they dealt with a more abstract system of numbers ('Arabic' numerals). Some discoveries made in India in the early period were unknown in Europe until the Renaissance or later.

In higher education there was some considerable development from the earlier period. Apart from Nalanda, there were many other institutes of learning in India which, though associated with religious sects especially Buddhist, seem also to have given some instruction in secular topics. The University of Takshashila (also known under the hellenized name of Taxila to which we have referred as the Mauryan capital of Gandhara, with its contacts with Persia) was an important institution of this kind, the 'intellectual capital of India', especially for Brahman scholars. It provided an exemplary education, well-esteemed by local kings. It attracted students mainly from the Brahman and warrior castes, but

[67] Jacquart 2005: 83.

from all over India. There was a certain democracy in the teaching, individuals from different groups meeting together for general discussion. Instruction included not only religious classics but also the Eighteen Arts and Sciences, which included elephant lore, hunting, archery, magical charms and various forms of divination. Medicine, law and military science were incorporated in schools that followed separate curricula. Today the ruins of the ancient city of Taxila can be found in the Punjab province of Pakistan, about thirty kilometres north-west of Islamabad. One of the oldest universities in the world, it was most revered in India, especially by Hindus and Buddhists. It is cherished by the former because the great strategist Chanakya (Kautilya), who appears later to have consolidated the realm of the emperor Chandragupta Maurya, was a senior professor there. His political treatise, the *Arthashastra* (Sanskrit for 'the knowledge of economics'), is said to have been composed in Takshashila itself, where the grammarian Panini also wrote. It is also revered by Buddhists because it is believed that the Mahayana form of the religion was founded at that school.

Some scholars date Takshashila's existence to c.700 BCE, perhaps to the very beginnings of alphabetic literacy in the far north, and it remained a centre of learning until the city was sacked by nomadic invaders from central Asia (the Hephthalites) in the fifth century CE. Students were normally sixteen years old when they entered the university and learnt the four Vedas and the Eighteen Arts, but in addition there were the specialist schools to which we have referred.

We have already mentioned one other early centre of higher education, that of Nalanda, a place which the Gautama Buddha is believed to have visited before it was established, giving sermons near 'the mango grove of Pavarika'. Whereas Taxila was largely Hindu, Nalanda was basically Buddhist. Education there was well endowed and in general free, attracting students of all sects from India and around, especially from China. It may possibly have been the earliest and certainly the largest residential centre of learning that the world had known. During its prosperous days it had over 10,000 students and 1,500 teachers, and its library was housed in a nine-storied building. The subjects taught there are said to have covered every field of learning. The name Nalanda means literally 'the place that confers the lotus'. According to a Tibetan biography, Nagarjuna (c.150–250) was taught at a monastery there. Ashoka had reputedly founded a temple there; it was also a holy place for the Jains and the founder Mahavira is said to have spent fourteen rainy seasons there.[68] However, historical studies indicate that the university was established only later

---

[68] Mookerji 1951: 557.

during the Gupta empire (c.320–546 CE), apparently by Kumaragupta. Later on we have more concrete records. A Buddhist traveller from Tang dynasty China, Xuan Zang, recorded his impressions of the university in the seventh century in great detail.[69] Then it was a 'school of discussion' where people of various faiths and sects could debate in public, and it was run by a 'democratic' management with teaching marked by tolerance and freedom; students could work at Brahman or Buddhist studies, in the arts or in the sciences.

To a large extent, Tibetan Buddhism (Vajrayana), along with the other variants of Mahayana Buddhism in the Far East, emerged from schools of thought at Nalanda in the late ninth to twelfth century. Theravada, the other main school of Buddhism, had a centre at Nagarjunakonda (named after Nagarjuna, who is said to have taught at Nalanda) in Andhra Pradesh, and was followed in Sri Lanka, Myanmar, Thailand, Cambodia and elsewhere, and the later Theravada schools also developed here. There were many foreign students who came to study and many Nalanda graduates who worked abroad. In 1193, the university complex was destroyed by Turkic Muslim invaders under Bakhtiyar Khalji, who according to a Persian historian had all the books burned. This has been viewed as the culminating moment in the near extinction of Buddhism in India, but in fact it was assimilated with the Brahmanic system of belief by the twelfth century.

Other important universities were at Vallabhi, which was especially important for Jains and is discussed by the Chinese traveller Itsing in the seventh century, as well as Odantapuri in Somapura Mahavihara, visited by many Tibetan monks but destroyed by Muslims in the thirteenth century, as was the Buddhist Vikramshila University. Varanasi, also known as Banaras, however, has continued as a centre of Hindu learning, and has been called the 'cultural capital of India'.

These institutes of higher education, which proliferated in India, were mainly centred around religious institutions, largely Buddhist, the teaching of which was later incorporated in Brahmanism, which eventually made them obvious targets for Muslim conquerors or their converts who tried to destroy them. Most such institutes were primarily engaged in religious instruction, using Sanskrit. For science, one often had to look elsewhere, to courts for example, and for technology to the guilds which flourished as the economy grew.[70] As temples or monasteries consequently became more complex, decorative art and sculpture flourished, for example in the murals of Ajanta, and appeared to spread from Buddhist sources.

[69] See Watters 1904.   [70] Thapar 1997: 50.

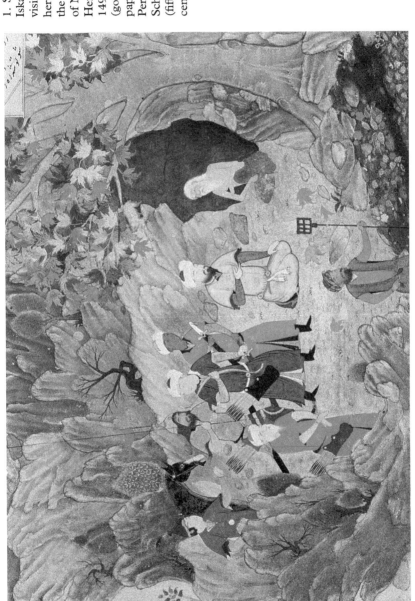

1. Sultan Iskandar visits a hermit, from the 'Khamsa' of Nizami, Herat, 1494–5 (gouache on paper) by Persian School (fifteenth century)

2. Ms Or 20 fol. 122r(a) Battle between Abu-l Qasim and the Samanid
Muntasir for the recovery of his dominion, in one of many clashes in 1003–4.
Miniature from the 'Jami' al-Tawarikh' of Rashid al-Din, c.1307 (vellum) by
Islamic School (fourteenth century)

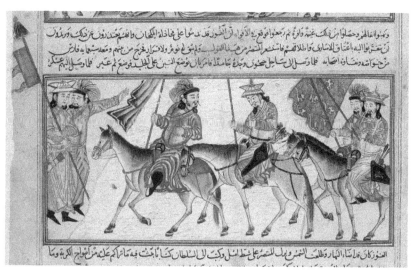

3. Ms Or 20 fol. 122r(b) The defeated al-Muntasir crosses the frozen river
Jayhun. Miniature from the 'Jami' al-Tawarikh' of Rashid al-Din, c.1307
(vellum) by Islamic school (fourteenth century)

4. Fountain in the Court of the Lions, Palace of the Alhambra, Granada, Spain

5. East Gate carving detail of a *salabhanjika* from the Great Stupa at Sanchi, Madhya Pradesh, c.50 BCE

6. Apsaras sculpture (stone), Chittaugarh, Rajasthan, India

7. Emperor Jahangir (1569–1627) with his consort and attendants in a garden, from the Small Clive Album (opaque watercolour on paper) by Mughal School (eighteenth century)

8. Silver and gilt Buddhist reliquary, Famen Temple, Fufeng, Shaanxi province

北宋范中
立軸山行旅
圖

9. Fan K'uan, *Travelling among Mountains and Streams* (c.990–1030)

10. Guo Zi, *Early Spring*, dated 1072

To speak of other achievements, physics was closely linked to religion, concerned as it was with understanding the world. For example, Indian scholars developed an atomic theory independent of the Greeks, but 'Indian ideas on the origin and evolution of the universe are rather a matter of religions than of sciences.'[71] The concept of a flat earth was rejected by the learned early in the Christian era, possibly influenced by the Greeks. It was a notion that represented the birth of a true sense of geography. Astronomical ideas were adopted, again perhaps from the Greeks, as they were needed for prognostication. In chemistry the Indians concentrated upon medical compounds, especially those using mercury. As we have seen, the country developed an empirically based science of surgery, remaining ahead of Europeans in this field until the eighteenth century. Calculation was obviously assisted by developments in Indian mathematics, especially the decimal system. The *Siddhantas* of the early Gupta period, which were composed in the late fourth and early fifth centuries largely on the subject of calculation in geometry and astronomy, are probably indebted to Greek mathematical treatises in some degree, as al-Biruni suggested; it is likely that Gupta patronage motivated the adoption of Greek astronomical models and sponsored their embellishment with Hindu content. There were observatories at Jyotishavedanga and Surya-prajnapati. The first properly scientific astronomer, Aryabhata, calculated *pi* and the length of the solar year as early as 499 BCE; he accepted the idea of an axially rotating earth, the shadow of the globe resulting in the moon's waning, and in the lunar cause of an eclipse. Sen writes of him as 'the head of the Hindu mathematical renaissance'[72] and he was followed very much later by a number of important mathematicians like Brahmagupta (598–668 CE) continuing right up to the modern period. Indian astronomy and mathematics in turn influenced Arab calculations and Indian supremacy in these fields depended significantly upon their use of a decimal place-value system. The Babylonians also had place-value but it was sexagesimal. However, the Indians had based their calculations on ten even in the Vedas and used zero at least by Aryabhata's time.

Although the achievements in Indian science were considerable and probably influenced the Greeks in medicine and later the whole of Europe in the early renascence, there does not seem to be much in the way of a sudden burst but rather a slow but general evolution. After the coming of the Muslims, science took different forms. Nevertheless, the Classical Age is said to represent a 'glorious period' in science and technology as in history generally. 'From about the fourth century A.D. to about

---

[71] Basham 1967: 490.   [72] Sen 1971: 165.

the eighth or ninth century and also a couple of centuries later, different branches of science made great headway and even became codified in . . . texts.'[73] Medical books were translated into other languages and the Persian doctor al-Razi incorporated such knowledge in his compendia, which was translated into Latin in the thirteenth century and became a standard work of reference in Europe in the later Middle Ages. It is also the case that in alchemy and chemistry, in atomic ideas (only revived in Europe in the seventeenth century), in impetus theory, in technological practices (especially in metalworking) and in agriculture, Indian science 'participated effectively in the evolution and even the transmission of scientific ideas and techniques'.[74] But this was an evolution rather than a 'scientific revolution'. It continued over time, and it influenced and was influenced by both Chinese and Arabic–Persian scholarship, and through al-Khwarizmi and others had its importance for 'Europe's mathematical renaissance', beginning in the thirteenth century with the publication of Pisano's work on the place-value system, which came from India.[75]

In the Gupta era, the reign of Chandragupta II 'perhaps marks the high watermark of ancient Indian culture';[76] it then 'reached a perfection which it was never again to attain'. This period is also described as a golden or classical age of literary and musical patronage, with Sanskrit being the elite language at court and among the aristocracy. It was also used for the writing of plays for that audience, especially romantic comedies, for the plays and poems of Kalidasa and for the one tragedy written by Shudraka.[77] In addition, biography and fables were popular literary forms. An element of literary criticism also developed as did legal writings that commented on the Code of Manu (*Manavadharmashastra*). This was a period in which the norms of Indian literature, art, architecture and philosophy were established, a time of 'renascent Hinduism' and of material prosperity.[78] During this period, which one writer speaks of as 'the great Brahman renaissance',[79] trade flourished and, for some, life was prosperous. The level of 'luxury' can be seen in the *Kamasutra*, a treatise on sexual love, which was characteristic of a liberalized upper echelon of society who were certainly not confined by the more puritanical elements in religion.

However, it has been said that 'although often referred to as the Indian Renaissance, the Gupta period is not properly understood as a rebirth, except in a political sense as a reappearance of a unified rule that had not

---

[73] Subbarayappa 1971: 584.   [74] Subbarayappa 1971: 592.   [75] Sen 1971: 212.
[76] Basham 1967: 66.   [77] Was Sanskrit drama partly inspired by the Bactrian Greeks?
[78] Thapar 1997: 47.   [79] M. R. Sastri, according to D. Chattopadhyaya 1959: 17.

been known since the extinction of the Maurya Dynasty'.[80] There was of course a reference back to Vedic religion and to Sanskrit literature and there was a flourishing of culture. After the fall of the Roman empire, India had little communication with the west; on its own it nevertheless experienced a 'florescence' after 'a long period of gradual development', a 'sophistication and complete assurance in expression in music, literature, the drama, and the plastic arts'.[81] So the period can be described as 'classic' in the sense of defining 'a norm or degree of perfection never achieved before or since, and in the perfect balance and harmony of all elements stylistic and iconographic'.[82] Once again there was movement as well as continuity. The great Indian epic, the *Mahabharata*, went through a final recension at this time and the *Ramayana* enjoyed renewed popularity.

Indeed, the Brahmanic Renaissance or the golden age of the Gupta period is compared by the art historian Rowland with the Italian Renaissance itself.[83] He specifically mentions the names of Leonardo, Giotto and El Greco. 'The richness and dramatic conception of relief', he writes of that period, 'are an unmistakable indication of the real renaissance that was taking place in the art of the Hindu Church.'[84] However, he also writes that '[s]culpture in the period of Gupta supremacy, like the allied arts of painting and architecture, must not in any sense be regarded as a revival or a rebirth, but rather as the logical culmination of several continuous traditions', mainly the Indian one of Mathura and the heritage of Graeco-Roman art.[85] It is marked by 'a finished mastery in execution and a majestic serenity in expression that *have seldom been equalled in any other school of art*' (my italics).[86] But in the Gupta period painting, like architecture and sculpture, is 'merely the culmination, not the renewal, of a very ancient tradition'.[87] Continuity is stressed throughout. At this time, three types of painting existed, which were appropriate for temples, palaces and for private dwellings, and were differentiated between the 'true', the 'lyrical' and 'secular' painting. The combination of sacred and secular art is intrinsic to the wall-paintings at Ajanta as well as to other Gupta forms which occupy 'a position corresponding to that of Greek and Roman art in the West'.[88] It was 'classic' in the same sense but was never rejected in the same way as was classical art in the west, and therefore had no need of a rebirth. There was greater continuity, but not stasis or immobility.

---

[80] Rowland 1953: 129.   [81] Rowland 1953: 129–30.   [82] Rowland 1953: 130.
[83] Rowland 1953: 129.   [84] Rowland 1953: 138.   [85] Rowland 1953: 138.
[86] Rowland 1953: 138.   [87] Rowland 1953: 145.   [88] Rowland 1953: 180.

As an example, the epics themselves were constantly reinterpreted in the course of this era. They long continued to be a source of inspiration. In the Sanskrit theatre of the Gupta period, many plays were based on that material while others used plots invented by the authors. There are some elements of secularity, while other plays consisted of material drawn entirely from sacred texts; later on, early in the eighth century Bhavabhuti wrote drama based on the *Ramayana*, a tradition that has continued down to the present day. That was also true in the Dravidian country in the south. During the Chola empire (tenth to twelfth century), we find an awakening of literatures from the tenth century in Kannada, Telugu and Malayalam, the first works being based upon the Sanskritic epics. In Telugu that was also the case with those of the Brahman Nannayya Bhattarakudu (c.1000–1100 CE), who began the *Andhra Mahabharatamu*, which was finished in the thirteenth century. In this way the Sanskritic epics became an integral part of a growing tradition of the regional languages.

Although India displays a considerable degree of cultural continuity in matters of religion, this was not the same for all spheres. The country came up with important developments in the economic field, especially in respect of the manufacture of cotton which from early times was exported both to the east and to the west. So too of culture in the more restricted sense, which went through definite periods of 'efflorescence'. Although there was a continuity of religious culture, there were some periods in which substantial change did take place. The rigidity of the Hindu caste system was amongst the prime factors in its rejection and the emergence of Buddhism and Jainism. The reabsorption of Mahayana Buddhism into Hinduism was a further striking instance of this change. There was also the appearance of the division between the Shaivite and Vaishnavite strands of Hinduism. The former was more concerned with orthodox Shiva worship, the second, directed more to Krishna, saw the emergence of *bhakti* cults dedicated to personal devotion and equality. We also find a limited, regional tendency to move from polytheism to a kind of monotheism.

The so-called feudal period[89] that followed between 700 and 1200 CE saw education in Brahmanic hands becoming increasingly theological and orthodox. Literature became rather sterile. Temple architecture, often a hallmark of classical achievement, did indeed reach heights of excellence, especially in the north and centre at large commercial and cultural

---

[89] This is no longer viewed as the feudal period but as that of regional kingdoms, markets and economic growth, population growth, 'peasantization' and the formation of many *jati* (caste) groups. See B. Chattopadhyaya 1994.

towns like Khajuraho, Bhubaneshwar, Patadakal, Aiholi and Ellora, and Kanchipuram and Thanjavur in the south. Religious culture was particularly strong at this time and there was little by way of general rebirth before the coming of the Muslim dynasties in about 1200. That invasion in itself did not lead to a renascence or reformation but resulted in a reinforcement of orthodox Hinduism. In the economy, the Chola kingdom in the south flourished, trading widely in south-east Asia, conquering Ceylon and sending out a naval expedition to Sumatra in Indonesia. Tamil culture was, if not democratic, at least popular.[90] In the north, Muslim rule expanded, reaching as far as Madurai in the south. But an important Hindu kingdom was also founded at Vijayanagara in the south which established relations with the invading Portuguese in Goa.

Vijayanagara did react to the Muslim threat to southern India by what Stein has called 'centralized prebendalism',[91] but its high culture was 'fundamentally conservative and accumulative, geared to the support of brahminical culture';[92] there is little evidence of innovation. For close on three centuries (from 1336 to 1565) this empire resisted the attacks of the Muslims from the north, and in particular of the Bahmanis (whose ruler destroyed the temples and colleges of the Brahmans as did Christians), fought for the cause of Hinduism and 'prescribed the ancient tradition of the country in its polity, its learning and its arts'.[93] Vijayanagara was largely a 'war-state' involved in constant struggles with the Muslims, and sometimes with Hindus, heavily dependent upon the import of cavalry horses from Arabia to the western ports, but at the same time it flourished with its rulers patronizing Hindu shrines and schools.[94] Ambassadors arrived from Persia and were sent to China; Krishnadeva Raya 'built a glorious age', for he was a great administrator, reorganized the army but was also a patron of the arts who 'added much to the beauty and amenities of the capital', being also a scholar and poet.[95] Much of the poetry was in Sanskrit, and some in local languages, mostly religious, but some was secular. Work in Kannada, often by Jains, was more concerned with secular subjects, including the scientific. But 'the division, within a European classical inheritance, between "Christian-religious" and "Latin-Greek secular" strands has no correspondence within the Hindu traditional sources'.[96] The two were intertwined.

When the Muslims came to India from the north, there was a certain amount of destruction not only of universities but also of monuments, although in general they were tolerant rulers. There was, however, little

[90] Basham 1967: 77.   [91] Stein 1989: 140–6.   [92] Rubiés 2000: 237.
[93] Sastri 1975: 264.   [94] Sastri 1975: 307, 274.
[95] Sastri 1975: 284.   [96] Rubiés 2000: 232.

of 'the fertilizing effect on Hindu culture that might have been expected' except with the growth of Sikhism.[97] Hinduism became yet more conservative in the face of the challenge. There was some political renewal of Hinduism with the Maratha Shuinji but again no 'real cultural revival'. That happened only later with the advent of the Europeans, especially with the founding of the Asiatick Society of Bengal and the return of foreign-educated Indians.

While Islam had entered the continent earlier (already the first Muslim roads were made in Sindh in the seventh century), the dynasties proper only begin with Delhi in 1206 with the conquest of the Turkic tribes, possibly to be dated to 1000 CE, who raided the subcontinent from Afghanistan. The real impact of the period of Turkic rule not only in north India but in the south too (with the Khiljis, after the Mamluks) began with that Mamluk (Slave) dynasty in Delhi. Sanskrit and Brahmanism obviously suffered from the coming of Islam, as did the sculpture in Hindu temples, step wells and other buildings through the Muslims' aversion to figurative representation. But Islam rapidly developed its own culture in the region, looking back to earlier Islamic achievement and particularly to Persian art forms, which, however, did include some secular painting at the court level, particularly of miniatures. In the early sixteenth century, the Safavid ruler in Persia, Shah Ismail, persecuted some Sufi orders, in consequence of which many members including poets emigrated to India, where they established an Indian–Persian literary school, known as *Sabq-i Hindi*, that is, Indian style.[98] The Muslim invasion also meant the import of Arabic and Persian texts on mathematics and astronomy, including translations from the Greek, of Euclid for example, which stimulated work in mathematics and led to many local commentaries.

In the north, the early Turkic invaders had to fend off a number of Mongol attacks, though in 1398 Timur (or Tamberlane) did eventually (but briefly) invade the country as far as Delhi. Despite these attacks the Turks continued to trade with the north for horses for their cavalry (and for canons coming from Turkey possibly in the second half of the fifteenth century) in exchange for textiles. Horses they needed for their particular type of warfare, textiles to effect the purchase. During this period, there were a number of advances in that industry with the introduction of the wooden cotton gin, the spinning wheel and possibly the treadle loom, as well as sericulture and improvements in construction technology. The production of paper came to India from China in the eighth century (well before Europe) and produced increased record-keeping and the

[97] Basham 1967: 481.   [98] Irwin 1996: 72–3.

widespread use of bills of exchange. But only after the fourteenth and fifteenth centuries, well into the Islamic period, did paper begin to be widely used. Before this, palm-leaves in south India and birch-bark in the north were the norm. Paper-production was later strongly encouraged by the Muslim rulers. Towns also flourished as centres of exchange, administration and intellectual activity, and in the thirteenth century Delhi became one of the largest in the Islamic world. As the economy grew, so did charities and educational establishments. In the country the Muslims created a number of canals, improving internal transport, with the regime also making considerable contributions to culture and to learning.

Although Muslims dominated the north, in the south some Hindu states continued to flourish, for example, that of Vijayanagar (1336–1646). While there was increasing militarization, here too there was also commercialization both with China to the east and with the Near East to the west. Even in the earlier period the Chola empire had intervened in Indonesia because Shrivijaya had interfered with trade going through the Malacca straits. In some respects Vijayanagar consciously represented itself as the last bastion of Hinduism against the forces of Islam. In it, there was a measure of scholarship, and the ruler, Krishnadeva Raya (1509–29), was noted for his learning and for his patronage of Telugu and Sanskrit literatures.

It was about this time that gunpowder came into use in India. According to Khan,[99] it is possible to make out a case that gunpowder was introduced to the Delhi sultanate in the thirteenth century through contact with the Mongols and was being first used for pyrotechnic displays, then in the fifteenth century for warfare. The history of firearms proper in India is far from straightforward, but he concludes that cannon and musket were present in the second half of the fifteenth century.

In the north of the country the Muslim Mughal empire (1526–1761) became a blend of Perso-Islamic and Indian elements. It was founded by Babur, a Turk from central Asia, a region that depended upon the expansion of trade with the outside world and upon the advent of new technologies and ideas from outside. Babur was succeeded by his son Humayun and then his grandson, Akbar (1542–1605), who ran a distinctly liberal regime and established a sound, secular, administrative framework; he even disestablished Islam as the religion of the state. Much later, in the seventeenth century, the reigns of Jahangir and Shah Jahan were noted not only for considerable economic activity but also for excellence in painting and architecture (plate 7). Increasing monetarization

---

[99] Khan 1981: 146.

took place, with the emperor owning shipping fleets and advancing funds for merchants with which to trade.

While Shah Jahan was a tolerant ruler, who patronized scholars and and poets in Sanskrit and Hindi as well as in Persian, his successor, Aurangzeb, reversed this policy, abandoned Akbar's secular rule and established an Islamic state, demolishing Hindu schools and temples, and imposing increased taxation on the followers of that religion. His actions encouraged the classic confrontation between Muslim law and legal pragmatism, between the religious and the secular, between the traditionalist and the modernist, between faith and reason.

The north, however, was not completely ruled by Muslims. The rivals of the Mughals in that area were the Hindu Marathas who played a political role of increasing importance. The earlier period saw a proliferation of small states, each with their own courts, a fragmentation that was culturally invigorating (as with the Taifas in Andalusia) since each court competed with one another. In the south, under the Marathas, Thanjavur was also a case of 'cultural efflorescence', producing high-quality literature in Tamil and Telugu, as well as in Sanskrit and Marathi. It was then that the Karnataka tradition of Indian classical music was created and a distinct style of painting developed. In the north, the same happened in Lahore with Punjabi and Persian. The mixing of Hindu and Islam was often very creative; indeed, much of India's 'traditional' culture is attributable to this period when 'tradition' was invented.

The existence of both Muslim and Hindu courts encouraged diversity. So too did the coming of the Europeans, who regarded their culture as vastly superior and introduced higher education in English, French and Portuguese as well as a new type of western Christianity. Other ideas were imported from abroad, westernization, with evangelicals, freethinking utilitarians and radical rationalists coming from France. These ideas led to Hindu reform and eventually to the independence movement; that reform prohibited *sati*, child marriage and infanticide. While most held on to either the Hindu or the Muslim religions, in its westernizing zeal the young Bengal movement even denied Hindu religion itself. However, most people managed to borrow from the world without any feelings of disloyalty to their creed.

An important part of this movement developed around Calcutta, headquarters of the British East India Company, and was soon described as the Bengal Renaissance. But the actors were not so much engaged in reviving Sanskrit, although this was included as one of the intentions of participants, as in encouraging the adoption of European (English) education.[100] Calcutta was the locus of much economic activity, and

[100] Chaudhuri 2004.

it was there that rentiers of agricultural land formed 'a fashionable and intellectual society' under the first governor-general, Warren Hastings.[101] India was of course a colonial asset, and hence its role as a source of revenue, commodities and trade was undoubtedly uppermost in the mind of Westminister. Yet it was Hastings's decisive move, liberal but also politically prudent, to pursue the day-to-day governance of British India with reference to indigenous practice and precedent that set the tone for a marked renascence of Hindu culture. Amongst the first practical gestures towards ruling the present by the dictates of tradition was the Hastings-sponsored project of a digest of Hindu law, the *Gentoo Code*, consisting of a body of excerpts from the main Hindu and Muslim legal tracts in use in the subcontinent with the aim of standardizing the legal precepts employed in the courts and excluding the capricious element arising from the constant use of ad hoc advisors. Though his Asiatic linguistic expertise was largely restricted to Persian, Hastings was, as his personal correspondence reveals, a considerable connoisseur of the Hindu scriptures, known to him in excerpt and in Persian translation. The impetus provided by his retrospective strategy quickly accelerated with the appointment of the talented philologist-lawyer William Jones as a puisne judge of the Calcutta Supreme Court. Shortly after he arrived in India, Jones brought together the indological element from among the Europeans in and around Calcutta along with whatever native sources he could summon and instigated the Asiatick Society of Bengal under Hastings's patronage. Jones recorded and set down in print from native or resident European sources all he could glean on a vast range of Indian cultural, historical, religious and scientific topics in the monumental journal, *Asiatick Researches*, which he edited through the last six years of his life and which also contained ethnological and other contributions on neighbouring regions of Asia. As time wore on Jones contributed more and more of this material himself.

Although Jones's actual pedigree as a Sanskrit scholar, even by the standards of the day, which were set largely by his subaltern Charles Wilkins and a handful of other members, is still a matter of discussion, he clearly initiated and to a large extent masterminded what might be called a renascence of Sanskritic learning when he set up the meetings and publications of the Asiatick Society; being centred in the capital of British India, having an extremely widespread pattern of contacts and sources, and using the method of book publication for propagating knowledge, fairly new for India, the Society made an impression among the English-speaking intelligentsia of the country, and no doubt among much of the educated class in Bengal and beyond. No one would suggest that the

[101] Percival Spear 1997: 95.

Andhrapradesh farmer in his rice-field or the herder on the grazing slopes of the northern *pahad*, or most of India, suddenly became aware of the activities of the Asiatick Society and were captivated by the realization that they were living in an age of renascence. But independence gradually became a widespread aim and that involved revival of the Hindu tradition and the use of the printed word.

But while this particular revival of Sanskrit was European-led, there was clearly an interest in the language among the local community, and had been for a long time. This was part of a wider political renascence of the idea of an independent India which took the form of an upsurge in cultural production later involved with the return of self-government. Some authors such as Shukla and his successors have traced the course of this upsurge, which included a great stirring of Brahmanical writing and of publishing activity extending right into the twentieth century.[102] There were many Sanskrit poetical tracts on current events, taking up both sides of the *sati*, widow-marriage and female education debates, the 1857 mutinies, the accession of Victoria as empress, as well as on cultural integrity and traditional morality; later in the nineteenth century, with the growing awareness of foreign readerships, there was a burst in the writing down of spiritual teachings, which were published in English and Sanskrit. There were allegorical plays written throughout the century on various subjects (usually satirical with a political edge); such writings often had a critical or negative, even a reactionary and anti-secularizing tone. After such beginnings, India did experience a gain in status, notably among the middle class, by looking back to Hindu culture; in this way a great nation was born, in principle secular but in fact dominantly Hindu.

Before this happened, the large component of princely India remained 'in a stagnant traditionalism'.[103] However, the colonial presence had opened up the country to the industrial mechanization of the west, to steamships, telegraph, scientific irrigation, railways, to a 'modernized' world that was to find political expression in the Indian National Congress and then in independence. But many of the conquerors were ambivalent about change. After the Indian mutiny of 1857–9 some thought that revolt was due to the 'secularizing inroads of utilitarian positivism and the proselytizing of Christian missionaries'.[104] So reform came to a halt to try to limit this process and much weight was put behind Queen Victoria's declaration that British policy involved perpetual support for native princes and for non-intervention in matters of religious belief. Despite the 'modernization' associated with the struggle for independence, there was a vigorous return to Hindu culture.

---

[102] Shukla 1969.   [103] Percival Spear 1997: 96.   [104] Wolpert 1997: 98.

The looking back in written culture did not prevent the movement forward; indeed, it was often an intrinsic part of the process. In a sense Indian culture had always retained this backward look at the classics which was seen as helping its onward flow. In the north that flow was profoundly modified by the advent of Islam, and the meeting of the two cultures, as well as of China to the east, itself resulted in a kind of efflorescence, especially in the Mughul period, with the production of a delicate court art of secular miniatures, of new varieties of architectural form, of astronomy, of medicine and of the whole influence of Islamic science and of Greek knowledge. The invasion of the British encouraged a revival of interest in ancient Hindu culture and this in turn formed a main theme of the independence struggle. In a sense the *swadeshi* (domestic or homeland) movement, associated with the name of Mahatma Gandhi, involved a looking back to the Indian past, for example in its return to handspun cotton rather than the imported cloth of Lancashire. In Pune, Bal Gangadhar ('Lokmanya') Tilak, a maths teacher at the European-style Fergusson College which he had helped to found, and an important nationalist leader,[105] looked to orthodox Hinduism and Maratha history as his twin sources of inspiration. He called upon his countrymen to take a keener interest in the religious, artistic, martial and political glories of pre-British Hindu India rather than focussing their attention on foreign learning and emulating the ideas and attitudes of the white Christian oppressors.[106] To this end, he helped found the popular Ganapati and Shivaji festivals in Pune in the 1890s. The orthodox character of Tilak's revival brought many Hindus into the movement but it led to strife with the Muslim community.

The Indian National Congress held its first meeting in Bombay in December 1885. Nationalism evolved in opposition to and in emulation of western achievement; many professional people and those, such as Tilak, who were educated in the new universities (founded from 1857) took a prominent part in reviving Hindu culture. Matters were not improved between Indians and the occupying power by the administrative division of Bengal into two states, Muslim and Hindu, to which the nationalists objected violently. They started a boycott of British goods and institutions, calling for the use of *swadeshi* or home-country products. The young leaders in Bombay also created a number of regional

[105] He was later jailed and sent to Mandalay, and was reprieved by the Privy Council at Max Müller's request.
[106] Not only Maratha history and orthodox Hinduism provided inspiration for him, but also Indian mathematics and astronomy. His book *Orion, or, Researches into the Antiquities of the Vedas* used astronomy (as many have done before and since) to date Vedic culture back to the fourth century BCE.

political associations and independent newspapers, as well as founding the Hindu reformist association, Prarthana Samaj (the Prayer Society). An important actor in all this was Swami Vivekananda, whose address to the Chicago World Conference of Religions in 1893 picked up the Upanishadic non-dualist strand of Hinduism for special consideration; many Indians regarded this as a crucial juncture in their own Renaissance as it redeemed Hinduism's image in the world community, emphasized universalism and rejected its understanding as a superstitious caste-ridden creed.[107]

It was the time before Congress was inaugurated that Helena Blavatsky (1831–91), co-founder of the Theosophical Society, came to India in 1879 to sit at the feet of Dayanand Saraswati, known as the Luther of Hinduism (for conducting a reformation), a religious leader who had founded his 'back to the Vedas' society, the Arya Samaj, in Bombay in 1875 with the intention of getting Hindus to reject what he regarded as the corrupt medieval additions to their faith, including idolatry. The independence movement was therefore heavily influenced by a looking back to former Hindu glories, modified by contact with the British world which had introduced a new university system to train graduates for the civil service. Blavatsky was succeeded by Annie Besant who became president of the Congress in 1917. The movement to boycott British goods developed at the same time a *swadeshi* culture and stimulated local production in a number of ways; Lancashire cottons were publicly burnt on a number of bonfires.

From the beginning, the Congress was supposed to have been a secular, all-Indian society for continental independence. But the Hindu–Muslim divide soon made itself felt in electoral and other matters. The Muslim leader, Sayyed Khan, convinced many by his writings that Hindus were primarily responsible for the Mutiny (though there is no evidence for this). He worked in the East India Company, visited Oxford and on his return in 1878 established what is now the Aligarth Muslim University, after which a Muslim movement began to develop quite separately from the Hindu.

The final struggle involved much sectarian looking back, especially in the thought of Mahatma Gandhi, who was committed to various aspects of Hindu doctrine, including *satyagraha* ('devotion to truth') and *ahimsa* (non-violence) as well as to modifications to the caste system. But he also laboured to achieve Hindu–Muslim unity, although eventually those religious divisions manifested themselves politically. The 'untouchables' broke away in considerable numbers to become neo-Buddhists. The

---

[107] We are indebted to Prof. A. Srinivasan for this observation.

Muslims broke away to establish Pakistan (and later Bangladesh), leading to a terrible massacre in the process. But independence did bring a kind of renascence, especially in Indian art and cinema, in which the revival of classical dancing, music, painting and writing played an important part. In this they were certainly looking back to look forward. Workers for independence rejected or modified 'corrupting' medieval aspects of the faith, to return to the 'original' purity of Vedic life. These 'medieval changes' were thought to have made India weak and disunited, destroying its capacity to resist foreign invasion, whereas the reform movement was part of the cleansing of Hinduism that encouraged modernization and independence. But there was also the influence from the west. Whatever reading Nehru, a Brahman and the first prime minister of India, had done in European political philosophy clearly dominated the actions he took and the policy he adopted; the Vedic literature did not play a great part.

There has thus been a consistent looking back to India's literate past, especially to Hinduism, in earlier times to Sanskrit, but also to a good part of its traditional culture, in dance, in music and in painting. But that looking back has not necessarily impeded the reform of religion, with the emergence of Shaivism and Vaishnavism, of Jainism and Buddhism, nor has it prevented change in the arts and certainly not in the sciences and technology which have proceeded throughout, albeit slowly. That is clear not only in the way that India and Pakistan today have their own nuclear weapons but in the way that Indian steel has become a superior or more efficient product than in the past and has even conquered Europe, while Indian cottons have long since seen off competition from Lancashire, from Roubaix and from other European centres. In earlier times too we have not experienced an Italian-type Renaissance since there was not the discontinuity displayed in Europe; there was not the breach in cultural achievement involved in the arrival of a hegemonic religion that already knew all the answers, about art as about nature, but rather a continuity of culture combined with a consistent looking back and the occasional cultural efflorescence. Scientific achievement was certainly seen in the Bronze Age itself, then with the coming of iron and later with the acquisition of alphabetic writing. The advent of the Brahmi script led to a period that included the creation of Buddhism and of Jainism. The time dominated by the founding of the Mauryan empire also saw the coming of the Greeks under Alexander, which led to the change in Buddhism from an aniconic to an iconic religion, starting the school of Gandharan (or Indo-Greek) art. The Mauryan empire disintegrated and was followed by a succession of small kingdoms including the Indo-Greek kings. But society nevertheless flourished, economically and in other ways, trade taking place with the Romans in the west as well as with the east. The sciences too expanded, especially in medicine, during the efflorescence of the Gupta period (c.240–550CE), which has been described as the Indian Renaissance. Higher education developed, as did the sciences of astronomy, medicine and mathematics. So too did playwriting with the court-drama of Kalidasa as well as in other literary forms, including commentaries on the laws of Manu and various works of 'luxury' culture such as the *Kamasutra*. The achievement of the visual arts have indeed been specifically compared with those of the Italian Renaissance. But there was no massive rebirth as no great hiatus had occurred, despite what historians refer to as a dark age. But there was always a harking back both to the Vedic myths and to the Sanskrit language.

The so-called feudal period (700–1200CE) saw a hardening of religious education (though philosophically always accompanied by a more secular element) until Hindu culture was thrown back on itself by the establishment of the Muslim dynasties in Delhi. Obviously Hinduism suffered; higher education was more confined, Indian arts were defaced in the aniconic zeal, but the Turkic invaders did impart a measure of Persian culture, including the language, as well as certain techniques like the production of paper. As a result, a new blend of Perso-Islamic and Indian elements emerged, especially under the Mughal empire (1526–1761) when trade and exchange with the outside world expanded considerably.

This expansion was partly connected with the British invasion of the continent, which eventually introduced new forms of production and mechanization as well as of education, for example, the first mechanism for drilling seed. But clearly many Hindus saw Christianity, like Islam, as a threat and as a result were thrown back on Indian language and culture. In fact the independence movement represented a true renascence of Indian culture in all its forms, as well as innovation, the expulsion of the Europeans and of most Muslims. Here there was in a sense a rebirth, since in many spheres the coming of Islam and then of Christian Europe had introduced something of a break with earlier Hindu culture.

The historian Romila Thapar has herself considered the problem of the appearance of a 'golden age' or a 'classical age' in Indian history.[108] The first she thinks occurs 'when virtually every manifestation of life reached a peak of excellence'.[109] The second, often an elusive concept, 'sets the standards for assessing forms' and is marked by 'enduring excellence'.[110] The first description has been applied to the Gupta period because of its impressive literary and scientific works in Sanskrit and the high quality of its art. It was assumed that the whole society prospered in this way

[108] Thapar 2002: 280.   [109] Thapar 2002: 280.   [110] Thapar 2002: 281.

but in fact the discussion of all renaissances refers to high culture. 'There are at least three epochs when artistic and literary expression achieved impressive standards' she writes, though she does not mention the sciences here, the post-Mauryan and Gupta periods, the Cholas and the Mughals.[111] It could be argued that we have not one classical age here but that every regional culture had one, for all differed. There is an inevitable tendency to concentrate on Brahmanism and on Sanskritic culture, but, as we have seen, Buddhism was very important intellectually as well as religiously and its art was significant in the Gupta period. And much too was written in local languages, in Prakrit, Telugu and others, apart from Sanskrit itself.

Thapar's conclusion about the Gupta period is that the classicism was not an innovation so much as the 'culmination of a process that began earlier'.[112] Classicism is 'an evolving continuum' which is a 'transition towards a uniform, elite culture' but 'becomes a catalyst for many others. The Gupta period is therefore the threshold to a marked mutation of north Indian society during the late-first millennium AD, rather than a revival or a renaissance.'[113] In other words you have cultural continuity but one that allows for periods of 'efflorescence' which also occurred at other times. A renaissance in the stricter sense was not called for, but one had a renewal in the wider usage of that term.

---

[111] Thapar 2002: 281.   [112] Thapar 2002: 281.   [113] Thapar 2002: 282.

7   Renaissance in China

with S. Fennell

In Gernet's *A History of Chinese Civilization*, there is no ambiguity about a renaissance in China. He writes of Antiquity before the Qin period, of the 'intellectual renaissance' at the end of the following Han, of the 'great upsurge' of Buddhism of the 'golden age' of the Tang and after their decline, of the beginning of the Chinese 'Renaissance' following the proscription of Buddhism about 845 CE, of the subsequent 'ancient style' movement, and the 'return to the classical tradition' of the Song period about the year 1000. He declares that in this context he had adopted 'the term "Renaissance"', admitting that the usage is no doubt open to criticism, even though the analogies are numerous – the return to the classical tradition, the diffusion of knowledge, the upsurge of science and technology (printing, explosives, advance in seafaring techniques, the clock with escapement, and so on), a new philosophy, and a new view of the world'. He admits that the Chinese Renaissance, like its western counterpart, had its own distinctive characteristics. But this allusion to Europe is a reminder of 'the very general parallelism of the history of civilizations and the long-term fellowship which has united them during the course of their development'.[1] This statement represents exactly the conclusions I would make, with others, except that the parallelism was also partly due to the system of communications and the fellowship was a matter of socio-economic development, both of which today's world brings very much to the fore.

What happened in China involved a constant looking back, usually to the works of Confucius (Kongzi, 551–479 BCE) dating from the sixth to fifth century BCE. Unlike Islam (or Judaism or Christianity) this looking back did not involve a hegemonic, monotheistic religion which in its day swept all before it and then needed to be modified for the revival of some more pagan, classically inspired, culture. In India, that process of revival involved a pluralistic and less hegemonic form of supernaturalism. In China on the other hand, while in some contexts the gods flourished and

---

[1] Gernet 2002 [1982]: 298.

so too did Buddhism until partly repressed about 843–5, Confucianism meant a looking back to a secular programme of personal and societal conduct.[2] Indeed, in what has been called the Renaissance of the Song (in which some have included the late Tang), there were educated Chinese who tended to set aside the earlier intervention of Buddhist otherworldly thought from India in order to revive a modified Confucianism of indigenous origin and to develop a strongly secular culture, in the arts as in the sciences.[3]

China was one of the great Bronze Age cultures of Eurasia. It had a complex 'civilization' in the sense of a culture of cities and an Urban Revolution, long before Europe. Early on, it had achieved much, in science, technology and the arts, which was significantly facilitated by the invention of a logographic script that contributed to the unity of the country. At this point in time China was in no way 'backward' compared with the major societies of Eurasia. Marks on pottery date from 4000 BCE, but essentially the written language developed from the late Shang (eighteenth to eleventh century BCE). In the capital near Anyang in present-day Henan province, inscribed oracle bones have been discovered that provided its kings with instructions of a divinatory and sacrificial nature. Writing was to become very important for the Chinese, later preserving and disseminating their culture (wen, wen hua). For it was this that distinguished the civilized Chinese from those they called 'barbarians' ('northern'), and it became critical to the running of the state, probably around the time of Confucius in the sixth century, as well as being important in the intellectual sphere. The standardization of the script was endorsed by the Qin at the end of the third century BCE, and writing then became an even more important instrument of political unification and cultural incorporation.[4] Literacy was also dominant in intellectual affairs. In early Tang times (seventh century CE), we hear not only of the imperial library but of a state university (kwo-tzu-chien).[5] That was after the time the Han (206 BCE–220 CE) institution of bureaucratic

---

[2] It is often thought nowadays that the 843–5 suppression of Buddhism was only a temporary set back and that Chan (Zen) Buddhism flourished in the Song dynasty. The institutional decline of Buddhism was hastened in the late tenth century because from 983 all Buddhist monks and ex-monks were banned from taking the exams. Really destructive attacks occurred in the early and mid Ming when central government ordered the closure of most temples. Local government attacked temple property, lineages took over what remained, including ancestral graves and attached fields previously looked after by monks.

[3] There was no such term as Neo-Confucianism until the 1950s (in the USA). In Chinese it is called Daouve (learning of the way) or Lixue (learning of moral principle).

[4] Recently this point has been questioned on both textual and archaeological grounds as the sole Chinese text is very vague, simply saying 'characters were made the same'.

[5] Gernet 2002 [1982]: 244.

examinations came to play an important role in making appointments to the upper levels of the civil service.

Chinese literacy warrants a further comment. As a logographic script, the equivalent of our mathematical notation, it could represent the diversity of languages existing within the borders of China, and thus served to hold this immense and complex country together and to provide a unified 'market' for intellectual goods. The USA has achieved the same unity by insisting upon a single language, English, and thus demoting other languages and cultures. The European Union (EU) has tried to establish a single market and to retain the languages and cultures of all the participants. At less cultural cost than the first and with greater efficiency than the second, China pursued a different course. It could be argued that the EU might consider whether a phonetic script was best adapted to a multilingual community, and whether we might adopt the Chinese alternative, despite Lenin's pronouncement that the alphabet was to be the revolution of the east, difficult as such a script may be for the keyboard.

In the arts, as early as 500 BCE much verse was written and anthologized in the 'Book of Odes' (*Shi jing*) and has been composed by the 'classically literate' ever since. At the same time, China developed a tradition of historical chronicles that later provided a model for the writing of popular historical romances (which were very different from the stories and folk tales of purely oral cultures). However, the widespread use of writing only developed in the Han dynasty, when calligraphy became an art form.[6]

Writing was important for the humanities generally as well as specifically for the arts. In the Near East, writing eventually produced a burst of religions of the Book, Judaism, Christianity and Islam, monotheistic religions of conversion and conviction whose doctrine firmly laid down the way the world was supposed to work. But writing was also used in Mesopotamia and the classical world for other scientific purposes, as well as for less authoritarian polytheistic creeds. Over time, China experienced the gradual development of thinking about nature that played down the supernatural factor. While it had initially no organized hegemonic religion, from the fifth century BCE it did have a dominant secular ideology in the shape of Confucianism. Later there was the intervention of the Buddhist religion from India, although it only penetrated the country in the first and second centuries, becoming the subject of religious fervour from the fourth to the ninth. However, it never became totally dominant

[6] Fu *et al.* 1986.

and anyhow did something to counter beliefs about the supernatural.[7] There was a further element of secularization with the suppression of Buddhism in the mid ninth century but this religion never represented anything as dominant as what had to be overturned with the Abrahamistic religions of Europe and the Near East.

And it is important for the history of science that China had more than one religion and ideology, and was not monotheistic. Not only did it have Confucianism, which was non-theistic, but it also had Buddhism, Daoism, ancestor worship and a plethora of local and imperial cults. The plurality meant that none was dominant, virtually all could be made compatible, even with the non-transcendental view that 'one of the important features of nearly all Chinese natural philosophy was its immunity to the perennial debates of Europe between the theistic world-view and that of mechanical materialism – an antithesis which the West has not yet fully resolved'.[8] Needham, the great historian of science in China, saw the interest in the natural world as specifically associated with Daoism, which in this respect seems to have resembled Tantrism in India. Particularly important was 'the Taoist contribution to the deeply organic and non-mechanical quality of Chinese naturalism'. Like Confucianism, Daoism accepted the world, which Buddhism rejected. The Daoists

refused to give up their naturalistic and realistic world-picture. The external world was, for them, real and no illusion... A sexual element was at the heart of all things, and asceticism... was simply a means to an end, the attainment of material immortality, so that the enjoyment of Nature and her beauty might have no end.

Here is the key note. One of the pre-conditions absolutely necessary for the development of science is an acceptance of Nature, not a turning away from her... But other-worldly rejection of this world seems to be formally and psychologically incompatible with the development of science.[9]

Needham's thesis about Daoism has been generally rejected. Confucianism, he argued, encouraged an ambivalent attitude towards science. That philosophy was largely concerned with people, with affairs, not at all with objects which would have led to the sciences. 'On one side Confucianism was basically rationalistic and opposed to any superstitious or even supernatural forms of religion... But on the other side its intense

[7] The Chinese language had no character for religion until about a century ago when a Japanese neologism *zongjiao* was adopted. It used the character *jiao*, meaning 'teachings', to indicate what ideas were proposed by Confucians, Daoists and Buddhists or other 'religious sects'.
[8] Needham 1956: xxiv.   [9] Needham 1956: 430–1.

concentration of interest upon human social life to the exclusion of non-human phenomena negatived all investigation of Things, as opposed to Affairs.'[10] He concedes, paradoxically, 'that rationalism proved itself less favourable than mysticism to the progress of science'. It is not clear why this should be so, nor indeed if it is true, for it has been strongly contested. Mote argues that it was Needham's emphasis on Daoism that led him to see Confucianism as inimical to science and to downplay some later achievements.[11] What is common to the historians of science and technology is that the major focal point is emphatically the Song dynasty, the great period of 'revolution' when educated males, nurtured by the study of Confucian books for the civil service examinations, increasingly tended to demote their interest in Buddhism, and Neo-Confucianism came to dominate and at the same time incorporate other systems.

So there were no periods in China where the dominance of the other-worldly dramatically interrupted the development of a more 'rationalistic' worldview as there were with the coming of Christianity in Europe, inter-mittently with Islam, and often with Judaism. Needham writes of China that there was nothing corresponding to the Dark Ages.[12] In geography, for example, just as Ptolemy's geography was falling into oblivion in Europe, in China 'it continued steadily with a consistent use of the rectangular grid right down to the coming of the Jesuits in the 17th century'.[13] One of the main reasons for this difference was connected with the nature of religion and of the worldview where China adopted 'an organic materialism'. 'Metaphysical idealism was never dominant in China, nor did the mechanical view of the world exist in Chinese thought... In some respects the philosophy of Nature may have helped the development of Chinese scientific thinking' (especially in encouraging field theories). More important was the fact that among the educated a supernaturally oriented theology did not inhibit science, as it did in Europe where a hegemonic religion oversaw most thinking about Nature. In science, the Jesuits who had such an influence in China were a post-Renaissance exception, in their belief system they adopted many of the recent discoveries of the west and tried to use them for religious purposes – to convert the heathen. To intervene like this, faith was mixed with secularism and rationalism without excluding the other-worldly.

Both Daoism and Confucianism had concerns that encouraged a concentration upon the material world, of either people or things. And materialism was associated with transforming materials, as in alchemy, which

---

[10] Needham 1956: 12.   [11] Mote 1999: 326.
[12] Needham 1981: 11 (although Thapar does speak of one in India).
[13] Needham 1981: 11.

was linked with Daoist seclusion rather than with orthodox teaching; this activity lay at the back not only of pharmacy in medical science but also of the invention of gunpowder in which China long preceded the west. This latter invention, which was 'one of the greatest achievements of the medieval Chinese world', was introduced towards the end of the Tang in the ninth century CE, but the first reference to the combination of saltpetre (potassium nitrate), charcoal and sulphur occurs in a Daoist book in 1044.[14] Its discovery appears to have something to do with the capacity to control smoke for military purposes, which is recorded as early as the fourth century BCE and was needed to conceal the movement of troops. But gunpowder was later used for 'flying fires' as well as for grenades and rockets. The invention was transmitted to Europe via Islam; in 1248 the Andalusian botanist Ibn al-Baytar mentioned saltpetre as the 'snow of China'.

However, this transformation of materials was not to everyone's taste and science did not have it all its own way. From the point of view of the scholar-gentry, certain sciences were orthodox, others were not. Interest in the calendar made astronomy valuable, as often in the west. But alchemy was 'distinctly unorthodox, the characteristic pursuit of disinterested Taoists and other recluses';[15] in pharmacy, certain types of medicine were equivocal, though as everywhere healing was always important in a practical sense even if the theories were not. The Chinese, Needham explains, displayed a 'fundamental practicality' and were 'inclined to distrust all theories', although 'Neo-Confucianism' in the eleventh–thirteenth centuries, as the philosophical basis of the Song revolution, was an exception.

While China may not have had a dark age in the European sense, it did have periods when 'civilization' was temporarily conquered by 'barbarians'. The cities of the plain and the valleys, where the civilization of the Bronze Age grew to maturity, were subject to attack from those who lived beyond and for whom the Great Wall would later be constructed to keep out. These intruders were the herders of the north, the breeders of cattle and horses, used to a rougher existence and capable of rapid movement. From the beginning of the eighth century BCE the incursion of these horsemen led the warring states to unite and about the third century BCE to take steps towards building the First Empire.

The first 'historical dynasty' in China was the Shang, with its circulating kingship, dating from the mid sixteenth to the eleventh century BCE. It fought against these northern 'barbarians', developed a metal (copper and bronze) technology out of the previous Neolithic (stone) culture with

[14] Needham 1981: 27ff.   [15] Needham 1981: 25.

high-heat processes already being used for ceramics.[16] The new age had its buildings of rammed earth fortifications, its palaces, its bronze for weapons, vessels and ornaments, its chariots and early writing on oracle bones (around 1200 BCE). The need for metals, unevenly distributed, would have led to contact with 'foreigners', possibly encouraging a more centralized political organization, with colonies and imperialism as well as a logographic script suitable for other languages. The wheeled chariots, used in burials, were probably at first primarily for hunting and seem to have come from the Caucasus in the west. But Shang ritual vessels of bronze show an advanced metal technology involving not only sophisticated knowledge of materials but a complex organization of production with large groups of ore miners, fuel gatherers, ceramic workers and foundry specialists coming together under central control. While many elaborate offerings of this kind were made to gods and ancestors, none were made to the High God, *Di*; as in many polytheistic religions, he received no cult of his own.

The Shang was followed by a regime whose political organization has been called feudal, that of the Zhou (1122–256 BCE or 1111–255 BCE); the dynasty continued until the third century BCE, when China was unified. It was during this latter period that we find the earliest documents from scribes of the royal or princely courts.[17] Before that happened, in the Spring and Autumn period (770–476 BCE) of the Zhou, there was a gradual diminution of feudal family relations. The culture of the Spring and Autumn period was exceptional in many ways and south China was eventually drawn into one sociopolitical, if not yet cultural, system, but the country flourished. Assimilating a number of 'barbarians', central control was now established, with a bureaucracy manned increasingly by educated men who expected the local prefectures to submit taxes and annual reports. Under this regime important changes took place in agriculture. In the north, wheat now became a major cereal while rice came from the south and the soya-bean was extensively grown everywhere. Fertilizing was carried out, fallow abandoned and rotation introduced. In the Central Plain agriculture became intensive and frequent weeding took place. In some areas irrigation developed to leach alkaline soil and to flood paddy fields, most of which was carried out by local authorities, not by the central government, as much of the theory of the Asiatic Mode of Production would maintain.

---

[16] Using archaeological findings, some western scholars have now traced the origin and development of bronze technology to the steppe in the third and second millennia BCE. Chinese scholars have not followed this approach, partly out of ignorance about research on these foreign sites.

[17] Gernet 2002 [1982]: 82.

Connected with these developments, inter-regional trade expanded and new cities provided markets for goods and luxuries. The big merchant entrepreneurs were the group making the largest contribution to the enrichment of the state and there was an upsurge of commerce and private industry, leading to this growth of towns. Advances in metal-smelting led to the first recorded blast furnaces and to the earliest steel, produced by a process that made some large fortunes. The use of iron proliferated, for agriculture, for warfare and for domestic purposes. The metal was produced relatively cheaply and on a large scale. As we have seen, this technology had developed from the high-heat processes used in ceramic production in the later Neolithic, which in the Bronze Age had produced metal for warfare as well as elaborate tripods for ritual offerings.

In the Western Zhou and Spring and Autumn periods (first half of the first millennium BCE) we see longer inscriptions on bronze vessels of up to several hundred characters. In the shape of these characters there was a steady erosion of pictographic realism in favour of more convenient linearity, evidence perhaps of the increasing frequency of their use or, as some scholars have argued, of a weakening of the religious ideas initially behind their production. In the following century and for half of the Warring States period that followed, the script came to be used by a greater cross-section of the population and we have a wide variety of commemorative, legal, military, commercial and other everyday documents from these decades. There was also evidence to show that bronzes were becoming wider luxury products in the sense that they could now be procured from imperial workshops and were no longer confined to royalty alone.[18]

A disintegration of the system followed during the period of the War-ring States (475–221 BCE) of the early Iron Age. In the fifth century (possibly before) standing professional armies were produced. The War-ring States period that followed saw military literature such as Sun Tzu's *Art of War*, and a considerable degree of urbanization took place, partic-ularly in the Central Plain near the Yellow River; technology advanced due to the needs of war. But political fragmentation also resulted in a diversification of writing practices amongst the various territories where archives were kept by scribes on silks and bamboo strips. Writing also took more creative forms that influenced future generations, in particular creating the classical corpus which was composed about this time. The Five Classics (*Wu jing*) are held in considerable reverence even to this day and have been compared to the works of Plato or the Bible in the west in

---

[18] Clunas 1997: 26.

terms of cultural influence; these comprised *Shi jing* (Classic of Poetry), the *Shu jing* (Classic of History), the *Yi jing* (the Book of Changes), the *Li ji* (the Book of Ritual) and the *Chunqiu* (Spring and Autumn Annals, a 722–479 BCE chronicle of the principality of Lu, Confucius's native state). It was in the time of Confucius that these works took on a definite form. It was then also that the notion of a Heavenly Bureaucracy was elaborated, with the mythical rulers under the supervision of the Jade Emperor, who ensured the proper running both of the earth and the heavens, the hierarchy of the one running parallel with that of the other so there was no sharp dichotomy between the sacred and the secular.

At this period there was also a growth of trade and of household land tax; and during the Warring States the decentralized government eventually disappeared in the face of central state control. These political and social changes were accompanied by what has been called an 'intellectual ferment',[19] when Confucius advocated social and cultural values that were to become central to later Chinese society, ideals whereby leadership combined ability and moral excellence rather than being derived solely or primarily from birth.[20] In this sense, 'feudalism' was weakened and education triumphed. And it was to this classic period of intellectual and cultural ferment that subsequent ages often looked back. Confucius was one of several important philosophers of this period, including Mencius (Mengzi, c.371–289 BCE), Mozi (fifth century BCE) and Xunzi (c.298–c.230 BCE). All were members of the *shi* (土) class of officials whose works became essential reading and study for civil servants in subsequent dynasties and were the basis of a classical education. This development took place at a time close to what the European regards as the supposed invention of philosophy in ancient Greece, the beginnings of what many westerners see as essentially theirs.

During the period of the Warring States, 'one of the richest known to history in technical innovations', life in the country had been much improved by various inventions, including the greater use of iron tools and even of the steel produced under the Zhou, leading to the development of markets, of textiles, to the appearance of metallic money and of a merchant class, one of whom, Li Si, became the prime minister of the First Emperor, Qin Shihuangdi.[21] It was he who unified China in 221 BCE, probably for the first time, with the ending of the Warring States. The new empire of the Qin was subject to a doctrine of legality (promoted

---

[19] Mote 1999: 737.
[20] Confucianism was primarily concerned with the family and so it never fully discarded birth even in official appointments.
[21] Gernet 2002 [1982]: 72.

by the Legalists) which placed law above ritual, as earlier laid down by the philosopher Han Feizi (290–234 BCE). It was this period of imperial unification that saw the gradual rise of the literati, the offspring of the earlier class of *shi*, partly to replace the great families of barons who had previously run the government. The demands of the state, changing according to circumstance, became more important than unchanging custom and even than Confucian 'humanism'. In accordance with these demands, the Qin regime constructed the Great Wall and started to organize Chinese territory by means of a series of massive works (in the course of which many died), digging canals, building a road network, as well as organizing a national system of writing, of money, of weights and measures, and the politically calculated movement of peoples. At the same time communications improved. Main roads were constructed at breakneck speed in the first decade of the third century by enormous levies of men and women. But in 213 BCE the government also decided upon a burning of books (the scale and import of the event have doubtless been exaggerated), because these writings were thought to hark back to the earlier regime. As Chinese children are taught, the emperor 'burnt the books and buried the scholars'.[22] However, his own writings remained, and he wanted to inaugurate a new intellectual order. Books dealing with subjects other than law, horticulture and herbal medicine (these subjects were also unhindered under Islam and Judaism) were kept out of public circulation because such knowledge was held to be dangerous.

The unified Chinese empire demanded a huge bureaucracy. Balazs estimates that under the Han 10 per cent of the population, i.e. 6 million persons, were bureaucrat-literati. This extensive network kept this huge empire together by an elaborate system of relay postal service, along the new roads, that was esssentially for government purposes.[23] This system was taken over by the west Mongol empire which stretched from the Pacific to the Baltic and brought its bureaucratic organization to parts of Europe.

In the thirteenth century this form of post was adopted by the Mamluk sultan Baibars (of Turkish origin) in Cairo, though of course there is evidence of earlier forms of distance communication. The post also encouraged the use of pigeons (which had also existed earlier) as well as a system of optical signals by smoke or by fire (which also had been present in earlier China). The transport included not only mail from Damascus but also ice for the sultan's drinks. Merchants were subsequently allowed to use not the post but the related caravanserais. In Europe this system of long-distance communication, which ceased to

---

[22] Clunas 1997: 29.   [23] Gazagnadou 1994: 23.

exist after the fall of the Roman empire, began again in the duchy of Milan in 1586, which had many interests in Muslim lands. It was even opened up to merchants and others, on payment of a contribution – a system that Gazagnadou sees as promoting a new mode of 'subjectification' compatible with modernization that marked the west rather than the east.[24] Important as this modern post was, it certainly did not initiate such communication at a distance and it seems a mistake to attribute that feature to its introduction. However, the Mongol advance to Europe may well have been the occasion for transfers of other Chinese inventions to Europe, including possibly the stimulus towards printing and the printing press. It was brought to France by Louis XI (r. 1461–83) (but without the private use), who was already allied to Milan and who also brought the manufacture of arms to Lyons and Tours and silk-weaving to Lyons.

In China, the First Emperor died in suspicious circumstances, and within a few years the dynasty ended in assassinations, political uprisings and chaos. From this collapse, the ascendancy of the Liu family initiated the Han dynasty in 206 BCE, and but for the brief Wang Mang interregnum these emperors ruled until 220 CE using the same imperial base as the previous dynasty. The new dynasty continued with yet larger-scale public works. Writing became more widely used and more practical. The period saw the development of the clerical script which now reached its 'full aesthetic flowering'.[25] The wide role of texts is evident from the fact that an increasing number of private individuals began to collect manuscripts which became subject to market transactions in the towns; they no longer existed only in the imperial library. The fact that texts were aimed at bureaucrats did not mean that the reading public was small. Despite the difficulties of the script, there was probably a larger readership than in the west with its alphabetic system.[26] One official is said to have owned a lot ('ten thousand chapters') of texts in scroll form, for there was a growing role for writing in all aspects of Chinese civilization.[27] To learn the characters, the well to do provided their sons with private tutors while the poor were taught in small schools on a more voluntary basis. Formal education was confined to the study of the Chinese classics (from which students learned their characters). For four or five years the boys began by memorizing characters, then learning letter writing and composition. Those pupils going into public service then attended government colleges in the main towns from which they took an

---

[24] Gazagnadou 1994.   [25] Goepper 1995: 281.   [26] Gernet 2002 [1982]: 32.
[27] Goepper 1995: 281. In the late eighth century, a chief minister had 30,000 scrolls in his library and at least three other men had 20,000.

open examination, for the more complex state needed to employ clerks and bureaucrats, trained in literacy, rather than using illiterate feudal dignitaries.

Before the second century BCE there was a lot of unrest involving a struggle between various groups of reformers. One party consisted of the 'tradition-bound Confucian literati, who advocated only "reasonable" or "justifiable" reforms as might be sanctioned by Holy Writ'.[28] This movement, in which many students took part, was carried out by the League of Literati, made up of a number of officials debarred from office, and was bloodily suppressed; the balance between training and employing literati was always a constant problem, right down to recent times. For others, Confucian ideas were dressed up to appear as revolutionary or anti-traditional; new ideas had to be given an old garb. The literati now became more important at court and this meant that books banned by the Qin came back into circulation.

Bureaucratic rule required summaries of texts and encyclopedias to sum up knowledge. Moreover, in examining changes over time in the topics that these works covered, a historian has seen a shift 'from the ritual to the functional', to 'emerging secularization, rationalization, bureaucratization'.[29] The educated, who were so often administrators, looked back to what had been written earlier, but especially in the broad field of politics; that explains the huge number of collections of documents and encyclopedias. These scholar-officials came from a very large country significantly held together by administration through this logographic script. In this situation, it was the literati (trained for government) which led the way. They were not without rivals, the eunuchs at court, the Buddhist and Daoist priests, but they held sway in the long run. After some hesitation, and not without some conflict and contradiction, they adopted Confucianist doctrines as being the ideology that best expressed their way of life. After that, even revolutionary changes, as we have seen, were disguised in historical costume and whatever new regime was established, the complexity of the country meant that the literati soon took over control of its civil administration.

The achievements of the Han in extending and consolidating the regime are associated with the emperor Han Wudi (141–87 BCE) when he was first taken under the wing of the Confucian school led by the great philosopher Dong Zhongshu (175–105 BCE). His long reign marked the extension of Chinese interests to central Asia as well as to the tropical south and the frontier with Vietnam. Much of his work lay in organizing the state to support this military activity, an important part of which was

[28] Balazs 1964: 175.   [29] Balazs 1964: 140.

financed by the state monopoly of salt and iron and then that of alcohol instituted in 119 BCE, as well as by the taxes on artisans and traders; some of these were payable in silk, which was subsequently marketed by the state with the proceeds being added to its revenue. It was not only the imperial courts but those of princes too that became centres of intellectual, literary, scientific and artistic achievement, all of which flourished. Courts were major centres of activity, especially in art which was later taken up by the bourgeoisie.[30]

The Han court of Wudi at Chang'an (present day Xi'an), at that time one of the largest and most populous cities in the world, attracted intellectuals as well as administrators from all over. It was dependent upon scholarly talent for its appointed bureaucratic officials, who were literate persons (rather than the feudal dignitaries of Confucius's day); but the bureaucracy nevertheless encouraged scientific discovery and technological achievement as well as artistic activity, and religious specialists were also found amongst these highly literate individuals. But the main aim of the educational system was not to provide clergy (as in the Abrahamistic or Hindu religions) so much as to rear administrators. Much historical writing, for example, was written by bureaucrats for bureaucrats and was intended to be a guide to administrative practice.

In 110 BCE the emperor created an Office of Music which completely re-edited the books of poetry, known as the Songs of the South and the Book of Odes (or Poetry). At the same time, one saw the greater assimilation into Confucian thought of the systems of correspondence associated with yin and yang as well as the malleable notion of the Five Agents. For official purposes many documents were produced using the revised script on bulky and fragile wood strips, or sometimes on silk. In this context, the invention of paper (no later than 105 CE) was especially useful and the circulation which this permitted further strengthened the position of the whole class of officials who, as specialists in written administration, relied on an extensive knowledge of technical terminology and a command of traditional writing. With paper this could be more readily reproduced. Competition in the official examinations by which such positions were filled was now open to other children, no longer merely to the members of the *shi* (scholar) class of bureaucrats, thus ensuring that merit played an increasing part. The activities of these literati included the explanation and writing of classical texts, the elaboration of works of reference (a bibliography, for example) and the composition of a dictionary (the *Shuo-wen jie-zi* by Xu Shen) about 100 CE. There was also the important historical work of Sima Qian (c.145–86 BCE), who wrote

---

[30] Clunas 1997: 43.

his *Record of History* (*Shiji*), complete with footnotes, to survey the whole length of Chinese history up to his time. Under such writers Chinese prose reached its 'full maturity'.[31]

Many of the achievements of the period were connected with government administration, such as a textbook on mathematics (the *Shu-shu ji-yi*, attributed to Xu Yue) used to assess officials, and a fragment of a medical work concerned with the care of troops and of horses. Water clocks were needed to time work assignments, for example for painters decorating palaces. The state's iron industries also prepared weaponry and the salt monopoly required the cutting of deep shafts for which engineers were needed, as well as to control water for transport and irrigation. The regime installed water wheels and mills for use with this latter which later were employed for industrial purposes; hydraulic power was then applied in forges to piston bellows. The wheel made its appearance in the third century and well before that came the adoption of the breast strap for harnessing horses.

Partly as a result of territorial expansion and of the consequent demographic and economic strains, throughout both the Western and Eastern phases of the Han dynasty, incursion from without, unrest from within, and succession wrangles at the top were amongst the periodic hazards that the regime had to weather. But its final end only became inevitable by the late second century CE with waves of rural rebellion, especially that of the Yellow Turbans, a messianic Daoist sect. In 190 CE the capital at Luoyang was sacked, including the library and the archives, leading to a loss of written texts greater than in the book-burning of the earlier regime. It was nevertheless a period of intense intellectual activity and Confucianism started to disappoint some members of the scholar-official class, who began to look elsewhere, above all into Daoism. Especially in its writings, that doctrine became increasingly influenced by Buddhism, now starting to make its mark in China. The Han showed various signs of cultural and scientific sophistication, as in the invention of new farming technologies and instruments, a heyday of engineering and public works, various new tendencies in medicine, a resurgence in Confucianist secularism, and a continuation of the upsurge in literacy and imperial administration initiated during the Qin, but the stability of the regime was highly variable; it lived in some ways 'on the edge' with all its military ambitions and civil liabilities.

All this activity would not have been possible without a flourishing economy, which was stimulated by the advent of Buddhism, a merchants' religion, by the conquests south and north, and by the opening up of the

[31] Gernet 2002 [1982]: 167.

Indo-Iranian trade, a move of the greatest importance which brought the Han in touch with the Roman empire as well as with Syrian merchants trading along the coasts of Vietnam. In this international exchange it was difficult to distinguish private trading from official commerce; both were involved, in one direction as in the other. It was this mercantile activity combined with increased production and technological progress that formed the background to Han military, diplomatic and commercial expansion, showing a vitality that is confirmed by literate and archaelogical evidence. Embassies from India appeared in the west and relationships with the rest of Asia proliferated. Here again, public and private enterprise existed side by side, as in silk-weaving and even in the nationalized monopolies of salt and iron. But that activity did not stop measures being taken in 199 CE, as in later Europe, to restrict the merchants' lifestyle; they were forbidden to wear silk, to ride horses and to carry arms.

When the Han fell, it was followed in 220 CE by the Three Kingdoms (San-guo, which were based in Luoyang, Chengdu and Nanjing), a period which began what is sometimes called 'the Chinese Middle Ages'. The Buddhist church had brought Hellenistic influences in the field of art and, as in later Christianity, many artists, painters, metalworkers, sculptors and architects lived on the commissions given to them in the name of religion (plate 8). In Chinese art there had been, as in Japan, a religious and a secular mode since Palaeolithic times (fifth millennium BCE), documented originally by rock paintings in scenes depicting aspects of everyday life. Then, in the second third of the first millennium CE, Buddhism became an important influence on art; although traces of Buddhist art survive from the Han period, it only became widespread from the Northern and Southern dynasties (386–589 CE) onward. From this period, religious art was dominated by Buddhist painting and secular art by drawings of humans and nature, stimulated by Daoism and Confucianism.[32] Buddhism gave rise to an important array of ornamentation, for repetition of the same motifs was a religious practice which even saw the birth of woodblock engravings and ultimately the appearance of the printed word by the same process which permitted endless ritual repetition; a million copies of one Buddhist charm were printed in Japan at the empress's orders in the eighth century.[33] That religion also contributed to the development of literature in the vernacular and between the fourth and the eighth centuries encouraged the advent from India of work in the secular sciences, especially in mathematics, astronomy and medicine. Though the original writings have disappeared, translations

---

[32] Lee 1991.   [33] Clunas 1997: 109.

from 'Brahmanical' texts were especially important in the latter part of this period.

The sinologist Balazs writes of the 'spiritual renaissance of the Middle Ages', and the total transformation of the country between 200 BCE and 600 CE (Qin to the beginning of Tang).[34] The salvationist creed of the Buddhism of the Great Vehicle (*Mahayana*), which had been introduced to China from India about the beginning of Christianity, became highly influential in the fourth century CE. Among the consequences of this influence was the acquisition of considerable property and power by the Buddhist establishment which also set up its learned monasteries and schools, though the learning was mainly religious and scriptural. It was in the north, at Luoyang, at Dunhuang and at Chang'an, that between the second and the early fifth centuries the Sanskrit texts of the Gautama were translated into Chinese, a stupendous task. The extension of Buddhism to the south took place under the Southern Liang dynasty (502–57 CE) founded in Nanjing, which prospered partly as the result of the great expansion of maritime commerce and the construction of south-eastern ports permitting the exchange of goods with the coastal towns of south-east Asia and the Indian Ocean. Many merchants from abroad visited these Chinese ports, the country became considerably richer and the Buddhist establishment benefited financially due to its privileged position.

After the decline of the Han until the coming of the Sui in 581 CE, despite or possibly because of the political fragmentation that marked the country, cultural and social life was 'one of the richest and most complex in the intellectual history of the Chinese world. It was astonishingly fertile and abounded in innovations' and in these respects has also been said to resemble Renaissance Italy[35] – its metaphysics, its religious fervour (mainly towards Buddhism), its interest in aesthetics and literary criticism, with painting becoming a skilled art, especially in landscape (influenced by the Daoist interest in nature), and an unprecedented 'efflorescence of poetry'. In the latter half of the second century there had been a 'renascence' of the thought of the Warring States period (of the fourth and third centuries BCE) but from a rather different point of view. The north of China saw an era of renewed 'barbarian' invasions and rule, dating from 304 CE. South of the Yangzi opposition of a disorganized sort took place. Although politically weak, 'these dynasties were characterized by cultural brilliance: in literature, art, philosophy, and religion, they constituted one of the most creative periods in Chinese history'.[36] Once again, political weakness did not appear to inhibit a

---

[34] Balazs 1964: 187.   [35] Gernet 2002 [1982]: 202.   [36] Twitchett 1997: 83.

cultural efflorescence, and cultural advances continued despite the problems with government and religion.

One of these southern regimes, the Liang, under which maritime commerce expanded, was followed by several short-lived dynasties. Eventually, the reunification of the country was carried out from Luoyang by the
partly 'barbarian' general Yang Jian (later known as the emperor Wendi),
founder of the Sui dynasty (581–618 CE) which ushered in what has
again been called a 'golden age' that lasted more than three centuries
(through the Tang); it was marked by an economic boom, the absence of
civil wars and a wide range of achievements not only in technology but
in literature, the plastic arts, in music and in dance. The Sui continued
to open up the waterways, vastly enhancing and expanding communication and commerce, completing the Grand Canal that linked north
and south; the canal encouraged the primary producers and markets
to exploit the agricultural potential of the Yangzi Valley and the Chinese started a flotilla for maritime expeditions to Korea and Sumatra.
Trade expanded. It was in 628 that Islam first came to China. With
the expansion of commerce that followed in the next dynasty, the Tang,
Wahb-Abi-Kabcha, a maternal uncle of the Prophet, was sent by sea
from Arabia to Canton, where the first Chinese mosque was built, with
presents for the emperor. Nestorian Christians also despatched a mission from Persia in 631. From the same country, Mazdaism had arrived
earlier that century and Manicheanism came later on in 694; a plethora
of religions was permitted. There were Brahman temples and merchants
in Canton in 750 CE.[37]

The Tang dynasty was founded in 618 by another general, the emperor
Taizu, in alliance with Turkic rebels; he was assassinated by his son, Li
Shimin, who became the emperor Taizong, reigning from 626 CE to
649. The first two Tang emperors once again unified the country; in the
main they carried on the administrative practices of the Sui regime but
in a more economical way. The period included an 'era of good government' very much looking back to Confucian ideals. While the court
administration consisted largely of military and aristocrats, it achieved
some regional balance and was supplemented by 10 per cent of examination candidates. These tests had been re-established following the Sui,
though candidacy was necessarily restricted since government schools,
teaching a standardized curriculum, were mainly limited to the sons of
nobility and of high officials; however, the system was soon to become
more open still. In the early Tang the economy grew under the leadership
of the capital, Chang'an, which at that time was the largest city in the

[37] Sastri 1975: 332.

world with at least 600,000 inhabitants. The desire to raise the resources with which to conquer new territories led to a reorganization of the agricultural system, with each family devoting a certain specified acreage to farm crops that provided a tax in cereals, silk or labour. A version of this 'equitable fields' land tenure and civil administration already functioned in the Sui and even earlier in the Northern Wei dynasty. The administration obviously involved a complex bureaucracy that regularly produced a large-scale census and cadastral surveys.

This period of 'good government' was noted for low prices and for general prosperity, following measures taken to rationalize taxation. Taizong undertook a new codification of law and provided for strong central control. The military reorganized under the Tang now extended their domination over the Turkic tribes to the north, giving rise to greater communication with the west. Embassies came from Byzantium (Rome had earlier sent a mission by ship under the Han in 166 CE); Nestorian temples and Buddhist monasteries were established in the larger towns.

Truly unique was the remarkable rule of the empress Wu Zhao (b. 627), known as Emperor Wu, a concubine of the previous emperor who had the capital moved to Luoyang and preferred examination-selected officials for the top positions. She dominated from 660, and ruled as emperor from 690 to 705, thrusting aside the legitimate heir. The administration expanded with the number of examination candidates whose presence necessarily diminished the role of the aristocracy, although many degree holders were aristocrats and 80 per cent of the officials still had no degrees; nevertheless half of the officials were ex-clerks promoted for good service from within the ranks of provincial government offices. The change of emphasis to examination candidates for top court appointments was probably important in the 'Renaissance' that followed. Their expansion again required new taxes, the unpopularity of which helped get rid of the ruler in 705. However, Japan (and Korea) did not have the same attachment to recruitment by examination as had later China. 'Japanese Confucianism remained committed to their native, aristocratic traditions.'[38] There was not the same meritocracy, although in China it was only in the fourteenth century that merchants' sons could compete, so that equality of (male) opportunity was a process slow to evolve. Subsequently the reign of Xuanzong, the 'Brilliant Emperor', was the high point of the Tang's material prosperity, its institutional progress and the 'flowering of the arts'. As part of his sweeping administrative reforms, taxpayers were now more effectively registered and, together with the

---

[38] Elman and Woodside 1994: 545.

repair of the Grand Canal system (which had fallen into neglect under Emperor Wu), his court enjoyed a great increase in imperial revenues. It was a period of extraordinary progress in engineering, in the building of canals, of roads and bridges, as well as in the arts. Even beyond the achievement of their illustrious contemporary Wang Wei, the *yang* and *yin* of Chinese poetry, Li Bai and Du Fu (widely known as Li Po and Tu Fu to English-language readers), are considered among the greatest poets of any age; this was seen 'like the Renaissance, linking the ancient to the modern world'.[39] Though as a 'civil servant poet' Du Fu leant distinctly more towards Confucian values, the reckless and brilliant Li Bai's work was unmistakably Daoist, and despite his repeated attempts to enter the civil service, and one brief period of appointment, the strident free-thinking exuberance of his poetry is as non-Confucian in tone as one could imagine. The poetry's editor, Cooper, describes this as 'the most golden of all the golden ages in the 3,000 years . . . of Chinese poetry',[40] resembling 'our Tudor times'.[41] This period is said to have been preceded by the 'Chinese Dark Ages' (despite Needham's assertion to the contrary) which occurred before the earlier Sui dynasty and has been thought of quite differently, but nevertheless there was 'a continuity of traditions unknown in any of the world's literatures'. Throughout the Three Kingdoms, the Jin and Southern and Northern dynasties periods between the Han and the Sui there was a dark age because of political fragmentation, invasions, rebellions, usurpations, territorial instability and the economic problems, but nevertheless a cultural efflorescence. Later Cooper speaks of the emergence of 'a Renaissance-like age', comparing Du Fu with Dante[42] and the surrounding society to fifteenth-century Florence,[43] while others have referred to the works of western classical Antiquity.[44]

While the Tang is known as the golden age of Chinese poetry, its composition was of course widely practised both before and after. In this 'golden age' of classical verse, the writers were original, personal poets.[45] But this was also a time of great achievement in a more vernacular prose, and notable for some early attempts to write fiction, 'tales of marvels'. The visual arts prospered, in architecture (though little remains) as in painting (though few originals are found). Minor arts were lively and colourful. Above all, there was an important shift in the means of communication. Printing appeared, first to multiply Buddhist scriptures, and later for calendars, almanacs and dictionaries. The appearance of

[39] Cooper 1973: 20.   [40] Cooper 1973: 20.   [41] Cooper 1973: 22.
[42] Cooper 1973: 37.   [43] Cooper 1973: 172.   [44] Demiéville 1962.
[45] Gernet 2002 [1982]: 275.

woodblock engravings presaged a more rapid diffusion of knowledge and the emergence of a popular literature, as well as the repetition of written prayers. 'The invention of printing made possible a general diffusion of knowledge hitherto impracticable, and made books available to the most modest of purses. The resultant increase in the number of libraries reinforced the bookish nature of education, fixed the literary character of the examinations, and helped Neo-Confucianism to inculcate the precepts of traditional conservatism and to disseminate respect for antiquity.'[46] Since the early Tang, and the travels of the brilliant Buddhist scholar, translator and historian Xuanzang (602–64), there had been a tradition of translation from Sanskrit and other Indian languages used for the Buddhist treatises; he himself even translated Laozi's *Dao-de jing*, the seminal Daoist classic, into Sanskrit.[47] The new intellectual climate led to a diversity of political philosophies, but it was not only learning but commercial life that blossomed during this period. Towns grew up, the range of luxuries expanded, agriculture improved, iron technology became widespread, taxation was regularized, artisans flourished. In the country itself the taxable base shifted to private land, taxes on commerce became more important, and the institution of state monopolies favoured the rise of a new class of merchants.

The Tang emperors officially supported Daoism since they were supposedly descendants from Laozi, the founder, but nevertheless Buddhism was favoured. As elsewhere, much wealth in land had been transferred to the church and this was necessarily withdrawn from ordinary circulation, grasped by its 'dead hand' (mortmain). The monasteries exploited these lands, either directly or indirectly, operated mills, provided hospitals, cared for the sick and ran their own schools. When in 843–5 the emperor Wuzong decided to suppress Buddhism, partly for financial reasons (as in the European Reformation), monasteries were closed, lands confiscated, some quarter of a million monks and nuns were sent away. The attack did not last long but this point marked the beginning of a decline in the influence of Buddhism and the revival of Confucianism in a new form.

There had been a period of strong religious influence with the building of many pagodas, which were towers functionally evolved from the stupa of India. At the time, as we have seen, several Chinese monks visited that country and left behind valuable accounts of life in those parts. But official circles became increasingly worried at the growth of Buddhist power, leading to persecutions and proscriptions and to a further 'sinification' of both popular and educated schools of thought. This was also the time when China came in contact with Muslims along the Silk

[46] Balazs 1964: 146.   [47] Gernet 2002 [1982]: 279–80.

Road, a great channel for the exchange not only of goods but of ideas in both directions, with India as well as with the west. However, the Chinese were defeated by those Muslims at the battle of the Talas River near Lake Balkhash in 751, where prisoners were said to have passed on the secrets of paper production, eighteen or nineteen years after the victory of Charles Martel over the Muslims at Poitiers. But the intellectual exchange with Asia was not all one way. There was an influx of astronomical, material and mathematical knowledge, of manufactured goods, music and crafts from western and central Asia, giving the culture a definite cosmopolitan aspect.

Despite the threat of Arabic and other forces invading the country, plus the vicissitudes of internal social pressures and periodic insurrections, the Tang (618–907 CE) continued to flourish until 755. Then the rebellion of the Turkic-Sogdian general An Lushang sacked the capital, put an end to the first phase of the dynasty and, despite the subsequent restoration of imperial rule, set the tone for a long but steady history of decline. When the central government eventually collapsed in 907, artists and craftsmen lost a powerful patron, for the imperial court had stimulated the 'golden age' of literature. The regional courts of the following Five Dynasties (907–960) tried to continue the same tradition in art and culture, especially in the kingdom of Sichuan; many poets, painters and scholars moved there to what constituted a miniature Tang court. There was the monk Guanxiu, for example, whose paintings of *arhats*, disciples of the Buddha, showed pain, suffering and consciousness of death, indeed brought out their spiritual experiences, subjects that were rarely treated in court-sponsored painting.

The main format of painting at the time was the wall-surface together with some screens, but in the following tenth century these types were challenged by smaller, more intimate portable paintings, leading in the following century to elegant miniatures. But in north China the great tradition of Tang wall-painting ended with the persecution of Buddhism, especially severe in 955, and was only taken up again in the later thirteenth and fourteenth centuries. The Tang influence continued in Jinling, as Nanjing was then called, which was the capital of the Southern Tang kingdom and achieved a remarkably high level of artistic culture, especially in the landscape paintings of the Buddhist priest Juran (active c.960–85) and of the court painter Dong Yuan (d. 962). The work of these men was very different from that of northern painters, produced as it was in the lush and distinctive natural surroundings of Jiangnan, the remaining Southern Tang territory; it spanned the Five Dynasties and the early Song years, and set the standard for much of the Song dynasty proper. While the Song which followed the Five Dynasties in

960 could not equal Tang achievements in figure and narrative painting, it would surpass it in its depictions of nature, in landscapes and in bird and flower painting.

It was the first half of the eighth century when Chinese influence in Asia was at its peak, with many missionaries arriving from India, central Asia and Iran. In the Tang of the early ninth century we find the development of 'the back to Antiquity' movement (*ku-wen*) that first made its mark in the literary field, then took up the interpretation of ancient texts, giving rise to a process of 'radical evolution' that led to 'the sort of renaissance constituted by "neo-Confucianism" under the Song in the eleventh and twelfth centuries'.[48] In a nationalistic way, that 'looking back' led to the proscription of foreign religions as early as 836 and finally in 845 under the Tang. This included the Mazdaist and Nestorian churches but it was Buddhists that suffered most because they had accumulated so much. Monks were secularized, lands were seized, copper bells and statues melted down and turned into coinage (as in the 'reforms' of Henry VIII). The measures were soon eased but Buddhism never again played so central a part in Chinese life and thought.[49]

The Song state emerged by conquest in 960 (–1279) and reunified the ancient empire by taking most of the fragmented territories by the late 970s. In doing so it saw that rebirth of traditional learning and education but used these not in order to retreat back but to move forward in many fields. All traditional Chinese education, ending up with the highest examination of all, the *jinshi*, involved mastering the ten or twelve basic Confucian classics. One of the leaders of the 'Neo-Confucian' movement in the Song was Zhu Xi (1130–1200), who had a great command of classical learning. Though his doctrines were not declared orthodox until more than a century after his death, his contribution to 'Neo-Confucianism' embraced a paedagogical synthesis which grouped together four of the central books of Confucian philosophy to form the basic educational texts, the *Doctrine of the Mean*, the *Great Learning*, the *Analects of Confucius* and the *Mencius*, together with his commentaries. They would remain standard for the civil service examinations right down to the time that these were abolished in 1905. Thus the Southern Song commentaries were a key element in the measure of ideological continuity that existed over a period of nearly 2500 years: at its heart was a secular ideology that did not hamper additions to knowledge in science nor achievement in the arts. And yet the social horizons of this ideology were limited in

---

[48] Gernet 2002 [1982]: 293.
[49] Some western scholars think Chan Buddhism in the Song reached the peak of its attainment.

several ways. For example, Zhu Xi is also said to have composed a book called *Family Rituals* which prescribed the ceremonies for key passages in a person's way of life; in these and other matters he placed increasing restrictions on women, tending to bring them under greater male control. Partly for this reason the learning of the 'Great Way' has been seen as stiff and unthinking, a factor in the supposed social and technological tardiness of later eras of Chinese culture. Nevertheless, '[t]he intellectual vigour of the Northern Song was generated by a rediscovery of Confucian values'[50] – in other words, by a looking back which brought with it a flowering of culture.

From the Song onwards, except for the Mongol era, the Chinese upper classes were no longer attracted to the military profession in the same way as before – that was for mercenaries. They rather concerned themselves with textual learning, and in their leisure they collected books and works of art, and practised literature, painting and calligraphy, developments which were assisted by the much earlier advent of woodblock printing.[51] The centre of the artistic activity of the Southern Song was the capital Hangzhou with its many examination candidates, bureaucrats, military men and Buddhist monks.[52] The lives of these persons showed what have been described as high consumption levels, lavish tastes and a love of exotic products. Much the same consumption patterns were evident in other large urban centres, since the elite were dispersed throughout the country and there was a high level of trade between cities. The entertainment quarters of these cities produced popular shows drawing large audiences of ordinary people, including those coming from the rural areas. There was also the expansion of amusements including the seeds of popular literature; storytellers, shadow-theatre, novels and plays flourished. In China there was always a difference between the classical works of the literati and the more rustic literature of the people, though with the latter providing much of the impetus for change. 'Every new form', wrote Hu Shih, '. . . had come . . . from the unlettered class of the countryside . . .'.[53]

According to Elvin, medieval China, by which he means the tenth to the fourteenth century, the late Tang and Song periods, experienced an extensive 'revolution'. Needham also speaks of the 'Golden Period' of natural science of the eleventh and twelfth centuries.[54] Technologically, Chinese agriculture was transformed; in the north improved milling machinery facilitated the shift from millet to wheat; in the south there

---

[50] Mote 1999: 323.   [51] Elvin 1973: 179.
[52] The major neo-Confucian figures did not live in Hangzhou.
[53] Hu Shih 1934: 52.   [54] Needham 1956: 493.

was increasing mastery of the technique of wet-field rice. The spread of new methods was encouraged by woodblock printing, especially with new seeds, double cropping, water control and its increased lifting (by means of the *noria*),[55] more careful preparation of the soil, and increased marketing. There was also a revolution in water transport which was very extensive, both inland by roads and rivers, and by sea from one part of China to another. By Song times, Chinese boats had become much more sophisticated, built with iron nails, waterproofed with oil, with watertight bulkheads, buoyancy chambers, axial rudders and compasses. Canals linked up inland waterways and the invention of the double lock in the eleventh century eased passage past difficult points. With advanced technology, merchant activity became more complex, with partnerships of various kinds exploiting the system of water transport. At the same time, roads were improved, some even being paved. Trade increased, as did the money supply on which it partially depended. In the eleventh century, paper money made an early appearance but the excessive use of notes led to inflation by the early twelfth and again in the thirteenth century. As a consequence, they were withdrawn. However, merchant credit still existed in the form of bills of exchange and other devices. The opening up of China to commercial activities, especially in the southern provinces and towards the Indian Ocean, meant a great upsurge in all spheres from the tenth to the thirteenth century.

A further merchant revolution, Elvin suggests, took place in market structure and urbanization. Commerce had long been important but now a long-distance market for daily goods developed. For the peasantry this meant increased exchange, not only for food and timber but also for paper and textiles. There was a strong growth in inter-regional trade as well as in international commerce with Japan, Korea and south-east Asia. Business activity as a whole became more complex and the towns developed, but Elvin nevertheless sees these centres as having a different historical role than those in Europe (meaning in his view they did not presage capitalism; only Europe did that).

From the tenth century it is clear that China went through a revolution in science and technology 'advancing to the threshold of a systematic experimental investigation of nature' and creating 'the world's earliest mechanised industry' in iron smithing and silk spinning.[56] Deforestation in the north led to the increased use of coal and iron, especially important for the manufacture of weaponry. In textile production, new machinery was developed for reeling silk; in the thirteenth century this was widely adopted for hemp and powered by the water in canals, which may well

[55] Elvin 1973: 113.   [56] Elvin 1973: 179.

have influenced the creation of European reeling machinery in Lucca and Bologna and thence its spread to England.[57] Advances also took place in intellectual matters, in mathematics, astronomy and medicine. The foundation again lay in the art of woodblock printing, invented by the seventh century and in general use by the eleventh. Even moveable type was created in the eleventh century, though it was never used to any large extent. Elvin writes of 'a renaissance of learning' driven by the government.[58] The Song dynasty edited and printed many texts, old as well as new, raising 'the national level of knowledge to new heights'.

The historian Gernet also sees a Chinese Renaissance as beginning around the year 1000, reinforcing much that Elvin suggested. The eleventh century was distinguished by a return to the classical Confucian tradition, and the end of the influence Buddhism had exercised since the fifth century CE.[59] The educated Chinese of the eleventh century, he claims, was 'as different from his Tang predecessors as Renaissance man from medieval man'.[60] Gernet discerns a practical rationalism based on experiment, a testing of everything, a curiosity in each realm of human knowledge, leading to an attempt to construct a synthesis and a naturalist philosophy. In fact, there was a complete 'renewal of intellectual life' based upon the urban economy and 'cheap means of reproducing written texts'.[61]

In this latter respect, the Chinese experience of printing was rather gradual and slow. Many documents and texts which consisted mainly of Buddhist writings and pictures were held in a repository in the northern caves of Dunhuang. Closed circa 1000, they were only opened in 1907 when they were found to contain almanacs, lexicons, a short popular encyclopedia, educational texts and model compositions, as well as historical and occult works. Interestingly, less than 1 per cent of these texts were imprints. The literati were slow to take advantage of the new process, but from 932 the Nine Classics were printed by a provincial government and soon afterwards the whole Buddhist canon by the Song dynasty, despite the control exercised over that religion.

In the Renaissance the west eventually made considerable advances in printing with moveable type, but the first full use of this technology in China is referred to c.1040. However, this did not involve a press, without which moveable type had little chance of supplementing the woodblock before the arrival of mechanical printing from Europe in the nineteenth

---

[57] Elvin 1973: 198.   [58] Elvin 1973: 180.
[59] Much recent western scholarship questions the end of Buddhist influence. It sees it flourish with the Song and abate in the Ming. But institutionally it was restricted.
[60] Gernet 2002[1982]: 330.   [61] Gernet 2002 [1982]: 331.

century. Until that time the creation of woodblocks was usually quicker and cheaper than setting moveable type. This technique nevertheless gave rise to a very lively book-trade which ensured a wider diffusion of knowledge. The main centres of learning had previously been Buddhist monasteries and the state schools in the capital. From the eleventh century, however, public and private schools multiplied together with libraries. One of the biggest libraries was that of the Imperial Palace founded in 978, later containing 80,000 scrolls or chapters (*juan*). This was a period of collections of texts, of large encyclopedias and of complex inventories. The age was also famous for the number of published works in the natural sciences. From the latter half of the twelfth century private publications flourished in south-east China, so that in the realms of medicine, geography, mathematics and astronomy 'remarkable progress was made'; in mathematics there was the development of algebra and evidence of the first Chinese use of the nought.[62] In addition, in 1090 there was the construction at Kaifeng of an astronomical machine activated by an escapement, which provided a slow, regular motion, and produced the most accurate piece of clockwork so far developed.

The Song also saw the awakening of an interest in antiquities and in the growth of archaeology which had already begun in the eighth century. That led in turn to the activity of copiers and forgers. The period is said to have seen the emergence of a movement towards critical reflection, especially in comparing versions of histories, an important aspect of literacy. This movement formed the basis of a 'positive renewal of historical studies' as well as the composition of historical encyclopedias.[63] Especially important was the work of Sima Guang (as in *The Complete Mirror*), which was marked by an exhaustive search of sources and a critical approach to documents.

At the same time Song writers formulated a philosophical system concerned with the basic characteristics of the human and the natural orders, which was definitely hostile to Buddhism though adapting some of its questions and methods of teaching in its return to what was considered the true Confucian tradition. In this way the new learning, as we have seen, was associated with an effort to jump over the previous age of religious restrictions and to go back to ancient sources, including the classics, an aim not so different from that of the 'humanists' in later Europe. In fact, this age is described as one 'of optimism and of faith in universal reason' with a belief in the benefits of education and in the possibility of improving society and the political system, together with a desire for a systematization of knowledge and a search for 'the good life'

[62] Gernet 2002 [1982]: 338.   [63] Gernet 2002 [1982]: 342.

to replace the ideology of Buddhism.[64] This task involved a return to the past and to the formulation of 'Neo-Confucianism', which thereafter had a stabilizing effect on Chinese thought comparable to that of Aristotle and Aquinas in the west.[65]

In sum, the eleventh to the thirteenth century saw 'an amazing economic and intellectual upsurge',[66] in contrast to the comparative 'backwardness' of Europe before the Italian cities took on new life at the other end of great commercial routes of the continent. For a time this trade by land and by sea avoided the invasions of the Mongols which did so much harm to the Islamic world, but established or resurrected connections between the Asiatic east and the west, though this suffered from the division of the Mongol empire in central Asia from the mid fourteenth century. After 1500, the west emerged from its relative isolation through its exploration of the east, especially maritime, whereas the Arabs, Indians, Chinese and others had long traded throughout the Indian Ocean and in the China seas.

In the more important towns, the state expanded education, largely of a literary kind but practical subjects were also taught. Medicine itself had its own independent training, as in the Near East (and eventually in Europe), which was supervised by the Office of Supreme Medicine. This unit established a college that offered instruction, supervised by the government, in four areas, general medicine, accupunture, massage and exorcism.[67] In 629 the Tang emperor had already established medical schools in every prefecture, and in the eleventh century copies of the materia medica and other texts were centrally printed; advanced and comprehensive pharmacopoeiae were published. Medical training took seven years of study in which knowledge was tested by examination. Part of the training involved the learning of ethical concepts, very much like those defined in the Hippocratic oath. Chinese medicine did not produce much surgery since, as in the west, it was thought that the body should be returned to God or the ancestors in the same condition as it had left. Consequently there was little investigation or research done in this area, but dissection did develop from 1045 CE. In this medical work Daoism played a strong part, especially that to do with exorcism; Buddhist clergy, however, were little involved except with the care of the poor and the sick, which was to some extent taken over by the Song government in the ninth and tenth centuries after the persecution of Buddhism. But apart from 'religious medicine' there were also 'Confucian doctors', that is, secular physicians who became more important in the Tang.[68]

---

[64] Gernet 2002 [1982]: 345.   [65] Gernet 2002 [1982]: 346.
[66] Gernet 2002 [1982]: 347.   [67] Benn 2004: 225.   [68] Benn 2004: 294.

Private printing flourished, not only for Buddhist scriptures but also for texts in agriculture and in mathematics, so that China became 'the most numerate as well as the most literate nation in the world'.[69] In writing of the 'revolution in science and technology' of the tenth to the fourteenth century, Elvin speaks of 'this renaissance of learning'.[70] This followed 'many preceding centuries of scientific and technical progress'[71] which had as their foundation the development of woodblock printing from the eighth century, ensuring the wide circulation of scientific texts. But 'the main driving force' was the government (except for astronomy which was 'classified' as possibly dangerous). Otherwise the Song government edited and printed standard texts not only on mathematics and agriculture, but also on medicine and warfare, as well as the Confucian scriptures, dynastic histories, law codes and philosophical writings. It also sponsored some new publications. In other words, as with Eisenstein[72] in the case of the Italian Renaissance, Elvin attributes an important role to printing (by woodblocks) from around the tenth century. Not everyone is in agreement. In his work on the Chinese book, McDermott thinks that the role of the printed book in the Song has been over-rated; nonetheless it was significant in diffusing old knowledge and in encouraging the new, which it was able to do some centuries before Gutenberg.[73]

The achievement in the realm of art was no less important and this became 'the foundation for all later dynasties'.[74] For during the Song 'the art of painting flourished as it never had before'.[75] Emperors themselves painted and it became one of the gentlemanly arts.[76] The great practioner of this period, who built on the work of earlier artists from the north and south, was the aristocratic Li Cheng (919–67), who became creator of the landscape style of the Song, painting the elegant world that became 'the most dynamic, cultivated, and richly accomplished in Chinese history'.[77] The classic breadth of the Northern Song aesthetic is visible in the stark contrast between Li Cheng's work and that of another great painter, Fan K'uan (955–1025), a 'mountain man' who produced one of the great surviving masterpieces of landscape, *Travelling among Mountains and Streams* (plate 9).

The emperor Huizong had organized an Imperial Academy for painting, an art which he himself practised along with poetry and calligraphy, where painters worked in excellent conditions, representing the birds and plants that surrounded them. Huizong was also an antiquarian with a respect for the past and his interest led ceramic artisans to reproduce

[69] Elvin 1973: 181.   [70] Elvin 1973: 180.   [71] Elvin 1973: 179.
[72] Eisenstein 1979.   [73] McDermott 2006.   [74] Barnhart 1997: 96.
[75] Barnhart 1997: 97.   [76] Mote 1976: 4.   [77] Barnhart 1997: 100.

the form of bronzes manufactured 3,000 years earlier. About the year 1110 manuscripts along with ancient inscriptions on stone, bronze or jade were edited under the Song, giving a great documentary insight into the cultural and political life of ancient China.

In his academy, Huizong, who brought more painters to the capital than anyone before, emphasized three aspects. The first was Daoist religion and the careful, direct enquiry into nature, the tradition of representing nature that was embodied in the work of Guo Zi, the greatest artist of this period (plate 10). He also insisted upon the systematic study of the classical painting traditions; the catalogue he produced of the government's collection was 'a major document in the process of canonisation'.[78] The third requirement was the attainment of 'a poetic idea'; Huizong's paintings themselves attain 'a classic beauty rooted in the past, in realistic observation, and in poetic ideals'.[79]

The political course of the Song dynasty was, once more, divided between a Northern (960–1126) and a Southern (1127–1279) phase. Of achievement in the arts, Mote sings the praises of the former:

the Northern Song is famed as an age of consummate poetry and strong belletristic and historical prose writing, of magnificent painting and calligraphy, of matchless ceramics, and of a full complement of what the Chinese looked upon as minor arts. The scholar-official elite . . . were the creators and producers of the poetry and other literature, as of the painting and calligraphy, and they patronized the craftsmen who made . . . the ceramics and all the beautiful objects they collected, treasured, and used in their daily lives . . . In some fields of humanistic learning the Song saw the beginnings of quite systematic scholarship that is strikingly modern in its methods and goals. It was an age when the systemizing and ordering of vast fields of knowledge in encyclopaedias was a characteristic undertaking. The study of the past saw advances in historical study, in linguistics, in the critical study of classical texts, in the collection and study of ancient inscriptions on bronze and stone, and in the beginnings of archaeology.

The Song elite

had progressed far beyond the 'cabinet of curiosities' stage, still current in Europe at a much later date, and were engaged in intelligent research concerned with identification, etymology, dating, and interpretation . . . From among the ranks of the same scholar-official elite that produced the artists, writers, and humanists also came the persons who delved into mathematics, science, medicine, and technology, making the Song a high point in those fields as well.[80]

Especially important at this time was the work of Shen Gua (1031–95), a 'highly individualistic' personality whose remarkable achievements are

---

[78] Barnhart 1997: 24.   [79] Barnhart 1997: 25.   [80] Mote 1999: 151.

listed by Mote.[81] He was known as a man of 'human letters', equally at home in sciences as in the arts. 'Of course there also were the unnamed non-elite persons who designed and built ships, applied maritime technology to sailing the seas, built the bridges, palaces, and temples, sculpted the great Buddhist figures and impressively decorated the temples, designed and manufactured weapons and the matériel of war, and contributed in innumerable ways to the life of the society.'[82]

In the late tenth and eleventh centuries the northern bureaucracy recruited widely and examinations became more important. Official salaries were increased and schools opened in every prefecture to prepare for the examinations; institutions of welfare grew. The collection of tax was improved both in efficiency and from the standpoint of social justice. At the same time the exploitation of salt, copper, iron and coal was increased. These measures taken by Emperor Shenzong's chief minister, Wang Anshi, were annulled by his successor 'in the name of Confucius'. Then the faction-ridden state in the north became a prey for the 'barbarians on horseback', the Jurchen warriors from a Tangut tribe who eventually took the emperor Huizong prisoner at the capital of Kaifeng in 1127.

The sacking of the capital led to a retreat southwards across the Yangzi to the picturesque city of Hangzhou, which became 'perhaps the most flourishing economic centre of the world during the twelfth and thirteenth centuries'.[83] In the eleventh century the south too had become richer partly through the cultivation of Champa (early) rice, which allowed two harvests in one season, and partly because its ports opened the way for the export of commodities to the world at large, bringing considerable benefits to the merchant class. Now they reconstituted the Painting Academy which supplied works to the rulers whose preferences were of great significance in promoting an artistic style for they laid down the themes for much of the art. The re-established dynasty was especially attentive to the power of art, 'concentrating upon a new image of classical revival',[84] particularly 'old historical narratives telling of imperial hardship, survival and rebirth'. Royal patronage dominated at this period for the merchants did not patronize paintings. Painting itself was largely in the hands of craftsman families whose interests were conservative. This was also true for the works done under the patronage or inspiration of the Buddhist temples, as with Chan (or Zen) painting.

Still threatened by northern invaders, the Southern Song constructed naval craft on the Yangzi River and, described in a manuscript on warfare

[81] Mote 1999: 326.   [82] Mote 1999: 151.
[83] Barnhart 1997: 28.   [84] Barnhart 1997: 28.

published in 1044, developed the use of gunpowder for war purposes. The Mongols from the north imitated this practice. The invention of gunpowder passed to the Arabs and then, at the end of the thirteenth century, to the Europeans. Under the Southern Song dynasty, the landed families in the vicinity of the capital became increasingly important until a reformist prime minister, Jia Sidao (1213–75), introduced a limitation of some 27 hectares in the size of estates, the remainder being confiscated by the state to support the army. However, his reforms came in the final gasp of the dynasty and affected only the lower Yangzi delta. For most of the first century the Southern Song prospered, commerce in the south-east becoming increasingly important. Towns grew, and agriculture prospered owing to the different strands of early ripening rice; trade increased both internally along the waterways, including in luxuries which were produced not only for palaces but now for the *nouveau riche* in private exchange, and externally with the outside world. From about 1200 CE, China had the biggest navy in the world, consisting of huge ships ('junks') with as many as a dozen sails, vertical keels and sealed compartments capable of carrying some 500–600 passengers and guided by the mariner's compass and by maps. The country also advanced astronomy and invented the first mechanical clock.[85] The age has been summed up as one in which 'a new culture' took form, although this was later seen as representing 'traditional China'. But there was 'a new spirit in learning and thought', not as 'unquestionable truths attained through some level of suprarational revelation'. The elite were achievement-oriented in a self-conscious fashion and their confidence was built upon prosperity. 'China was the richest, most orderly, most culturally and technologically advanced portion of the world throughout the more than three centuries of the Song',[86] especially in the south. It contained the largest cities, supported greater commerce than the rest of the world, printed thousands of books and had a growing rate of literacy. During this period, the Chinese probably had a higher percentage of educated people than the west.[87] That meant that China could 'effectively accumulate, present, and disseminate knowledge'[88] which improved lives and livelihoods. For it had an 'ever-surprising inventiveness in science and technology'.

It was then that China became the 'workshop of the world', with many significant industries especially in textiles, in tea, in porcelain where the

---

[85] By the late twelfth, if not the eleventh, century Chinese sea-going boats could carry as much as 5,000 piculs of cargo and 500–600 persons. Such boats were rare, however, and most big boats had two masts, 2,000 or more piculs of cargo and fewer than 100 crewmen.
[86] Mote 1999: 324, as is much of the paragraph.
[87] Gernet 2002 [1982]: chapter 15.   [88] Mote 1999: 328.

use of coal and hydraulic machines enabled them to produce at higher temperatures. This extensive exchange, both public and private, saw the widespread use of copper currency (sometimes melted down from Buddhist statues) and the beginnings of paper money. However, many Sinologists and others have been led to ask why China did not continue at that time (to capitalism?). It is Elvin's argument that despite its various revolutions China did not develop a 'modern' economy because it fell into 'a high-level equilibrium trap'; there was economic growth, but he claims that technological invention for production was almost entirely absent in the Ming and during the Qing. He analyses the dissolution of serfdom and of the manorial order, the multiplication of market towns and the industrialization of portions of the countryside and discusses conventional explanations of why China did not develop industrial capitalism, namely inadequate capital and a restricted market, political obstacles to economic growth, and enterprises that were small-scale and short-lived. These he sets aside and proposes the notion of the 'trap'. Nevertheless, there was still some entrepreneurship and some invention, although Elvin speaks of a phase which, while not altogether stationary, prevented the attainment of modernization.[89] He recognizes the growing strength of the guilds, so important in Europe, which in some areas 'became the municipal governments', involving a rather different concept of the eastern town than is often proposed.[90] But in speaking of the failure to achieve a bureaucratic 'modern' economy in this way the author seems to be referring in essence to recent western attainments, which now stand in danger of being overtaken, in the mass-manufacturing field, by a 'backward' China.[91]

Some attribute the supposed failure to continue in this process of 'modernization' to the fact that the dynasty of the Song was conquered by their former allies against the Jurchen, the Mongols under Genghis Khan (1167–1227) who invaded Beijing in 1215 (then under the Jin dynasty).

In the south the Mongols (1211–1368) defeated the Song in Hangzhou in 1276 and completed their conquest of China by 1279, which had the great advantage of unifying the divided country and easing communication between north and south. They established the Yuan dynasty, who stimulated water-borne trade and established a single (paper) currency (until inflation set in with the last ruler). Trade brought more contact with the Near East through the extensive Mongol empire while extending

---

[89] Elvin 1973: 314.   [90] Elvin 1973: 292.
[91] About capitalism, see Dixin and Chengming 2000 for quite a contrary view, interactions with the west being an important factor.

to Europe in the west. In many ways the intellectual and artistic tradition of the Song continued. In the twelfth century the commentaries on the Confucian classics made by Zhu Xi became increasingly influential among the educated, as the dynasty attempted to legitimize its rule by adhering to the Chinese classics and customs. At least in the south-east the flowering of culture continued, and, since the old elite were not in much demand administratively, they pursued scholarship. While legal, medical and fiscal specialities were taught during the Tang and Song dynasties, the ending of these examinations in civil service selection during the Southern Song marked the state's withdrawal of social and political patronage from technical subjects.[92] Thereafter such training became the preserve of common clerks and others who staffed the technical side of the bureaucracy. This did not conform to the amateur ideal of Confucian scholarship.

The Mongols had their own shamanistic religion, but they nonetheless supported Buddhism, and to a lesser degree Daoism and Confucianism. By and large, Yuan rule and achievement were conservative, with the Chinese section of the population clinging to earlier ways.[93] But in fact conservativism would mean a 'creative revival'.[94] Confucianism and its social hierarchy were not so rigidly enforced as previously, so that the merchants generally flourished in the community, providing an audience for and encouraging public performances, especially of the opera, for drama and for historical romances.

In this way, the Yuan or Mongol dynasty became 'one of the great ages for art...It was an age when the institutions of Confucian education, the academies, the publishing of books, the scholarly attention to exegetical texts, philosophical and political writings all displayed significant advancement; it was an age of high cultural attainment.'[95] In the sciences, it profited by the contact with western Asia, especially Persia, in the fields of mathematics, astronomy, medicine, hydraulics and in others, including military engineering. An Institute of Muslim Astronomy existed alongside the Chinese Institute for preparing calendars. The same happened with medicine. Much fruitful intercourse took place in these and other fields, as in the work of Guo Shoujing (1236–1316), who contributed to astronomy and constructed scientific instruments.

---

[92] Elman and Woodside 1994: 550.
[93] North China was so long under foreign rule that the commoners adopted a surprising amount of non-Chinese customs, thus horrifying the educated Chinese, particularly of the south. But this practice had of course been going on for centuries, in imperial times since at least the third century CE.
[94] Silbergeld 1997: 110.   [95] Mote 1999: 507.

This dynasty was followed by the Ming (1368–1644), which ruled up to the time of the Italian Renaissance in the west and re-established the native Chinese tradition. Its founder was an ex-Buddhist monk who became a successful rebel general and set himself the aim of freeing China from Mongol rule. The dynasty restored the country's international dominance by acquiring tribute from Japan, Ceylon and the Persian Gulf. Local government was extended along the lines of the Song model, though there was increased centralization at the top. Even more than in the Northern Song, the government itself was dominated by a largely non-hereditary civil service recruited by examination. The tests for the examinations required extensive knowledge of the classics, as interpreted by the Zhu Xi school of 'Neo-Confucianism', and the answers were written in the manner of the highly stylized 'eight-legged essay'. Feeding into this system of recruitment lay government-sponsored schools at the county level. Specially talented students were then promoted to a National University in the capital. In the later period there was also a proliferation of private academies where students gathered to discuss and prepare for examinations. While a father's position and wealth doubtless affected one's chances of recruitment, new blood was always entering officialdom.

It was under the early Ming that the remarkable maritime expeditions of Zheng He took place in the 1430s, to India and then to Africa, in a series of attempts to establish the emperor's legitimacy and the position of China as the centre of the world. For already in the Song and the Yuan it had been the world's greatest maritime power.[96] However, the government's expansive overseas expeditions came to a halt with these voyages and contact with foreigners was inhibited in order to avoid 'barbarian' influence. But this withdrawal did not in fact prevent the territorial expansion of the Chinese population overseas nor did it stop mercantile activity within China and even with its southerly neighbours, though much of the latter involved smuggling and piracy. At the same time, European commerce opened up and merchants came to be of greater importance as did the trade and the diplomatic routes to south-east Asia, India, the Persian Gulf and Africa. Their wealth and indeed often their family background enabled merchants to marry into the official class, becoming part of the establishment; indeed many sons of wealthy merchants acquired official degrees and appointments. Consequently they were less likely to challenge the status quo, as happened with the bourgeoisie in Enlightenment Europe. Mote writes of the late Ming as a lively society with vast towns; in the sixteenth century the rates of literacy were higher than in any other

[96] Mote 1991: 337.

pre-modern society, and China 'had the highest levels of literacy in the world'.[97] They used these skills for a wide range of activities and 'avoided the idea of revealed truth',[98] 'teaching in its place that men must study the past, observe the world about them – especially the human world – and apply the lessons . . . to solving present problems'. That view was highly significant for the future.

Political weakness in the Ming even seemed to contribute to a certain 'cultural flowering'.[99] There was a growth of 'literary associations' which stimulated social and political debate, and a significant proportion of the literati were involved in activities outside the political arena. In the 'extraordinary' period of the late Ming, modernism was prefigured in many ways, with expressionism and abstraction in art, social freedom, companiate marriage and emotive literature. The increased market for cheaper books meant that there was more information about people's private lives, and hence more knowledge of women, of individuals and of individualism. It was an age of lavish consumption for the upper echelons but also one that in some circles emphasized Confucian 'puritanism' in conserving earlier practices.

It was also one of the great periods of literary theory and criticism. Poetry was especially important and 'all agreed that the ancient Book of Odes . . . was the fountainhead of literary creations';[100] poets employed historically established forms and, as with Confucian norms, were again looking back in time, though that did not prevent them also from going forward. The manner of early Ming was gradually rejected in favour of a more vigorous style that meant restoring archaic models, but 'it was an archaism of a reforming, almost revolutionary, kind', as with the use by some twentieth-century English poets of Anglo-Saxon.[101] The rigid simplicity of early Ming prose gave way to two, often conflicting developments by the early sixteenth century: a highly literate classicism with much use of allusions to canonical texts and a more direct and vivid vernacular that itself often drew on classical texts that served as primers for those gaining literacy. Once again, one was looking back to reform the present, as happened so often in literate societies.

Writers experimented with drama and fiction, and the former included Tang Xianzia (1550–1616), often known as the Chinese Shakespeare, who was his contemporary; the most celebrated of Tang's four

---

[97] Mote 1999: 775. This is unlikely, in comparison to the Dutch and English from the sixteenth century and the Japanese from the eighteenth century. Of course, it is difficult to compare 'literacy' in the two scripts as they mean quite different things. Dutch, English and Swedish literacy were of course tied to religion.
[98] Mote 1991: 338.   [99] Mote 1999: 769.
[100] Mote 1999: 772.   [101] Mote 1999: 773.

dream-dramas (still widely performed in various forms), the twenty-hour-long *Mudan ting* ('The Peony Pavillion') ends with the morbidly lovesick dreamer Liu Mengmei, whose very name refers to his beautiful dream, topping the imperial exam and being pardoned by the emperor for grave-robbing! In fiction, four of China's five greatest novels were written or rewritten during this period;[102] all were set historically in earlier dynasties, and all appear to have been written anonymously, as it was not considered proper for ambitious literati to produce these vernacular forms of entertainment.

Buddhism continued to have an important influence on art. As in Japan there was a religious and a secular mode. The first consisted predominantly of Buddhist painting, the latter of drawings of humans and nature, stimulated by Daoism and Confucianism.[103] In China, Lee writes of the literati (*wenren*) painters in the Yuan who were an example of 'dramatic revisionism' and took part in the 're-writing of history'.[104] This rewriting was virtually wiped out by the early Ming (1368–1644) but revived later on. That early period was dominated by 'traditional painters building creatively on the past' in an attempt to legitimize their own dynasty and consisting of both court and professional artists. After 1450, the literati style of landscape painting was taken up again, notably by Shen Zhou and the Wu school, which 'utterly changed the appearance of Chinese art',[105] using paper (rather than silk), pale washes and self-expression. Looking back to the history of art through their paintings, these painters of the lower Yangzi delta consciously commented on past art and its history in an effort to imbue their work with 'the spirit of antiquity' and with a 'new tradition', to which they brought 'concepts derived from Confucian, Daoist and Chan Buddhist thought'.[106] In the north the Ming emperor encouraged the professionalism of court painters, while in the south the gentry promoted literati and professional artists working on the landscape and in decorative art. Late Ming China was 'a great age for painting and calligraphy' which also developed the essay as a literary genre. At the same time, 'book culture' flourished both in printing and in collecting; connoisseurship and antiquarianism developed as did new branches of learning.

---

[102] These were: the sexually explicit pioneer work *The Plum in the Golden Vase* (*Jinpingmei*, after parts of the names of the three main characters), written in prose with snippets of classical poetry, *The Water Margins* (*Shuihu zhuan*, a book on banditry, on which one of the central scenes in *The Plum in the Golden Vase* is based), *Journey to the West* (*Xiyou-ji*) and the *Romance of the Three Kingdoms* (*Sanguo yanyi*). The other great classic Chinese novel, *The Dream of the Red Chamber*, would come in the Qing dynasty.
[103] Lee 1991.   [104] Lee 1991: 352.
[105] Lee 1991: 355.   [106] Lee 1991: 356.

Like many other sinologists, Mote too confronts the question of why China did not become 'capitalist' or indeed 'modern', like post-Renaissance Europe, an issue which he sees in the context of late Ming society of the sixteenth and early seventeenth centuries, whereas Elvin, as we have seen, discusses this problem for the Song and after. Scholars place weight on the fact that Chinese towns did not develop institutions of self-government in ways like the west and were more autonomous with regard to the countryside. Yet, as he argues, they functioned much as cities did elsewhere. We have already referred to the role of some guilds in local government which were used for taxing specialist groups; they played a political role. In any case, these cities were complex, and served as centres of cultural activity; '[l]iterature and scholarship, book publishing and book collecting, art and drama, music and entertainment, and the indulgence in rich elite modes of life were present in all of them'.[107] They functioned as cities elsewhere and the Weberian argument about their relevant differences seems wrong.

All of this has made some see the late Ming as showing 'the sprouts of capitalism', in an 'elite' form in which were found new types of money and instruments of credit, a growth of commerce, market agriculture, complex industrial processes, an improvement in medicine and a freer labour market. Mote argues that if capitalism is defined by what happened in western Europe, China's trajectory was indeed different in entrepreneurial and legislative terms. Nevertheless, economic progress did take place, some before and some a little later than in the west, as we can see clearly from present developments.

Balazs too asks why China never made it to capitalism, though in fact he sees tendencies already from the Zhou dynasty (Warring States period). But the scholarly elite who governed the country were 'unable to formulate any program of social reform without cloaking it in a reference to the golden age of antiquity'.[108] However, whatever Hegel, Marx and Weber might have thought, Chinese continuity was never a matter of stasis. There was abundant change of all kinds in a mobile society. But what remained virtually continuous in its history was a bureaucratic stratum of scholar-officials, the members of which ran the state from 221 CE and saw to its own reproduction as a group by controlling the educational system. Its ideology was Confucian, secular but rigid in many respects, providing an ideology within which scholars were continuously looking back (and sometimes going forward). However, the continuity he sees was a reactionary one that eventually came into conflict with the resurgent 'capitalism' of the west.

---

[107] Mote 1999: 763.   [108] Balazs 1964: 102.

Following the Ming, there was another period of foreign rule by the Manchus, sinicized Tungusic conquerors descended from the Jurchen people of the Jin dynasty (1115–1232) who struggled to acquire legitimacy under the name of Qing (1644–1911). The Manchus conquered China from the north in 1644, when they were joined at the Great Wall by an army under General Wu Sangui, who retook the capital of Beijing from 'bandits', that is, from peasants who had rebelled under Li Zicheng. Claiming to be the legitimate rulers of China, the Manchu recognized they could only rule the Chinese if they followed local practices. They staged an 'orderly succession' and became more Chinese than the Chinese, honouring Confucian values and restoring good government, inheriting the Mandate of Heaven and condemning the licence of late Ming society. Nevertheless their ordinance that all Han men should shave the front of their heads and wear a pigtail in the Manchu fashion was initially deeply unpopular.

There is a widespread idea in traditional history that the Qing period in China was backward in comparison with the west, in terms of its lack of democracy, of science, of technology and of military knowledge. But revisionist analysis has shown that 'the usual laundry list of Chinese faults', including Confucian disdain for commerce, are grossly inadequate in view of the growth of trade, the extension of political sovereignty in central Asia and elsewhere, the establishment of new arsenals with the development of military technology, and the increase in agrarian productivity.[109] Among the literati a discussion took place about whether western science (*xixue*) was something quite new and different from *gezhi* (pre-modern as distinct from modern science). However, despite the desire to avoid this dichotomy and to emphasize the continuing elements, many late Qing intellectuals in fact ended up voting for modern knowledge and neglecting the efforts the Qing had made to combine the two. These efforts were not helped by the sectarian rebellions of the nineteenth century leading to the death of some 20,000,000 people, by the defeat by the Japanese in 1895, and by the shortage of silver as the result of revolutions in South America. However, China could not be considered to be all that behind other nations. Often vaunted as 'culturally' closer to 'capitalist' Britain, Japan received much of its information on western science and technology through China; the difference was not all that great, even though China was defeated in the Sino-Japanese conflict because of the superior military training of the enemy.

Nevertheless, Confucian scholarship in the Qing was substantially different from Song Neo-Confucianism, and constituted a phase which

[109] Zurndorfer 2006.

consisted in going back and critically examining the earlier texts in the light of what was called 'Han dynasty knowledge' or 'empirical research'. The Qianlong emperor (r. 1736–95) made copies of his vast collection of Chinese texts available to scholars, thereby encouraging what has been called 'a late flowering of thought and learning'.[110] Once again, looking back promoted a forward movement. 'Empirical research' led to a correcting of Song metaphysics, especially in Confucian scholarship, which the empiricist *kaozheng* ('test-evidence')[111] movement saw as overly influenced by later Buddhism. An attempt was made to revitalize Confucian thought by going back to the beginnings, to the text itself, which the emperor had made available. This was an example of 'revolutionary criticism', a renewal of intellectual life by reverting to the 'original' Confucius. For example, among the leading lights in this Confucian resurgence of the early–mid Qing was Dai Zhen (1724–77), who turned away from the Buddhists' fascination with self-examination and their devaluation of human desire; for Dai Zhen, an understanding of reality presupposed an active empirical engagement with the world outside,[112] an approach that is borne out in his work in a variety of scientific fields. So there was then a 'flowering of scholarship and Confucian learning' in the mid Qing. However, poetry did not greatly thrive; until quite recently the Ming and Qing poets have been absent from all but the most dutiful anthologies. However, prose prospered, and the period produced such fine works as *The Scholars* and Cao Xueqin's (1715–63) *The Dream of the Red Chamber*, the last and, for many, the greatest of the classical Chinese novels.

The Qing also extended its rule territorially as far as Cambodia, for they had the best-equipped fleet in the region. The three 'enlightened emperors' of the Qing (1662–1795) maintained the examination system, tightened the fiscal and monetary system, and the mandarinate once again took as its model the teaching of Confucius. At this time, the 'modernization' of China did not preclude looking back to earlier norms. In place of what they considered 'Ming licence' as far as writers were concerned, the Qing decided in 1778 to have a book-burning, partly of anti-Manchu literature, partly of books on forbidden subjects including the erotic, in an attempt to re-establish orthodox Confucian morality. In the bigger towns the public recitation of Confucian principles was

---

[110] Mote 1999: 928.

[111] The strength of this movement's connection between empirical science and textual examination is still visible in the modern use of the term *kaozheng*考証 for textual criticism.

[112] The philosophical side of these convictions is most clearly brought out in his work *Yuan shan* ('Inquiry into Goodness'). His text-critical acumen is forcefully demonstrated in his semantic commentary on Mencius.

carried out at street corners, with an emphasis placed on responsibility, virtue and obedience. Other creeds were condemned; even Manchu princes converting to Christianity were censured. The emperors made every effort to encourage the arts and traditional Chinese culture more generally. The nostalgia in early Qing court painting was either largely Ming-oriented or eclectic, a symptom of the underlying notion that the past was a major object of interest: it was in that sense a continuation of the Ming itself. Despite the lingering resentment of many Han intellectuals and artists, the levels of imperial patronage of schools of both metropolitan and regional painting (mostly in a traditional literati style, though often with a new exuberance of colour) reached a new apogee under Kangxi, and continued under Qianlong with the growing influence of western engravings, oils and frescoe styles. The practice of inscribing paintings with dedications and sometimes quite lengthy poems continued from the Ming. But especially in the large centres in the south like Yangzhou, the merchant clientele commissioned bolder, more free-style works.

From 1679, the long-reigning emperor Kangxi (r. 1662–1722) compiled not only the official *History of the Ming* (almost every post-Sui regime did this for its predecessor) but also a comprehensive dictionary (known as the *Kangxi Dictionary*) and an enormous illustrated encyclopedia. The Qianlong emperor then collected a copy of every extant title, about 10,000 in all, recopied by some 15,000 copyists. In the practical aspects of the empiricist school, in engineering, mathematics and other sciences, and in the bibliophile and encyclopedic works, what we have are the projects of a renascence of Chinese Confucian learning, some of which was sponsored centrally (and some, indeed, by the emperor's own person).

For China, the eighteenth century was a period of considerable prosperity. The Manchus favoured the small peasantry against the big landowners and brought about an improvement in agriculture and in other productive technologies. The country was not only the great workshop of the world but also a great market, externally as well as internally. Its growth was in textiles and in copper; tea, silk, porcelain and lacquer were exported in large quantities, giving China a positive balance of payments. It is estimated that in the two centuries before 1771 about half of all the silver coming from the Americas ended up in China.

However, the success of the economy seems to have resulted in an over-population of the core territories and the transfer of Han peoples to the north and south to less populated areas in the process of empire-building. At the same time, the administration became more corrupt and inefficient. During this period, there was considerable pressure from the west, first from the Russians in the north, and later from the British and other European powers along the coast. The damaging opium wars led to further invasions by European gunboats, to the imposition of 'unequal treaties', to the humiliation of the Chinese, and then to an effort to 'modernize' in the western manner, and eventually to the founding of the Republic in 1912. The attacks of the Europeans led to a weakening of the Manchu regime and its near collapse in the face of the Taiping rebels. Court and provincial officials realized that the west had made distinct advances in science, in manufacturing, in military power and in railway and telegraph communications, but they disagreed strongly on how to adopt them. In Hu Shih's view the Chinese Renaissance is that brought about by this contact with the west. A strong reformist movement on the Japanese model eventually arose leading to the foundation of the Republic by Sun Yat-sen, who had been educated in western fashion in Hawaii and Hong Kong. In 1894 he founded a small republican party, significantly called the Society for the Renaissance of China, which eventually evolved into the Nationalist Party (or the Guomindang). As far as visual and other arts were concerned, after the coming of the Republican Revolution in 1911, there was a period in which westernization again battled with traditional approaches. The founding of the People's Republic in 1949 saw a move to a socialist art which at first owed much to the Soviet Union, as in many other ways. This was followed, under Mao Zedong, by a more nationalistic trend that emphasized Chinese traditions and that led to the dramatic events of the Cultural Revolution (1966–76). After Mao's death in 1976, a more relaxed period began, with a more distinct 'search for roots' and a revival of the Chinese past, for instance in the cinema of Zhang Yimou, the director of *Raise the Red Lantern* (1991).[113]

Characteristic of the cultural history of China has been a constant looking back to the Confucian classics, to 'Antiquity', providing a continuous point of reference for both conservatives and reformers and establishing the legitimacy of each. There was never a time when this Confucian tradition was totally set aside, as the classical tradition had been in the west by the Christian and other hegemonic religions whose new faiths effectively outlawed the earlier ones. The nearest China came to that experience was with the advent of Buddhism, which although of fundamental importance never became dominant in the same way, partly due to the opposition of the mandarinate and partly because the populace stuck to a plurality of creeds, including Daoist and local cults. In the Song, Buddhism became one set of beliefs among several and did not play a particularly restrictive role in intellectual life.

---

[113] Clunas 1997: 223.

In the west the inhibiting effects of hegemonic religion had been experienced differently in the arts and in the sciences. In the arts these were initially aniconic, and all the major religions had to overcome profound objections before they could 'represent' the world, either in visual arts or in the theatre. While there were some inhibitions at times in Chinese and Indian art, with the use of colour in literati painting for example (and perhaps with figuration in early Buddhism, before the advent of Greek sculpture), there was never the same kind of sharp divide between the religious and the secular as in the west. Painting and sculpture were confined to religious subjects for nearly a millennium, as was the theatre, rejecting the great achievements of Greece and Rome in these spheres.[114] However, in China there was no similar rejection of a tradition involving a subsequent retracing of footsteps (a rebirth).[115] The same was true in the sciences, which were to some extent set aside under Christianity, Judaism and at times Islam, at least in certain major spheres.[116] Science continued in China and as Needham has shown in a graph of the botanical sciences, the activity proceeded steadily there even when there was a hiatus in the west.[117] There was no sudden burst forward after a gap as there was in the Italian Renaissance, but rather a number of periods in which these activities flourished more than in others.

Mote's account of late Imperial China (900–1800) concludes that 'slowly renovating changes' characterized its history.[118] His words deserve to be recalled:

Self-renovating change was constant and gradual, not sudden and disruptive, and was always justified by reference to past models. Chinese society looked backward in order to move steadily if slowly forward, overcame institutional lag from time to time in the name of recovering antique values, obviated the need for explosive adaptations, and comfortably convinced itself that it was virtually unchanging, while in fact it was growing with the times... This presents the fascinating enigma of archaism serving the course of renovating change.[119]

---

[114] Restrictions existed at times on popular 'representations' of images of past and present emperors, especially with long dead ones, but this law originating in the Ming was enforced only half-heartedly.

[115] There was actually no classical theatre in China; that was not evident until the twelfth–thirteenth centuries, especially in the cities. Drama in China came from village festivals of which records of their performances for the village tutelary or another god date back to the Song. Then under the Mongols, especially in north China, drama was written by literati and performed in cities.

[116] That is to say, they did not punish such research, as the church at times did in early modern Europe; nor did they actively reward it. They rewarded, with government office and its endless privileges, those who mastered, and often spent much of their lives mastering, non-scientific learning, i.e. Confucian texts, that did not encourage questioning these arrangements.

[117] Needham 1986: 11–12.   [118] Mote 1999: 965.   [119] Mote 1999: 966.

Thus China has also been described as 'an open society' and as an 'achieving society', although these terms have been queried. It was particularly open in certain intellectual matters. While it constantly looked back to early Confucian learning and to traditional family rituals, religious beliefs remained eclectic and, outside Confucianism, there was no overriding credo which might have held back intellectual enquiry – hence the remarkable progress in the sciences in earlier times. The high culture of elite Chinese was maintained by an education which concentrated on the Confucian classics and tended to inculcate values more than doctrine. It was a high culture diffused through a mastery of complex strands of literacy, attained and shared by the governing classes as well as by many of the emperors themselves. That remained true of the 'scholar-official class' until the twentieth century, when there was the establishment of a set of radical doctrines and of far-reaching social changes. But even then Mao Zedong composed traditional poetry and calligraphy, and Confucianism was not dead. By the start of the twenty-first century, voices in support of that doctrine, if only as a form of cultural nationalism, were heard from the top-most levels of this Communist government as well as from an increasing number of ordinary citizens. Today, in 2008, the resurrection of Confucianism has taken an extravagantly popular turn.[120] Looking back to a secular ideology has not prevented a total 'modernization'.

---

[120] I am indebted to Dr McDermott, who has recently travelled in China, for this observation.

8   Were renascences only European?

Was the Italian Renaissance unique? Historically for Europe it clearly was. But sociologically? There are two major characteristics of a renaissance or renascences, a looking back and an efflorescence. Cross-culturally, these phenomena are not necessarily coincidental. One can have a look-ing back, especially in religious discourse, which produces little in the way of going forward, simply a restatement, perhaps a reformulation, of doctrines about the transcendental. It is, in other words, conservative or conserving. That happened to art in the European Reformation, which saw a recrudescence of Judaic aniconism in the Calvinistic community. But one can also find an efflorescence, as with Jewish culture at the Emancipation, that does not involve looking back. In the Italian Renaissance you found the two together.

From the historical standpoint, the Italian Renaissance was obviously unique. Sociologically, however, we should view it as not only a European experience, but as one of a larger class of events that occur in all literate cultures and involve a looking back and a burst forward, not always combined in one. Periods of efflorescence were not uncommon in literate societies (and often known as 'golden ages') where the speed of cultural change was obviously affected by the mode of communication; the going forward not always but often involved a measure of looking back. Even in Europe the Italian Renaissance was not the first of these periods. If the European humanist claims to have 'reshaped the world' by looking back to classical literature that had been set aside, what does this say about the Renaissance or about the world? The Renaissance was not unique, nor was humanism in the sense of a revival of earlier literature. This happened elsewhere and is a function of literacy.

There were earlier instances in Europe which have actually been given the name of Renaissance or renascence. Scholars speak of the Carolin-gian renascence of the eighth to the ninth century, of the renascence of the twelfth-century when Roman law became established in Bologna accompanied by a revival of Latin poetry and an interest in Greek science especially in Aristotle, as well as progress in medicine, much of

the stimulation for which came from Muslim sources. An early humanism also developed at Padua under Venetian rule and in other Italian
city states where the renewal of commerce, especially with the Mediterranean east, resulted in the breakdown of the ecclesiastical monopoly
on learning. Merchants as well as clerics needed literacy and their con-
tacts with the east widened and deepened many cultural perspectives.
By the fifteenth century, the Council of Florence (1438–45) brought in
Greek scholars to that town from the ecclesiastical and trading city of
Constantinople and that led to the formation of the so-called Platonic
Academy; their visit was followed by a strong revival of interest in
Greek learning in the Latin west from which it had largely disappeared.
Much earlier in Asia Minor, after the Fourth Crusade, Byzantium under
Genoese influence is said to have experienced the Palaeologue Renais-
sance, so called after the name of the dynastic family of the emperor,
when scholarship flowered and artistic activity flourished, including
the building of the beautiful frescoed church of St Saviour in Chora,
Constantinople. All these cases are confined to Christianity.

As a historian of art, Panofsky already saw two European renascences
in their twelfth century, what he called the 'proto-Renaissance' and the
'proto-humanism'. The first, the revival of classical art, was a Mediterranean phenomenon, arising in southern France, Italy and Spain where
the classical element was still important in daily life and at a time when
trade and urbanization were beginning to pick up again. Islam was significant in this development which, as we have seen, encouraged the birth
of medicine in Europe both as an academic and as a practical subject. So
there too the influence of the east was significant in the rebirth of the arts.
Poetry flourished, fiction returned, the minor arts were renewed. Probably beginning in Norman Sicily with artists from Islam and Byzantium,
'the ancient art of the sculptor regained the status of a living practice in
the Western world'.[1] Then too further north in Europe, there was the
advocacy of a liberal education by such as John of Salisbury, cultivating
the classical tradition from the point of view of the men of letters. That
humanistic movement involved looking back to 'pagan' writers and a
loosening of some of the restraints of religion, which was a more northern phenomenon than the rebirth in the arts. But that movement also had
its own detractors. 'In Paris', wrote a contemporary, 'they display care
for the liberal arts; in Orleans for literature; in Bologna for law books;
in Salerno for pill boxes, and in Toledo for demons; but nowhere for
morals.'[2] All these cases are from Christian Europe. But the phenomenon
was not only Christian. The Turks too, who later captured the Greek city

[1] Panofsky 1972 [1960]: 155.   [2] Quoted Panofsky 1972 [1960]: 69.

of Constantinople, underwent what has been called the Timurid Renaissance under Babur (1483–1530). The author of an important memoir, *Baburnama*, he eventually led the Mughal conquest of India and was at the same time a great patron of the arts and sciences, often described as a Renaissance prince.[3]

In Europe the situation gave rise to a plurality of renascences but, as we have seen in earlier chapters, these periods occurred in Asia as well, not always involving such a sudden efflorescence as we find in the Italian version but nevertheless representing a step towards 'modernization' in its varied forms. Historians have long suggested that in Europe there had been earlier times which had tried to rescue the manuscripts of classical works. This effort inevitably stirred up interest in pre-Christian gods and in pre-Christian times. That is to say, it encouraged a modicum of secular thinking as well as suggesting the existence of alternatives to Christian belief. One of the reasons the European Renaissance stands out is because of the extent of the post-Roman collapse and the dominance of an Abrahamistic religion. The resulting gap in secular knowledge made a backward reference over many centuries more conspicuous than was the case elsewhere, especially if a certain measure of secularization that was required both in the sciences and the arts was to be encouraged. This particular feature, however, should not make us overlook the occurrence of Renaissance-like features in places and at times which we do not usually associate with the idea of rebirth of an earlier culture. There were times when such an efflorescence happened with the neighbouring Muslims, which contributed significantly to these European renascences. And we have seen that similar processes were to be found in other literate cultures in parts of Eurasia which were economically on roughly the same level.

Using the term 'Renaissance' or 'renascence' in the west involves a notion of European history as a more or less continuous cultural process from ancient times, with a previous period of eclipse, a sort of historical depression, during which the culture lost its natural course but from which it recovered after a transition (to 'capitalism'), to flow once more in its expected channel, with added wisdom and a renewed vigour. The consequences of this view – and it cannot be stressed enough how powerfully this reading is encoded in the very use of the capitalized 'Renaissance' – are several. Firstly, one consequence is that it secures a European monopoly for the achievements of Antiquity. We have seen earlier that while Europe had a need to revive ancient knowledge (for it had largely disappeared or gone underground during the Middle Ages), this had to some extent survived outside that continent in Arabic

---

[3] Dale 1996: 78.

translation. But Europe claimed for itself the heritage of Greek and Roman Antiquity which in this view it had lent to others, for safe-keeping as it were, during the Middle Ages. This belief is sometimes espoused outright, and sometimes merely implicit in the terminology we use, but in each case it neglects the simple fact that as far as Greek Antiquity was concerned, northern Europe as we know it hardly existed – theirs was rather a Mediterranean world, which extended to the Near East and Persia. But in addition to being an heir to its triumphs and a candidate for its rebirth, European historiography created the ancient world as its dominant and unique ancestry.

There are two problems of nomenclature involved if we are looking at the question of comparability. Firstly, what other movements have been spoken of as renascences by those western scholars who have made an explicit comparison? Secondly, what movements have been so described by indigenous scholars? Thirdly, what other movements might we see as renascences and might have some of the characteristics we have listed in chapter 1, involving the looking back and the cultural rebirth, or simply the efflorescence? In his remarkable survey of Islam, Hodgson does not use the term Renaissance or renascence in a comparative way but he writes of 'a vigorous flowering of Persian literature' in the fifteenth century,[4] of the 'tremendous thrust' of Chinese culture under the Song,[5] of the 'great florescences' of Islam in the Caliphal period, which 'did not exceed, in its creativity or in its basic institutional novelty', that of the European Renaissance.[6] Here we are concerned with the sociological definitions of renascence.

Rebirths of culture go back much further in recorded history. Childe writes of Dark Ages occurring in the literate societies of Egypt, Mesopotamia and India when eras of prosperity were succeeded by periods 'from which few buildings or inscriptions survive'.[7] As a consequence, there was alternation. In the first two cases, cultural activity re-emerged 'liberated from some of the shackles of ancestral barbarism [in the technical sense] and deepened so as to benefit more fully new classes in society'. In other words, the Dark Ages were followed by a cultural efflorescence. There is no evidence I know of that suggests a deliberate looking back although the foundation myth itself often provides some account of an earlier 'golden age' which might influence future events. But as these were all Bronze Age cultures with a written tradition, such a looking back was always possible, so the past could be called upon to revitalize the present. There was a more specific Dark

---

[4] Hodgson 1974 2: 490.   [5] Hodgson 1974 2: 570.
[6] Hodgson 1974 2: 571.   [7] Childe 1942: 159.

Age in Sumeria where an efflorescence had emerged following the unification of the cities of Sumer and Akkad by the kings of Mesopotamia;
for there had earlier been the attack of the 'semi-barbarian Amorites'[8]
that established Babylonia. Soon the ruler, Hammurabi, consolidated the
new kingdom and gave it a written code of laws as well as better transport
(with lighter wheels); a complex culture bloomed again after a definite
setback. But the Dark Age gave hope for a revival, as Childe wrote in the
Second World War (even faced with the Nazis). It 'was not a bottomless
cleft in which all traditions of culture were engulfed'.[9]

In more recent times we find other renascences or efflorescences in
the literate societies of Eurasia. We did not examine the history of Japan
in detail nor yet that of Persia,[10] both literate Eurasian societies, though
we have touched upon both since the word has been employed, but in
China, in India and in Islam, similar periods of florescence did occur and
even the term Renaissance has on occasion been used. It has for instance
been applied to Islam in the nineteenth century in what has gone by the
name of *nahda*, but at that time this referred not so much to a going
back as to a rebirth of cultural activity following the Napoleonic invasion of Egypt with its important cultural consequences. That activity was
expressly following modernization in the west. There was also a constant
looking back in Islam, not only to the Quran (because that was what a
written religion of the Book involved) but also among the Abbasids to the
translations of Greek, Indian and other texts; for in conquering the Near
East Islam had taken over lands near the Mediterranean where Greek
and Persian knowledge of a written kind was of current concern. Subsequently there were various contexts under Islam when secular knowledge
predominated, in periods that alternated with those emphasizing a religious account, and in these it had been easier to pursue a form of enquiry
in a tradition that looked back to Aristotle and to Plato, among others.
These times have been described as renascences in the sense of cultural
efflorescences, of a renewal and an expansion of human activity. Such
periods occurred at intervals as at Cordoba in the tenth century. But
they were temporary, subject to the return of phases of religious dominance. It was only with the institutionalization of secular knowledge in
universities, schools and academies as distinct from that of theological

---

[8] Childe 1942: 160.   [9] Childe 1958: 73; Gathercole 1994: 34.
[10] Both of course were literate societies and certainly looked back. However, the first looked
   back to China, the second originally to the Sasanid past and then to Islamic culture. On
   the Sasanian empire (226 CE – Islam), see the summary in Hodgson, vol. I, 1974: 137ff.,
   especially for its literary efforts, its agricultural (irrigation) and commercial (eastwards)
   success, its relationship with north India (Buddhism and medicine) and with China
   (silk).

(or other) beliefs that mankind achieved a more permanent and progres-
sive accumulation of such learning. Otherwise knowledge of the world
was inhibited by the intervention of supernaturally determined views
about the nature of the universe. This process of partial secularization
did not happen immediately with the foundation of the universities, for
initially these were heavily influenced by the need to teach priests. The
early library of Cambridge University (and of St John's College) where
I am was very small (especially as compared with Chinese and Islamic
libraries), with the holdings there largely devoted to religious books rather
than to secular literature or knowledge generally. *Beowulf* and Chaucer
were both absent.

In Hindu India one again found periods of cultural upsurge to which
the name Renaissance has been given by various writers. This happened
both in the Mauryan (360–185 BCE) and in the Gupta (c.320–540 CE)
periods, and these represented a cultural upsurge that did not really
derive from a looking back. That was again the case, according to
Thappar, in the Chola and Mughal periods. A looking back occurred
constantly with Vedic texts when the process of knowledge acquisition
was more the preservation of existing (sacred) writings than the creation
of new, innovating information. That was also the problem for many earlier schools in the Abrahamistic religions which were in the hands of the
church, since they were established in order that people would be able to
read or understand the scriptures, to learn about the old rather than the
new. As Furet and Ozouf noted for rural eighteenth-century education
in France, education was largely directed to the reproduction of existing
religious knowledge.[11] The same would be true of a yeshiva in Israel
today; consequently it is not only the number of schools that counts for
'modernization' but the nature and quality of the knowledge that is being
handed down or accumulated in them. In medieval Europe, in contemporary Islam, in the present-day yeshiva, this is not high; innovation is
not on the agenda, conservation is.

If one examines the other major societies in Eurasia, as we have tried
to do, at a certain point they all look back to earlier writings, Confucian
in China's case, Vedic in India, and in Islam, when it was not the Greek,
it was Muhammad's own words in the Quran. The reference was to a
canon, usually religious, but there were also intermittent periods when
the object of review was more secular knowledge. The context of such
a looking back was often an economic burst which benefited the town-
dwellers and the merchants (the 'bourgeoisie') above all, but inevitably
the countryside participated in the longer run. And these activities could

---

[11] Furet and Ozouf 1977.

result in a cultural efflorescence which might take a variety of forms and to which the name Renaissance has often been given by western scholars.

Sometimes as we have seen this looking back was to a sacred (or quasi-sacred) text, as in the case of Islam. In which case the process did not involve an outburst of new cultural activity but rather a stasis. This happened in medieval Christianity and it was rather the same with Buddhism, which dominated much of Indian education from an early period and established a number of famous universities. But these were largely concerned to teach Buddhist texts. On quite another level, the idea of rebirth is intrinsic to Buddhist religion, but it is linked to the notion of personal renewal in the sense of reincarnation as well as in a metaphysical sense of 'renaissance' to indicate the revitalization of ideas and images.[12] This idea has to do with an individual's trajectory continually passing through various incarnations before the emergence of a perfect person. But here we are talking about cultural not personal rebirth. In Buddhism there was some reading of texts other than these religious ones, and mathematics and astronomy did develop at courts, if not at universities, the first being useful for taxation purposes, the second for calendrical ones. In medicine there was some increase in conceptualization as well as in the capacity to heal, since this was knowledge of which all had need and which to a certain extent was independent of a specific religion. As I have pointed out, there were periods in Indian history, sometimes centred on the court of an enlightened monarch as in the Mauryan or Gupta dynasties, which opened the way to scientific and cultural achievement. That was also the case in Baghdad with the Abbasid caliph al-Mamun (813–33), whose achievement was based upon a rebirth of classical knowledge. In the Indian case there was no similar period of retrospective reference (although the Greeks were again partly involved at Gandhara) but there was a definite burst forward. However, with later Hindu oppositions to the Muslim and British regimes, there was certainly a looking back to earlier Indian society and a revival of interest in their traditions of independent rule. More recently the foundation of an independent state was itself followed by a birth of intellectual, artistic and now economic activity. This included a looking back to the Vedic scriptures which had a largely symbolic effect for Hindus without acting as much of a practical guide.

That was not true of the looking back to Confucian writings in China, especially at the end of the Tang (618–907) and during the Song dynasty (960–1279). Confucianism, or Neo-Confucianism, provided guiding texts for the conduct of state business as well as a non-transcendental

[12] Brinker 2001: 13.

counterpart to Buddhism. That religion had been so important for intellectual life earlier in the Tang, although to some extent it had served as an inhibition on secular knowledge just as the Christian church had done in Europe and Islam in the Near East. The Song period has been called a Renaissance and it certainly appears as such.[13] Not only did it look back to Confucian times for political purposes where those writings were an important part of the examination system but there was a flowering in art, in science and in technology. Later on the looking back to the Confucians continued, but then there was not a spectacular move forward in quite the same way.

I did not begin by trying to explain all the various periods of looking back, nor yet all the bursts forward; to identify all the relevant factors in 'other cultures' would be an immense task, for the reasons are complex and too many. Nevertheless some thoughts have emerged. Clearly one important factor is the creation of wealth which leads not only to exchange but to conspicuous and luxury expenditure, and that affects the pursuit of both the sciences and the arts, not to speak of the growth of production and exchange. That economic element was of great significance in the Italian Renaissance, and in the opening up of trade with the east, as Lisa Jardine has emphasized.[14] Then there was the encouragement of rulers and their courts (including ecclesiastical ones), for example, in Mauryan and Gupta India, in the Carolingian Renaissance in Europe, in the Abbasid 'Revolution' in Iraq, places which were at the same time the centres of trading activity. The enjoyment of such wealth and leisure may be confined largely to the upper reaches of society with relatively little downward impact, as seems to have been the case in the Buyid Renaissance in Iran and possibly even in Renaissance Europe, though pageants and plays were addressed to a wider audience. That raises the political dimension. For the change of regimes could itself lead to a burst forward, as it did in the French or in the English Revolutions.

So there are two general aspects I want to link with renaissances, firstly, literacy which enables one to look back, secondly, trade and economic prosperity, which provides the leisure time to do so. In most of these various periods to which I have referred, there was an expansion of the means of communication, as in the original development of writing, of printing, of paper or similar advances. In addition, there was a certain freeing of the intellect in that weight was taken off fixed religious appeals to knowledge in favour, in some compartments at least, of more flexible secular ones. And in addition there was a measure of commercial success which was important in producing contacts with the outside world and in giving rise to enough wealth to sustain those 'leisure' activities so

[13] Elvin 1973.   [14] Jardine 1996.

necessary for the pursuit of both the arts and the sciences. Renaissances were initially for the rich, but there was a downward drip. These then are general factors behind all such effloresences.

Such 'rebirth' I have linked to literacy. But clearly material objects other than books could be copied by later peoples without the aid of writing, such as ceramics, metal objects, buildings. One could therefore theoretically find a renaissance of Roman architecture (as in Romanesque) derived from the continued presence of Roman buildings. Undoubtedly such a renewal occurred, perhaps in the form of deliberate antiquarianism. But this process was unlikely to have been generally significant before writing had been invented. In any case it would comprise only a very partial renaissance of a culture, a partial rebirth of the kind that occupied Toynbee.[15]

One feature that was of central importance in all these renascences was an increase in the flow of information, especially in writing. That did not happen in all cases of looking back, for transcendental writings had a more conservative impact. But there was an accumulation of secular knowledge. Basic to all looking back is the question of literacy and the importance of the written word. But important too is not simply the existence of the written word but the degree of its circulation, especially if we are moving from a minority possessing an ability to read and write to a wider 'democratic' one in which the majority can. The increased circulation of information may depend partly on printing, as was the case in the Italian or in the Bengali Renaissance, and in China too during the Tang and Song periods, but this also varied with the materials used, for example the shift to paper that occurred not only in first-century China but also in eighth-century Islam and in later Europe. That cheaper material meant that the book was much more widely available, being made from vegetable or waste materials rather than from the expensive parchment or papyrus used in early Europe. Another important factor was of course what was written, especially the language used. In many areas where Arabic was not a spoken language, Islamic literacy was hampered by having to write in that tongue. So too in the medieval period in Europe where higher literacy was more concerned with the learning of Latin than of the vernacular. Such a preference for another language was clearly associated with religion (as in Islam with Arabic), which commanded a special place for the languages of the Book or of the Church service. In Europe, as a consequence, until the early Renaissance literacy was largely in the hands of the ecclesiastical ministry, the *clerici*. Before the thirteenth century in England a small literate elite was scattered through a large non-literate population. The languages of everyday use were not

---

[15] Toynbee 1954.

always written and the acquisition of the skill of literacy involved learning an elite language, often dead.[16] In the literary world that elite tongue
gradually gave way to the vernacular, which had always been the currency
of ordinary speech, but for humanists and for many of the Renaissance
scholars, Latin remained the language of the 'learned' man (which few
women acquired). Even today, Cambridge University (which until 1947
excluded woman from degrees) presents its recommendations for honorary degrees and recites its College graces in Latin, not as the word
spoken but as the word written. Formerly there was a hiatus between
Latin and the vernacular, one being the written, the other spoken, but
this has now been largely abandoned. So too with classical Arabic for
many Muslims and with Hebrew for most Jews (but not in reconstructed
Israel); in earlier times for the 'learned', the scriptural or written language took precedence over the oral. The Renaissance changed all that;
indeed, the vernacularization of the written happened earlier since Dante
wrote in Italian and Chaucer in English (and long before there were the
Anglo-Saxon poets). But in Chinese the problem never existed since the
script was not phonetic and could represent any language in unaltered
form, including a changing one; in the written language there was not
the same division between the classical and the vernacular.

The contention here is that the nature of literacy itself, the preservation
over time of invisible speech in writing, or rather the development of
'transformed speech', means that there can always be a looking back,
whether that occurs in the arts, back to Homer or to Shakespeare, in
the sciences, back to Aristotle or to Darwin, or in religion, back to the
Book. For the word has become a material object. In the sciences we
look back partly in order to build on earlier work but in the arts to
celebrate and perform what has been achieved. In the religious context, in
which the words are sacred, we often look back over even longer periods,
not so much to construct anew but to conserve, as well as for some
guidance in everyday life. But while this looking back may lead to religious
reformations, it is essentially a process that concentrates on rehabilitating
the eternal word of God. Of course, literate societies frequently looked
back in order to preserve things as they were, or as they should be. This
conservatism was particularly the case in the religious field, even for
instance with the Reformation in western Europe which involved looking
back to the true religion of the Book; once again the Reformation was
a unique event historically but not sociologically. Judaism, Islam and
Buddhism underwent reformations of this kind that went back to the
Book.

---

[16] Niezen 1991: 230.

However, such a looking back also occurs not only with the transcendental but in China with more or less secular Confucianism. Over the centuries the writings of this philosopher have served as a guide to morality and to government. His work has not only been revived but, especially with Neo-Confucianism, has been brought back to reform ways of acting. Where this looking back differs from the Renaissance in the west is that it did not involve a leap back over a culture that had rejected what now became the centre of attention. In the case of the Jewish Enlightenment it was a looking around rather than a looking back, much influenced by the activity and consequences of the Italian Renaissance or in Spain by Andalusian Islam. And the same experience occurred with Muslims in the Near East, for the practice of miniature painting ultimately derived from China; and even with the 'foreign sciences' which they had translated from Greek and Sanskrit. In both China and India, looking back involved more continuity than in Europe, which experienced its 'catastrophic regression'. That had meant the disappearance and later the revival of aspects of a culture that in some respects had been virtually forbidden, a revival of classical learning, and an art that represented nature as such and not simply the religious landscape. China had fewer problems of this kind because even following the invasion of the northern nomads, who were mostly sinified and sometimes more Han than the Han themselves, there was a degree of cultural continuity in both the sciences and the arts and a continuous, not a heavily interrupted, looking back.

It was similar in India where the Vedic scriptures, less clearly datable than the relevant Chinese texts, formed a background for continuous reference, helped by the persistence of the Sanskrit language.[17] Traditional India looked to the past in many ways and even the independence movement itself glanced backwards as well as forwards, to a time when India was both independent and Hindu. The Muslim conquest had obviously changed all that, especially politically. In art it meant for them an absence of representational, figurative work, though there was a certain reformulation of both Muslim and Hindu traditions, deriving from Mughal influence coming originally from China, that led to a new 'flowering' of miniature painting. In poetry and in science, the now dominant Islam of the north made its own contribution. There had been ups and downs in both the Indian and the Chinese achievement, periods of florescence in both the arts and in the sciences, but there had been no long-term setbacks similar to that in western Europe with the coming of Christianity, a monotheistic Abrahamistic religion, that took its stand not only against

[17] See Pollock 2006.

classical science and learning more generally but also condemned figurative representation – except later in a religious context. Hindu India
never underwent such a period of denial, although in a way the coming of
Buddhism and of the Muslim and British invasions presented problems
for the continuity of their own cultural development as well as providing
a certain stimulation.

While China looked back, it did so to Confucianism which was largely
secular, anyhow for the literati. Needham thought this doctrine was
antipathetic to science but others have disagreed.[18] Science continued
to develop, and artistically there was nothing to restrict the subject matter of naturalistic painting, although some literati preferred to work in
ink rather than colour. Chinese society constantly looked back to the
classics, even when it was conquered by northern nomads (e.g. the Mongols), and their classics were basically secular; and certainly there was no
dominant religious ideology (except in the case of some individuals) to
hold up the advance of science which needed at least a partially secular
framework for its expansion. A fixed religious view of the world would
only have prevented this. Buddhism might have done so in China when it
arrived from India in the first century CE, but it never achieved a totally
dominant status in society before being controlled under the Song; then
it was partly set aside in favour of a secular Neo-Confucianism that in
most fields promoted free enquiry.

In considering these other periods of rebirth, or even of humanism,
we should take into account another aspect of the Renaissance that has
recently been emphasized by Jardine, namely, the economic.[19] In the pro-
logue to her account she writes: 'It is this entrepreneurial spirit which I
shall be pursuing in the chapters that follow, in order to sustain my claim
that the seeds of our own exuberant multiculturalism and bravura consumerism were planted in the European Renaissance.'[20] In other words,
to a significant extent its achievement was rooted in mercantile activity.
This view is certainly a long way from Burckhardt's claim that it was the
combination of the revival of Antiquity with the Italian spirit 'that under-
lay the Renaissance'.[21] His mode of 'essentialism' is no longer academi-
cally acceptable, though often it is still used on an even wider scale (for
the European rather than the Italian 'spirit' or 'genius'). Even Jardine's
more entrepreneurial approach is somewhat ethnocentric in regarding the
European Renaissance as founding our 'exuberant multiculturalism' and
'bravura consumerism'. Multiculturalism was surely characteristic of all
empires, political or commercial, that incorporate a plurality of peoples,

---

[18] Needham 1956.   [19] Jardine 1996.   [20] Jardine 1996: 34.
[21] Burckhardt 1990 [1860]; Burke 1998: 2.

some of them being more bent on a 'civilizing mission' than others. The second feature, an early form of consumerism, marked the blossoming of trade and manufacture in the east as in the west; as Jardine infers, this was a feature of capitalism in the west but Europe was certainly not the only example. It is true that in the nineteenth century both features were found there more extensively, largely as a result of the Industrial Revolution. But in concentrating on Europe, which its natives are virtually bound to do, we must avoid assuming that these features were characteristic only of that continent. Mercantile activity was intercontinental. China already displayed a measure of multiculturalism, and, with commerce, consumerism had been developing since the Bronze Age. Jardine brings in a new emphasis but she still essentializes the European Renaissance as the sower of the seeds of modernity. For 'our own' modernity that is certainly the case, but it is implied that modernization in general depended upon this development. That is not so evident.

In emphasizing the entrepreneurial and commercial aspects, Jardine is obviously calling attention to the fact that the Italian Renaissance happened in a culture of production and exchange, an economic context that manifested increasing prosperity, a major contributor to which was trade with the east (and south) and hence outside Europe. That is surely part of the significance of the Renaissance bazaar, which Brotton and Jardine note involved not only importing Turkish carpets and hangings, which decorate so many European paintings of the time, but also the temporary export of certain painters, like Gentile Bellini, whose portrait of Mehmet (1481) today hangs in the National Gallery in London, having been sold as idolatrous by a subsequent sultan.[22] The introduction of representational art to the rulers of a Muslim country and the history of Bellini's portrait, discarded in an Istanbul market where it was picked up by English merchants, is a dramatic instance of what was going on in that bazaar. Royal courts often saw themselves as outside even the religious inhibitions, as a law unto themselves, but it was a fragile encounter as far as others were concerned. And it was an encounter based on commercial exchange.

To recall the Turkish contribution to the Italian Renaissance is to bring to mind a related aspect, the importance of the revival of the Venetian (and more generally the Italian) trade with the rest of the Mediterranean. For it is essential to remember that despite the severe downturn in westwards commerce in post-Roman times, the Near East continued to display the urban culture that had decayed in so much of Europe, not in the Roman towns of Palmyra and Apanamea but in Alexandria, Aleppo

[22] Brotton and Jardine 2000.

and Constantinople. Moreover, it continued to trade vigorously with India and China throughout this time. In the ninth century there were said to be over 100,000 Muslim merchants in Canton;[23] there were many too seeking spices and other luxuries in the south of India that resulted in permanent settlements in Cochin long before the arrival of the Portuguese.

International trade was fundamental to the later European Renaissance, as it was in many other instances of an efflorescence; that mercantile activity brought about the exchange of information. However, the essentialist emphasis on internal growth may sometimes obscure the role of external contributors to these periods of greater cultural activity. Such periods were partly made possible by the growth of trade and manufacture. Not only were textiles of silk and cotton brought to Europe on a large scale but wool was widely exported (as well as being used locally), providing the wealth to build the fine churches of East Anglia, for the reception and development of the northern Renaissance among the weavers in Bruges (which was part of Burgundy), Flanders and Antwerp, and for the kind of commercial activity that centred upon Prato, Florence and other Italian towns such as Venice and Genoa. As in the case of the Medicis, this commerce was essential in providing the wealth for the patronage not only by the high bourgeoisie but also by the court and by the church; later on, a demand for visual art among a yet wider number of people was created when consumerism and secularization took command (literature, which could be read aloud, and theatre, which could be watched publicly, were already more democratic).

It is obvious to Europeans that their Renaissance was intrinsic to their modernization. In themselves their Middle Ages would not have led to 'modernization', it is argued, without such a break with tradition (a 'transition'), which was creative in a general way. The change also involved the secular, with religion being confined to narrower channels, leaving more room for developments in the sciences and in the arts as well as encouraging the production and exchange of the 'worldly goods' on which so much of this activity was based. In its particular details this break with tradition involved the revival of classical culture, but this revival did little directly to advance the expansion of Europe, the trade that expansion encouraged, nor the later development of mass production in the Industrial Revolution. Yet 'early modern Europe' is characterized by all three of these features, although not in any exclusive way for each appeared elsewhere. With trade this is obvious, since it was reciprocal. The desire to expand and explore new worlds was present earlier, notably in the Greek and Roman empires, but also in the Asian civilizations; in the

[23] Irwin 1996: 53.

extraordinary spread of Islam with an economic network and political-religious domain stretching from Andalusia to the further Mongolian border; in the Chinese expansion into central and south-east Asia, especially under the emperor Kublai Khan, not to speak of in the remarkable voyages of Zheng He; in the Hindu move into southern India, into Indonesia and again into south-east Asia. As for the development of mass production, we see its climax in the European factory, but we find elements of it in the earlier manufacture of porcelain in China as well as in the weaving of the cotton textiles of India; both were products exported to Europe and elsewhere on a mass scale and were taken up in the Industrial Revolution as industries with more developed but clearly linked technologies. However, at this time societies in the east enjoyed a consumerism which was initially far greater than in the west, illustrated in the practice of connoisseurship,[24] in the preparation of food and in the cultivation and use of flowers.[25] After the Industrial Revolution, Europe became more developed economically and other ways than the east, but many westerners regard this advantage as existing long beforehand, manifesting a strongly teleological perspective on the past. In fact in comparative terms the European continent went backwards economically and in a wider sense after the Romans, and only really picked up again in the period leading up to the Renaissance and the re-establishment of trade with the east.

But there was something particular about the European Renaissance, a feature that had its correspondence elsewhere and which can be stated in general terms. The feature of the European Renaissance that marks it out is that in looking back, it did so to texts from the classical period, which were certainly not in the Christian nor even Abrahamistic tradition but were often more secular, certainly pagan, some being also specifically atheistic, materialistic, as with Epicurus on whom the young Marx wrote his thesis. In other words, by looking back they were not conserving medieval culture but jumping over the restrictions placed upon them by the earlier religious creed to one with a very different emphasis. That was important for thought generally but especially so in the arts, for the Abrahamistic religions had effectively forbidden representation, although forms of Christianity later permitted this to happen in the sacred sphere, in visual painting, in sculpture and in drama. So too under certain circumstances did Judaism and Islam, but by and large iconophobia remained the order of the day.

There is a further question. All the Abrahamistic religions, Judaism and Islam as well as Christianity, had initial problems in that these monotheistic creeds inhibited not only the arts (through iconophobia) but the

[24] Clunas 1991.   [25] Goody 1998, 1993.

sciences (because the unique God was omniscient). Before a cultural efflorescence could manifest itself in either of these spheres, there had to be a break-away, a partial secularization. On the other hand, neither Islam nor Judaism had their own classical past to revive in quite the same way as did Europe, though Islam went back in its translation movement and in its link with other ancient civilizations, such as the Persian.

Until very recently Jewish communities were largely iconophobic, since when they have dominated figurative representation and the media in many parts of the world. We can hardly speak of this development as a 'renascence' since there is little evidence of an explicit reaching back to earlier periods when these forms of representations were encouraged for their own sake (although there was always the Golden Calf). They too looked back to Greece and Rome, but as pagan not to revive, as indeed did earlier Christianity. Their later emancipation certainly meant a flowering of 'culture' but one that owed most to the surrounding community in which they were embedded, not to a rebirth of something in their past.

Islam provides a roughly similar situation. However, while there is no equivalent of a declared and programmatic return to an earlier icono-graphic tradition from the determinedly iconophobic one of the Quran, there were alternative models in the background of the lands they occu-pied, classical art on the Ionian coast, in Syria, in the Arabian peninsular and elsewhere, Assyrian art in the land between the two rivers, Chi-nese art along the Silk Road, which influenced Persia and the Turks above all, and Iranian art over the plateau. Representation did some-times emerge, especially in court contexts as with the painting of the Mughal rulers (through Persian, Afghan and Chinese influences and usually as miniatures rather than as full-sized representations). In the sciences and in secular learning generally they looked back to the 'sci-ences of the ancients' which they periodically revived and augmented in a way that later benefited the European Renaissance. They went ahead on their own particularly in medicine, generally in communication, in technology, especially water control, in astronomy and in mathematics.

In the sciences, the looking back and the revival, as Joseph Need-ham among others has explained, were necessary as scholars needed the freedom to explore. In their work scientists cannot afford to be transcen-dentalists; they have to enquire into nature as it is. In other words, they had to become 'naturalists', pushing the deity further and further from their work space into being perhaps a first cause rather than an omnipo-tent presence. In the face of this situation, the church fought a rearguard action, indeed is sometimes still doing so. Nevertheless Copernicus and Galileo eventually came out on top, despite the ecclesiastical condem-nation of heliocentric theories, and more recently Darwinism, which has largely won over 'creationism'. Naturalism, perhaps agnosticism, were central to scientific activity. And in Europe this trend was reinforced by looking back to the writings of the classical period, when philosophy was effectively independent of religion. Science and technology, which led to a definite advance in human knowledge, required freedom to operate and that only came through partially setting aside the current version of religion.

When we are comparing renascences and their effects, a major factor is the going back to some earlier phase in the culture. In Europe the return involved a pagan Antiquity, which while that world had its own polytheistic gods it was certainly secular or pagan in the context of Christianity, so that this return had the effect of loosening the bonds of a hegemonic religion. The whole process of such a loosening may be influenced by surrounding cultures, as was the case with the Jewish Enlightenment in Europe, and earlier with the relationship of that group to Islamic Spain. Though dominant in religious terms, Islam too had periods of its own form of humanism which involved a recourse to 'reason' as well as to faith (or in some cases to one instead of the other, though the two were rarely exclusive), and in certain cases this going back was accompanied by a going forward which was not unrelated. Indeed, at the very beginning a significant aspect of intellectual life among the Arabs was the desire of the Abbasid court, and later some merchants and scholars, to collect and translate Greek manuscripts (secular and scientific but neither literary nor religious), as well as work from India, with knowledge coming even from China (as the Prophet himself recognized). In Europe one result of the encounter of one hegemonic religion with another was to produce a form of partial secularization, or at least a querying of the bases of one's own faith, as perhaps in Toledo after the reconquest, where Christian clerics met with Muslim texts and with Jewish translators. However, another contradictory result of such a meeting was to reinforce existing belief in a reassertion following cognitive dissonance.[26] Much later on, the encounter of Islam with later western culture (in Turkey, for example) led to a recognition of many among the former that their society had to 'modernize', that is, to adapt, while in many cases trying to keep a Muslim identity (although not Ataturk, who insisted on secularization). At that time the authority of the *ulama*, of the Sharia, was severely challenged and a measure of secularization was introduced. In both Iraq and Syria, the Baath party, whose name meant Resurrection, was openly secular and displayed a radical Arab nationalism. In much of the new Arab nationalism of a modernizing kind, a

[26] See Festinger 1957.

common thread was the idea that one was resurrecting an earlier pre-Islamic identity, not without God but without the authoritarianism of monotheism.

The specific revival of Antiquity was of course critical to the Italian Renaissance and, as we have seen, that revival has been related to the difference between Japan and Europe. Despite the common inheritance of 'feudalism', contends Anderson,[27] this difference lay in 'the perdurable inheritance of classical antiquity' which existed in Europe but not in the east. The ancient world was itself incapable of the transition to capitalism and was followed by a 'catastrophic regression', unparalleled in the history of civilization. However, the medieval age saw a slow gestation which culminated in the birth of capitalism that arose from the '*the concatenation of antiquity and feudalism*', from the internal contradictions of the previous regime. In other words, going back to the classics helped produce this major change. But he argues there was no gradual evolution from one mode to another; the process can only be understood 'by breaking with any purely linear notion of historical time as a whole'.[28] We have to think in terms of 'a renascence' or 'concatenation', because the 'advantage' of Europe over Japan 'lay in its classical antecedence'; for this process a backward look to Antiquity was essential. 'The Renaissance remains – despite easy criticism and revision – the crux of European history as a whole: the double movement of an equally unexampled expansion of space, and recovery of time.'[29] That is, 'the rediscovery of the Ancient world and the discovery of the New World', these two aspects were essential to the Renaissance and to the growth of 'capitalism'.

On this account the Italian Renaissance was not simply any historical rebirth, but an essential step on the road between a European Antiquity and a European capitalism. In many nineteenth-century versions of history Europe was unique in discovering (or obtaining) 'capitalism'. Therefore the Renaissance and Antiquity were sociologically unique. Yet the sinologist Elvin is constantly comparing China with Rome in the years contemporary with that empire, that is, in Antiquity. If this comparison is valid, then obviously China cannot have diverged far from the main stream of social development, not as far as the notion of Asiatic nor yet of European exceptionalism presupposes. In another view there was no such early divergence, nor did that take place immediately afterwards. As Elvin remarks, the east had run a 'nearly parallel' course to the west for 'over a millennium',[30] a course that included bursts forward as well as periods of stasis. The alternative argument of Europeanists holds that

[27] Anderson 1974a: 420.   [28] Anderson 1974a: 421 (author's italics).
[29] Anderson 1974a: 422.   [30] Elvin 1973: 69.

before Antiquity the systems of east and west diverged, but on political as much as economic criteria. China remained a single empire; Europe formed competitive 'networks'. Both regimes developed manorialism, but in China the unitary state retained control of defence, whereas in Europe this task was left to different feudal lords.[31] About subsequent modernization and the growth of capitalism, Elvin remarks 'there is so much evidence... of the heightened tempo of economic activity from the later sixteenth century that we are forced to ask "Why did China not break through to modern economic growth at about the same time as Europe?"'.[32] Of course, that date is much later than the 'revolution of the Song', the period of the so-called Chinese Renaissance, but it follows from it. So that Elvin is led to ask '[o]ut of so widespread a mastery of the pre-modern mechanical arts it seems strange that no further technological progress should have come'.[33]

The answer does not lie in China's past because that country was at least as entrepeneurial as any other and had all the cultural requisites for continued growth. Both in the east and in the west there were periods in which one region had the advantage over the other. But for most Europeans the Renaissance was clearly critical on the general path to 'capitalism'. This period of retrospection and of change was indeed essential to modern life as a whole. But other major Eurasian cultures also had periods of reflection and rebirth, not perhaps as radical for reasons of the medieval 'backwardness' of the west, which was crucial for their, and in some cases for our, modernization too. The importance of these other experiences of Renaissances is to emphasize that there is not simply one route to 'modernity', that is, via Christianity, but other paths which have been taken by the societies we have considered. These periods involving the rejection or compartmentalization of transcendental beliefs implied a recognition that 'man makes himself', to use the title of a book by the prehistorian Gordon Childe.[34] One thinks of the invention of printing, of paper, of gunpowder and of the compass, and perhaps of Indian numerals and mathematics as well as of Chinese ceramics, of silk-weaving and of Indian steel. The changes in the means of production, of communication, of destruction, of transport, of knowledge systems themselves, set human culture on a different course. In science this is clearer than in the arts for obvious reasons, but there too substantial changes took place that can be viewed in some sense as developments, in painting, in sculpture, in the novel, in the theatre. As we have remarked, what made the Italian Renaissance stand out was the reversal in some spheres, the modification in others, of the earlier dominance of a hegemonic religion

---

[31] Elvin 1973: 69.   [32] Elvin 1973: 284.   [33] Elvin 1973: 286.   [34] Childe 1956.

and its monotheistic God, with its resistance to representation in the visual arts (except for Christian themes) and with its earlier reluctance to pursue certain lines of enquiry about the world, in science (for example, in the case of Galileo) although technology was usually freer. The Italian Renaissance made some dramatic changes in this situation, partly through a leap back to a pagan or secular past, in many respects quite distinct from the present, and then moving forward – rather than going back to the continuity with one's own past as often happened in China and in India. Islam displayed something akin in its early efforts to re-establish Greek science, but this scarcely affected the arts and did little to modify the influence of Abrahamistic religion over time.

Nobody else could repeat this rediscovery of Antiquity because nobody else had lost their past in quite the same way. From their Abrahamistic standpoint most Jews, like most Christians and at times most Muslims, set aside Greek knowledge as pagan, but India and China, as we have seen, kept an intermittent faith with past achievements, slowly accumulating, not requiring to make up for lost time in a rush as took place in the Italian Renaissance, in the Jewish Enlightenment, to some extent in the periods of Arab humanism. In the European case, much of the tradition deriving from Rome had been specifically demoted at the coming of Christianity and in what are referred to as the Dark Ages. But Judaism and Islam stood in a rather different relationship to the classical period, which was specifically an enemy of the first and largely foreign to the second. It is true that those societies adapted to a common Near Eastern legal tradition, which was akin to Roman law, whereas Europe had also to take account of the Germanic codes. That 'feudal' period was followed by a distinct rebirth; the early Renaissance saw a determined revival of Roman law. This process has been considered by some as intrinsic to economic change. Take the example of the concepts of private property which have been seen by Marx and others as preparing the way for capitalism. Roman law was held to incorporate the shift from 'conditional' to 'absolute' private property, believed to be intrinsic to the development of capitalism (or 'modernity') and hence singular to western Europe. But the argument failed to give sufficient weight to Sir Henry Maine's notion of a hierarchy of rights, that is, the idea not of an outright opposition between the two forms of property, 'modern' and 'primitive', but of differences of degree based upon hierarchy. Which societies do not have some notion of more or less 'absolute ownership' for some objects and a more qualified one for others? But the belief that Roman law was singular in this way meant that its revival was seen as essential to the development of capitalism and modernity, which could happen here and nowhere else. That argument was based upon a simplistic analysis of the legal system, since in essence broadly similar concepts already existed in the Near East and elsewhere.

For the historian Perry Anderson, this revival of Roman law and the assumed changes were accompanied by the reappropriation of the whole of the cultural heritage of Antiquity, that is, its 'philosophical, historical, political and scientific thought – not to speak of its literature or architecture – suddenly acquired a new potency' in which 'the critical and rational components' jumped over the great 'religious divide'; 'it always retained an antagonistic and corrosive context as a non-Christian universe'.[35] That was a very important factor, as we have seen; the classical supplemented, in some spheres set aside, the Christian (sacred) universe and promoted secularization. The result was 'an intellectual and creative revolution', 'because the classical dominated the medieval. The increasingly analytical and secular cultures that gradually unfolded, still with many theological blockages and reversions', singled out Europe.[36] In many fields the hegemonic religion of medieval times no longer held sway. However, in other areas of Eurasia that had no such authoritarian religion, similar blockages did not take place; secular and analytical thinking were not restrained in the same absolute way.

With the fall of the Roman empire the European economy had also collapsed, a process that affected the whole continent. But culturally the problem came with the advent of Christianity and the Abrahamistic religions. The God of Abraham was not only the one God (unlike the multiplicity in the supernatural regimes in south and central Asia) but he was also omnipotent, omniscient. His writings (or the works of those he inspired) contained the whole truth and there was no point in looking for other answers. So the sciences, which had flourished in the ancient world, were no longer needed with the religious hegemony of monotheism, although in various fields such as agriculture, warfare and medicine technology continued to advance. It continued surreptitiously, as alchemy, as magic. There may of course be a cultural release from such religious domination without any going back, as happened with the Jewish Enlightenment discussed in chapter 5. Such a release was the result of the influence of the surrounding cultures. Nevertheless, like the earlier European renascence of the twelfth century or like 'humanist' movements in Islam, this was an instance of the temporary confinement of an Abrahamistic religion which otherwise held back the advance of the 'information society', in science and in the arts.

What is the importance for world history or sociology of showing the parallels of the Italian Renaissance, the similar moments in other

[35] Anderson 1974a: 426. [36] Anderson 1974a: 426.

Eurasian societies? The Renaissance in Europe has been seen as critical to the development of the modern world and to the subsequent domination of that continent in world affairs. So in one way it was, but in an important sense that was because in many ways the continent had been relatively 'backward' in the earlier centuries, intellectually and commercially. Needham has shown, for example, how in botany China had greater knowledge of plants than Europe in the medieval period as distinct from the fifth century BCE. That was but a minor aspect. The hegemonic weight of Abrahamistic religion made an enormous difference to the accumulation of knowledge about the universe, for it laid down its own definitive version of events. In this context it was important that the Renaissance represented a catching up with the achievement of the eastern powers, who because they had never experienced the same problems of divine omniscience, looked back to earlier times in a different spirit.

We can view the Italian Renaissance as making up for the backwardness that resulted in part from earlier restrictions but also building on that and making a sudden burst forward, having overcome some of the constraints of Abrahamistic religion, to 'modernization', to industrial production, to 'capitalism'. These various processes the Chinese had already started, not only with knowledge, especially science, but with the economy, with the manufacture and export of ceramics and to some extent with silk and paper. In the new environment Europe developed these industrial processes further in these and other spheres, using techniques and knowledge some of which originally came from the east (as with reeling fibres by water power). But this was not at first a complete takeover. China remained the greatest exporting economy throughout the eighteenth century. It was overtaken by the west in the Industrial Revolution of the nineteenth century, but it still continued to produce both economically and intellectually, albeit in a less outstanding manner. This economic and cultural dominance led to Europeans adopting an ethnocentric and teleological account of the world. But it has been no surprise to see China again becoming so important in the world economy in recent years. This is a fact for which the dominant thesis in the west does not allow, for it tends rather in the essentialist direction taken by Toynbee when he sees in the Renaissance 'the natural expression of the western spirit'.[37] That is essentialism of the crudest kind.

The Renaissance in Europe represented a clearing of the air which allowed for a burst forward in science, in knowledge generally, as well as in the arts. Almost by definition, that permitted the growth of the modern world which owing to our institutions of learning and training

---

[37] Toynbee 1954: 84.

was self-sustaining. But this was not the growth of capitalism per se, for this had existed elsewhere in the shape of mercantile activity and production for exchange, including some industrial and mechanized production. Certainly there were important developments in Europe in the late eighteenth and nineteenth centuries, but these soon become transferred to the east, just as the east had transferred much beforehand to the west. These transfers fell on fertile soil; before the end of the nineteenth century India began exporting more machine-made cotton cloth to England than it imported. Japan and now China have done the same with other industrial goods. It was not the notion of capitalism that was exported but factory production; some mercantile and industrial activity was in place and ready to expand. Western capitalism is not as unique as those in the west once thought. It is not simply Japan but China, India and the rest of south-east Asia that are nowadays making inroads into the world economy. Nor is this only a result of exporting 'western' capitalism to these areas. For, in some significant ways, they had already industrialized or mechanized parts of the process of production to create more commodities. Not only was China the largest exporter in the world until the beginning of the nineteenth century, but India too had a positive balance with the export of cotton goods and of luxury items.

The Italian Renaissance is critical not only to the history of Europe but of the world. But was it the only one of its type? Writing of Japan in his important study on the emergence of 'capitalism' in Europe, Anderson argues that 'nothing remotely comparable to the Renaissance had touched its shores'.[38] Japanese education he argues was backward; 'there was no growth of science, little development of law, scarcely any philosophy, political and economic theory, and a virtual complete absence of critical history'. Yet in the west the florescence of these fields was not primordial nor continuous, not a characteristic of its 'culture' over time. All had existed in Antiquity but subsequently what was notable was their relative absence until their re-emergence in the early renascence which happened, as we have seen in chapter 2, in the wake of contact not only with their own past but with Islam. For European society to emerge from this 'backwardness', the renascence had to rediscover the society and culture of the classics and, in doing so, to rediscover a modified secularism. Moreover, Japan was not totally without the fields mentioned by Anderson, for in all those various areas it had access to and depended upon Chinese achievements as well as upon its own. Yet not till recently has China been given a place in the discussion of modernity. Japan received

[38] Anderson 1974b: 416. See also Veblen (1925 [1899]: 1) for an automatic equating of 'feudal' Europe and Japan; both had a 'leisure class'.

some attention, partly because of its early performance in industry and in 'modernization', which was stimulated by the American attack under Commodore Perry. More 'theoretically' it was said to be another society like Europe which emerged from 'feudalism', a regime China is supposed not to have had (though some such as Needham have argued for 'bureaucratic feudalism' in that country).

So for many western writers the importance of Japanese feudalism lay in its similar history to the west. For Anderson, the parallelism is most arrestingly confirmed 'in the posterior destiny of each zone. European feudalism . . . proved the gateway to capitalism.'[39] Outside Europe, only Japan achieved 'an advanced industrial capitalism'. 'The socio-economic preconditions . . . live deep in the Nipponic feudalism which so struck Marx.'[40] Thus the similarities are teleologically determined. Japanese society had to resemble Europe in the past because of its later attainment of capitalism. In fact the course of its history was much closer to that of China; it also had its own 'Enlightenment' but that was one, like the later Jewish *Haskala* and the Islamic *Nahda*, based on the deliberate imitation of the west.[41] But Anderson claims it had nothing 'comparable to the Renaissance'. How dated the whole argument about Japan's 'feudalism' and the development of capitalism now seems after the extraordinary growth of China, the Little Tigers of south-east Asia and of India too! True, the Japanese engaged in industrial production at a relatively early date. But, apart from their own achievements in industrial and mechanical production, China and India did not lag far behind in global time, despite the claim that they lacked large-scale 'feudalism'.

This leads to another particular aspect of the problem that is paralleled in other renaissances. In both Islam and Judaism, as we have seen, there were periods of 'humanism'. In the Islamic east, apart from the translation movement itself, there were the humanists of the Buyid age in Iraq.[42] The golden age of Hispano-Maghrebian culture in the west saw the writings of Averroës and Maimonides, one Muslim, one Jewish, both of Cordoba in Andalusia. The work of the two writers influenced in turn the European 'renascence' of the twelfth century, that of Averroës in particular as he had been entrusted by the sultan with the mission of exploring the work of Aristotle, for this was a period when the court among others was open to secular scholarship. Both Jews and Muslims were of course also engaged in promoting their own religious traditions but at this time they gave a prominent place to philosophy, to medicine, mathematics, astronomy and to a range of 'secondary' sciences, called

---

[39] Anderson 1974b: 414.   [40] Anderson 1974b: 415.
[41] Blacker 1964.   [42] Kraemer 1986.

speculative; in doing this they followed new lines of thinking, contributing to one of the alternative 'humanistic' periods of which I have spoken.

In Europe too some elements of a secular outlook were always present even under the hegemonic religion, but an agnostic view never dominated, for the prevalent ideology was always subject to strong ecclesiastical control. For example, in Béziers, not far from Montpellier where one of the first schools of medicine in Europe developed, an element of tolerance and laicity was to be found in the thirteenth century. That ended in 1209 when the town was invaded from the north by the Albigensian Crusade and many of the inhabitants were massacred. Intellectually, Béziers became a different place as the result of increased ecclesiastical control. The consequences of such control are now difficult to imagine but they were very extensive in European society. It has been written of education in Cambridge University for a much later period, '[i]n the days when Cambridge's main function was training ministers for the Church of England and college fellows resigned on marriage, there were no laboratories and no formal scientific careers. Great Scientists needed independent means to pursue their goals...'[43] That is to say, even in the nineteenth century religion and science did not get on well together, although in most contexts one had to adapt to the other. But intrinsic to most advances in knowledge of the world, as well as to creativity in the arts, was an element of secularity, or at least the compartmentalization of religion. This position was often difficult to obtain within traditional religions, especially as monotheistic ones did not easily relinquish the claim to have all the answers.

However, an important change took place in Europe in the Renaissance. But what was it that instigated this shift? On one level the economy, especially in Italy and the Mediterranean, and trade with the east. This advance was central to much cultural activity, of science and of art. But it was perhaps the looking back that released that continent in an explosive way from part at least of its religious hegemony into adopting a more enquiring and a more secular approach. That release could not take place in the same dramatic manner in cultures that had not adopted so dominant a religion. Nor could it occur in the absence of secular institutions in the fields of learning and training. Of this advent of secularity, either in science or in art, Anderson like others does not perhaps make enough.

A more secular approach to the world was not confined to Europe. But the problem with hegemonic religions, especially monotheistic ones, is they allocate supreme power and knowledge to God. All that men

[43] Emsley 2006: 14–16.

and women require to know is contained in the scriptures. Such systems of belief discourage interference with God's creations, whereas science demands some freedom to experiment and to enquire. The religious, on the other hand, developed forms of mysticism, like Sufism, the Kabbala or the Christian equivalents, which allocated an extraordinary role to the supernatural. Heaven knows all, can do all, is beyond all. In extreme cases there is no need of other learning than is contained in the Book or in the mystical sect. You can get lost in mystical thought and practice; you dance and sing your way out of whatever else is going on.

It is clear that this kind of attitude has to be modified if change is to take place, in the sciences as in the arts. In the latter, Semitic aniconism was gradually breached. In Christianity, the freedom of painting began with the portraits of holy individuals, such as that reputedly made of Christ himself, his human rather than his divine nature, by the evangelist Luke.[44] That was the focus of Byzantine art, the icon, the holy portrait without figurative background. Byzantine art had a strong influence in western Europe. But the west produced the idea of a background, especially in the early Renaissance when perspective was developed (or redeveloped). The background itself was already a secularizing factor, for it promoted an interest in landscape in addition to that in holy persons, though of course in a religious context. Eventually the Italian Renaissance extended 'holy persons' to include royalty, ecclesiasts and other patrons but also took in classical subjects, as in Botticelli's famous *Birth of Venus*. A painter like Poussin (1594–1665) gave increasing emphasis to nature, but his works remained 'classical', inhabited by Roman statues and by distant people. Later on, the people often disappear, giving place to the romantic concentration upon nature, culminating perhaps in the work of Paul Cézanne (1839–1906), who in a controlled manner wanted to put the true colours into such paintings and 'faire du Poussin sur nature',[45] that is, to paint in 'natural' colours and without the figures. Indeed, the last period of Cézanne had a strong link with early abstract painting and the absence of representation, in France, in Russia and elsewhere.

In this development of art it is not easy to appreciate how central religion had been to life in earlier times, how different from the post-Renaissance, post-Enlightenment, world in the west. That was true in all spheres of activity. Writing of marriage among the Jewish communities in Morocco, Zafrani describes it as 'an institution of religious law',[46] sanctified by a nuptial benediction and consisting of a series of rituals

---

[44] As Toynbee remarks, Christianity betrayed the Jewish principles of aniconism and monotheism (1954: 86).
[45] Coulange 2006: 71.   [46] Zafrani 1996: 119.

spelt out in religious terms; so too it was (and in some limited respects still is) in Christianity and Islam. If marriage involved a religious ceremony, it stands to reason that the choice of spouse should not be left to the partners alone and that the education of children should be organized by the prevailing creed, largely for its own ends rather than for acquiring secular knowledge. Marriage meant religious endogamy, you married within, outside love was not approved, and young male children at least learnt how to read and write mainly for cultic reasons. Secular knowledge had often to be acquired in a different context, not primarily in the schools of the Abrahamistic religions but often in the house or informally, if at all. The child followed the parent and learnt his or her trade at home. Education was for religious socialization, not for offering new vistas, different opportunities. That is why the Renaissance was such a breakthrough in the Christian communities of Europe, in seeking inspiration from a pagan source and reducing the field of religions which had hitherto been so dominant partly because they were monotheistic. And it remained like this for many people and in many contexts. What the Renaissance did not do was to free the western world altogether from religion, but it did place limits on its sway, especially in the artistic and scientific spheres.

This dominance, as I have remarked, is difficult for people in the west fully to comprehend today, whatever branch of the Abrahamistic religions they acknowledge. For example, the writing of Indian history by the west was much influenced by the Enlightenment, a movement that carried secular thinking a stage further than the Renaissance. This meant that European historians 'were baffled by a religion that was . . . not monotheistic, there was no historical founder, or single sacred text, or dogma or ecclesiastical organization'.[47] In my own terms, Indian religion was not hegemonic and did not inhibit cultural or intellectual difference in the same way; 'diverse and multiple religions were practised'.[48] But post-Enlightenment European historians failed to give proper weight even to this less prescriptive creed; the influence of religion could not be properly evaluated. On the other hand, the study of oriental cultures did give some members of the west the promise of another renaissance different in kind from the rationalist revival of the Greek, where the 'spiritual' east would compensate for the discipline, rationality and materialism of Europe, an idea embodied in German (and to some extent British) Romanticism.[49] That was a sort of renaissance that went in quite a different direction than what happened earlier in the west and was a reaction to its secularizing tone.

[47] Thapar 2002: 3.   [48] Thapar 2002: 3.   [49] Thapar 2002: 4.

The incomprehension of the 'modern' historian in the face of India, however, was partly the outcome of the residual attachment to a monotheistic creed and to a written religion of conversion. In oral societies the supernatural world is more eclectic. So too are polytheistic religions, as in the case of Hinduism, which in India virtually absorbed Buddhism. Their explanation of the world still pertained to the supernatural, to the transcendental. Even so, in such societies there were certain periods of cultural effervescence when more secular forms of reasoning came to the fore, at least in selected sectors of activity. In China, which had its full share of beliefs in gods among the bulk of the people, it was the Confucianism of the elite that produced the ancestral canon (apart from the Buddhist one) to which the literati constantly looked back. At this level Confucianism was largely a secular creed that left enquiry with a freer reign than under transcendental doctrines. In this regime there was a relatively continuous development of science, as Joseph Needham has shown for example with regard to the knowledge of plants and animals. There were periods of effervescence, but there were downs as well as ups, relating to the state of the polity, the economy and to ideological factors.

There is the theoretical possibility that these various periods of efflorescence throughout Eurasia were not altogether independent of one another. We have already spoken of the impact of Christianity on the Jewish Emancipation and of Islam on the Christian Renaissance. But I refer to yet wider influences. After all, by the sixteenth century, in some cases much earlier, the major societies throughout Eurasia had long been in communication with one another, direct and indirect, largely through trade or other forms of exchange, but also by conquest, especially of the 'Huns' and the Mongols of Europe. Trade, however, was dependent upon production, even in the case of prime materials, gold, silver and other metals, the exchange of which required prior production but not manufacture. But in each case interchange was involved which could also include a 'cultural' transfer of the kind that was implicated in the birth of new items and techniques, as with paper, printing, the compass, gunpowder, in one direction, and counter-transfers such as perspective and clocks in the other. Relations developed, hostile as well as amicable. But commerce continued and so did the movements of merchants: the Turks had their *fondacio* (inn) complete with *hammam* (bath house) and mosque, which were distributed along the trade routes east and west (e.g. at Venice) and where justice was meted out, as at Istanbul. All were in constant communication, like Italian bankers and merchants in London's Lombard Street and in the Hanseatic towns of north Germany.

This commerce comprised many commodities, but as we see from wool in Florence (the Medicis were cloth merchants), from silk-cloth in

Lucca and Bologna, from linen in Egypt, from cotton in India and from silk again in China, textiles were an essential feature in this trade, the profits of which fed into various renascences. The historian of Jewish Cairo, Goitein, notes that 'the major industry of medieval times in the Mediterranean area' was textiles to be used in this exchange;[50] early on, the Egyptian production of linen was most important, becoming the basis of the economic prosperity of its golden age in the Tulinid period (868–903) and subsequently in that of the Fatimids. Linen was produced on the estates of great landholders who reinvested in the industry and had the textiles made in state or private 'factories' (as at Tinnis) and then widely used for exchange, including exports. This was also the case in Europe. 'The role of the textile industry in the economic growth and development of medieval and renaissance Italian cities, the Low Countries, and in England has . . . been central to the study of the economic history of medieval Europe.'[51]

This exchange led to the establishment of merchant and manufacturing communities throughout. In the Near East, Goitein speaks of a bourgeois revolution in the eighth and ninth centuries;[52] that revolution was especially important for the merchants but also gave rise to the possibility of learned men among the rich, as with the family of the philosopher Maimonides, who were involved in the trade in precious stones with India. Similar communities existed in the Far East, as we have seen, both in China and in India, and with rather similar ideologies. For these merchant regimes were more important in those parts of the world than has often been thought. 'The ideals of ancient India, while not perhaps the same as those in the west, by no means excluded money-making. India not only had a class of luxury-loving and pleasure-seeking dilettanti, but also one of wealth-seeking merchants and prosperous craftsmen, who, if less respected than the brāhmans and warriors, had an honourable place in society.'[53] That was also the case in China and Japan where in many parts merchants developed a rich urban culture, even though they suffered discrimination from time to time.

Under these mercantile conditions production was not based on family activity alone but took place in other institutions. The Mauryan state owned not only spinning and weaving workshops, but also those for the manufacture of weapons and other military supplies, employing salaried craftsmen for the purpose. Larger mines were also worked by the state. Yet there was ample scope for individual producers as well, some of whom were involved in large-scale manufacture for an extensive market (and

[50] Goitein 1967: 101.   [51] Frantz-Murphy 1981: 280.
[52] Goitein 1967.   [53] Basham 1967: 218.

were therefore 'individualistic'). One form of industrial organization, which involved an elaborate division of labour, consisted of cooperative groups of workmen employed in the building trade and elsewhere. Such work was often regulated by guilds (*shreni*) which played a big part in the economy of most towns, where they also enjoyed a political role as some of them had their own militia at least as early as Buddhist times (from the fifth century BCE).

Such extensive trade was clearly facilitated by the use of an acceptable medium of exchange that eventually included paper money, which depended upon literacy and upon trust. Metal coinage may have been first introduced to India from the Near East but money equivalents such as cowries existed earlier. Lending money on interest was also widespread, as in Islam and Judaism despite restrictions on usury; bankers (*shresthin*) were numerous, often being leading members of guilds who represented their members on the local council and thus participated in political decisions. Mercantile companies, which often consisted of temporary *commenda*-type associations, got together for maritime expeditions, trading widely with the west as well as with south-east Asia. Embassies were sent to Rome and elsewhere and merchants regularly visited the Near East, establishing a sizeable Indian colony on the island of Socotra. To the Near East went cloth and various luxuries including sugar and rice, as well as fortune tellers and prostitutes. In return India wanted little but gold, although Roman pottery (*sigillata* ware) was exported to Arikamedu in the south-east, as well as some wine, gold and slave-girls, all luxury items. Whenever and wherever extensive trade of this kind occurred, it is obvious that literacy played a part in the reckoning, especially in long-distance trade, since one of its advantages was to make interpersonal communication possible over space, without the necessity of face-to-face interaction.

I have argued for the very widespread appearance of early mercantile activity whose extent was facilitated by the innovation of writing. Indeed, it has been proposed that exchange was of vital importance in elaborating the early writing system of Mesopotamia in which physical tokens were represented by written marks (symbols) on the outside of the clay envelopes that contained them.[54] Of course, exchange had long been present, but writing encouraged more complex forms of credit, especially later on with paper money. For there is plenty of evidence to show the way in which 'functional literacy' has been of importance in elaborating mercantile transactions.[55] Hence, while we have argued that writing was significant for political and religious affairs, especially for the

[54] Schmandt-Besserat 1996.   [55] See Goody 1986 for this use of Arabic writing.

Abrahamistic religions where the teaching of reading and writing was the virtual monopoly of their personnel and hence schools were originally heavily skewed in favour of religious literacy, nevertheless merchants, as parents of some of the pupils in these establishments, also exercised an influence in favour of practical teaching for their own ends. The school was never simply religious in any of the major literate societies since a percentage of the children would always become merchants who required writing skills for their work. Therefore there was instruction in calculation and in letter writing, while other students needed writing for the administration of complex states, especially in China for the bureaucracy.

The drive for a secular literacy among merchants was especially strong in China, but also in India where the accounting system used in large-scale commerce was of course predicated on writing. That skill was also important for Islam not only in religion and in translation, in trading, in administration and in science but in a quite different context where, as Rodinson demonstrates, it enabled merchants to build up a collection of recipes and thus to elaborate their cuisine, as well as their culture more generally.[56] And it was obviously so in Europe, where Nicholas has shown the importance of schooling for the children of Flemish merchants, who were among those leading the way in the economic recovery of the north.[57] In the Elizabethan period in England, when the Reformation had taken them away from the monopoly of the Catholic Church, the grammar schools were developed by royal charters and patronized by the children of merchants whose future activities inevitably had a strong influence on the curriculum, despite instruction still being in many ways heavily ecclesiastical. Hence there was an increasingly secular aspect to education, even though this facet had never been entirely absent.

We have given fundamental importance to literacy and to the mode of communication in this process of rebirth. But, as we have seen, literacy may be very restricted. One thinks of a form of script in Persia that was only used for royal inscriptions.[58] One thinks of the early script in Mesopotamia that may have been elaborated by merchants for merchants. One thinks of the uses of writing in earlier Christianity, Judaism and Islam which were largely for religious purposes. It was mainly when script was employed by the bourgeoisie that it became really transformative of the wider culture and led to an efflorescence. Of course, its presence had earlier made a significant difference to political/legal, economic and religious systems, as I have tried to outline elsewhere,[59] but to be effective in the broad cultural sense we have discussed, it had to be more widely

[56] Rodinson 1974 [1966].   [57] Nicholas 1996.
[58] Herrenschmidt 2007.   [59] Goody 1986.

available. What is important in any rebirth is what you look back to. Clearly with some monumental scripts there are only public inscriptions to examine (though there were other forms of writing in Persia). Recalling the contents of this script would not produce a cultural efflorescence. That depends upon the uses made of writing, which had to cover a wide spectrum of social life. Transcendental usage alone will not do, except for a reformation of religious knowledge. Of course, looking back in a literary mode may descend into pure mimicry, as with many scholarly attempts to reproduce Greek or Latin verse, or as in the efforts of Byzantine scholars to compose the equivalents of texts in Ancient Greek. This process then comes near to counterfeiting, but in any case it represents an extreme form of conservation or reproduction.[60]

In this account I have also stressed the role of trade for obvious reasons. Firstly, it seems to me of crucial importance in the European Renaissance, especially with the renewal of exchange within Europe and in the Mediterranean, the ending of Arab control of that sea, the growing commerce of Venice and other Italian cities with the Near East, and from the Near East to Persia, India and China. Secondly, the history of the east has tended to emphasize political aspects, or alternatively the internal economies, rather than the external communication. As Thapar has said of her colleagues, 'histories of India in the past have been essentially land-based, with maritime trade playing a marginal role'.[61] That bias needs to be overcome in considering the wider history of exchange and of renascences. In India, there was a very vigorous trade with the Persian Gulf, with Arabia, with Egypt and Turkey by the Red Sea, with the eastern shores of Ethiopia and Africa. Some of the commodities involved in this commerce continued overland to North Africa, to Africa south of the Sahara and to Europe. A series of exchanges were encouraged that were of fundamental importance to the Italian Renaissance, for trade meant that intellectual goods too were involved.

But there is little reason to think that all fields made such a burst forward at the same time, in the arts and in the sciences. I have argued that for enquiries into the natural world around us and for the expansion of the arts from a religious context, it was essential to have a measure of secularization in those areas, although transcendental beliefs continued to be present in other restricted spheres. The arts were rather different and religion simply became one topic among many. The uniqueness of the Italian Renaissance came in its historical setting and the fact that in looking back it was reviewing a 'pagan' culture and avoiding the many restrictions that Christianity had placed upon scientific and artistic activity. There was

---

[60] See Toynbee 1954: 59.   [61] Thapar 2002: xxvii.

also a loosening up of relations both in trade and in intellectual exchange with the cultures of the east, infidel as they were. This loosening of the bonds also occurred from time to time in Islam and in Judaism, as well as in Song China; in India there was more cultural continuity. Nevertheless, an important element of continuity did exist in Arabic and Chinese, as well as Sanskrit, where looking back involved linguistically a constant rapprochement between the past and the present, whereas in Europe (and in early Islam) looking back was dependent upon translation from and sometimes to another language (such as Latin), which was obviously not available to the majority. That indigenous process was quite different from that in societies where the renascence was of a culture that expressed itself in quite another tongue. In the latter case, while the rebirth concerned translations from other languages, the progress of the Renaissance lay in the shift of knowledge and creative activity to the local languages, in other words to a vernacularization. Therein lay the background of this more permanent burst forward to 'modernization', certainly as far as the wider participation of other people, especially technologists and artisans, was concerned. Learning, as Bolgar says, became familiar to all who could read, not only all who could read classical languages.[62]

It was in instituting and institutionalizing the possibility of a secular approach to the arts and especially to sciences that the Italian Renaissance helped to change the world.

This institutionalization was partly the result of non-transcendental knowledge being conserved in universities and academies. It also had to do with the changes in the internal economy which supported these colleges, and the means of communication were also heavily involved. The printing press certainly had a role in enabling humankind to build on what had been learnt; 'Humanism may indeed have owed the ultimate survival of its ideas to Gutenberg's discovery.' Otherwise, like the renascence of the twelfth century, it might have been 'transmogrified by a new Scholasticism'. It did not create the Renaissance, Bolgar argues, but 'helped to keep alive revolutionary ideas'.[63]

The external economy was also important, for this expanded with the discovery of America and the colonization of other parts of the world, allowing for an enormous growth of production and of exchange activity. Together with the harnessing of energy and the organization of work necessary to drive the machines, this larger market meant the development of larger-scale industrial enterprises.

My thesis is then that all societies with writing, which was an important skill for merchants, administrators and scholars as well as for clerics, look

---

[62] Bolgar 1954: 302. [63] Bolgar 1954: 280.

back to what was composed at an earlier period and that looking back was followed at times by a burst forward. However, the looking back was especially important in the religious domain where progress and change are hardly welcomed. All literate religions looked back, the Abrahamistic ones to the Jewish Bible and to later accretions, the polytheistic Hindus to the Vedic scripture, the Buddhists to their canon, the Jains to theirs. But so too in the more secular case of China, people harked back to Confucius and to other scholars of that period, who were constantly referred to as authorities; all literate societies looked back whether or not to religious texts. This process did not always lead to a rebirth; it might occasionally involve conservation and continuity although the reference to past writings could also stimulate new cultural activity or even provide for a breakthrough. A more important stimulus came when the looking back involved reviving a culture that had a different ideology, as happened in Europe when the non-Christian world of the classics was available for recall and encouraged a more secular approach to many aspects of life. The decline of the Roman empire had led to a collapse in the urban economy of the west. Towns became of less importance and trade between them suffered. The Mediterranean was no longer the hub of economic activity, until commerce took up once again with the east and the south, where an urban and mercantile culture had continued to exist leading beyond to Persia, India and to China, to the whole of the Eurasian continent. In those regions there had not been quite the same regression that western Europe had experienced; though not uninterrupted, India and China had seen a more continuous development. And aside from Islam they were more pluralistic. Contact with these eastern cultures helped stimulate the changes leading to the Italian Renaissance, that is to a resumption of trade, the rebirth of a wider approach, and a renewal of cultural contacts with the past and with the present. But each of these other literate societies had its own period of looking back, its own cultural efflorescence, its own renascence, when supernatural explanations were challenged at times and a more secular humanism flourished. From a sociological standpoint, renascences were multiple and not confined to 'capitalism' nor to the west. Europe was not alone, nor was it a cultural island.

Appendix 1: Chronologies of Islam, India and China

Dynasties of Islam

Egypt and Syria	Arabia and Mesopotamia	Persia and Central Asia	Spain and Maghreb	Turkey	Afghanistan and India
Byzantine and Persian rule	Hijra (622) Muhammad's death (632)	Sasanian rule	Christian kingdoms in Spain		
Early caliphate (632–61)					Muslim incursions in Sindh (711)
Arab conquest (646)				Anatolia under Christian rule	
Umayyad caliphate (661–750)			Conquests in North Africa		
Abbasid dynasty (750–1258)			Spanish Umayyads (756–1031)		
Tulunids (868–905)		Samanid amirs (819–999)			
Abbasids in Egypt again (905–35)					
Ikhshidids (935–69)		Karakhanid amirs (999–1211)			
Fatimid dynasty (910–1171)			Taifa kingdoms (mid 11th – early 12th century)		Ghaznavid dynasty (975–1187)
Seljuq dynasty (1068–1141)			Almoravid dynasty (1073–1147)	Seljuqs of Rum (1077–1307)	

First Crusade (1095)

Ayyubid dynasty (1169–1271)

Mongol invasion (1258)

    Mongol Ilkhans (1256–1335)

        Almohad dynasty (1147–1269)

        Kingdom of Granada (1228–1492)

                Ghurid dynasty (1148–1215)

                Minor Muslim dynasties (Slave, Khilji, Tughlaq, Sayyid, Lodhi)

Mamluk dynasty (1250–1517)

Ottoman empire (1453–1918)

        Safavid dynasty (1502–1722)   Fall of Granada (1492)   Ottoman empire (1453–1918)

                Mughal empire (1504–1707)

Napoleonic invasion (1798)

        Qajar dynasty (1781–1925)   Persian invasion

                Incursions by Russia, Austria, France, etc.   British incursions

                Effective British Rule (from 1770s)

British protectorate (1882–1922)

World War I Arab revolt (1916–18)

                World War I Defeat (1918)

Syria (French protectorate 1920–46)

        Pahlavi dynasty (1925–79)   Revolution under Atatürk (1920)

Independence (1922)

    Saudi royalty (1932)

        Khomeini revolution (1979)

                Independence (1947)

Events in Islamic history, 622–1334

622 Muhammad's hijra to Medina

632 Muhammad's death (Islam dominates most of Arab peninsula)

632–61 Early caliphate (Abu Bakr, Umar, Uthman, Ali), followed by dynastic caliphates

> Abu Bakr, companion of Muhammad
>
> Umar, companion of Muhammad
>
> Uthman, early convert, conquered Iran, Cyprus, Caucasus, most of North Africa
>
> Ali (r. 656–61), warrior, lieutenant and later son-in-law of Muhammad, first imam of the Shia sect

661–750 Umayyad caliphate (from Damascus)
(expansion of Islam to Atlantic and Indian and Chinese borders)

> First Umayyad has Ali assassinated in a coup and conquers Egypt

750–1258 Abbasid caliphate (from Baghdad)

> Tahirids, Saffarids, Samanids (Persia); Central Asia from c.850 caliphate under effective control of Turkic military (Iranian) Buyid renaissance in ninth and tenth centuries

756–1031 Spanish Umayyads (from Cordoba)

909–1171 Fatimid dynasty of Ismaili Shia caliphs, from Maghreb (the only Shia ever caliphs)

972 Fatimids conquer Egypt, found Cairo, continue to Syria, to Sicily and southern Italy, independent dynasties in Morocco, Tunisia, Egypt

1050?– Turkish sultanate (incl. India, Central Asia)

1064–71 Seljuq Turks annexe Armenia, Georgia and Anatolia; Fatimid territory shrinks to Egypt under Seljuq and Maghribi Sunni pressures

1072–92 Great Seljuq Malikshah extends to Syria, Chinese border; vizier in Baghdad

1087 Malikshah, ruling from Isfahan, is proclaimed Sultan of East and West

1090–1272 Assassin sect active, mainly against Seljuq and other Muslim targets

1092 Death of Malikshah, sultanate dissolves into warring dynastic states

1095 First Crusade arrives to take Holy Land from Seljuq and Fatimid hands

1099– Crusader states throughout Levant

Cultural golden age in Persia in eleventh and twelfth centuries

1171 Saladin (a Kurdish Ayyubid) deposes last Fatimid caliph

1171– Ayyubid (Kurdish) dynasty of caliphs, ruling western Arabia, Syria, Egypt

1182 Badlis dynasty of khans of Kurdistan emerges; rule till 1847

1187 Jerusalem falls to Saladin

1193 Saladin's treaty with Richard I, restoring Ascalon–Antioch strip; Saladin dies

1291 Mamluks terminate Christian kingdoms in Levant

1206 Mamluk (slave) general Qutb-uddin Aibak establishes sultanate in Delhi (till 1290)

1250 last Ayyubid sultan of Egypt supplanted by slave general Aibak; Mamluk sultans of Egypt till 1517; 'Bahri' dynasty is named after their ('sea') regiment; Mamluk (Bahri) sultanate begins shortly after Aibak is murdered

1260–63 last residues of Ayyubid sultanate of Damascus and emirate of Homs lapse; Ayyubid remnants resist from emirate of Hamah till 1334

Periods of Indian history

Mehrgarh and related sites

> Early food producing era c.7000–5500 BCE, followed by region-alization phase or the 'Early Harappan' period 5500–2600 BCE

c.2600–1700 BCE Indus civilization (Harappan-Mohenjodaro culture)

> Urban phase, the so-called 'Mature' Harappan period and/or the 'Integration Era' 2600–1900 BCE
>
> 'Late' Harappan phase or Localization Era 1900–1300 BCE

1500–700 BCE The so-called Vedic Age

> Iron Age, megalithic burials in South India, Grey Ware in upper Ganga plains. Early dynasties in Magadha (Bihar, Orissa, Bengal) from c.1200 BCE

700–320s BCE The Classical Age

> Mahajanapadas and Bimbisara dynasty in the Magadha from sixth century BCE when, from then onwards, the Black North-ern Polished Ware (700–200 BCE) makes its appearance
>
> 600–300 BCE Urbanization, emergence of cities on nodal routes of trade – e.g. Kausambi, Sravasti, Vatsa, Champa, Anga, Ahicchatra, Rajghat, Vaishali, Ujjaini on the Ganges and

its tributaries, and Taxila, Hathial, and Pushkalavati in the
northwest

Gana sanghas ('city states') and kingdoms; the rise of a state at
Magadha, where the Nanda rule is mentioned by the Puranas

Buddha: 486 BCE his Mahaparinirvana ('great, complete
Nirvana' at death)

Invasions in the north-west:

519 BCE Cyrus, the Achaemenid ruler of Persia

326–27 BCE Alexander of Macedon crosses the Indus

321–185 BCE Mauryan dynasty and the emergence of empire, emanating from Magadha and extending to all of north India

Chiefdoms in south: Cheras, Cholas Pandyas, Satyputras mentioned in
Asokan Pillars and in the Sangam literature

185 BCE–c.300 CE Reign of the Shungas (Magadha), Kharavela
(Kalinga), and existence of oligarchies such as Kunindas, Sibhis, Yaud-
heyas, Malavas, Abhiras in north India

c.230 BCE Rise of Satavahana power in the Deccan

c.50 BCE–c.50 CE Peak of Roman trade with India

In the north-west:

180–165 BCE Indo-Greek in Hazra, Swat and Punjab

c.150–135 BCE King Menander

1st BCE (c.80 BCE) the Sakas with King Maues

The Parthians – Gondophernes (d. 46 CE)

1st CE Kushanas

Date of Kanishka controversial (c.78 CE, or else 122–40 CE)

In the west, i.e. Gujarat and the Deccan:

1st CE Saka Ksatrapa dynasty – Rudradaman (c.150 CE)

1st – mid 3rd CE Satavahana

followed by the Abihras and Traikutakas

300–700 CE northern India: with Magadha as base of empire

319–c.455 CE the Gupta dynasty

405–11 CE visit of Chinese traveller Fa-Hsien

606–647 CE empire of Harshavardhana (northern India)

630–643 CE the Chinese traveller Xuanxang in India

Western India:

c.4th/5th CE Vakataka dynasty

mid 6th CE Chalukyas of Badami, Pulakesin I (543–566 CE)

712 CE Arab conquest of Sind

7th CE – 9th CE Rashtrakutas
10th/11th CE Silaharas
12th CE Yadavas of Devagiri
1347–1538 CE Bahamani

South India:
c.574–731 CE Pallava dynasty of Kanchi
Continuous warfare among the Pallavas, Chalukyas and Pandyas
c.900 CE to 13th CE Chola dynasty in Tamil Nadu
985–1070 Chola imperialism at its height.
1110 CE Rise of Hoysala power under Vishnuvardhana
(Hoysalas of Dwarasmaudra c.12th–13th CE)
13th CE Pandyas
16th CE onwards – Nayakas
1336–1565 CE Vijayanagara

For east:
Palas, Senas

Back to north:
Gurjara Pratihara, Parmara, Chauhans, Chahamanas, i.e the so-called
Rajput kingdoms
1000–26 CE Mahmud of Ghazni's invasion
1206–1526 Delhi sultanate
1526–1757 Mughal empire

Power shared from early eighteenth century in both south and north
amongst various nawabs; following Clive's campaigns in the 1750s,
the power and independence of the Mughals declined drastically; last
Mughal exiled 1858
1739 Nadir Shah's invasion of Delhi
Regional states of the 18th century
1674–1818 Maratha empire
1716–99 Sikh Confederacy in north-west India, Oudh, Hyderabad,
    Nawabs of Carnatic, Mysore, Bengal, Jats, Rohillas
1757 Beginning of European rule and expansion after battle of Plassey
1757–1857 Company Raj
1857–1947 British India: power passes formally from East India
    Company following 1857 rebellion
1877 Imperial British hegemony formalized
1947 Modern states, following independence

Chinese dynasties

1700–1045 BCE Shang dynasty
1045–221 BCE Zhou dynasty

> Western Zhou (1045–771 BCE)
> Eastern Zhou (770–221 BCE)
>
> Spring and Autumn (770–476 BCE)
> Warring States (475–221 BCE)

221–207 BCE Qin dynasty
206 BCE – 220 CE Han dynasty

> Western Han (206 BCE – 23 CE)
> Eastern Han (25–220)

220–80 Three Kingdoms

> Wei (220–65)
> Shu Han (221–63)
> Wu (222–80)

265–420 Jin dynasty

> Western Jin (265–316)
> Eastern Jin (317–420)

386–589 Northern and Southern dynasties
386–581 Northern dynasties

> Northern Wei (386–534)
> Eastern Wei (534–50)
> Northern Qi (550–77)
> Western Wei (535–56)
> Northern Zhou (557–81)

430–589 Southern dynasties

> Song (420–79)
> Qi (479–502)
> Liang (502–57)
> Chen (557–89)

581–618 Sui dynasty
618–907 Tang dynasty
907–60 Five dynasties

Later Liang (907–23)
Later Tang (923–36)
Later Jin (936–46)
Later Han (947–50)
Later Zhou (951–60)

960–1279 Song dynasty

Northern Song (960–1127 CE)
Southern Song (1127–1279 CE)

916–1125 Liao dynasty
1115–1234 Jin dynasty
1232–1368 Yuan dynasty
1368–1644 Ming dynasty
1644–1911 Qing dynasty
1912– The Republic

Appendix 2: Four learned men

A brief examination of the biographies of four learned men – two from an Islamic background, and two of the great names in European theology and philosophy – will illustrate the general climate of intellectual exchange and interaction within which subsequent advances in medicine and knowledge more generally are to be situated. The first was also a doctor and all were involved in the struggle between faith (religion) and reason (rationality, even 'science'), attempting to reconcile the two.

Avicenna (981–1037) came from Persia and worked in the great library of the Samanids in Baghdad that was later destroyed by the Mongol invasion. He was a physician who wrote *The Book of Healing*, translated into Latin in the twelfth century, as well as *The Course of Medicine*, an encyclopedia drawing from Greek and Arabic sources together with work of his own. He taught the quadrivium and learnt from Aristotle as well as from Neoplatonism, and in turn influenced Aquinas and the Scholastics.

Averroës (Ibn Rushd, born 1126, Cordoba – died 1198, Marakesh) was from the west and attempted to integrate Arab and Greek thought. While accepting the authority of the Quran, he argued that an integration of faith and reason could not be established by the dialectical arguments of theologians but required proof by philosophers who were capable of explaining the true meaning of religion. For his philosophy he too drew upon Aristotle and Plato, writing commentaries and summaries of most of the former's works, some of which represent the only versions now in existence. His arguments brought him up against the clerics and in 1195 he was temporarily banished by his patron, the ruler at Cordoba, Abu Yusuf (Yaqub al-Mansur), at the time of a holy war against Christian Spain.

Albertus Magnus (c.1200–80) taught at Paris and was greatly influenced by Averroës's work on Aristotle. One of his pupils was Thomas Aquinas. He distinguished the path of knowledge by revelation and faith from that of philosophy and science. The latter follow the authorities of the past according to their competence but also make use of observation and proceed by way of reason and intellect to the highest degree of abstraction. But these approaches were not seen as opposed and should come together in harmony.

Thomas Aquinas (1225–74) began his studies at the University of Naples, where he was exposed to the scientific and philosophical translations being undertaken from Greek and Arabic. He then studied under Albertus Magnus at Paris from 1245, and moved with him to Cologne in 1248, returning to Paris twenty years later to teach. He was influenced by both Aristotle and Averroës, but moderated the latter's dualism of faith and reason. In his *Summa Theologica* (c.1265–73), he argued that reason was able to follow its own laws within faith. Nature was determined by structures that could be apprehended by reason, and knowledge was based on sense experience leading up to a reflective appreciation of Providence. To study the laws of nature was to study the perfection of God's creative power.

Appendix 3: The Bagre

The Bagre consists of two parts, the account of the rituals in the White and the more esoteric Black which deals with the myth behind the ceremonies. Looking at the Bagre in a comparative way, I do not now see the Ngmangbili Bagre ('the Third Bagre') (Goody and Gandah 2002: 139) as being a version of the Black but of the White as it is concerned with the ceremonies involved in the performances of the Bagre society. Such ceremonies (beginning at 1.125) are discussed at length though this recitation is listed as Black (Goody and Gandah 1980: 46). On the other hand, it does begin with the building of a house, as happens in the Gomble and Biro (Black) version ('the Third Bagre', 2002: 5 and 101).

None of the later versions of the Black (except the first) have retained the visit to Heaven (where man was created or born), an incident which seemed so important in my original version. How something which I conceived as so central to the structure could disappear made me reconsider the problem of memory in purely oral societies as well as the structure of myth. In the beginning of the first version (Goody 1972), two men cross a river, meet an old man and are shown by the 'beings of the wild' how to eat guinea-corn (sorghum), smelt iron and make fire. The younger of the two then climbs up to Heaven with the help of the spider where he meets God ('an old man' again). He encounters a slender girl and in front of them God creates a child (symbolically from one point of view) about whose ownership they quarrel.

The second version of the Bagre (1980) begins with a man and his wife who build a house themselves. They brew beer for the helpers and make iron to forge an arrow. They kill an animal and divide it out. No one helps them except their neighbours. In fact, God and the beings of the wild play very little part. It is the Bagre god who comes down in the course of the ceremonies, for which this Black Bagre provides an account of them all. But the whole recitation is very much of the here and now with a great deal of attention being paid to all those present, especially to the relations (paternal and maternal) of Gandaa, the late chief, in whose compound the recitation took place. In this Second Bagre the man crosses a river and meets the red-haired beings of the wild as well as a man (*daba*, 1.1803) who is not 'an old man' (God). However, the incident with the flying animals (1.1829) may possibly represent a severe shortening of the visit to Heaven: if so, only my earlier version can clarify. The child is taught to poison his arrows in the proper manner, which he could not do. But there is no quarrel between the parents about ownership. The boy shoots, his sister is excised. There is still some dispute about a child but this difficulty is much clearer in the subsequent versions 3 and 4 from Gomble and Biro, which are very close to one another ('the Third Bagre', 2002). God does assist the man and the woman to build a house. They have intercourse and a child is born. The mother and father quarrel about their offspring. The boy goes hunting. Trouble strikes the son and they have to perform the Bagre.

References

Abulafia, D. 1977. *The Two Italies: economic relations between the Norman kingdom of Sicily and the Northern Communes*. Cambridge: Cambridge University Press

Abu'l Fazl ibn Mubārak 1977–8 [1868–94]. *The Āʾīn-i Akbarī*, vol. 3, trans. H. Blochmann and H. S. Jarrett, corrected by Sir Judanath Sarkar; 2nd edn, revised and edited by D. C. Phillott. New Delhi: Oriental Books Reprint Corporation

Achebe, I. 2001. Religion and politics in Igboland from the 18th century to 1930: earth, God, and power. Unpublished PhD dissertation, University of Cambridge

Achour, M. 1995. L'invention dans les arts. In D. Chevalier and A. Miquel (eds.), *Les Arabes du message à l'histoire*. Paris: Fayard

Adams, R. M. 1966. *The Evolution of Urban Society: early Mesopotamia and pre-hispanic Mexico*. Chicago: Aldine

Almaqqari 1855–61. *Analectes sur l'histoire et la littérature des Arabes d'Espagne*, trans. R. P. A. Dozy. Leiden: Brill

Amado, C. 1986. De la cité visigothique à la ville mediévale (de la XIIe siècle). In J. Sagnes (ed.), *Histoire de Béziers*. Toulouse: Privat

Anderson, P. 1974a. *Passages from Antiquity to Feudalism*. London: Verso
1974b. *Lineages of the Absolutist State*. London: Verso

Anon. 1957. *Le Livre de Kalila et Dimna*, trans. al-Muqaffa, trans. from Arabic by André Miquel. Paris: Éditions Klincksieck

Assman, J. 2001 [1984]. *The Search for God in Ancient Egypt*, trans. D. Lorton. Ithaca, NY: Cornell University Press

Atil, E. 1975. *Art of the Arab World*. Washington, DC: Smithsonian Institution
1981. *Renaissance of Islam: art of the Mamluks*. Washington, DC: Smithsonian Institution Press

Augustine, St 1945. *The City of God*, vol. 1, trans. 1610, J. Healey. London: Dent
1991. *Confessions*, trans. H. Chadwick. Oxford: Oxford University Press

Bakhle, J. 2008. Music as the sound of the secular. *Comparative Studies in Society and History* 50: 256–84

Balazs, E. 1964. *Chinese Civilisation and Bureaucracy*. New Haven, CT: Yale University Press

Barnhart, R. M. 1997. The Five Dynasties (907–960) and the Song Period (960–1279). In R. M. Barnhart *et al.*, *Three Thousand Years of Chinese Painting*. New Haven, CT: Yale University Press

Baron, H. 1966. *The Crisis of the Early Italian Renaissance: civic humanism and republican liberty in an age of classicism and tyranny.* Princeton, NJ: Princeton University Press

Basham, A. L. 1967. *The Wonder that Was India: a survey of the history and culture of the Indian sub-continent before the coming of the Muslims.* London: Fontana

Bashar ibn Burd 1972. *Baššār et son expérience courtoise,* trans. A. Roman. Beirut: Dar El-Machreq

Bayle, P. 1697. *Dictionnaire historique et critique.* Rotterdam: R. Leers

Beck, J. H. 1999. *Italian Renaissance Painting.* Cologne: Konemann

Bell, J. 2007. *Mirror of the World: a new history of art.* London: Thames & Hudson

Belting, H. 2008. *Florenz und Bagdad: eine westöstliche Geschichte des Blicks.* Munich: Verlag C. H. Beck

Benn, C. 2004. *China's Golden Age: everyday life in the Tang Dynasty.* Oxford: Oxford University Press

Berenson, B. 1950. *Aesthetics and History.* London: Constable

1952. *Italian Painters of the Renaissance.* London: Phaidon Press

Bernal, J. D. 1954. *Science in History.* London: Watts

Bernal, M. 1987. *Black Athena: the Afroasiatic roots of classical civilisation,* vol. 1. London: Free Association Books

2005. India in the making of Europe. *Journal of the Asiatic Society* 46: 37–66

Bhatia, S. L. 1972. *Medical Science in Ancient India.* Bangalore: Bangalore University Press

Blacker, C. 1964. *The Japanese Enlightenment: a study of the writing of Fukazawa Yukichi.* Cambridge: Cambridge University Press

Blazy, G. (ed.) 2001. *Guide des collections: Musée des tissus de Lyons.* Lyons: Éditions Lyonnaises d'Art et d'Histoire

Bolgar, R. R. 1954. *The Classical Heritage and its Beneficiaries.* Cambridge: Cambridge University Press

Bonnet, H. 1992. *La Faculté de Médecine de Montpellier: huit siècles d'histoire et d'éclat.* Montpellier: Sauramps

Boorstin, D. 1991. The realms of pride and awe. In J. A. Levenson (ed.), *Circa 1492: art in the age of exploration.* New Haven, CT: Yale University Press

Bose, D. M. *et al.* (eds.) 1971. *A Concise History of Science in India.* New Delhi: Indian National Science Academy

Bourain, M. 1986. Le massacre de 1209. In J. Sagnes (ed.), *Histoire de Béziers.* Toulouse: Privat

Bousma, W. J. 2002. *The Waning of the Renaissance, 1550–1640.* New Haven, CT: Yale University Press

Braudel, F. 1981–4a [1979]. *Civilisation and Capitalism, 15th–18th Century,* vol. 1: *The Structures of Everyday Life.* London: Phoenix Press

1981–4b [1979]. *Civilisation and Capitalism, 15th–18th Century,* vol. 2: *The Wheels of Commerce.* London: Phoenix Press

1981–4c [1979]. *Civilisation and Capitalism, 15th–18th Century,* vol. 3: *The Perspective of the World.* London: Phoenix Press

Bray, F. 2000. *Technology and Society in Ming China (1368–1644).* Washington, DC: American Historical Society

Brinker, H. 2001. The rebirth of Zen images and ideas in medieval Japan. In N. C. Rousmaniere (ed.), *Births and Rebirths in Japanese Art*. Leiden: Hotei Publishing

Brook, T. 1981. The merchant network in 16th century China: a discussion and translation of Zhang Han's 'On Merchants'. *Journal of Social and Economic History of the Orient* 24: 165–214

Brotons, R. 1997. *L'Histoire de Lunel, de ses Juifs et de sa Grande École: du 1er au XIVème siècles*, part I. Montpellier: Arceaux

   2005. *L'Histoire de Lunel, de ses Juifs et de sa Grande École: du 1er au XIVème siècles*, part II. Nîmes: Thierry

Brotton, J. 2002. *The Renaissance Bazaar*. London: Oxford University Press

Brotton, J. and Jardine, L. 2000. *Global Interests: Renaissance art between East and West*. Ithaca, NY: Cornell University Press

Brunet, G., Tremblay, A. and Pare, P. 1933. *La Rénaissance du XIIe siècle: les écoles et l'enseignement*. Paris: J. Vrin

Brunschvig, R. and Von Grunebaum, G. E. (eds.) 1957. *Classicisme et déclin culturel dans l'histoire de l'Islam. Actes du symposium international d'histoire de la civilisation musulmane (Bordeaux, juin 1956)*. Paris: Besson Chantemerle

Burckhardt, J. 1990 [1860]. *The Civilisation of the Renaissance in Italy*. New York: Penguin

Burke, P. 1998. *The European Renaissance: centres and peripheries*. Oxford: Blackwell

Burns, R. I. 1981. The paper revolution in Europe: Valencia's paper industry: a technological and behavioural breakthrough. *Pacific Historical Review* 50: 1–30

Bury, J. B. 1924. *The Idea of Progress*. London: Macmillan

Carboni, S. 2007. Moments of vision: Venice and the Islamic world, 828–1797. In S. Carboni (ed.), *Venice and the Islamic World, 828–1797*. New Haven, CT: Yale University Press

Caskey, J. 2004. *Art as Patronage in the Medieval Mediterranean: merchant customs in the region of Amalfi*. Cambridge: Cambridge University Press

Chadwick, H. M. and N. K. 1932. *The Growth of Literature*, vol. 1: *The Ancient Literatures of Europe*. Cambridge: Cambridge University Press

Chakrabarti, D. K. 1990. *The External Trade of the Indus Civilization*. New Delhi: Munshiram Manoharlal

   2006. *The Oxford Companion to Indian Archaeology: the archaeological foundations of ancient India*. New Delhi: Oxford University Press

Chaliand, G. 2004. *Nomadic Empires: from Mongolia to the Danube*, trans. A. M. Berrett. New Brunswick: Transaction Publishers

Chambers, E. K. 1903. *The Medieval Stage*. Oxford: Clarendon Press

Charbonnat, P. 2007. *Histoire des philosophies matérialistes*. Paris: Syllepse

Chardin, Sir John 1988. *Travels in Persia 1673–1713*. London: Constable

Chattopadhyaya, B. 1994. *The Making of Early Medieval India*. Delhi: Oxford University Press

Chattopadhyaya, D. 1959. *Lokāyata: a study in ancient Indian materialism*. Delhi: People's Publishing House

Chaudhuri, S. 2004. *Renaissance and Renaissances: Europe and Bengal.* Cambridge: Centre of South Asian Studies Occasional Paper
2004 forthcoming. *Humanism and Orientalism.* Calcutta: Jadavpur University
Chevalier, D. and Miquel, A. (eds.) 1995. *Les Arabes du message à l'histoire.* Paris: Fayard
Childe, V. G. 1942. *What Happened in History.* Harmondsworth: Penguin
1956. *Man Makes Himself.* London: Watts & Co.
1958. Retrospect. *Antiquity* 32: 69–74
Clot, A. 1999. *L'Espagne musulmane.* Paris: Perrin
Clunas, C. 1991. *Superfluous Things: material culture and social status in early modern China.* Cambridge: Polity Press
1997. *Art in China.* Oxford: Oxford University Press
Cohen, G. D. 1997. Rabbinic Judaism (2nd–18th centuries). *Encyclopædia Britannica*, 22: 393–99. Chicago, IL: Encyclopædia Britannica
Colebrook, H. T. 1817. *Algebra, with Arithmetic and Mensuration, from the Sanskrit of Brahmagupta and Bhaskara.* London: J. Murray
Collcutt, M. 1991. Art in Japan 1450–1550. In J. A. Levenson (ed.), *Circa 1492: art in the age of exploration.* New Haven, CT: Yale University Press
Cooper, A. R. V. (trans.) 1973. *Li Po and Tu Fu.* Harmondsworth: Penguin
Coulange, A. 2006. *Cézanne.* Paris: Le Monde
Crone, P. 1996. The rise of Islam in the world. In F. Robinson (ed.), *The Cambridge Illustrated History of the Islamic World.* Cambridge: Cambridge University Press
Crouzet-Pavan, E. 2007. *Renaissances Italiennes 1380–1500.* Paris: Albin Michel
Dale, S. F. 1996. The Islamic world in the age of European expansion 1500–1800. In F. Robinson (ed.), *The Cambridge Illustrated History of the Islamic World.* Cambridge: Cambridge University Press
Datta, B. and Singh, A. N. 1962. *History of Hindu Mathematics, a source book.* Bombay: Asia Publishing House
Demiéville, P. 1962. *Anthologie de la poésie chinoise classique.* Paris: Gallimard
Dharampal. 1971. *Indian Science and Technology – the Eighteenth Century.* Delhi: Impex India
Diderot, D. (ed.) 1772. *Encylopédie, ou dictionnaire raisonné des sciences, des arts et des métiers, par une société de gens de lettres*, 17 vols. Geneva
Dixin, X. and Chengming, W. 2000. *Chinese Capitalism, 1522–1840.* Basingstoke: Macmillan
Djebbar, A. 2005. *L'Âge d'or des sciences arabes.* Paris: Le Pommier
Dols, M. W. 1977. *The Black Death in the Middle East.* Princeton, NJ: Princeton University Press
Doutté, E. 1908. *Magie et religion en Afrique du Nord.* Alger: Adolphe Jourdan
Dudley, D. R. 1937. *A History of Cynicism: from Diogenes to the 6th century AD.* London: Methuen
Dumont, L. 1963. *Essais sur l'individualisme: une perspective anthropologique sur l'idéologie moderne.* Paris: Le Seuil
Dupont, A. L. 1995. L'Islam dans une nouvelle réflexion historique arabe. In D. Chevalier and A. Miquel (eds.), *Les Arabes du message à l'histoire.* Paris: Fayard

Durkheim, E. and Mauss, M. 1967 [1903]. *Primitive Classification*, trans. R. Needham. Chicago, IL: University of Chicago Press
Eckstein, N. 2005. Study of Italian Renaissance society in Australia: the state of play. *Bulletin of the Society for Renaissance Studies* 22: 2
Eco, U. 1992. *The Name of the Rose*. London: Mandarin
Eisenstein, E. L. 1979. *The Printing Press as an Agent of Change*, 2 vols. Cambridge: Cambridge University Press
   2002. An unacknowledged revolution revisited. *American Historical Review* 107: 87–105
Elgood, C. 1951. *A Medical History of Persia and the Eastern Caliphate from the Earliest Times until the Year AD 1932*. Cambridge: Cambridge University Press
Elias, N. 1994 [1978]. *The Civilizing Process*. Oxford: Blackwell
Elman, B. A. and Woodside, A. 1994. *Education and Society in Late Imperial China, 1600–1900*. Berkeley, CA: University of California Press
El-Rouayheb, K. 2005. Opening the gate of verification: the forgotten Arabic-Islamic florescence of the 17th century. *International Journal of Middle East Studies* 38: 263–81
Elsner, J. 1998. *Imperial Rome and Christian Triumph: the art of the Roman Empire AD 100–450*. Oxford: Oxford University Press
Elvin, M. 1973. *The Pattern of the Chinese Past*. London: Eyre Methuen
   2004. Ave atque vale. In J. Needham, *Science and Civilisation in China*, part 2, vol. 7. Cambridge: Cambridge University Press
Emsley, J. 2006. Unweaving the rainbow. *CAM, Cambridge Alumni Magazine* 49: 14–16
Erdosy, G. (ed.) 1995. *The Indo-Aryans of Ancient South Asia*. Berlin: de Gruyter
Etienne, R. (ed.) 1990. *Histoire de Bourdeaux*, new edn. Toulouse: Privat
Ettinghausen, R. 1970. The flowering of Seljuq art. *Metropolitan Museum Journal* 3: 113–31
Evans-Pritchard, E. E. 1940. *The Nuer*. Oxford: Clarendon Press
Ezra, Moseh Ibn 1993. *Antologia Poetica*, trans. R. Castillo. Madrid: Hiperion
Falk, T. (ed.) 1985. *Treasures of Islam*. London: Sotheby's
Fahmy, A. M. 1966. *Muslim Seapower in the Eastern Mediterranean from the Seventh to the Tenth Century AD*. Cairo: National Publication and Print House
Felliozat, J. 1949. *La Doctrine classique de la médecine indienne: ses origines et ses parallèles grecs*. Paris: Imprimerie Nationale
Fennell, S. 2005. Asian literature as a tool for cultural identity creation in Europe: Goethe's Hafiz. *Asia Europe Journal* 3: 229–46
Festinger, L. 1957. *A Theory of Cognitive Dissonance*. Stanford, CA: Stanford University Press
Finley, M. I. 1972. *Introduction to Thucydides, History of the Peloponnesian War*. Harmondsworth: Penguin
   1973. *The Ancient Economy*. London: Chatto & Windus
   1985. *Democracy Ancient and Modern*. London: Hogarth
Fontenelle, B. 1716 [1688]. Une digression sur les anciens et les modernes. In *Poësies pastorales, avec un traité sur la nature de l'eclogue et une digression sur les anciens et les modernes*, 4th edn. Amsterdam: Etienne Roger

Frantz-Murphy, G. 1981. A new interpretation of the economic history of medieval Egypt. *Journal of the Economic and Social History of the Orient* 24: 274–97

French, R. 2003. *Medicine before Science: the business of medicine from the Middle Ages to the Enlightenment.* Cambridge: Cambridge University Press

Frèches, J. 2005. *Il était une fois la Chine, 4500 ans d'histoire.* Paris: XO Éditions

Frye, R. N. 1965. The new Persian Renaissance in Western Iran. In G. Makdisi (ed.), *Arabic and Islamic Studies in Honour of Hamilton A. R. Gibb.* Cambridge, MA: Harvard University Press

Fu, Shen, Lowry, G. D. and Yonemura, A. 1986. *From Context to Concept: approaches to Asian and Islamic calligraphy.* Washington, DC: Smithsonian Institution Press

Furet, F. and Ozouf, J. 1977. *Lire et écrire, l'alphabétisation des français de Calvin à Jules Ferry.* Paris: Éditions de Minuit

Gallagher, N. E. 1993. Islamic and Indian medicine. In K. F. Kiple (ed.), *The Cambridge World History of Human Disease.* Cambridge: Cambridge University Press

Gathercole, P. 1994. Childe in History. *Bulletin of the Institute of British Archaeology* 31: 25–52

Gazagnadou, D. 1994. *La Poste à relais.* Paris: Kimé

Gernet, J. 2002 [1982]. *A History of Chinese Civilisation,* rev. 2nd edn, trans. J. R. Foster and C. Hartman. Cambridge: Cambridge University Press

Ghosh, A. 1992. *In an Antique Land.* New York: Vintage Books

Gibb, H. A. R. 1950. *Islamic Society and the West.* London: Oxford University Press

Gilli, P. 2004. Les formes de l'anticléricalisme humaniste: antimonarchisme, antipontificalisme ou antichristianisme? In P. Gilli (ed.), *Humanisme et église en Italie et en France méridionale (XV siècle – milieu du XVIe siècle).* Rome: École Française

Gilson, E. 1944. *La Philosophie au moyen âge: des origines patristiques à la fin du XIVème siècle.* Paris: Payot

Ginzburg, C. 1992 [1976]. *The Cheese and the Worms.* Harmondsworth: Penguin

Goepper, R. 1995. Precursors and early stages of the Chinese script. In J. Rawson (ed.), *Mysteries of Ancient China: new discoveries from the early dynasties.* London: British Museum Press

Goitein, S. D. 1963. Letters and documents on the India trade in medieval times. *Islamic Culture* 37: 96

  1967. *A Mediterranean Society: the Jewish communities of the Arab world as portrayed in the documents of the Cairo Geniza,* vol. 1. Berkeley, CA: University of California Press

  1971. Sicily and southern Italy in the Cairo Geniza documents. *Archivio Storico per la Sicilia Orientale* 67: 9–93

Goldstein, D. 1965. *The Jewish Poets of Spain.* Harmondsworth: Penguin

Goody, J. 1967. *The Social Organisation of the LoWiili,* 2nd edn. Oxford: Oxford University Press

  1968. Introduction to *Literacy in Traditional Societies,* ed. J. Goody. Cambridge: Cambridge University Press

1972. *The Myth of the Bagre*. Oxford: Clarendon Press

1976. *Production and Reproduction*. Cambridge: Cambridge University Press

1977. *The Domestication of the Savage Mind*. Cambridge: Cambridge University Press

1982. *Cooking, Class and Cuisine*. Cambridge: Cambridge University Press

1983. *The Development of Marriage and the Family in Europe*. Cambridge: Cambridge University Press

1986. *The Logic of Writing and the Organisation of Society*. Cambridge: Cambridge University Press

1987. *The Interface between the Written and the Oral*. Cambridge: Cambridge University Press

1993. *The Culture of Flowers*. Cambridge: Cambridge University Press

1997a. *Representations and Contradictions*. Oxford: Blackwell

1997b. A kernel of doubt: agnosticism in cross-cultural perspective. The Huxley Lecture. *Journal of the Royal Anthropological Institute* 2: 667–681. Reprinted in *Food and Love*, 1998

1998. *Food and Love*. London: Verso

2004. *Capitalism and Modernity*. Cambridge: Polity Press

2006. *The Theft of History*. Cambridge: Cambridge University Press

2009. *The Eurasian Miracle*. Cambridge: Polity Press

forthcoming. Towards a knowledge society: something old, something new. Berne

Goody, J. and Watt, I. P. 1963. The consequences of literacy. *Comparative Studies in Society and History* 5: 304–45

Goody, J. and Gandah, S. W. D. K. 1980. *Une récitation du Bagre*. Paris: Colin and Gandah, S. W. D. K. 2002. *The Third Bagre: a myth revisited*. Durham, NC: Carolina Academic Press

Gopal, S. 1969. Social set-up of science and technology in Mughal India. *Indian Journal of the History of Science* 4: 52–58

Grabar, O. 1968. The visual arts, 1050–1350. *The Cambridge History of Islam*, vol. 5: *The Seljuq and Mongol Periods*. Cambridge: Cambridge University Press

Grendler, P. F. 1989. *Schooling in Renaissance Italy: literacy and learning 1300–1600*. Baltimore, MD: John Hopkins University Press

2004. *The Universities of the Italian Renaissance*. Baltimore, MD: John Hopkins University Press

Grunebaum, G. E. von 1953. *Medieval Islam: a study in cultural orientation*. Chicago, IL: University of Chicago Press

Guha, S. 2005. Negotiating evidence: history, archaeology and the Indus civilisation. *Modern Asian Studies* 39: 399–426

Gutas, D. 1998. *Greek Thought, Arabic Culture: the Graeco-Arabic translation movement in Baghdad and early 'Abbāsid society (2nd–4th/8th–10th centuries)*. London: Routledge

Habib, I. 1969. Potentialities of capitalistic development in the economy of Mughal India. *Journal of Economic History* 29: 32–78

1992. Pursuing the history of Indian technology: pre-modern modes of transmission of power. *Social Scientist* 20: 1–22

Hajnal, J. 1965. European marriage patterns in perspective. In D.V. Glass and D. E. C. Eversley (eds.), *Population in History*. London: Aldine

Hariz, J. 1922. *La Part de la médecine arabe dans l'evolution de la médecine française*. Paris: Geuthner

Havelock, E. A. 1963. *Preface to Plato*. Oxford: Blackwell

Herrenschmidt, C. 2007. *Les Trois Écritures: langue, nombre, code*. Paris: Gallimard

Hobsbawm, E. 2005. Benefits of diaspora. *London Review of Books* (20 October), 16–19

Hodgson, M. G. S. 1974. *The Venture of Islam: conscience and history in a world civilization*, 3 vols. Chicago, IL: University of Chicago Press

Howard, D. 2000. *Venice and the East: the impact of the Islamic world on European architecture 1100–1500*. New Haven, CT: Yale University Press
    2007. Venice and the Mamluks. In S. Carboni (ed.), *Venice and the Islamic World, 828–1797*. New Haven, CT: Yale University Press

Iancu, D. and C. 1995. *Les Juifs du Midi: une histoire millénaire*. Avignon: Barthélemy

Ibn Khaldun 1951. *Al-Ta'rīf bi Ibn Khaldūn wa Riḥlatuhu Gharbān wa Sharqān*. Cairo: Muḥammad ibn-Tāwīt at-Tanjī
    1967. *The Muqaddimah*. Princeton, NJ: Princeton University Press

Inalcik, H. 1969. Capital formation in the Ottoman empire. *Journal of Economic History* 29: 97–140

Innis, H. A. 1951. *The Bias of Communication*. Toronto: University of Toronto Press

Irwin, R. 1996. The emergence of the Islamic World System 1000–1500. In F. Robinson (ed.), *The Cambridge Illustrated History of the Islamic World*. Cambridge: Cambridge University Press

Isakhan, B. 2007. Engaging 'primitive democracy': mideast roots of collective governance. *Middle East Policy* 14, 3: 97–117

I-Tsing 1896. *A Record of the Buddhist Religion as Practised in India and the Malay Archipelago (AD 671–695)*, trans. J. Takakusu. Oxford: Clarendon Press

Jacquart, D. 2005. *L'Épopée de la science arabe*. Paris: Gallimard

Jardine, L. 1996. *Worldly Goods: a new history of the Renaissance*. London: Macmillan

Jayyusi, S. K. (ed.) 1987. *Modern Arabic Poetry: an anthology*. Oxford: Columbia University Press
    (ed.) 1992. *The Legacy of Muslim Spain*. Leiden: Brill

Johns, A. 2002. How to acknowledge a revolution. *American Historical Review* 107: 106–25

Josephus, F. 1848. *Works*, 3 vols., ed. and trans. W. Whiston. London: G. Auld

Julius, A. 2000. *Idolizing Pictures: idolatry, iconoclasm and Jewish art*. London: Thames & Hudson

Jurdjevich, M. 2007. Hedgehogs and foxes: the present and future of Italian Renaissance intellectual history. *Past and Present* 195: 197–239

Kaye, G. R. 1924. *Hindu Astronomy*. Calcutta: Govt. of India, Central Publication Branch

Keith, A. B. 1928. *A History of Sanskrit Literature*. Oxford: Clarendon Press

Kennedy, K. A. R. 1995. Have Aryans been identified in the prehistoric skeletal record from South Asia? Biological anthropology and concepts of ancient races. In G. Erdosy (ed.), *The Indo-Aryans of Ancient South Asia: language, material culture and ethnicity.* Berlin and New York: de Gruyter

Kenoyer, J. M. 1998. *Ancient Cities of the Indus Valley Civilization.* Oxford: Oxford University Press

Kettle, B. 1970. The flowering of Seljuq art. *Metropolitan Museum Journal* 3: 113–31

Khairallah, A. A. 1946. *Outline of Arabic Contributions to Medicine.* Beirut: American Press

Khalidi, M. A. 2005. *Medieval Islamic Philosophical Writings.* Cambridge: Cambridge University Press

Khan, I. A. 1981. Early use of canon and musket in India: AD 1442–1526. *Journal of Social and Economic History of the Orient* 24: 146–64

Kraemer, J. L. 1986. *Philosophy in the Renaissance of Islam: Abū Sulaymān Al-Sijistānī and his circle.* Leiden: Brill

  1992. *Humanism in the Renaissance of Islam: the cultural revival during the Buyid age.* Leiden: Brill

Kraye, J. 1996. *The Cambridge Companion to Renaissance Humanism.* Cambridge: Cambridge University Press

Kristeller, P. O. 1956–96. *Studies in Renaissance Thought and Letters,* 4 vols. Rome: Edizioni di Storia e Letteratura

  1990. *Renaissance Thought and the Arts: collected essays.* Princeton, NJ: Princeton University Press

Labib, S. Y. 1969. Capitalism in medieval Islam. *Journal of Economic History* 29: 79–96

Labouysse, G. 2005. *Les Wisigoths.* Porter-sur-Garonne: Loubatières

Laertius, Diogenes 1925. *Lives of Eminent Philosophers,* 2 vols., Loeb edn, trans. R. D. Hicks. London: Heinemann

Lal, B. B. 1997. *The Earliest Civilisation in South Asia.* New Delhi: Aryan Books International

Lambton, A. K. S. 1962. The merchant in medieval Islam. In W. B. Henning and E. Yarshater (eds.), *A Locust's Leg: studies in honour of S. H. Taqizadeh.* London: Percy Lund, Humphries

Landau, J. M. 1997. [Islâmic] dance and theatre. *Encyclopædia Britannica,* 22: 68–74. Chicago, IL: Encyclopædia Britannica

Laslett, P. and Walls, R. (eds.) 1972. *Household and Family in Past Times.* Cambridge: Cambridge University Press

Leclerc, L. 1876. *Histoire de la médecine arabe,* 2 vols. Paris: E. Leroux

Ledderose, L. 1983. Module and mass production. In *International Colloquium on Chinese Art History, 1991, Proceedings: paintings, part 2.* Taipei: National Palace Museum

Lee, J. Z. and Wang, Feng 1999. *One Quarter of Humanity: Malthusian mythology and Chinese realities 1700–2000.* Cambridge, MA: Harvard University Press

Lee, S. E. 1991. China in the age of Columbus. In J. A. Levenson (ed.), *Circa 1492: art in the age of exploration.* New Haven, CT: Yale University Press

Lemerle, P. 1986 [1971]. *Byzantine Humanism: the first phase: notes and remarks on education and culture in Byzantium from its origins to the 10th century*, trans. H. Lindsay and A. Moffatt. Canberra: Australian Association for Byzantine Studies

Levenson, J. A. (ed.) 1991. *Circa 1492: art in the age of exploration*. New Haven, CT: Yale University Press

Lévi-Strauss, C. 1949. *Les Structures élémentaires de la parenté*. Paris: Presses Universitaires de France

Lewis, B. (ed.) 1976. *The World of Islam: faith, people, culture*. London: Thames & Hudson

2002. *What Went Wrong? Western impact and Middle Eastern response*. London: Orion House

Lopez, R. S. 1951. Still another Renaissance? *American Historical Review* 57: 1–21

1962. Hard times and investment in culture. In W. K. Ferguson (ed.), *The Renaissance: six essays*. New York: Harper & Row

Macdonell, A. A. 1993 [1917]. *A Vedic Reader for Students*. Oxford: Oxford University Press

Madhava, Acharya 1914. *Sarva-Darśana-Saṃgraha*, trans. E. B Cowell and A. E. Gough. London: Kegan Paul

Maimon, S. 1954. *The Autobiography of Solomon Maimon*, trans. J. C. Murray. London: The East and West Library

Majumdar, R. C. 1971. Medicine. In D. M. Bose *et al.* (eds.), *A Concise History of Science in India*. New Delhi: Indian National Science Academy

Makdisi, G. 1990. *The Rise of Humanism: classical Islam and the Christian West*. Edinburgh: Edinburgh University Press

Mâles, E. 1933. Les influences arabes dans l'art roman. *Revue des Deux Mondes* 18: 311–43

Malinowski, B. 1935. *Coral Gardens and their Magic: a study of the methods of tilling the soil and of agricultural rites in the Trobriand Islands*. London: Allen & Unwin

Malthus, T. T. 1958 [1798]. *An Essay on the Principle of Population*. London: Dent

Martindale, A. 1966. *Man and the Renaissance*. London: Hamlyn

McDermott, J. P. 2006. *A Social History of the Chinese Book: books and literati culture in Late Imperial China*. Hong Kong: Hong Kong University Press

McLuhan, M. 1962. *The Gutenberg Galaxy: the making of typographic man*. Toronto: University of Toronto Press

Mez, A. 1937 [1922]. *The Renaissance of Islam*, trans. S. K. Bukhsh and D. S. Margoliouth. London: Luzac and Co.

Mikami, Y. 1913. *The Development of Mathematics in China and Japan*. Leipzig: Teubner

Miquel, A. 1995. De la foi au pouvoir. In D. Chevalier and A. Miquel (eds.), *Les Arabes du message à l'histoire*. Paris: Fayard

Miller, A. 2006. *The Earl of Petticoat Lane*. Heinemann: London

Miller, E. 1961. *The Portrait of a College*. Cambridge: Cambridge University Press

Mir-Hosseini, Z. and Tapper, R. 2006. *Islam and Democracy in Iran: Eshkevari and the quest for reform*. London: Tauris

Mitter, P. 2001. *Indian Art*. Oxford: Oxford University Press

Modena, Rabbi L. 1637. *Historia de gli riti hebraici: dove si ha breve, e total relatione di tutta la vita, costumi, riti, et osservanze, de gl'Hebrei di questi tempi*. Paris

Mookerji, R. K. 1951. *Ancient Indian Education (Brahmanical and Buddhist)*. London: Macmillan

Mote, F. W. 1977. Yuan and Ming. In K. C. Chang (ed.), *Food in Chinese Culture: authropological and historical perspectives*. New Haven, CT: Yale University Press

   1991. Art in China 1450–1550. In J. A. Levenson (ed.), *Circa 1492: art in the age of exploration*. New Haven, CT: Yale University Press

   1999. *Imperial China, 900–1800*. Cambridge, MA: Harvard University Press

Mukhopadhyaya, G. 1993. *History of Indian Medicine*. Cambridge: Cambridge University Press

Musallam, B. 1996. The ordering of Muslim societies. In F. Robinson (ed.), *The Cambridge Illustrated History of the Islamic World*. Cambridge: Cambridge University Press

Needham, J. (ed.) 1954–. *Science and Civilisation in China*. Cambridge: Cambridge University Press

   1956. *Science and Civilisation in China*, vol. 2: *History of Scientific Thought*. Cambridge: Cambridge University Press

   1969. *The Grand Titration, science and society in east and west*. London: Allen & Unwin

   1981. *Science in Traditional China: a comparative perspective*. Hong Kong: Chinese University Press

   1986. *Science and Civilisation in China*, vol. 6: *Biology and Biological Technology*, part 1: *Botany*. Cambridge: Cambridge University Press

Nicholas, D. 1996. *Trade, Urbanisation and the Family: studies in the history of medieval Flanders*. Aldershot: Variorum

Niezen, R. W. 1991. Hot literacy in cold societies: a comparative study of the sacred value of writing. *Comparative Studies in Society and History* 33, 2: 225–54

North, D. C. 2005. *Understanding the Process of Economic Change*. New York: Academic Press

Núñez Guarde, J. A. (ed.) 1989. *Ver y comprender La Alhambra y el Generalife*. Granada: Edilux

Olmstead, A. T. 1948. *A History of the Persian Empire*. Chicago, IL: Chicago University Press

Ong, W. 1974. *Ramus, Method and the Decay of Dialogue*. New York: Octagon Books

Oppenheim, A. L. 1964. *Ancient Mesopotamia*. Chicago, IL: Chicago University Press

Pamuk, O. 2001 [1998]. *My Name Is Red*, trans. E. M. Göknar. London: Faber & Faber

Panofsky, E. 1972 [1960]. *Renaissance and Renascences in Western Art*. New York: Icon Editions

Parpola, A. 1994. *Deciphering the Indus Script*. Cambridge: Cambridge University Press

Pellat, C. 1976. Jewellers with words. In B. Lewis (ed.), *The World of Islam: faith, people, culture*. London: Thames & Hudson

Percival Spear, T. G. 1997. India and European expansion, *c.* 1500–1858. *Encyclopædia Britannica*, vol. 21: 82–98. Chicago, IL: Encyclopædia Britannica

Peters, R. F. 1968. *Aristotle and the Arabs: the Aristotelian tradition in Islam*. New York: New York University Press

Pingree, D. 1970–81. *Census of the Exact Sciences in Sanskrit*, 4 vols. Philadelphia: American Philosophical Society

Pollock, S. 2006. *The Language of the Gods in the World of Men: Sanskrit, culture, and power in premodern India*. Berkeley, CA: University of California Press

Pokorny, R. 2009. The Arabs got there first. *The Art Newspaper* 201: 51

Pomeranz, K. 2000. *The Great Divergence: China, Europe and the making of the modern world economy*. Princeton, NJ: Princeton University Press

Porter, R. 1997. *The Greatest Benefit to Mankind: a medical history of humanity*. London: Harper Collins

Quinet, E. 1842. *Du Génie des religions*. Paris: Charpentier

Rahman, A. (ed.) 1999. *History of Indian Science, Technology, and Culture, AD 1000–1800*. New Delhi: Oxford University Press

Raju, C. K. 2007. Cultural foundations of mathematics: the nature of mathematical proof: the transmission of the calculus from India to Europe in the 16th century CE. In D. P. Chattopadhyaya (ed.), *The History of Science, Philosophy and Culture in Indian Civilisation*, vol. 10. New Delhi: Pearson Longman

Rawson, J. (ed.) 1992. *The British Museum Book of Chinese Art*. London: British Museum Press

 (ed.) 1995. *Mysteries of Ancient China: new discoveries from the early dynasties*. London: British Museum Press

Rashid al-Din 1951. *Histoire universelle de Rašīd al-Dīn Faḍl Allāh Abul-Khair*, 5 vols., trans. K. Jahn. Leiden: Brill

Rawski, E. S. 1979. *Education and Popular Literacy in Ch'ing China*. Ann Arbor, MI: University of Michigan Press

Ray, P. C. 1909. *A History of Hindu Chemistry, from the earliest times to the middle of the sixteenth century, AD*, 2 vols. London: Williams & Norgate

Renan, E. 2003 [1852]. *Averroès et l'averroïsme*. Rennes: Ennoia

Reynolds, L. D. and Wilson, N. G. 1968. *Scribes and Scholars*. London: Oxford University Press

Riquer, M. de 1975. *Los trovadores: historia literaria y textos*, vol. 1. Barcelona: Ariel

Robinson, F. 1996. Knowledge, its transmission and the making of Muslim societies. In F. Robinson (ed.), *The Cambridge Illustrated History of the Islamic World*. Cambridge: Cambridge University Press

Rodinson, M. 1974 [1966]. *Islam and Capitalism*, trans. B. Pearce. London: Allen Lane

Rosenthal, F. 1947. *The Technique and Approach to Muslim Scholarship*. Roma: Pontificum Institutum Biblicum

 1975 [1965]. *The Classical Heritage in Islam*, trans. E. and J. Marmorstein. London: Routledge & Kegan Paul

Rostow, W. W. 1959. The stages of economic growth. *Economic History Review* 1: 1–16

Roy, T. 2008. The guild in modern South Asia. *International Review of Social History* 53: 95–120

Rowland, B. 1953. *The Art and Architecture of India: Hindu, Buddhist, Jain*. Harmondsworth: Penguin

Rubiés, J. P. 2000. *Travel and Ethnology in the Renaissance: South India through European eyes, 1250–1265*. Cambridge: Cambridge University Press

Rublack, U. 2005. *Reformation Europe*. Cambridge: Cambridge University Press

Sabra, A. I. 1996. Situating Arabic science: locality versus essence. *Isis* 87: 654–70

Sagnes, J. (ed.) 1986. *Histoire de Béziers*. Toulouse: Privat

Sahlins, M. 2004. *Apologies to Thucydides: understanding history as culture and vice versa*. Chicago, IL: Chicago University Press

Saliba, G. 2007. *Islamic Science and the Making of the European Renaissance*. Cambridge, MA: MIT Press

Sarton, G. 1927. *Introduction to the History of Science*, vol. I. Baltimore, MD: Williams & Wilkins

Sastri, N. 1975. *A History of South India: from prehistoric times to the fall of Vijayanagar*. Delhi: Oxford University Press

Sayli, A. 1960. *The Observatory in Islam and its Place in the General History of the Observatory*. Ankara: Turk Tarih Kurumu

Schimmel, A. 1997. Islâmic literature. *Encyclopædia Britannica*, 22: 46–64. Chicago, IL: Encyclopædia Britannica

Schönig, H. 1985. *Das Sendschreiben des Abdalhamid B. Yahya (gest. 132/750) an den Kronprinzen Abdallah B. Marwan II*. Stuttgart: Steiner Verlag

Schmandt-Besserat, D. 1996. *How Writing Came About*. Austin, TX: University of Texas Press

Schwab, R. 1984. *The Oriental Renaissance: Europe's rediscovery of India and the East, 1680–1880*. New York: Columbia University Press

Sen, S. N. 1963. The transmission of scientific ideas between India and foreign countries in ancient and medieval times. *Bulletin N. I. Science in India* 21: 8–30

   1966. An estimate of Indian science in ancient and medieval times. *Scientia* (March and April)

   1967. Indian elements in European Renaissance. *Organon* 4: 55–59

   1971. A survey of source materials. In D. M. Bose *et al.* (eds.), *A Concise History of Science in India*. New Delhi: Indian National Science Academy

Serjeant, R. B. 1948. Material for the history of Islamic textiles up to the Mongol conquest. *Ars Islamica* 13/24: 75–117

Sharma, J. P. 1968. *Republics in Ancient India c. 1500 BC–500 BC*. Leiden: Brill

Shastri, D. 1930. *A Short History of Indian Materialism, Sensationalism and Hedonism*. Calcutta: The Book Company

Shih, Hu 1934. *The Chinese Renaissance: the Haskell Lectures, 1933*. Chicago, IL: Chicago University Press

Shukla, H. L. 1969. *Renaissance in Modern Sanskrit Literature*. Raipur: Yugadharma Press

Siban, S. 1999. Jews and the arts. In P. F. Grendler (ed.), *The Encyclopedia of the Renaissance*, 3: 338–42. New York: Scribner

Siddiqi, M. Z. 1959. *Studies in Arabic and Persian Medical Literature*. Calcutta: Calcutta University Press

Silbergeld, J. 1997. The Yüan, or Mongol, dynasty: the arts. *Encyclopædia Britannica*, 16: 110–11. Chicago, IL: Encyclopædia Britannica

Sisam, K. (ed.) 1953 [1921]. *Fourteenth Century Verse and Prose*. Oxford: Clarendon Press

Skinner, Q. 1978. *The Foundations of Modern Political Thought*, vol. 1: *The Renaissance*. Cambridge: Cambridge University Press

Smith, D. E. and Karpinski, L. C. 1911. *The Hindu-Arabic Numerals*. Boston: Ginn

Sombart, W. 1913 [1911]. *The Jews and Modern Capitalism*, trans. M. Epstein. London: T. Fischer Unwin

Southern, R. W. 1953. *The Making of the Middle Ages*. New York: Hutchinson's Library

1970. *Medieval Humanism and Other Studies*. Oxford: Blackwell

Spufford, P. 2002. *Power and Profit: the merchant in medieval Europe*. London: Thames & Hudson

Stein, B. 1989. *Vijayanagara*. Cambridge: Cambridge University Press

Strong, R. (ed.) 1982. *Indian Heritage: court life and arts under Mughal rule*. London: Victoria and Albert Museum

Subbarayappa, B. V. 1971. Arts. Chemical practices and alchemy. The physical world: views and concepts. Résumé. In D. M. Bose *et al.* (eds.), *A Concise History of Science in India*. New Delhi: Indian National Science Academy

Swann, P. C. 1958. *Chinese Painting*. Paris: Pierre Tisne

Swift, J. 1704. *A Tale of a Tub: written for the universal improvement of mankind. To which is added, an account of a battle between the antient and modern books in St James's Library*, 3rd edn. London: J. Nutt

Thapar, R. 1968. *A History of India*, 2 vols. Harmondsworth: Penguin

1997. The development of Indian civilisation from c. 1500 BC to c. AD 1200. *Encyclopædia Britannica*, 21: 36–54. Chicago, IL: Encyclopædia Britannica

2002. *The Penguin History of Early India, from the Origins to AD 1300*. New Delhi: Penguin

Thrower, J. 1980. *The Alternative Tradition: religion and the rejection of religion in the ancient world*. The Hague: Mouton

Toaff, A. 2000. *Mangiare alla Giudia: la cucina ebraica in Italia dal Rinascimento*. Bologna: Il Mulino

Toynbee, A. J. 1954. *A Study of History*, vol. 9. London: Oxford University Press

Trinkaus, C. 1982. Themes for a Renaissance anthropology. In A. Chastel *et al.* (eds.), *The Renaissance: essays in interpretation*. New York: Methuen

Troupeau, G. 1995. *Études sur le christianisme arabe au Moyen Âge*. Aldershot: Variorum

Twitchett, D. C. 1997. The Sui Dynasty. The T'ang Dynasty. *Encyclopædia Britannica*, 16: 85–95. Chicago, IL: Encyclopædia Britannica

Udovitch, A. L. 1970a. The 'law merchant' of the medieval Islamic world. In G. E. von Grunebaum (ed.), *Logic in Classical Islamic Culture*. Wiesbaden: O. Harrassowitz
  1970b. *Partnership and Profit in Medieval Islam*. Princeton, NJ: Princeton University Press
Ullman, W. 1977. *Medieval Foundations of Renaissance Humanism*. Ithaca, NY: Cornell University Press
Van Gennep, A. 1960 [1909]. *The Rites of Passage*. London: Routledge & Kegan Paul
Varadpande, M. L. 1981. *Ancient Indian and Indo-Greek Theatre*. New Delhi: Abhinav Publications
Veblen, T. 1925 [1899]. *The Theory of the Leisure Class: an economic study in the evolution of institutions*. London: Allen & Unwin
Vernant, J-P. 2006 [1979]. *Religions, histoires, raisons*. Paris: La Decouverte
Waldman, M. R. 1997. The Islâmic world. *Encyclopædia Britannica*, 22: 103–33. Chicago, IL: Encyclopædia Britannica
Walker, P. E. 1993. *Early Philosophical Shiism: the Ismaili Neoplatonism of Abu Yaqub al-Sijistani*. Cambridge: Cambridge University Press
Walzer, R. 1962. *Greek into Arabic*. Cambridge, MA: Harvard University Press
Washbrook, D. 1990. South Asia, world system, and world capitalism. *Journal of Asian Studies* 49: 479–508
  1997. From comparative sociology to global history: Britain and India in the pre-history of modernity. *Journal of the Economic and Social History of the Orient* 40: 410–43
Watters, T. 1904. *On Yuan Chwang's Travels in India, 629–645 AD*, ed. T. W. Davids and S. W. Bushell. London: Royal Asiatic Society
Weber, M. 1966 [1921]. *The City*, trans. D. Martindale and G. Neuwirth. New York: Free Press
Welch, A. 1985. The arts of the book. In T. Falk (ed.), *Treasures of Islam*. London: Sotheby's
Whipple, A. O. 1936. The role of the Nestorians as the connecting link between Greek and Arabic medicine. *Annals of Medicine* 8 (NS): 313–23
Wiet, G. 1961. *Grandeur d'Islam: de Mahomet à François Ier*. Paris: la Table Ronde
Wilson, N. G. 1983. *Scholars of Byzantium*. London: Duckworth
Winternitz, M. 1981 [1907]. *A History of Indian Literature*, 3 vols., trans. V. S. Sarma. Delhi: Motilal Banarsidass
Witt, R. G. 2000. *In the Footsteps of the Ancients: the origins of humanism from Lovato to Bruni*. Boston, MA: Brill
Witzel, M. (ed.) 1997. *Inside the Texts, Beyond the Texts: new approaches to the study of the Vedas*. Harvard Oriental Series. Opera Minora, vol. 2. Cambridge, MA: Harvard University Press
Wolpert, S. A. 1997. British imperial power, 1858–1947. *Encyclopædia Britannica*, 21: 98–116. Chicago, IL: Encyclopædia Britannica
Worsley, P. 1997. *Knowledges: what different peoples make of the world*. London: Profile
Wotton, W. 1694. *Reflections upon Ancient and Modern Learning*. London
Wroe, A. 1995. *A Fool and His Money Are Soon Parted*. London: Cape

Zafrani, H. 1996. *Juifs d'Andalusia et du Maghreb*. Paris: Maisonneuve Larose
   1995. Les Juifs. In D. Chevalier and A. Miquel (eds.), *Les Arabes du message à
   l'histoire*. Paris: Fayard
Zeevi, D. 2006. *Producing Desire: changing sexual discourse in the Ottoman Middle
   East 1500–1900*. Berkeley, CA: University of California Press
Zhang, W. 2006. *Heidegger, Rorty and the Eastern Thinkers: a hermeneutics of cross-
   cultural understanding*. Albany, NY: State University of Albany Press
Zuckerman, A. J. 1972. *Jewish Princedom in Feudal France, 768–900*. New York:
   Columbia University Press
Zurndorfer, H. 2006. Regimes of scientific and military knowledge: a revi-
   sionist perspective. Paper presented at Global Economic History Network
   (GEHN) Conference 9: Taiwan, May 2006. Online. Retrieved 20 July
   2007 from www.lse.ac.uk/collections/economicHistory/GEHN/GEHNPDF/
   GEHN9Zurndorfer.pdf

Index

technology 31, 35, 81, 85, 90, 100, 138,
    141, 157, 170, 182–3, 188, 195,
    198–9, 202–4, 204n, 205, 214, 217,
    221–2, 225–8, 235, 248, 256–7,
    260–1
telescopes 105
Templars 133
Terence 16, 62
textiles 29–30, 95, 135–6, 164, 188,
    206, 221, 228, 237, 254–5, 269
Thales 68–71
Thanjavur 187, 190
Thapar, Romila 5, 163, 165, 167, 170,
    196–7, 272
theatre 11, 13, 16, 26, 42–3, 77, 123–5,
    148, 239, 254, 259
    Chinese 239n
    'clerk's plays' 16, 77
    Elizabethan 92
    folk theatre 16, 77
    Jewish 32, 155–6
    kabuki 42, 92
    'mumming' 16
    mystery plays 11, 16, 77–8, 155
    No plays 42
    Sanskrit 42, 186
    secular 42, 77
Theft of History, The (Goody) 3
theology 9, 37, 49, 51, 67–8, 72, 84–5,
    97–8, 104, 163, 172, 186, 202, 261,
    284–5
    experience rather than 64
Theosophical Society 194
Thomas, Keith 36
Thomas, St 41
Three Kingdoms, the 212, 216, 282
Thucydides 67
Tigers, Little 264
Tigris, river 34, 118, 118n
Tilak 193
Timbuktu 138
time, reckoning of 26, 58, 62
Timur 54, 121n, 123, 129, 188
Toledo 45–7, 49, 51, 59, 113, 113n,
    127–8, 141, 148–9, 242, 257
Topkapi Saray 138
Torah 118n, 154, 156
torture, of thinkers 73
Toulouse 49n, 82, 85, 108n
towns 10, 19, 27, 40, 75, 80, 82, 99,
    110–11, 120–1, 147, 166, 189, 205,
    217, 221, 228–9, 231, 234, 246,
    254, 270, 274
Toynbee, Arnold 8, 8n, 9, 9n, 172, 249,
    262, 266n

trade 27–9, 31, 37, 39–41, 45–6, 53, 60,
    64, 70, 81, 91–2, 94–6, 107, 110,
    120–2, 125–6, 131, 133–4, 136,
    138, 142, 144, 159, 163, 165–6,
    176–9, 184, 188–91, 195–6, 205–6,
    212, 214, 220–1, 224, 228–9, 231,
    235, 242, 248, 253–5, 265, 267–70,
    272–4, 279–80
    western collapse 27, 29, 95
    western revival 27–9, 31, 91
traditionalism 113, 192
translation 60, 96–7, 99, 102–3, 105,
    107, 117, 128, 256, 264, 271, 273
    from Arabic 59, 84, 102, 108, 126,
    128, 285
    of Bible 87
    from Greek 6, 22, 48, 55, 59–61, 80,
    83–4, 90, 94, 96, 99, 102–5, 107–8,
    111, 113, 128, 143, 145–6, 159,
    188, 244–5, 256, 264, 285
    from Indian 103n, 104, 115, 212–13,
    217, 245
    medical texts
transport, means of 35, 189, 207, 211,
    221, 245, 259
Trobriands, the 68
Tu Fu 216
Tulinid period 269
Tunisia 40, 118, 123, 125, 278
Turkey 15, 31, 40, 48, 86, 89, 94, 100n,
    136–8, 140, 188, 257, 272, 276
    Ottoman 94, 100n, 125, 136–8, 142,
    277
Turkic 109, 122, 129, 132, 134, 182,
    188, 196, 214–15, 218, 278
Tyre 39–40, 46

Ugarit 40, 169
ulama 97–8, 100–1, 120, 127, 136, 138,
    140, 257
Umayyads 94–7, 114–15, 118, 126, 129,
    276, 278
uniqueness, European 3, 7–8, 11, 24,
    32–3, 38, 42, 60–1, 69, 86, 88,
    90–1, 241, 244, 250, 258, 263, 272
university, the 20, 33, 35, 92, 180–2,
    194, 199, 231, 246, 250, 265
    and medicine 43–61
Upanishad 194
Urban Revolution 2, 19, 87, 199
usury 270

vaccination 137
Valencia 22, 139
Vallabhi 182

Lightning Source UK Ltd.
Milton Keynes UK
UKHW020617120919
349633UK00011B/160/P